Living Systems

My Decades-Long Odyssey
through Bowen Family System Theory

by

Wayne F. Regina, Psy.D.

Theory-to-Practice Press

ALSO BY WAYNE F. REGINA

Applying Family Systems Theory to Mediation

A Practitioner's Guide

CONTENTS

Dedicated to

My wife, Janet, and our children, Carly and Sage,
for being the light and love of my life.

My parents, siblings, and family,
for helping me learn about and appreciate family systems.

My friends and colleagues,
who assisted me with this book in so many ways.

My clinical and mediation couples and families
for their courage to change.

My students,
from whom I learned as much as I offered.

Acknowledgements

When I started to write the second of three books in my "Bowen theory trilogy," little did I know of all the significant events that would conspire to delay its completion. In the twelve years since the publication of my last book, *Applying family systems theory mediation*, both of our children launched and moved to Philadelphia to attend graduate schools and to work; my father-in-law, Lou, had a significant stroke that necessitated him living with us for seven years until his passing in December 2019; and my wife, Janet, and I retired both from our teaching positions as well as our work as mediators at the Superior Court in Yavapai County. Then, there were the four hell years of unstable political turmoil and chaos, an overpowering recession fueled by the largest pandemic in over a hundred years, and, of course, the ever-evolving Covid-19 pandemic itself.

Several years ago, I realized that I needed to give up on any timeline, revised many times, and trust that "slow and steady" would complete this project, which it did.

In acknowledging the many people who assisted me with this professional memoir, in particular, I want to thank my two editors, my best friend and colleague K.L. (Kenny) Cook and my colleague and friend Melanie Bishop. Kenny, Melanie, and I were all professors at Prescott College, where we worked closely for decades. Like any author, after reading the same material time and time again, fresh eyes can make all of the difference. Their insights and suggestions were invaluable.

The first drafts of this book were largely produced during the annual writing retreats that Tim Crews, K.L. Cook, and I attended over the years. Those raw gems were edited and tweaked for years, though their origins remain from these productive retreats. For us, the retreats themselves have produced numerous books, chapters, and articles over its eighteen-year history. I'm pleased to add this work to our impressive collection.

I want to thank the co-writers whose work appears in Section Five. Kenny Cook, Sally LeBoy, Steve Pace, and Gina Simmons are all talented writers and professionals with whom I worked with over the years. They were all involved in editing the original publications, improving language structure and flow, while preserving the essence of those articles written at specific times in our professional histories.

I want to also thank the owners of the beautiful homes we occupied for offering up these "retreat centers." They include my brother Ronald Regina and brother-in-law Bart Broome for contributing no less than six different locations in northern and southern California over the years. Also, thanks to other friends of friends for allowing us to spend time in a lake home in Northern Minnesota (in the winter, no less), in a family retreat home in beautiful Durango, Colorado, and a lovely family compound outside of Salina, Kansas. Each locale was more beautiful than the next, and the enhanced aesthetics of our surroundings contributed to our collective creativity and productivity.

I want to thank my friends and colleagues, including Tim Crews, for their unwavering support and assistance over the years. I want to also thank my parents, Eugene Regina and Antoinette Regina, my extended family, Gary, Susie, and Jesse Regina, Ronald Regina and Bart Broome, and Debra Regina for always believing in me.

I want to thank United States International University (U.S.I.U, now Alliant University); the Mediation Program at the Superior Court in Yavapai County, Arizona; Prescott College, and Skyview School for providing numerous opportunities to test the application of Bowen family systems theory in real-world situations.

I want to thank all of the individual, couples, and family therapy clients, as well as the mediation and conciliation clients with whom I worked for almost four decades. Their courage and commitment to making their lives and the lives of their families better remain with me always.

Lastly, though importantly, I want to thank my students over the decades. Both the graduate students at U.S.I.U. and the undergraduates at Prescott College were enthusiastic learners, willing to suspend disbelief and embrace a new theory for a new time. I learned as much from them as they learned from me. It has been a glorious exchange of ideas and insights.

PROLOGUE

LIVING SYSTEMS

My Decades-Long Odyssey through Bowen Family System Theory

Professionally, I get bored easily. I used to think that this was a problem. After a few years of doing the same thing, I'm always looking for a new challenge. Over the years and decades, I have learned to appreciate my sense of being unsettled professionally as a gift in that I have explored a variety of professional paths. These careers have included college professor, marriage and family therapist, psychologist, trainer, supervisor, mediator, conciliator, educational leader, writer, and systems theorist. Through all of these professional incarnations, Murray Bowen's family systems theory–alternately referred to as Bowen theory and Bowen family systems theory–has been my constant companion and theoretical guide in navigating my internal and external worlds.

I wrote this book as a way of detailing this professional odyssey and as a way of articulating how Bowen theory has influenced my work over time. In writing this book, I struggled with identifying my audience. Should I write it for a lay audience? Current research suggests that millennials will have a number of careers over the course of their lifetimes. Certainly, a professional memoir by someone who has done just that, using a specific theoretical framework, might have appeal to this transformative generation. Should I write for a specialized, professional audience that already has familiarity with Bowen theory? That population understands the power and significance of family systems theory. Perhaps, a professional memoir using Bowen theory as a theoretical system would be of interest to and have resonance with those already using the theory in their own work.

In the end, I decided that my audience included both groups, those without a background in Bowen family systems theory who might find value and inspiration in examining this all-inclusive theory, as well as those more familiar with the theory who might enjoy an odyssey into Bowen theory that also explores its power outside of the more traditional therapeutic realm. In this way, rather than narrowing my focus, I hope to reach a larger audience. What that means, for example, is that those interested in applying Bowen theory to leadership will value the chapters focused on differentiated leadership. Those interested in higher education will value the chapters on teaching Bowen theory to undergraduates. Those interested in supervision will value how I re-conceptualize supervision using Bowen theory as a guide. Those interested in alternative dispute resolution will value how I have applied Bowen theory to mediations, conciliations, and peacemaking. And those interested in learning more about the theory and its application will find value in the entire professional memoir.

There may be times when some of the material, especially its dense theoretical basis, may appear too heavily textured for the lay audience. I trust that they will put in the time and effort needed to understand the theory enough to begin using it. And, reciprocally, there will be times when some of the material may seem too basic for those more familiar with Bowen's work. My hope is that these more experienced theorists and practitioners will find value in reviewing the theory and finding new ways to apply it.

Finally, this book is both theoretical and practical. Understanding the theory is essential: its scope, as well as its challenges and extensions. Understanding how to apply the theory to a variety of disciplines and careers is equally important. Theory and application are not mutually exclusive, of course. The value of theory is its sensible functionality. Kurt Lewin, a founder of social psychology, was fond of saying, "There is nothing so practical as a good theory." And application requires a firm foundation in theory. Theory application necessitates a continuous return to and reevaluation of one's work through the theory.

Throughout, I try to humanize and articulate the theory with many examples. Most times, these examples are composite cases from my collected experiences. They are altered or combined to protect the privacy of those with whom I worked. I have changed names when needed and, to the degree possible, provided anonymity for those involved. This is especially important in a memoir when referring to real people. Sometimes, these examples are cases that I have significantly altered from the original so as to essentially be fictional. *Any resemblance to persons living or dead is purely coincidental.* At all times, I use examples to highlight important aspects of the theory in order to better personalize and clarify what I'm trying to say.

In addition to charting my professional journey, I have also included chapters, journal articles, and professional presentation papers that I have authored, which are relevant to this voyage. As such, this book also serves as my "selected works" and demonstrates many of the ways that I have applied Bowen theory to particular populations and specific workplace, educational, and therapeutic environments.

I hope this book provides you with a comprehensive understanding of Bowen family systems theory's significance and how it can help you in your personal and professional life.

So, who am I and how did I get to this point?

I was born in 1955 to second-generation Italian-American immigrants in New York City. My mother, Antoinette (Toni), was the second of six children. Born in 1929, she was the oldest female and the second oldest child, a fortunate sibling position on my mother's extended side of the family. Antoinette was motivated to succeed beyond the economic circumstances of her parents, who struggled during the Great Depression after her father lost his auto repair shop. At the age of fifteen, Antoinette's mother, Genevese ("Jennie"), withdrew her from high school, despite her pleas and tears. She would work to help support the family. Antoinette's two younger sisters, Josephine ("Josie") and Angelina ("Angie"), wanted her married as soon as possible. As Italian tradition dictated, they couldn't marry until their oldest sister married. So, they waited. Antoinette married Eugene in 1953 at the ripe old age of twenty-four. (Her two sisters quickly married after her. Josephine was twenty and Angelina was eighteen.) Antoinette was restless and didn't want to raise her family in the Bronx, close to all of the extended family in the Italian immigrant neighborhood where she was raised. First moving to South Floral Park, Long Island, then to Kings Park, Long Island, my mother was the first of her family to move away, and also the first of her family to establish a separateness beyond that which was typical in her community.

My father, Eugene (Gene), was born in 1927. He was a hardworking but reluctant provider. As a teen, he dropped out of high school and cherished his free time, working on cars, going to the beach, dating, playing football in the neighborhood league, and enjoying life. World War II arrived and, with his father's approval and signature, since he was only seventeen, Gene enlisted in the Navy. The year was 1944. Father and son made this decision without his mother's knowledge and to her great protest and anger when she found out. This was a rare time that Gene and his father, Frank, quietly collaborated against Gene's mother, Anna. Gene served in the Navy for eighteen months, and then the war ended. He returned to the Bronx with a tattooed "Mother" and heart on his arm, an attempt to appease the angry Queen Regina.

Gene married when he was twenty-six. He followed Antoinette's initiatives to move away from their Italian families and neighborhood. He worked as a mail carrier for thirty years. On his 55th birthday, in 1982, the first day he was eligible for a full pension, he walked into his supervisor's office and tendered his resignation. This he did on his own, without discussing it with Antoinette. You can imagine her reaction when she found out. Such was their communication back then. From my father's perspective, he had fulfilled his obligations as a provider, father, and husband, and he had successfully launched four children. Gene was eligible for a full pension, and he was done working. Antoinette felt that they still had a mortgage and other financial responsibilities. She knew the finances; she paid the bills. They could not afford to stay in their home in Kings Park without Gene's income. Antoinette was not happy.

In the long run, though, Gene's retirement forced them to slow down and enjoy life more. This was good. A few years later, Antoinette retired after decades of back-breaking work in the garment industry, and they moved to West Palm Beach, Florida to be closer to Gene's sister, Dorothy, and her family. Four years later, they moved to Northern California to be closer to my siblings, who had all migrated there over the years, and to be closer to my wife Janet, me, and eventually their grandchildren, in San Diego.

My parents instilled in us the value of family, quality work, and, of particular importance, education to improve our standing in life. As a garment worker sewing heavy winter coats in hot factories, my mother knew what hard labor was. She had sacrificed a career as a clothing designer because my father felt threatened by her success and did not want her making more money than him. Instead, it was grueling factory piece work, with pay based on how many coats you produced. Nonetheless, Antoinette was committed to providing a middle-class life for her family.

My father often worked two jobs, doing what he needed to do to provide for us as well. I remember him waking up at 5:30 AM for work, getting home at 3:30 PM, and then leaving at 4:00 PM for the factory job of assembling and shipping transmission repair kits. He'd work until 10:00 PM, be home by 10:30 PM, and up again at 5:30 AM. He did this for years. Eventually, he ended his factory shift at 8:00 PM. He worked this shift for additional years.

While my mother's family all spoke Italian, her children would only speak English. (I regret that I could have been naturally bi-lingual.) Her children would all have American names, bucking the cultural trend of Italian immigrants in naming children after fathers, grandfathers, and other important family members. We were, in birth order, Gary, Wayne, Ronald, and Anne and not Anthony, Frank, Michael, and Anna. We would to be raised to assimilate as Americans, with little cultural or ethnic ties to the old neighborhood...except for food. You cannot escape the importance of food to an Italian-American household.

We settled in Kings Park, on the North Shore of Long Island in Suffolk County. It was there that I met my future wife, Janet. In middle school, she was friends with my younger brother, Ronald, as they worked together on the school yearbook. We met as youngsters, dated in high school, grew up together, fell in love, and eventually married in 1979. She is my partner in life, my one and only true love.

While most North Shore towns on Long Island were prosperous and cultured, Kings Park was an exception. It was a working-class community with deep economic ties to the psychiatric institution that was the economic base of the town. Irish and Italian mostly, with many Jewish families in the mix as well. Kings Park had the feel of a mid-island or south shore Long Island community on the 1960s and 70s—blue collar, conservative Republican, and white.

I was always fascinated by the psychiatric hospital. It covered many, many acres, existed in the heart of the community, and provided a buffer against residential encroachment. Its presence was felt throughout the town. While most buildings were locked, many residents were free to roam. The institution was not separated from the surrounding homes. In fact, we had to walk past one of the entrances of the psychiatric facility in order to attend our elementary school. This could be intimidating for children. My sister, Anne, was in kindergarten when we moved to Kings Park. Walking to and from school was always very scary for her. At six years old, this residence was much different than our suburban home in South Floral Park.

In effect, the psychiatric facility was fully integrated into the area. It was common to see the patients walking the grounds, walking the local streets, or walking throughout the town. They were simply a part of the place where I lived and grew up. In retrospect, it seems like most residents were suffering from a variety of chronic schizophrenias. Many had the capacity to walk about and return for meals and bedtime. Some were sweet; some were scary, especially for an eleven-year-old boy who had never seen mental illness. Why were they so different? Why did they move that way? Speak that way?

Fertile ground for a future psychologist, indeed.

Kings Park High School was tolerable, mostly because I took honors classes; at least the students wanted to learn, even if we were arrogant and not always appreciative.

I graduated high school and attended Stony Brook University on Long Island. It was and remains the most well regarded in the New York state university system, and it has a national reputation. This was fortunate, since it was only twenty minutes from my home. I commuted and worked off campus at the hardware department of Rickles department store my first year. I took a variety of liberal arts courses and became immediately attracted to psychology–motivation, perception, memory and learning, psychopathology, psychotherapy, neurology. This was great stuff. I was hooked! I graduated with a B.A. in psychology. I was interested in counseling and psychotherapeutic work, and I began thinking about graduate school.

I took a year off as I waited for Janet to finish her B.A. in Arts for Children at Brockport State College in upstate New York. I ran a low-vision clinic as an administrator and counselor for a year, living in Brockport and working in Rochester: too much snow, too much ice on the roads for too many days. After Janet graduated, we married at her home on Long Island and moved to San Diego, California. I was another second child who moved far away from home and community. In the end, Gary, Ronald, and Anne all followed, as did my parents. They settled, respectively, in Santa Cruz, San Francisco, San Rafael, and Windsor, cities and towns in Northern California.

Originally, Janet and I thought that we would live in San Diego for only a few years, until I completed my graduate studies. We were wrong. We never left the Southwest, and I'm not sure that we ever will. There is something about the landscape, the wilderness. "More nature than people," as Janet likes to say.

In 1979, I enrolled in the M.A. program for marriage and family therapy (MFT) at United States International University (U.S.I.U., now Alliant University) in San Diego. I followed up my master's degree by enrolling in their Ph.D. program in psychology with a specialization in marriage and family therapy. Eventually, I transferred into the new Psy.D. program with MFT specialization since I wanted a psychotherapy rather than research career. Even then, I was fascinated with intimate relationships and family systems. My graduate education was mostly adequate. There were some brilliant faculty and some not so brilliant. My cohort group was exceptional, and we learned a great deal from each other.

I was first exposed to systems theories in my graduate education. These were some of my most interesting and enlightening courses. I came to U.S.I.U. to learn how to work with couples and families. I was learning just that. I was enthralled by how family systems worked. Systems thinking appealed to my love of meta-thinking and "big picture" questions, such as with astrophysics and evolution.

My first introduction to Bowen theory was as a graduate student through the course Theories of Marriage and Family Therapy. While I was initially curious about Bowen family systems theory, it wasn't until years later that I had the opportunity to study the theory in more depth and with greater intentionality.

After graduating in 1982 with a doctorate in psychology (Psy.D.), I stayed on at U.S.I.U. as a lecturer. I was promoted to assistant professor and again to associate professor. I was moving up the academic ranks. In 1986, the college president asked me to direct the M.A. and doctoral psychology/marriage and family therapy programs at the university.

The university's president wanted to bring in the most important marriage and family therapists and theorists of the day for guest residencies and classes, so he offered the MFT faculty the funds to bring in eminent visiting professors from across the profession. One of our faculty members, distinguished professor and MFT pioneer James Framo, knew all of the first- and second-generation MFT founders, so we looked to Framo to help us secure distinguished visiting professors to enliven, deepen, and enrich the program.

This was a remarkable opportunity. The department set out to bring a host of prominent MFT luminaries to campus for two-to-four-week residencies. During my years as program director, I hosted these remarkable individuals, as well as provided logistical and educational support. In effect, I trained with and learned from them. As a part of this visiting faculty series, we brought in such notables as Carl Whitaker, Virginia Satir, Norm Paul and Betty Paul, Israel Charney, Maurizio Andolphi, and Edwin Friedman. This was an exciting time in the field, and U.S.I.U. was at the vanguard of MFT programs with our strong faculty and superstar residencies. While all of these prominent individuals were unique and provocative, it wasn't until April of 1989, when Edwin Friedman came to the university, that my life changed.

After Murray Bowen and Michael Kerr, Friedman was perhaps the most prominent Bowen theorist and therapist at the time, and probably the most widely-read and in-demand of the Bowen theorists and practitioner outside of the marriage and family therapy field. For years, Friedman had been making quite a name for himself as an organizational, congregational, and business consultant. In 1985, Ed published his landmark book on congregational systems called *Generation to Generation*. It remains the definitive text on Bowen theory and congregational systems. After the release of *Generation to Generation*, Friedman was in demand on the lecture and consultation circuit. We were fortunate to have him with us for a two-week residency for graduate students and local mental health practitioners and clergy.

It was then that I had the opportunity to work with Ed, and I got to know him personally. As program director, I served as his host and course assistant. In this capacity, we worked closely together for the duration of his residency. Ed was a fascinating man. He died in 1996, much too young and greatly missed. His mind was brilliant. He was able to see patterns of systems across disciplines in ways that were novel, imaginative, integrative, and profound. When Ed came to U.S.I.U., he had studied and applied Bowen theory for over twenty years as a rabbi, family therapist, White House consultant, government and business trainer, and educator. He was a radical thinker promoting subversive ideas about humans, systems, and the nature of change. People either loved him or hated him. The image that sticks in my mind is meeting Ed on the beach in 1992 at the American Association for Marriage and Family Therapy annual conference in Miami Beach, Florida. Here was Ed, unself-consciously walking the beach with this thin hair askew and wearing his shorts, knee-high socks, and dress shoes. He was an original. I have never met a man quite like him. To this day, he remains my most important Bowen family systems theory mentor.

My true introduction to Bowen theory stemmed from these initial discussions and encounters with him during his residency. Over the next several years and until his death in 1997, I had occasion to work with Ed as my supervisor in a difficult situation as a college dean at Prescott College when I was caught in an emotional triangle between the Board of Trustees and the outgoing president. Also, Ed solicited my feedback for a draft copy of his then upcoming chapter in Alan Gurman and David Kniskern's *Handbook of Family Therapy, Volume II*, which was published in 1991.

Ed provided me with generous and insightful perspectives on Bowen's theory that extended the theory to larger human systems such as the government, military, and other organizations. His approach also expanded Bowen theory in his own way, using fresh language that built on Bowen's work and providing imaginative perspectives that were uniquely his. Nonetheless, I always believed that Ed maintained a deep affinity for Bowen and his theory, going so far as to call himself a "disciple" of Murray Bowen. (This term "disciple" gets at his sly and provocative humor, since the term "disciple" from a rabbi provides a unique twist.)

I had read about Bowen family systems theory prior to Ed's residency. For some reason, it didn't grab me. I think that this might have been because most secondary sources do a poor job in articulating the theory. The few primary source readings that I had read didn't really affect me either.

But on the first night of Ed's residency, he gave a lecture and slideshow on maps to help the audience understand what emotional systems are and how they shape our thinking and our world. Ed uncovered a series of ancient, historical maps. He projected these maps and discussed how civilizations can get stuck, refusing to integrate new knowledge because of the power of emotional reactivity to nullify the thinking brain and flood the self and society with anxiety. Often, older maps were more accurate than newer maps. Cartographic knowledge did not always translate to more accuracy. Sometimes new knowledge conflicted with myth, religious teachings, or superstition. Knowledge itself didn't always confer greater precision with newer maps when compared with much older maps. There were even periods in history where maps varied wildly, again, despite the knowledge and exactitude of cartographers.

Ed used this extended metaphor to teach us about systems. It worked. I experienced an "aha" moment of exhilaration. I know that sounds dramatic. It was. I "got" what Ed was saying and where he was going. He understood that to *see* systems we had to *think* systems. We had to understand the fundamental forces that have shaped us throughout history, forces perhaps even older than life itself. It was bold and heady stuff. He reached me. So, too, did he grab many–though not all–of his audience of graduate students, faculty, and community professionals who were taking the seminar.

There are moments when I can see the bigger picture of systems. Like a dance, like a pulse, an almost "all at once" moment. This was the first of these moments: an understanding that knowledge and reality are dramatically influenced by set and setting, by perception and context. A second moment of revelation was when Ed introduced the emotional triangle. Emotional triangles are game changers. How can you not see an emotional triangle after you learn about them? There are emotional triangles everywhere: in this movie, on that cable show, in this book, in that art piece, in this relationship, in the political debate, in the legacy of racism and oppression, in the Palestinian-Israeli dispute, in the entire Syria debacle. These exceptional experiences through Ed's presentations are part of what changed me.

Bowen's theoretical concepts weren't all new to me. Some were, some weren't. I had been exposed to central concepts like differentiation and chronic anxiety before. Many theorists and therapists have taken parts of Bowen's theory and therapy and used them for their own purposes and in their own ways. And many of the pioneers were friends and colleagues so they freely used each other's language and ideas, sometimes slightly modifying a name or concept, sometimes not.

With Ed's presentation and a crash course in primary source readings in Bowen theory, I realized the profundity of the theory, the potential vastness of its possibilities. By the end of his residency, there was a palpable energetic among the faculty, students, and many of my friends and colleagues from the local community about the power and substance of Bowen family systems theory. Call it an emotional field shift. We wanted to keep this excitement alive, so we informally created a peer-group network based on Bowen theory. We continued to meet to discuss theory, review cases, and find other ways to apply Bowen's theory to our professional and personal lives. Over the years, I have maintained contact with several members of this group. Bowen theory changed them, as it did me.

By 1991, I was getting restless again. Plus, my wife and I had two young daughters–Carly, born in 1989, and Sage, born in 1991–and we wanted to raise them in a smaller community. San Diego was getting too large. I began looking for another faculty appointment and was immediately taken by an advertisement in the *Chronicle of Higher Education* for Prescott College. Prescott College is a small, four-year liberal arts college located in the central highlands, the pine-forested mountains of north-central Arizona. Prescott is a special community in so many ways. For a small city of less than 45,000 residents, it hosts Prescott College, a private, four-year liberal arts college; Yavapai College, a community college; and Embry-Riddle Aeronautical University, a private university. Prescott has four mild seasons, is a mile high, and boasts more culture than is typical for a town its size.

At the time, the tagline for Prescott College was "For the Liberal Arts and the Environment." The ad emphasized teaching as central to the job. Prescott College understood the value of collaborative, interdisciplinary learning. It prized small classes of less than fifteen students and promoted field studies across the curriculum. Prescott College was seeking teachers with experience and knowledge of "experiential education" or active pedagogy and thematic learning. It had a strong environmental component and, remarkably, they said that they also wanted someone with a good sense of humor. I was intrigued and excited!

During my interview, when asked about what I wanted to bring to the college, I answered that as an environmental, liberal arts college the faculty understood the importance of systemic processes, such as ecosystems and other Earth-based systems. I wanted to bring an equally important focus on human systems, in the form of family systems theory. I wanted to develop a series of courses to teach students about human, emotional systems. My thinking was that if I expose students to and trained them in understanding and seeing human systems as undergraduates, then they can take their systems thinking into their professional and personal lives. Since Prescott College students become activists, wilderness guides, artists, entrepreneurs, counselors, and others seeking to make the world a better place, I offered my belief that understanding human systems was an essential component in educating students and promoting the college's mission. To my delight, the committee agreed, as did the dean and the faculty. They hired me. Janet and I were ecstatic!

We moved to Prescott, Arizona in the summer of 1992 and, as I write this in 2020, I still live here. After I arrived, I taught for several years, creating new courses such as Family Systems Theory, Men's Studies, Counseling Skills, and Family Systems in Film and Literature and teaching other core classes in the human development-psychology curriculum. After a few years, the dean left, and I applied and prevailed in the search, becoming dean of the Resident Degree Program (RDP), serving more traditional college-aged students. I served in this capacity from 1995-2000. Here was another opportunity to bring Bowen theory, in particular the concept of differentiated leadership, to a new context. I used my time to train the faculty in the basics of the theory. Communication improved as people became aware of how emotional triangles are formed and how emotional reactivity can infect a group. I promoted personal responsibility and accountability throughout the system, including for the faculty, staff, students, and me.

Program Council, my management team, was especially open to learning about family systems theory. As program coordinators, they took their new understandings about emotional systems back to their departments. I wanted people to understand important concepts like triangulation, how everyone does it, how destructive it can be, and how to get out of an emotional triangle. I helped the management team learn family systems theory and understand the nature of emotional reactivity. We discussed systemic anxiety and how it can infect and flood a system. We provided vision for the RDP and worked closely with other faculty, students, staff, and administrators to become more differentiated leaders. These were some of the most productive and fun years of my life, and the Resident Degree Program thrived. My management team consisted mostly of friends. We were all raising our families together, growing the college in new and exciting ways, and enjoying life.

By 2000, I was growing unsettled and wanted a new challenge. The directorship of Skyview School opened up, and I decided to try my hand at executive leadership of an entire organization. Located in Prescott, Skyview School is a K-8 charter school based on Howard Gardner's theory of multiple intelligences. I had been involved with Skyview since the initial meeting of interested parents and community members in 1993. I helped to write and edit the original charter. I served on the board, including as board president, and provided on-going educational leadership training, using Bowen theory and differentiated leadership as guides, for the staff, faculty, and board.

In 2000, I became Skyview School's director for twenty-six months. This was a CEO-level position, and the school and I flourished, receiving state and national recognition. I taught the teachers and staff Bowen theory and differentiated leadership so that we could all use the same vocabulary and work toward the same academic and emotional goals. The teachers worked to apply differentiated leadership in their classrooms. Differentiation is synonymous with Gardner's personal intelligences—the interpersonal intelligence and the intrapersonal intelligence—so the re-focus to a larger conceptual system made sense to most of the teachers and staff.

Janet was also deeply involved at Skyview. She was a co-founder and original board member. Over the years she served in a variety of roles, including director for two years, integrated arts coordinator, and creative movement teacher. Years later, she taught kindergarten for six years.

Our children attended Skyview School as well. Those were special years, all of us walking to school together and sharing our lives in parallel and intersecting spaces. For twenty-six months, I applied Bowen theory to educational leadership as a charter school CEO, worked with my wife and partner, saw my children on a regular basis during the week, and led the school as director. What more could I ask?

By 2002, the dean who replaced me was pressuring me to return to Prescott College or resign. I always saw my primary career as a teacher and educator, so I returned to Prescott College in the autumn of 2002. I wasn't ready for fulltime, permanent administration. Back at Prescott College, I was free to continue developing a series of Bowen theory and Bowen theory-infused courses. I got to co-teach with some of our best faculty. I kept myself engaged with new classes and refurbished older ones. I presented at conferences, wrote papers, published work, and taught full time as a professor of peace studies and psychology.

My next sabbatical was in 2005-2006. I wasn't seeking to return to Skyview School as director. But it was struggling once again and, again, the board of directors offered me the directorship. I felt excited by the offer and the new challenge. In the ensuing twenty-eight months, I helped to resolve the leadership crisis and to stabilize the school emotionally and financially. Then, with the help of teachers, parents, students, and staff, we expanded enrollment and facilities, and returned Skyview School to its original mission as a multiple intelligences school with an active pedagogy and a thematic approach to integrating curriculum. This was my third experience with executive administration, and it was particularly rewarding. I had matured over the preceding ten years and, eventually, the work was easier and less fraught.

In 2000, my mediation career began in earnest as I started mediating at the Superior Court of Arizona, Yavapai County. Prescott is the county seat. I mediated domestic cases to develop parenting plans for divorcing parents and mediated victim-offender cases for adolescent offenders and their victims. I also provided conciliation counseling for those questioning whether or not to divorce. Here was a fresh and satisfying way of serving the community, developing new skills, and translating Bowen's theory to the mediation and conciliation room. This was exciting stuff! I first wrote about applying Bowen theory to mediation in *Mediation Quarterly* and in 2011 published a book about it, *Applying Family Systems Theory to Mediation: A Practitioner's Guide*. The thing about Bowen theory is that once you understand emotional triangles, you cannot *not* see them; they are all around us. Once you understand the power of chronic and acute anxiety, you recognize that learning how to self-sooth is the best way to calm the hyper-aroused brain. Once you understand Bowen theory, you understand the weight of multi-generational legacies, and you come to realize that we can feel powerless, deny them, or choose how to use them for our advantage and for that of our descendants. These understandings can be applied to all human systems. They are ubiquitous.

For eighteen years, I worked with the Alternative Dispute Resolution program as a trainer, mediator, and conciliator. For over a decade, I co-mediated with Janet. We worked with adolescents in diversion programs, victims and offenders, divorcing parents, and grandparents seeking designated time with their grandchildren. The work was deeply rewarding.

I returned to Prescott College in 2006. It was changing. In 2008, there was a "perfect storm" that hit the country and deeply shook the foundations of small, liberal arts colleges. The Great Recession reverberated across the nation, including higher education. Families were going underwater in the housing crisis and no longer able to finance their children's education with home equity loans. Students were reluctant to take on debt. Students were staying closer to home, especially for the first two years of college. Enrollments at Prescott College plummeted. Across the country, small colleges were closing.

Prescott College was struggling, and as I said, it was changing. The limited residence and online programs now have larger enrollments than the resident program. Suffice it to say that it is still here, smaller and trying to find a way to successfully transition in the new economy and economic realities of our times. It is still a college "For the Liberal Arts and the Environment." Now, though, the tagline reads, "For the Liberal Arts, the Environment, and Social Justice." I hope that it finds a way to survive and prosper. It is a valuable jewel in the progressive education movement.

My personal circumstances changed in February of 2012 when my father-in-law, Louis Bicknese, had a major stroke. He moved in with Janet and me. While he recovered much of his functioning, at eighty-nine, he needed to live with us and not live alone. My wife and I wanted to find a way to support him and transition to a new phase of our lives after being in education for over thirty years each.

I was ready for another change, and so I accepted what became an exit sabbatical for 2014-2015. I retired from Prescott College in June, 2015. I was sixty. As I age, I become more and more conscious of time as a non-renewable resource. I was tired of working in a place that was in constant crisis, and, perhaps more importantly, I wanted a change. I didn't want to continue a life pace that was "in fifth gear" all of the time.

In 2017, Janet and I resigned from the Superior Court. A change in leadership brought a new director whose vision for the mediation program differed from ours. Also, Lou was aging and becoming more impaired. We knew that it was only a matter of time until he needed a higher level of care. Retiring from the courthouse afforded us the opportunity to offer that greater assistance and to pursue other interests.

Currently, I am licensed in California as a marriage and family therapist and licensed in Arizona as a psychologist. I received my Advanced Mediator Practitioner certification from the national organization Association for Conflict Resolution. These professional endorsements have allowed me to work in a variety of environments with a wide range of clients over the decades.

While I have been writing this book since the publication of my last one in 2011, it wasn't until I retired from Prescott College that I had significant time to devote to this project. (There is little discretionary time as a college professor.) After a professional lifetime of mentorship, training, and application through Bowen theory, I wanted to reflect on what I learned: my successes and my challenges.

The sections of the book are divided into general topic areas. Section One begins with an introduction and theory overview, including comprehensive descriptions of the central concepts. I have included some of the neurological evidence in support of the theory. Here, I also address theory expansion. After a third of a century steeping myself in and using Bowen theory in both my professional and personal life, I explore the question: Is Bowen theory a "living theory"? And, if it is, how does the theory evolve after the passing of the founder?

Section Two details how I taught Bowen theory to undergraduates. I include the courses that I created at Prescott College, which were designed to infuse Bowen theory into a progressive undergraduate curriculum.

Section Three explore the application of Bowen theory to differentiated leadership. I include my work as an educational leader in two institutions, as dean at Prescott College and director of Skyview School.

In Section Four, I apply Bowen family systems theory to supervision and training.

Section Five is a collection of selected chapters, journal articles, and professional presentation papers that I wrote over the years. These writings provide a window into my thinking as a practicing Bowen theorist and practitioner. I also wanted my most important writings collected in one location. These include specific case history chapters on teaching family systems theory through film and literature, as well as training undergraduate mediators using Bowen theory as a guide. This section also includes chapters on Bowen theory and mediation, conceptualizing addiction and recovery through a Bowen theory framework, Bowen theory and peacemaking, Bowen theory and conciliations, and working with incest families using a Bowen theory model.

I believe that my life experiences and different careers provide a unique perspective on the possibilities and the applications of Bowen family systems theory. I aspire to inspire you with this unique and valuable theory.

SECTION ONE

INTRODUCTION, HISTORY, THEORY OVERVIEW, AND THEORY EXPANSION

CHAPTER ONE: INTRODUCTION

WHY BOWEN FAMILY SYSTEMS THEORY?

Bowen's family systems theory proposes a universal way to understand how people think, feel, and behave, regardless of race, gender, ethnicity, socio-economic status, religion, or other categories of identity. Understanding and applying Bowen theory professionally and personally has been my life work, as well as the life work of others.

About Bowen and the Development of Family Systems Theory

Murray Bowen was trained as a physician and practiced as a psychiatrist. As such, he was a medical doctor committed to the science of human development and behavior. He was one of the first-generation pioneers in the emerging field of marriage and family therapy in the 1950s. Bowen rejected what he saw as the "pseudo-science" of psychoanalysis and the acontextual approaches of both behaviorism and "third force" psychology. Instead, he chose another way, linking human behavior to evolutionary biology. His theory is an ecological theory of the human, as it sought to incorporate people into the circle of life on the planet. That is, rather than seeing humans as unique and different, Bowen placed humans squarely in the evolutionary history of planetary life.

In this way, Bowen family systems theory examines the similarities and differences between human and non-human life. Bowen's theory remains distinctive in incorporating evolutionary biology in the understanding of human systems. For example, Bowen saw humans as a part of the rich tapestry of evolutionary development, rather than being apart from it. Whereas most psychological theories of humans conceptualize Homo sapiens as unique life forms, Bowen theory views humans as imbedded in the evolution of life on Earth. In this way, the theory parallels systems theories and evolutionary theories in biology and cosmology.

Bowen lived from 1913 to 1990. Initially trained as a traditional psychoanalyst, Bowen also mentored with Harry Stack Sullivan, a psychiatrist who was concerned with the more social features of psychiatry, instead of simply searching for the interior, intrapsychic factors of humanity common with psychodynamic approaches. Sullivan's influence and Bowen's own curiosity about the human condition and the natural world shaped the development of his theory, which observed the links between people and nature. As a scientist, Bowen rejected conjecture and inference about the inner states of the human psyche. He believed that speculation and assumption was insufficiently thorough as it lacked the more objective analysis that clinical observation provided.

In this way, Bowen began developing a theory of family functioning that was, in his mind, more observable and therefore more scientific. His approach was rooted in current and multigenerational observations of human and family interactions. His theory did not require suppositions regarding interior states. With his focal point on evident and observable systems, Bowen developed a theory of human systems that was remarkably different from Freud's theory and the dominant psychoanalytical/psychodynamic models that required assumptions and speculation. In these ways, Bowen family systems theory may be considered the first significant ecological theory of human systems.

Bowen's approach was always different than that of his contemporaries who, along with him, were formatting the incipient field of marriage and family therapy at the time. Unlike his colleagues, Bowen wanted to develop a family systems theory that was rooted in science, specifically evolutionary biology. Up to that point, most psychological theories focused on the individual's internal conflicts, motivations, and desires.

What this meant was that Bowen's theory was more generally a theory about how we function in the world as humans and not simply a theory about human families and psychiatric symptoms. In this way, Bowen theory always had a theoretical scope and range that stretched far beyond its original parameters in family therapy. In truth, what I discovered is that Bowen family systems theory is a theory of humans that is just as applicable to leadership, organizations, societies, international relations, health, and the arts, as it is to individuals, couples, and families in treatment.

It was the magnitude, depth, breadth, and sheer audacity of Bowen's theory that initially fascinated me as a graduate student and later as a program director, systems therapist, mediator, and professor. Here was an approach trying to do more than simply help individuals, couples, and families eliminate toxic symptoms and improve their functioning. Here was a theory that could advance the lives of *all* humans in *any* relationship, regardless of culture, race, gender, socio-economic status, religion, and other categories of identity. From my perspective and that of many other Bowen theory practitioners, Bowen theory seemed to be a theory of everything. And, as such, if the theory was correct, Bowen theory could also be used for the benefit of non-symptomatic, "well" people to deepen and enrich lives by improving individual and social functioning, helping us become more mindful in our thinking, more intentional in our actions, and more responsible in our relationships. In fact, I align myself most closely with Bowen theorist, rabbi, and leadership consultant Edwin Friedman who viewed Bowen theory as a template to evolve the species. No small task indeed. But it was exactly this grandiosity that attracted me to this theory. Bowen family systems theory seems to have it all.

Bowen's theory has occupied a particularly unique and tantalizing niche among social science theories over the past sixty plus years. Originally conceptualized as a way of understanding humans and human relationships, particularly the relationship system of human families in distress, Murray Bowen received inspiration from his observations of natural systems, his study of evolutionary biology, and his insatiable curiosity about the human condition.

As such, though Bowen's theory was first proposed as a comprehensive way of conceptualizing and treating people and families who were suffering, it was always capable of articulating a more inclusive, broad-based understanding of all relationship systems. It wasn't long, then, until theorists and practitioners began applying Bowen family systems theory to business, health care, education, leadership, congregational systems, mediation, and other human endeavors.

In a seminal article, "Towards the Differentiation of Self in Administrative Systems" presented in 1972 at the Georgetown Family Symposium, Bowen applies his theory outside the family therapy realm and to his work as the Director of the Georgetown Center for the Study of the Family. Here, Bowen explores important applications of and implications for the theory to himself, as a leader, which included the following insight: focusing on one's own emotional integrity creates an emotional resonance in which other people are able to focus on theirs. That is, from Bowen's perspective, the more he paid attention in his directorship to his own responsibilities and self-management, and the more he stayed authentically involved with and connected to others in the organization, the more he promoted the effective functioning of others. Then, they, too, could develop greater responsibility for *their* selves and the work that *they* needed to accomplish in order to become essential leaders in their own right.

Bowen also pointed out several other important considerations in developing functional and effectual administrative systems. For example, Bowen said that he didn't care what others thought, that is, whether or not a colleague agreed or disagreed with him, he just wanted to know about it. What was important to Bowen was that differences didn't go "underground," where gossip and innuendo can cause havoc in the organization. In addition, Bowen used his own theory to articulate several other important components of effective organizational functioning, including the significance of direct communication, a unity of vision, and a hierarchical structure that clarifies the positions and roles of those in the system, while simultaneously allowing for flexibility and fluidity.

A successful implementation of his theory in an organizational context means that anyone in an administrative system can implement parts of the vision, take a leadership role with others, and find meaning and value in the institution's work. In essence, Murray Bowen found that by promoting his own effective functioning and staying appropriately linked to the organizational body, others were free to do the same.

Over the years, Bowen theorists and practitioners recognized what Bowen did–that his theory was applicable across a wide-range of human disciplines and endeavors. Adherents began finding new and innovative uses for Bowen family systems theory outside traditional therapeutic treatment systems. For example, since 1965, the Bowen Center for the Study of the Family has hosted annual conferences and symposia devoted to expanding Bowen theory across the disciplines and professions, as well as articulating important links between Bowen theory and findings in other areas of inquiry. Compendium books on Bowen theory's expanded applications were published from two of these conferences. The first collection was 1982's *Understanding Organizations: Applications of Bowen Family Systems Theory;* the second compilation was 1996's *The Emotional Side of Organizations: Applications of Bowen Theory.* Disciplines and fields included classroom education, nursing, organizational leadership, corrections (crime and punishment), international relations, the clergy and congregations, primatologist, and ornithology, among others.

Also, one only has to peruse the annual conferences and symposia of the Bowen Center over the years and examine the leading Bowen theory journal, *Family Systems: A Journal of Natural Systems Thinking in Psychiatry and the Sciences*, to appreciate the significant work that has gone into broadening and integrating Bowen theory into non-human and non-clinical systems.

In his pivotal 1988 article, "Darwin to Freud to Bowen," originally published in *The Georgetown Magazine*, psychiatrist Michael Kerr, Bowen's direct "heir" and perhaps the most important living figure in the field of Bowen theory today, compares the significance of Bowen's theory to both Darwin's theory of evolution and Freud's psychoanalytic theory of human development. Kerr discusses how it took decades for Darwin's findings, as articulated in *Origin of the Species,* to be accepted into mainstream scientific thought and by the general public.

In addition, Kerr offers Freudian theory as a necessary but insufficient advancement in understanding the science of human behavior. While many aspects of Freud's thinking have been modified or even rejected over the decades, Freud promoted the scientific study of human behavior and the treatment of maladies of the human condition through a theoretical and treatment system that eventually garnered a place of greater scientific support and public acceptance. Though today few psychotherapists offer the traditional "talking cure" practiced by Freudian psychoanalysts, millions of people still receive psychotherapeutic treatment from counselors and psychotherapists in modified forms of the talking cure.

And while Freud's work has not always been validated through greater scientific scrutiny and social critique over the past century, the significance of his thinking to promote a more biological and hence scientific understanding of mental and emotional processes, functioning, and psychopathology has gained considerable ground over the last few decades.

In fact, some psychiatrists and researchers have renewed their interest in Freudian theory through their investigations in neuroscience. The new branch of Freudian theory, neuropsycho-analysis, is one such attempt to bridge the insights gained from psychoanalysis with the science of neurobiology into a workable psychotherapy based on the latest findings on the brain. The journal, *Neuropsychoanalysis: An Interdisciplinary Journal for Psychoanalysis and the Neurosciences*, is one such leader in this new integration.

The evolution of Bowen's theory may be similar. In a radical departure from the traditional treatment of psychological and psychiatric disorders that historically involved the individual patient and the doctor, the theory and practice of Bowen's family systems theory have expanded our understanding of the human condition. This critical shift from psychoanalytic theory to family systems theory included the shift from inferred intrapsychic forces acting almost acontextually within the person to observable personal, interpersonal, and relationship forces that affect a person and related symptoms. This change also included the importance of understanding people as a part of a multigenerational legacy of influences, as well as the central focus on current systemic processes and stressors in the current family/nuclear family, work system, non-human environment, and other professional and personal relationships.

In this way, the study of human behavior "from Freud to Bowen" may be more properly conceptualized as altering the entire field of psychology, psychiatry, and counseling. The implications for this change provide the basis for a paradigm shift as, articulated by Thomas Kuhn in his seminal 1962 essay, "The Structure of Scientific Revolutions." For Kuhn, a paradigm shift in science was a fundamental dislocation from one foundational scientific theory to another, an essential alteration in how science understands and addresses an issue or a theory. The evolution from Newtonian physics to Einsteinian physics is one such paradigm shift. Bowen theory can be understood in a similar way, as a paradigm shift not only from individual to systems thinking in psychiatry but a far-reaching and fundamental alteration in how human development is conceptualized, our inescapable connection to nature and evolution, and how emotional maladies are comprehended and treated.

As an example, today it may seem obvious that providing therapeutic services to a couple together in relationship therapy is often preferred to treating a couple individually. Or, similarly, it may appear self-evident that working with an entire family with a troubled adolescent makes "systemic sense" in that it is a more integrated approach to affecting change than simply treating the symptomatic adolescent in isolation or removing her from the context where the problematic behavior developed and flourished. These are fundamental alterations in assessment and treatment brought on by the family theory and therapy movement. They were ushered in by the radical psychiatrists and psychologists–including Bowen–in the middle and late part of the 20th century. But these shifts in thinking about and treating psychiatric and systemic disorders are a relatively recent phenomenon. Before this time in Western culture, couples and families were never treated together, lest the psychotherapist "contaminate the transference" between patient and psychotherapist and hence regress the patient's progress.

Nonetheless, while there have been fundamental changes in the way that individuals, couples, and families are conceptualized and treated, a true understanding of human emotional systems and their effects on family members remains a rather limited endeavor. It has been more than sixty years since the beginning of the family therapy revolution. Even so, it is still more common today to bring in a family adjunctively to support the changes in an addict's lifestyle, behavior, and affect in order to promote his sobriety than it is to understand the multigenerational and nuclear family forces that promoted and enhanced addiction and addictive behaviors in the first place.

In contrast, a family systems approach to treating the addict provides a systemic restructuring of the family's interactions and a maturation of the family's emotional system. This systemic approach, in turn, promotes second-order, or systemic change, instead of simply providing symptom relief, or first-order change. Using a family systems theory and therapy approach, the family context alters and evolves so as to encourage and support more differentiated individual and family functioning rather than only providing an acontextual, cursory support to reinforce the addict's recovery.

Unfortunately, Bowen theorists and practitioners—even in the areas of psychology, psychiatry, and counseling—still face tremendous resistance within their professions in advocating for such a profound paradigmatic shift. We live in a world of limited and diminishing health care resources, and the emotionality of the culture is more attuned to a "quick fix" mentality and, as a consequence, time-limited, "evidence-based" treatments. In fact, this fast fix approach is common with societies in emotional regression, which we seem a part of currently. The kind of in-depth, systemic investigation, coaching, and treatment required by a Bowen family systems theory practitioner is often at odds with the current mandates of the culture. As a result, we often confront tremendous opposition and obstacles when undertaking this profound work. The culture and the times are more habituated to eliminating the symptom—which offers first-order change—instead of providing the resources to affect generations-deep, systemic, second-order change. Bowen family systems theorists, therapists, and practitioners are, nonetheless, working across communities to affect this very kind of long-term change and transformation.

And, because all humans interact with multiple social systems—work, family, school, friendships, government, and so on—these relationships all influence the health and wellbeing of the participants in these human systems. It seems that family systems themselves are nested within larger and smaller systems. As such, Bowen's family systems theory provides an instructive lens through which we can understand personal and societal evolution (and dysevolution) through a reliable, comprehensive model that is consistent or isomorphic across levels and scales of systems.

Family systems therapists are still treating distressed individuals, couples, and families through a systemic lens. In addition, Bowen theory practitioners are using what they learned from the theory to their work in other disciplines, including leadership, education, mediation, supervision, ministry, health care, business, art, and a host of disciplinary, interdisciplinary, and multidisciplinary endeavors.

In the spirit of Bowen's pioneering and visionary efforts in offering a more comprehensive, universal, and integrated theory of human systems and human functioning, I wrote this book as a way of charting my odyssey in applying Bowen family systems theory over the past thirty-five years to a variety of disciplines and settings. These include my work in conducting individual, couples, and family therapy; mediation and conciliation; training and supervision; educational leadership as a college dean and charter school director; and professor, writer, and theorist.

I didn't want to duplicate something that had been published before. Rather than try to replicate, for example, the excellent work of Ona Cohen Bregman and Charles M. White in their book *Bringing Systems Thinking to Life: Expanding the Horizons for Bowen Family Systems Theory*, I wrote this book using a more narrative approach whenever possible, describing case studies, articulating personal reflections on my journey in understanding and applying Bowen theory over the decades, and proposing possibilities to expand Bowen's theory. I hope that these stories and perspectives inspire you to find ways of applying this remarkable theory to your own work and your own life in seeking a more effective and evolutionarily progressive way of affecting positive change in yourself and in our world.

The next chapter provides a comprehensive overview of Murray Bowen's central concepts in family systems theory, as well as some current neurological research supporting aspects of the theory and my thoughts on Bowen theory expansion and evolution. This chapter offers an overview of Bowen family systems theory for those less familiar with the material and a review for those who have a basic understanding of the theory.

CHAPTER TWO

BOWEN FAMILY SYSTEMS THEORY: A HISTORY AND INDIVIDUAL CORE CONCEPTS

Murray Bowen formulated his family systems theory from the mid-1950s until his death in 1990. Bowen family systems theory is complex and extensive, and, much has been written about it. Bowen theory is insightful, logical, intricate, well-designed, multifaceted, and straightforward. Murray Bowen formulated his theory to comprehend human and family functioning and to treat families in clinical settings. This clinical application of Bowen theory to individual, couple, and family psychotherapy continues, and, over time, applications expanded into non-family, non-clinical populations and settings as well.

As Bowen theory relies on the intersection and overlay of all of its central concepts, it can be challenging to articulate individual components. Nevertheless, what follows is a brief history of Bowen's theory and my overview of its central concepts.

Family systems theory was the unappreciated stepchild of the mental health and mental illness professions in the 1950s and 1960s, which were dominated by the psychoanalytic and psychodynamic theories of Sigmund Freud and his colleagues. After World War II, behaviorism was in ascendance. Initially based in B.F. Skinner's theories, behaviorism was developed, in part, to counter the "unscientific" approach of psychoanalysis and was designed to provide a more observable scientific methodology for the study of psychology and the individual.

At the time, the most dominant perspective to challenge both psychodynamic theories and behaviorism was the "third force," humanistic theories and therapies of Carl Rogers, Abraham Maslow, Victor Frankl, and their contemporaries. Third force psychology and counseling challenged the dominance of both psychodynamic and behavioral thinking by offering a more hopeful, growth-focused, expansive, and positive view of human development and psychology. All of these early and mid-20th century approaches to psychology and psychiatry, though, viewed the individual as the primary focus in assessment, diagnosis, and treatment. At the time, the quality and dynamics of a person's relationships weren't a part of assessment, diagnosis, and treatment. Fortunately, for a growing number of psychiatrists, psychologists, and social workers, isolating the individual was seen as limited at best and destructive at worst.

It was in the late 1940s, within this environment saturated with individual-based clinical theories and therapies, that Murray Bowen began his professional career as a psychiatrist. By the 1950s, something was afoot in the psychiatric community, at least with some of its more restless, innovative, and creative thinkers and practitioners. Bowen and his contemporaries rejected the individual, non-contextual approaches to assessment, diagnosis, and treatment, and they started to incorporate novel advancements in understanding and treating humans through a relationship lens. From this imaginative perspective, these innovators created theories about the family system. Truly, this was an exciting and ground-breaking time for the field of mental health.

James Framo and Henry Dicks created Object Relations Family Therapy. Gregory Bateson, Don Jackson, Jay Haley, John Weakland, Virginia Satir, and others fashioned Communications Family Therapy. Carl Whittaker and Thomas Malone founded Symbolic-Experiential Family Therapy. Jay Haley was responsible for originating Strategic Family Therapy. Haley also influenced the development of both Structural Family Therapy with Salvador Minuchin and the family life-cycle with Betty Carter and Monica McGoldrick. Other schools of family therapy were also born during these years as well.

Even within this creative nexus, however, Murray Bowen's approach was unique. Instead of simply designing another theory of the human family and the development of family symptoms, Bowen boldly expressed an inclusive, systemically-based theory of human development and functioning that was centered on his observations of families and other natural systems.

Bowen Family Systems Theory Concepts

Bowen presented eight central concepts to his theory. Over time, Bowen and Kerr altered several of these concepts, expanded a few, and consolidated others. Conceptualizing the theory as articulated by Michael Kerr in Kerr and Bowen's 1988 landmark presentation of Bowen theory, *Family Evaluation*, these include:

1. The emotional system
2. Individuality and togetherness
3. Differentiation
4. Chronic anxiety
5. Triangles (emotional triangles)
6. Nuclear family emotional process
7. Multigenerational emotional process

While not a central concept in Kerr's presentation of the theory, Bowen offered societal regression as essential to understanding the vast scope of Bowen theory. As such, I include it in my review and in several of my chapters through the more expansive concept of societal emotional process.

The Emotional System

One day I was observing my cat, Midnight, looking through the window at some birds on the balcony. Midnight started making deep-throated sounds and began walking closer to the window. It seemed to me that her hunting instincts had been activated. Cat owners know what I'm talking about. We see it often. This hunting activation is a part of the species' innate capacity to hunt. This hunting instinct has not been eliminated despite thousands of years of domestication. This reaction exists through the emotional system, a system of behaviors and actions based on a combination of nature and nurture that has been "inherited" by mammals and other living organisms through millions if not billions of years of evolution.

Bowen did not specifically cite the emotional system as one of his central concepts. Nevertheless, like Kerr, I find it useful to begin with the emotional system in order to better understand the integration and complexity of the theory, as well as the emotional system's roots in evolutionary biology.

To better differentiate Bowen theory from Freud's theory of psychoanalysis and other psychodynamic approaches—which are largely off-shoots of Freudian theory—Bowen highlighted natural processes and forces that unite humans with evolutionary history. Through his years of observing families and natural systems, along with his extensive readings in the natural sciences, especially evolutionary theory, Bowen understood that human behavior is a part of evolutionary history. That history is a part of us and lives on in us.

In effect, Bowen presupposed that we cannot escape our evolutionary legacy, especially when we experience threat. It is what makes us *Homo sapiens*, the descendants of *Homo erectus*. This heritage is ever present and manifests in multiple ways and especially during times of challenge and stress. To this end, Bowen theorized that much human behavior is not merely the result of conditioned stimulus-response behavioral sequences or from interior-laden conflicts presupposed and inferred. Rather, Bowen viewed a good deal of human behavior as largely automatic, deeply embedded in evolutionary history. Bowen believed that much human behavior and ascribed motivation are more a function of habitual, "instinctual" development and less a function of thoughtfully cognating or consciously feeling. While not all human behavior is instinctual or automatic, from Bowen's perspective, a fair amount of human functioning is reactive to these ancient evolutionary, hard-wired forces and the cues that activate them in our environment.

Emotional reactivity, then, is the reflexive thinking, feeling, and acting that is driven by our evolutionary history and that of our ancestors. Emotional reactivity is a function of limbic activation to perceived or actual threat; it is a behavior that is part of most species. It is what often governs behavior when things get intense.

For Bowen, reactive behaviors are automatic and not a part of our conscious choosing. In *Family Evaluation*, Kerr identified this intensity of habitual functioning and reactivity as the *emotional system*. He distinguished this system from the feeling system and the thinking or intellectual system. Like the bee attracted to a flower, the cat whose hunting instinct is activated by the presence of a bird, or the child crying for his mother when lost in a grocery store, functioning through the emotional system represents behavior that is involuntary, unthinking, and automatic. Emotional reactivity is a constant in the human behavior repertoire, and it is ever-present across time, cultures, and people.

Through the emotional system, Bowen theory conceptualizes humans as a part of the natural world and governed by the same evolutionary processes that govern all life. While we often ascribe motivation and reasoning to our behaviors based on perceived or assumed internal states or external circumstances, Bowen said that such attributions are difficult to verify. Instead, he suggested that our "instinctual" behavior is a function of that which has been "written" in nature for billions of years. Experiences and culture certainly influence and shape how many of these behaviors are expressed, but emotional reactivity is universal across time, space, people, and cultures. A product of evolution, our emotional system is in large part a function of our most primitive, "reptilian" brain, though it is not merely an expression of brain functioning.

Ed Friedman, in his 2007 publication *A Failure of Nerve*, states that reactivity in the emotional system is a cellular phenomenon. He reminds us that emotionally reactive feelings and actions are experienced throughout the entire body. Bowen believed that all humans share this reflexive process with each other and with non-human life. Though humans often attribute their actions to a variety of thinking-based or feeling-based stimuli, Bowen suggested that these are rationalizations that represent surface perceptions and justifications. In fact, emotional reactivity is the result of evolutionarily ancient processes. From this perspective, human behavior, including our exchanges with other people, is often a function of something much "deeper" than intellectual or feeling expression. Bowen theory assumes that much human behavior, actions, and reactions are expressions that go beyond the human. They are, rather, what binds humankind with all life.

Bowen theory recognizes that experiences, including context, shape the person as well. Genetics are complicated, though it is increasingly clear that there is rarely a one-to-one correspondence between a behavior or trait and a single gene. Rather, there is a "gene pool," with genes activated and quieted often based on experiences. Human "nature," through the emotional system, then, is a complicated amalgamation of nature *and* nurture, and these variables incorporate the expression of genes from the gene pool; current environmental circumstances including life experiences and conditions; intergenerational patterns and legacies; the qualitative functioning of the family; sibling position; epigenetic factors affecting gene expression, and a host of other important social, ecological, and emotional factors.

The expression of the emotional system is particularly automatic in difficult and stressful circumstances. This emotional reactivity clearly has its roots in survival. While some of these automatic reactions are obvious "evolutionary mismatches"–for example, we may become hyper-aroused in the same way for an important speech as we would fleeing and escaping the saber tooth tiger–the fact is that through our evolutionary "programming" we can react similarly to both life-threatening circumstances and uncomfortable, but non-life-threatening events.

An example: two people, Leslie and Martin, are both rushing to get out of the grocery store. Both spot a newly opened check-out lane, head for the lane and arrive at the same time. Both believe they arrived first and think that the other is being unfair and selfish in trying to cut into the line. They begin to raise their voices and yell at one another. The situation escalates and neither backs down.

A variety of dynamics in his emotional system influences Martin to intensify the quarrel. They include a genetic predilection to violence, a family background of conflict, and current issues such as a relationship breakup. Because of these factors, Martin is more likely to become automatically hyper-aroused as this incident activates his fight-flight-freeze reactions, and he experiences threat. Consequently, Martin is looking for a fight and, in the circumstances at the store, he gets one. Martin's life experiences do not predispose him to assume individual accountability for his behaviors. People who know Martin call him hotheaded, rash, and immature. In this way, Martin's ability for successful self-reflection and self-containment of anxiety in challenging situations is diminished, and his actions can be thought of as more reactive or "mindless." When the interaction ends, Martin will probably defend his behavior as justified. These excuses, though, are a part of his reactive thinking, since they are neither complete nor accurate. Rather, Martin's actions are emotional reactions to what he automatically and unthinkingly experiences as a danger or threat. His ability to soothe himself is limited by the assortment of emotional features listed above, and his level of emotional maturity (or basic differentiation) is fairly low. He is deficient in his capacity to stop his anxiety from escalating after the initial activating event.

Like Martin, Leslie reacts similarly. She initially feels danger. Her threat activation system is also engaged, and she, too, raises her voice, yells, and demands his capitulation. While she also gets hyper-aroused, Leslie's collective life experiences lead her to accept greater personal responsibility for her behaviors. She has an increased capacity for both self-reflection and self-management, and so when Martin gets red in the face and begins to hyperventilate, she realizes that the situation is getting out of hand. She tries to achieve some equanimity and think her way out of the cycle of aggression. Leslie raises her hands in a sign of appeasement, and she apologizes to Martin for her actions and for increasing the conflict. Leslie's composed bearing and acceptance of personal accountability assists Martin in calming down, and the intensity around their situation quickly evaporates.

Leslie clearly displays an elevated degree of basic differentiation compared to Martin, and her capacity to remain reasonably composed—to regulate her emotions, assume more personal accountability, and interact with Martin more appropriately—soothes the situation and eliminates the dispute. Leslie exhibits a heightened ability for reflective thinking and acting instead of just allowing her reactivity to dominate throughout the crisis.

While highlighting humans' interwoven relationship with all life and to basic evolutionary development, Bowen also focused on what makes us unique from other organisms on the planet. Indeed, Bowen recognized that we possess a unique potential to manage our emotionality in intense situations and respond with greater mindfulness. Bowen theory highlights our species' distinctiveness when discussing the development of an advanced feeling system (in contrast with the more ancient emotional system), as well as a highly evolved thinking or intellectual system.

Bowen believed that, for humans, the intellectual system and its cerebral cortex were the pinnacle of biological evolution. In particular, he regarded our pre-frontal lobe as the crown jewel of the brain's development. This is the seat of abstract thinking. It is where we recognize the future consequences of our actions and our ability to reflect and learn from our behaviors. Our pre-frontal lobe is where planning and foresight occur. It is where we can regulate or at least manage some of our more "primitive" reactions. And, it is the cerebral cortex and the pre-frontal lobe that allow us to respond in a different way from our animal ancestors.

Bowen realized that while much of our behavior is automatic and reactive, humans have acquired an impressive capacity to step back and think about what we are doing and what will occur as a result of our actions, even in challenging environments. While we may not always respond based on reflective thinking, our evolutionary inheritance is such that we can nurture the ability to think more clearly and act with greater conscious intention. We can appreciate that our choices matter, and we can develop greater agency for ourselves in the world. As a result, our behaviors can be more thoughtful and mindful, even in difficult, threatening situations.

Viewing humans through these dual lenses is important. On the one hand, we are an intricate part of processes handed down over billions of years of evolutionary history. That history is "written" into our bodies, our genetic makeup, our brains, and our minds. We are connected to the very fabric of all life. We are, literally, star stuff created from the explosion of ancient suns. This evolutionary history is forged deeply in our cellular, genetic, and neurological make-up. And, through the limbic brain's amygdala, we react as any other animal reacts when threatened. In this way, survival behaviors themselves may be the most "hard wired" of our reactions.

Bowen theory also established that part of this evolutionary development is a richly complex feeling system and intellectual system. While these two systems evolved from the emotional system, they are not inherently better or more important. They are not even distinctly separate systems. Rather, our feeling and intellectual systems are best seen as evolutionary extensions of our emotional system. Even within the brain, the intricate neural connections between the brain structures corresponding to the emotional system, the feeling system, and the intellectual system—roughly corresponding to the ancient R-complex brain, the limbic brain, and the cortex—demonstrate that separating them into distinct components is not fully accurate or possible and, consequently, of only limited usefulness.

In *Failure of Nerve*, Friedman highlighted the emotional system's existence at a cellular level throughout the body and hence any demarcation between the intellectual, feeling, and emotional systems is somewhat artificial and arbitrary. Nonetheless, Bowen theory suggests that nurturing and developing our intellectual system can create opportunities for self-regulation that are not always fully developed in humans. This does not mean that thinking is more essential than feeling or emoting. It means, instead, that under stressful and challenging circumstances, we may want to choose a response or behavior that is less automatic and mindless and more autonomous and mindful.

And so, with concerted attempts and practice over years and decades, we are able to alter some of our more "instinctual" and therefore reactive behaviors so that we can think and act with more deliberateness and agency. In the above example, Leslie expressed this ability for more self-directed actions.

Friedman supports this point about managing emotional reactivity. He said that humans have the capability to evolve further than our biological imperatives. We can train ourselves to respond more thoughtfully in highly anxious situations so that we are not always reacting emotionally. While it is true that, as humans, we can develop a greater ability for autonomous thinking and acting, it takes time and effort to differentiate these responses. When we are under pressure, or when we perceive a threat, we are more likely to react emotionally. Over time, we can carefully cultivate more emotional coherence, intentional thinking, and conscious behaving so that we can respond more creatively and individually. Bowen described this ability for increased autonomy as *differentiation*.

Differentiation is essentially the outcome of competing and compelling life forces in action over time. These life forces are the *individuality life force* and the *togetherness life force*.

Individuality Life Force and Togetherness Life Force

As a mediator and conciliator at the courthouse, I worked with a wide spectrum of society. I saw Bowen theory alive and in front of me constantly. I watched frightened and hurt parents, partners, and spouses trying to figure out how to best protect and care for their children in the midst of chaos, pain, and dislocation. I believe that the vast majority of these parents wanted what was best for their children. They started with the same interest. Unfortunately, the degree to which they could see and act on this universal interest varied. Most parents worked through their dread, hurt, anger, and confusion enough to develop a parenting plan that was in the best interests of the children. These parents were able to separate themselves from their children enough so that they didn't equate the best interests of the children with their own best interests. They preserved the "I" within the "we." This capacity varied wildly.

An example: It is common for a parent who provides more care and who raises the child without much help from the second parent to experience anger, fear, and confusion when the less involved parent asks for additional parenting time with the child. (This is common after a parent is released from prison or if a parent is in recovery and now wants to re-enter or enter a child's life.)

Often, the primary parent believes that it is best for the child to have little or no contact with the other parent or contact based solely on what's best for the primary parent. The parent struggles to separate the "self" from the child. Her thinking is what is best for the mother is best for the child. (Or, what's best for the father is best for the child if the father is the primary parent. While I worked with both men and women who were primary parents, I mediated more disputes where women were primary parents.) (I use the female pronoun here to reflect my experience and for ease in writing with one gender pronoun. I alter this gender primacy throughout the book.) While the primary parent has the principal caretaking relationship with the child, the state of Arizona promotes regular and consistent contact between parents and children.

High levels of emotionality—almost universal in these cases—can work against the clear-headedness necessary for parents to work together cooperatively. Unraveling their intimate relationship makes forging a separate parental partnership difficult. It requires a certain level of differentiation to effectively part the interests and needs of self from the others (child and other parent in this case), and manage emotionality, especially in families with young children, and especially in the middle of the wrenching loss of the marriage or partnership. The forces of individuality and togetherness are ever-present in mediation cases. Bowen believed that they are fundamental and universal energies in nature.

In the 1950s and 1960s, Bowen's budding theory was essentially dissimilar from Freudian and psychodynamic theories in another important way. Bowen was an ardent observer of the natural world. He investigated the interwoven and interconnected association between the human and non-human worlds. His comprehensive theory of family systems was based on his conclusion that identical forces in nature preside over all life and that these processes also govern humans as well. Bowen labeled these forces the *individuality life force* and the *togetherness life force*.

In *Family Evaluation*, Kerr portrays the individuality life force as a universal, biological life energy that enfolds the uniqueness, discreteness, and separateness of living organisms. He views all of life as exhibiting this drive toward becoming biologically distinct entities. Kerr explicates the togetherness life force as the corresponding, universal, biological life force that impels living organisms toward attachment, connectedness, and relationship. Bowen believed that, for humans, it was the association between these opposing and dialectic life forces in action that establishes our unique level of *differentiation*, that is, our ability to operate as a separate organism, while at the same time staying in reasonable and close association with other people and the environment. Bowen saw humans as just one illustration of how these basic life forces manifested themselves in the natural world.

In this way, Bowen viewed humans as an expansion of innate processes already present in nature instead of us operating as if disconnected from evolution and the non-human world. Bowen theory is therefore an ecological theory that attempts to integrate humans into the natural ecosystem. Most other psychological theories, by contrast, are largely concerned with our exceptionalism as a species, with our growth and struggle a function of interior conflicts and internal processes. These alternate theories view humans as more distinctive and thus further apart from nature and the non-human world.

Differentiation: Basic and Functional

I have worked with a lot of deans in my academic life. There is one dean that stands head and shoulders above the others—literally and figuratively. Ron Liddle was dean during my initial years as lecturer and assistant professor at United States International University (U.S.I.U.) in San Diego. Well published and regarded as an accomplished academic in anthropology, Dean Liddle was also beloved by the faculty. That is a rare achievement. When I think about why this man was such an important figure in my life as a leader and mentor, several attributes come to mind. Ron was an imposing figure at over six feet six. Large hands and a big smile, he always made time for me. As a junior lecturer, Ron coached me on several occasions. I valued his knowledge and was thankful for his open door and gentle spirit. Ron was a deeply spiritual man. He was calm, thoughtful, funny, hardworking, and respected as a scholar, a leader, and a person.

It wasn't until Ron stepped down from the deanship and into the faculty that we found out how much Ron advocated for us as a faculty and staff.

He also protected us from a harsh and dictatorial administration, allowing us to do our jobs and teach. After Ron stepped down, we had a series of deans. It was never the same.

As I learned more about Bowen theory and differentiated leadership, I came to realize that Ron was both a highly differentiated leader and a highly differentiated man. What does this mean?

Differentiation is perhaps Bowen family systems theory's most significant theoretical contribution. It is a complex concept. Think of differentiation as the relationship and interaction between the two life forces "in motion." It signifies our aptitude for knowing who we are. This includes our capacity to manage and regulate our emotionality, our thinking, and our behavior. Differentiation is the degree to which we accept personal responsibility for our actions and personal accountability for our choices. It signifies living life with emotional maturity and distinctiveness.

Differentiation is about our relationship to self and other: clarifying who we are and also promoting close relationships with important people in our world. It includes our capacity for self-reflection as we define ourselves more precisely. The higher our differentiation, the more emotionally separate from our family of origin. Emotional separation is the degree that we can live our lives independent from what others want or expect from us, while preserving and enhancing important relationships.

Differentiation also includes the ability to consciously self-regulate our thinking, feelings, and actions when needed. It is understanding and respecting boundaries between self and others as individuals. Feminist Bowen therapist Harriet Lerner says differentiation is knowing where we end and others begin. Differentiation is concerned about encouraging others to develop their own separateness and successfully supporting intimacy with others without losing our "self" in the process. Differentiation is about maintaining the "I" within the "we," as well as the willingness and capacity to accept personal responsibility for our own emotional being and destiny.

When I think of Ron as a leader and as a man, I see those core characteristics present in his being. It's what Friedman refers to as "the power of presence" in more highly differentiated leaders. This is not the same as charisma. While some charismatic leaders are more highly differentiated, many are not. Ron listened with 100% focus and respect, he advocated for his faculty without putting us in the middle of his struggles with the president, he provided leadership and encouragement, and when he could no longer do his job with the integrity and independence that he needed, he stepped down without blame or acrimony. Individuality, togetherness, direction, focus, flexibility, care, respect, warmth, and integrity: Ron lived that more differentiated presence.

Our "core" or basic differentiation level is fairly set once we reach adulthood and the brain has fully matured. Full brain development for women is usually completed in the early to mid-20s. For men, full brain myelination and therefore maturity often occurs several years later by the mid to late-20s. Differentiation is, though, highly idiosyncratic, meaning each person expresses his or her differentiation in unique ways.

Friedman offers a distinctive way to understand differentiation. In his view, differentiation is analogous to the immune response. Differentiation is the body's capacity to separate "self" from "not self." This is an existential category of being. As differentiation increases, so too does our ability and capacity to know where "I" end and "you" begin. This is exactly what the immune system is always doing. "Not self" activates the body's immune system, a defensive reactive that recognizes that the "not self" virus, bacteria, fungus, or foreign object needs elimination.

From this vantage point, strengthening differentiation *is* strengthening the immune system. And the stronger our immune system, the more capable we become of experiencing intimacy, since we no longer fear a permanent "fusion" and hence loss of self within another. Preserving and enhancing our personal integrity, then, allow greater connection with another spiritually, emotionally, psychologically, socially, and sexually.

Bowen conceptualized differentiation existing on a theoretical scale of 0–100, with 0 as a theoretical person totally devoid of an independently functioning "self," and 100 being a theoretical person who has achieved full emotional separation from the family of origin and who exists in the world but is not reactive its forces and foibles.

Our core or *basic differentiation* is a result of a variety of features, including that which we emotionally "inherit" from our original families. It usually stays consistent over time and circumstances throughout the life cycle unless we consciously strive to increase it. Successful efforts often take years and decades of concerted effort. Exceptions include nodal or key events in our lives such as births, weddings, deaths, retirement, geographic relocation, and divorce. During these times the emotional system of the family, including the individuals within it, is more open to change, and we have the opportunity to move more freely and independently within our family system.

Life conditions that put us in new contexts, such as international travel and wilderness experiences, can provide opportunities to adapt and mature. Extreme life events—natural disasters, war, social disruptions such as mass migrations, and other traumatic challenges—are so intense that we can be inundated with anxiety. In these dangerous situations, some may experience rapid changes in basic differentiation. A few may move more progressively, rising to the challenge. Many others regress in their ability to successfully adapt (see more on this in chapter four, The Evolving Nature of Bowen Family Systems Theory).

By comparison, *functional differentiation* can alter more quickly as a consequence of the pressures and vicissitudes of our lives. As an example, Halle has been privileged to live a moderately tranquil and secure life. Consequently, she seems quite healthy emotionally and fairly well differentiated. Her life takes a sad turn: she loses her job and her father becomes acutely ill. Pressures increase and Halle becomes more intense and emotional. Now, she appears less able to adjust to her life situation. Halle starts to drink more in order to alleviate her stress.

As a result, Halle's functional differentiation decreases in reaction to these outside challenges. Initially, she was functioning at a higher level than her basic differentiation. Halle's world had order and consistency.

Her life was manageable. Now, her world is no longer as predictable as it once was, and she struggles to manage her increasing sense of anxiety and dread. As we can see, functional differentiation is different than basic differentiation in that functional differentiation is more variable over time and circumstances, while basic differentiation is more constant over time and most circumstances.

Higher levels of basic differentiation can offer some "protection" from the randomness and vagaries of life through increased resiliency. The higher our basic differentiation, the less fluctuation there is in functional differentiation over time and across situations as we are more flexible and have more resources. We adapt. In this way, moderate and higher levels of "core" emotional maturity safeguard us from some of the more extreme, harmful effects of anxiety. As basic differentiation decreases, however, functional differentiation oscillates more and more over time and across situations. Resiliency and adaptability diminish. Anxiety soars.

Halle is an illustration of a how a person with a lower level of basic differentiation can seem quite functional in the right circumstances. As her situation changes for the worse, insecurity and stress increase beyond her capacity to adapt. Whereas once Halle seemed poised and capable of managing her life, now, with anxiety and uncertainty mounting, she seems apprehensive and fearful. This, in turn, negatively impacts Halle's ability to adjust to what life has in store for her.

Bowen conceptualized differentiation on a theoretical scale. He detailed this scale as operating from 0 to 100. In Bowen's system, a scale score of 0 represents an individual with no core self, no integrated self, and an inability to relate to others. This is obviously a theoretical location, as most individuals are able to manage and relate to others in some capacity. At the other end, a scale score of 100 symbolizes an individual who is fully authentic, self-responsible, and interacts well with all people in all situations. Both extremes of 0 and 100 are unlikely theoretical positions.

The scale is sometimes divided into quadrants, with 0–25 as the quadrant of least differentiation. Those in this quadrant struggle in life and in relationships. Those at the higher end of the quadrant may have somewhat stable lives if they live in favorable circumstances. Those at the lower end are often mentally ill, homeless, severely addicted, and/or deeply entangled in the legal and social services systems.

Persons in the 25–50 quadrant function better than those at the lower end. Those at the higher end of this quadrant, like Halle, do best with favorable consistency in their lives, careers, and relationships. They have some ability to adapt, though this capacity decreases for those lower in the quadrant. People in the 50–75 quadrant are more capable of adapting and are more resilient. According to Bowen, given our imperfect natures, most humans do not exist beyond 65–75 on this scale. Those at the higher end are fairly differentiated, having achieved a good deal of emotional separation from their original families. Those in the 75–100 quadrant are people with the greatest degree of emotional maturity. Not many individuals achieve this. Nonetheless, in real life even the most emotionally mature human is not perfect and so is not fully separate from others. There is still relationship dependency and chronic anxiety even at the lower end of the upper quadrant.

The scale is a theoretical instrument used to highlight similarity and differences; it is not a clinical research tool. It suggests that humans function on a continuum, with different individuals existing at various positions on the scale. Bowen's differentiation scale facilitates our understanding of how diverse human functioning is, as well as the many variables that affect human behavior. Differentiation can be equated with emotional maturity, personal integrity, resilience, and adaptability. It is our ability to adjust to life's assorted situations and challenges, and our readiness to accept personal accountability for our emotional being and destiny.

The concept of differentiation seems similar to concepts proposed and hypothesized by other researchers and theoreticians. Howard Gardner, for example, is an educator who proposes a theory of eight multiple intelligences (MI). He suggests that two particular "intelligences"–the interpersonal intelligence and the intrapersonal intelligence, sometimes referred to as the personal intelligences–are essential for a happy and successful life. Gardner and his colleagues believe that cultivating the personal intelligences can fashion constructive environments for learning and growth.

German-Jewish religious scholar and philosopher, Martin Buber, discussed the "I-Thou" relationship, highlighting the essential nature and importance between the "you" in relationship to the "me." Science writer Daniel Goleman and his associates have written at length about and conducted research on emotional intelligence and social intelligence. Emotional intelligence and social intelligence include our ability to manage self in difficult situations, the capacity for self-containment, as well as our willingness and ability to appreciate, understand, and effectively deal with others. The theories of Gardner, Buber, and Goleman sound similar to Bowen's concept of differentiation.

These theoreticians, philosophers, and practitioners all essentially believe that a successful life is primarily a function of the capacity to develop and support an "I" that is distinct from the "we"; to assume greater personal responsibility for our thinking, feeling, and acting; and to increase our self-soothing when things get intense. This more differentiated presence requires a willingness and ability to self-reflect and manage our emotions, as well as a readiness to promote and nurture important relationships with others. Effective relationships with others increase our compassion. They develop our skills at acting selflessly when needed. Relationships encourage our understanding of how to get along with others individually and in groups without compromising our integrity.

As levels of basic differentiation rise, so too does adaptability. Increasing basic differentiation is associated with less emotional reactivity. Our responses become more consistent, intentional, and thoughtful in a variety of anxious environments. We are more emotionally free to think, feel, and act as needed. That is, as our basic differentiation rises, there is an enhanced ability to stay focused on the self and our responses in diverse circumstances and with various adaptive behaviors. Well-differentiated people, therefore, have more resources, are more spontaneous, and can express thoughts and feelings more clearly and concisely. In short, more highly differentiated individuals are more emotionally mature humans. Such people are more willing and capable of taking personal responsibility for their lives and decisions.

In contrast, as basic differentiation decreases, people have fewer resources. They are less capable of adjusting to the challenges that life throws their way. With lower levels of differentiation comes a diminished capacity to "bounce back" after life difficulties and challenges. This means that emotional reactions become more reflexive and automatic. There is less resilience than with more highly differentiated people. As a result, such individuals are less able to recover from difficult situations. More poorly differentiated humans are less free and more bound by reactive "instincts." This heightened emotional reactivity can take many forms, including reactive thinking, reactive feeling, and reactive behaving. They are less attentive to their internal compasses and are not as able or willing to accept personal responsibility. Their inclination is to criticize and blame. The focus becomes getting others to change, not the self. More emotionally immature individuals are strongly affected by those in the present and past. They are more likely to use *cutoff, emotional distance,* and *triangulation*—all key Bowen theory concepts—to manage problems and fault others for their circumstances instead of becoming accountable for managing life's happenstances.

Chronic Anxiety

Aunt Angie was my mother's younger sister. Angie was the youngest of twins; the older twin was Vito. She was also the youngest child. The youngest daughter is not a favored sibling position on my mother's side of the family. Angie was always an intense person. Her first husband, Donald, died of a heart attack while the two of them were physically fighting each other. They were in their early 20s. Angie's life followed a pattern of relationship and child abuse, raging, distancing, and cutting off. Angie was also a lot of fun. She was adventurous, daring, displayed a biting sense of humor, and would give you her last dollar if you needed it. In fact, she either loved you or hated you; there was little in between.

At one point, Angie cut off her oldest son, Michael, when he was twenty-four, and she refused to communicate with him any longer. She said, "He's dead to me." Michael had only been five when his father died. He witnessed his parents physically fighting and then his father falling over dead. To a five-year old, his mother had killed his father. He kept that secret locked away for decades. His deeply conflictual relationship with his mother over the years had its roots in Michael's childhood trauma of watching his father die.

A year after his mother cut him off, Michael was murdered in a drug deal gone badly. His head was split open with a baseball bat. Angie flew down to Florida from New York to be with Michael while he spent his last hours in a deep coma from which he never recovered.

In traditional psychiatric nomenclature, I believe that Angie suffered from borderline personality disorder. Her symptoms, as well as the way she lived her life, support this diagnosis. Perhaps more importantly, though, from a Bowen family systems theory perspective, Angie carried around a great deal of the family anger, especially the anger that existed between her parents. Michael Sr. and Genevese had a high conflict relationship, and this was particularly acute when my grandfather would come home drunk on the weekends.

My mother told us how the children would hide the knives before their father came home and how their parents fought, verbally and physically. My grandmother, while abusive herself, also protected her children from Michael's drunken rages.

It's common for a vulnerable child—for a variety of emotional reasons from sibling position to multigenerational influences—to absorb a disproportionate amount of unresolved, blocked, and/or amplified intensity from the nuclear and extended family. Angie was that person in my mother's sibling system of six. Her son, Michael, then "inherited" this transmitted chronic anxiety and carried it with him during his short life. While there was a good deal of chronic anxiety throughout my mother's nuclear family, it was Angie who bore the heaviest burden of it throughout her life. Her relationships were always messy. My mother and she were always close, but my mother would often "absorb" a lot of Angie's intensity. In fact, my siblings and I always knew when my mother had recently spoken with Angie. We all felt her emotional dislocation after one of these conversations between the sisters.

Angie died alone, penniless, cut off from most of her four remaining children and some of her siblings whom she pushed away over the course of her life. She paid a high price with having absorbed a disproportionate share of multigenerational chronic anxiety. She also generated and amplified a great deal of anxiety. Angie was a disturbed person, and she needed the love and support of family, which she wanted, feared, and rejected all at once. Her chronic anxiety was high; her differentiation level was low.

This story helps illuminate a fourth concept that is essential to understanding the richness and complexity of Bowen family systems theory, *chronic anxiety*. Think of chronic anxiety as the opposite side of the differentiation coin.

Kerr and Bowen believe that chronic anxiety is the extent to which we react to a *perceived* threat. In this way, chronic anxiety is unlike acute anxiety, which is a more surface feeling involved in reactions to an *actual* threat. Like the central concept of differentiation, chronic anxiety is something that H. sapiens share with all living organisms, since all creatures continuously react to alterations in their surroundings and to existential threats to their existence. In this way, chronic anxiety is deeply connected to the more ancient emotional system. It is also inversely related to differentiation level. As our basic differentiation goes up, our chronic anxiety goes down. This makes sense. As we expand our commitment to effective relationships, self-responsibility, and self-management, we carry lower levels of "life angst." We worry less, exist more in the moment, and find ways to take life as it comes. We are resilient. On the other hand, as chronic anxiety rises and basic differentiation decreases, the quality of our relationships, as well as our ability for self-care, self-containment of emotionality, and self-regulation of reactivity diminish.

Like differentiation, there are many factors that contribute to chronic anxiety. Our level of chronic anxiety is correlated with the degree of chronic anxiety in our parents, which is, in turn, highly related to the degree of chronic anxiety in the multigenerational family. High chronic anxiety is expressed through physical, emotional, and/or social symptoms. These symptomatic manifestations of chronic anxiety are also associated with the repetitive expressions of symptoms or patterns in our nuclear and extended families. That is, certain imprints and associations from the current and past generations—including biological factors such as gene expression and environmental influences such as current and historical stressors—affect how we generate, amplify, absorb, manage, transmit, and express chronic anxiety. How chronic anxiety is manifested through emotional reactivity is of significant importance for all interactions with the human and non-human world. As tolerance for uncertainty, emotional intensity, and perceived threats decreases, our chronic anxiety increases.

Differentiation suffers as chronic anxiety increases. Chronic anxiety can be conceptualized as the level of general wellbeing or lack thereof that we carry around with us. Another way to think about chronic anxiety is static in the broadcast. As Friedman said, you can't hear the broadcast better by turning up the volume, since this merely increases the static. Focusing on self—decreasing personal reactivity and increasing personal resilience—decreases the static and increases our personal integrity so that our true voice can more clearly heard. Differentiation levels rise as well when we feel more centered, more whole, and more "solid." A more solid self means that we can stand on our own two feet, even as the winds of change try to blow us down.

Chronic anxiety can also be expressed person to person. Most people today acknowledge the importance of the mind—body connection. Many believe that the mind—body divide is an artificial distinction and that it may be wise to discard it altogether. In fact, in *Failure of Nerve*, Friedman argues for the mind—body or brain-body as one unit of study. He references Candice Pert, the former head of brain chemistry at the National Institute for Mental Health, who, through her research and before her death in 2013, rejected the brain and body as distinct. Instead, she used the term "brain/body" when referencing the interconnections between them. In essence, this use of the term "brain/body" signifies that they are one and the same or inseparable.

As standard and seemingly non-controversial as this connection appears today, what is less understood or appreciated is the person-to-person connection proposed by Bowen theory and expressed through chronic anxiety. Bowen theory suggests that we can be expressing the chronic anxiety *for* another and *in* another. This is what happened to Angie and then later with Michael. This expression of chronic anxiety is seen through Kerr's notion of a "uni-disease." The uni-disease concept says that anxiety can overload a system and be expressed in physical, emotional (psychiatric/psychological), and/or social symptoms. A symptom's severity is a function of the total amount of chronic anxiety a person carries, along with the current acute anxiety and strain experienced.

An example: Elizabeth exhibits a phobia about leaving the home that reflects both her and her wife Delia's relationship conflicts and the accumulated chronic anxiety in their system. From a linear, non-systemic perspective, Elizabeth is "the problem" because she is phobic about leaving home. From a systems perspective, Elizabeth is expressing anxiety for both herself and Delia. She is the canary in the coalmine for the relationship and not "the problem." The problem is the relationship and the unresolved intensity and conflict that exist between them. The energy that drives this emotionality is chronic anxiety, which is a function of what each has inherited from their families and brought to the relationship. Elizabeth expresses the reactivity and conflict in the relationship through her symptoms.

As you can see, chronic anxiety is deeply related to the other Bowen theory concepts discussed so far, and it is also the "energy" that fuels emotional triangles.

Emotional Triangles

When teaching the course Family Systems in Film and Literature, one of the films that we watch and analyze is Woody Allen's brilliant movie *Hannah and Her Sisters*. In it, oldest daughter Hannah is the "golden gal" in the family system. She displays characteristics common of the oldest daughter of daughters: a super-responsible over-functioner for her parents, her sisters, her husband, her children, and others. Her husband, Elliot, believes that he cannot compete with the important people in Hannah's life and her over-functioning nature. Elliot courts and eventually seduces Hannah's youngest sister, the vulnerable Lee.

Sensing that they are drifting apart, Hannah asks Elliot if they should have another child, a common, ill-conceived strategy that many troubled couples use in an attempt to stabilize their relationship. While Elliot rejects this proposal, the central emotional triangle between Elliot and Hannah remains, through the secret affair between husband and youngest sister.

Love triangles are merely one example of emotional triangles. Love triangles, of course, are nothing new. Authors have written about them for centuries. They have appeared in books, film, and television for years. Bowen theory provides an understanding and explanation of *emotional triangles*, the next concept of Bowen theory that is relevant to our discussion.

Bowen believed that the triangle is the basic "emotional building block" of human relationships. He noticed that a two-person relationship system is intrinsically unsteady and will, in times of anxiety and stress, and by design, seek to re-stabilize itself by adding a third. This automatic effort to alleviate relationship anxiety is called *triangulation* or *triangling*. The third point on the emotional triangle can vary. This third point often becomes the point of bound anxiety for the system, a place that seems to be the problem. This *anxiety binder* can be another individual. In *Hannah and Her Sisters*, the anxiety binder for Hannah and Elliot is Lee.

Another example: Instead of speaking to her wife about her marital concerns, Delia calls her mother to discuss these problems. This creates an emotional triangle. Two people often triangulate another person into their relationship, and a three-person emotional triangle has all of the characteristics present in emotional triangles. Two people might also triangulate something physical, other than a person, like a pet, clothing, or house. Triangulation can even extend to ideologies, religious beliefs, money, and "causes." People can get quite creative in what they triangulate into a two-person relationship. Legal and illegal substances such as alcohol and drugs are common. So, too, is food. Think of these bindings of chronic anxiety as attachments that are meant, at some level, to "stabilize" things when there is a rough patch in the relationship.

The problem is, though, that triangulation is only a temporary solution to a more complex, longer-term problem. For example, while an affair like the Hannah–Elliot–Lee triangle may temporarily provide stability as the intensity between Hannah and Elliot is diverted, the marriage/intimate relationship becomes more and more undercut as the affair continues. So, what starts out as an automatic process that initially *reduces* intensity and provides some temporary stability becomes more and more what appears to be "the problem" to the outside world. When the affair comes to light, the aggrieved partner and supporters will often blame "the other man/woman," the acting out spouse, and the affair itself. Rarely will the couple or others focus on the disturbance in the relationship system as the primary "cause" of the affair. When couples do focus on the relationship, however, they have the opportunity to transform their relationship in ways they hadn't even considered prior to the affair. The natural blaming response, though, often undercuts the committed relationship, and, for many couples, the relationship doesn't survive.

Through Bowen theory, we can re-conceptualize the role that anxiety binders play in emotional triangles. Think of a drug or alcohol problem. *Silver begins drinking more and more as Willie stays at work later and later.* Over the course of the year, her nightly glass of wine has turned into a nightly bottle, then a nightly two bottles. Willie notices that Silver is usually asleep when he arrives home late from work. At some level he is grateful, since he doesn't have to defend himself about coming home so late because *Willie stays at work later and later as Silver begins drinking more.* This is the other side of the equation, of course, the flip side of the relationship coin. The relationship is reciprocal: each has a role and function in how it continues. Willie cleans up the bottles and puts away the wine glass and snacks. At another level, he is growing increasingly concerned about what he perceives as "the problem" now: the triangulated point of agglutinated chronic anxiety, the drinking, and not the "source" of the problem, their relationship deterioration.

Triangles exist cross-culturally, of course, as significant objects and archetypal symbols. There are many such cross-cultural symbols, including the circle, the cross, the pyramid, the square, the cube, and the sphere. Bowen's observation pointed to the triangle as the "sacred" symbol of human relationships.

Bowen theory conceptualizes the triangle's sides as conduits through which the chronic anxiety or emotional energy flows. People and points on the triangle assume either inside or outside positions. When things are relatively calm, the two people on the inside position want to stay that way. The inside position becomes less comfortable as intensity and anxiety increase between the two parties. One person on the inside position (or even both people) may seek the comfort of an outside position to alleviate this intensity. Alternatively, like Elliot, one person may seek a new inside position with another person, allowing the outsider to assume an insider role, like Lee. The third person, Hannah, then assumes the outside position in this emotional triangle. Again, this may work temporarily, but it is not a permanent solution. In the film, the affair temporarily stabilizes the marriage between Elliot and Hannah, but that stability is fragile, risky, and impermanent.

In fact, while triangulation is universal, and therefore not "pathological," it can, indeed, be quite regressive. A little triangulation might help us get clear about a relationship and our role in it by giving us some distance and someone to talk to, but, if this becomes the default pattern in the relationship, then triangulation can undercut differentiation.

Let's look at another example. Beth and Giselle are employees together in a small business. Beth attends her annual review, which is carried out by her supervisor, Alexandra. During Beth's review, Alexandra uncovers some serious work performance problems. The review reveals that Beth is chronically late to work. Beth has a moderately low level of basic differentiation. Consequently, rather than assuming personal responsibility and committing to change her behavior or talking openly and honestly to her supervisor, Beth remains quiet. Instead, she grumbles to her colleague Giselle that she was targeted by Alexandra. Giselle sides with Beth against Alexandra. This is an emotional triangle.

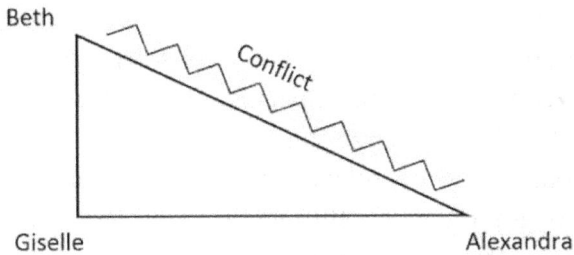

Beth · Conflict · Giselle · Alexandra

Whatever actual concerns exist here, they are between Beth and Alexandra. Rather than deal with those concerns directly, Beth brings in Giselle to temporarily stabilize the conflict. Giselle "absorbs" the tension and intensity from Beth concerning Alexandra. Giselle "feels" worse and is now agitated herself. Beth "feels" better, having "dumped" her anxiety on Giselle. Feeling better, Beth has no motivation to resolve her concerns with her supervisor. Instead, Giselle and she commiserate about Alexandra and what a problem she is. They join together to nurture their resentments, but the primary relationship issues between Beth and Alexandra remain the same. Giselle and Beth both occupy the inside position of this triangle.

Alexandra, not knowing about the problems Beth had with the review, feels like something is off with Beth. She also senses that Giselle is now acting coldly to her as well and wonders why. This temporary "solution," as we can see, has a price, since Beth feels better at the expense of both her association with Alexandra and her capacity to correct an obvious employment issue.

As discussed earlier, when the intensity amplifies between two people occupying the inside position of a triangle, one individual may seek the company of a person on the outside position of the triangle to escape the intensity. This creates a new inside position with the third person, originally on the inside, now on the outside. This is what happened between Beth, Alexandra, and Giselle. Giselle and Beth are now insiders, with Alexandra on the outside position of the emotional triangle.

Triangulation is a natural process. As far as we can observe, emotional triangles are created and present in all cultures, by all people, regardless of nationality, creed, race, gender, or other categories of identity. Emotional triangles are complex and vibrant. The main triangle is referred to as the central emotional triangle. It is the "origin point" of the conflict or at least the current origin point in this time or this generation. The essence of the conflict lies with and in the central emotional triangle. Other, related conflicts that are spawned by the original issue are managed through *interlocking triangles*. This is particularly problematic when the original three-person system is further strained, resulting in the need to disperse even more anxiety. Then, when a central emotional triangle "overheats" with intensity and the anxiety within the three-person relationship system cannot be contained and has not been resolved, an interlocking triangle can form that will assist in relieving pressure and calming the system, at least in the short run.

Remember that triangulation is an automatic, "instinctual" process that operates mostly outside of conscious awareness. It is simply something that people commonly do to reduce conflict in the short term.

Let's continue with our example: Alexandra finds out that Beth has been complaining to Giselle about her evaluation and supposed mistreatment. Instead of addressing her frustrations directly to Beth, which may have actually reduced some of the intensity generated and amplified between them, she, instead, vigorously complains to her own supervisor, Bennie. Bennie has had her own difficulties when she was Beth's supervisor. Unfortunately, in what now seems like the business model in this company, Bennie sympathizes with Alexandra about Beth.

Maybe if Bennie had directly confronted and hence managed this tardiness when she was supervising Beth, this concern may have been resolved. But, Bennie never managed this issue with Beth, so the best she has to offer now is to acknowledge Alexandra's misery. The two women bond over their dislike of Beth and her incompetence. Alexandria and Bennie have formed an interlocking emotional triangle that absorbed the anxiety that "overflowed" from the central emotional triangle of Beth–Alexandra–Giselle. While the conflicts shift through the binding of anxiety in the different parties at different times, there remains no satisfactory resolution.

Beth   Bennie

Giselle   Alexandra

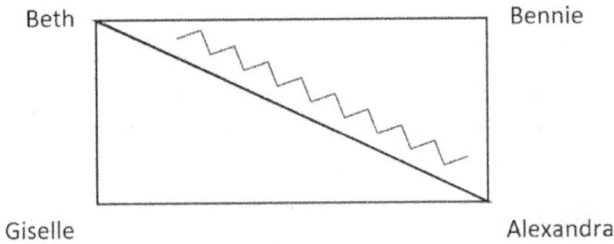

Chronic anxiety is the emotional energy that animates triangulation. If chronic anxiety appends to an individual, physical entity, drug, alcohol, symptom, or belief, this is called *anxiety binding*. Anxiety binders are the different ways we stay connected to the intensity of the conflict through our emotional attachments. Triangulation is, by definition, usually regressive, since the intensity doesn't decrease between the two in dispute. Rather, it gets "shuffled around," goes underground, and is displaced on another. This is regressive since it undercuts people's ability to think lucidly and act thoughtfully. Instead, thinking itself can become reactive and subjective. It is this reactive thinking and feeling that activates emotional triangling and keeps it alive, amplifying the anxiety in the system in some areas and dampening, but not resolving, the anxiety in other areas.

We can avoid or at least minimize triangulation by calmly, thoughtfully, and compassionately discussing the real issues between two people. This is scary in the short term, but it is the most promising strategy for effective conflict resolution. The problem is that most people will seek out the short-term solution, emotional triangling, since it seems the path of least resistance, the easier way out. If, however, the two parties can face each other in composed, alert conversation, the conflict will often lessen and the stress will be reduced.

Emotional triangling results if the intensity between the two individuals increases and the situation is not managed directly. This temporary solution lessens anxiety in the moment but increases it long-term. Triangulation is regressive because it undercuts clarity, directness, compassion, relationships, and personal responsibility.

Let's say that two partners want to grow their business. To do so, they decide to hire another worker. Partner Juan wants to hire

Enrico, and Partner Sarah does not. Let's also say that Juan and Sarah have had multiple differences of opinion and argued often over the years. These conflicts are not discussed and remain largely underground. As a result, the emotionality between them gets transferred and expressed through the new hire. The partners calcify their stances around this hiring: Juan wants to hire Enrico and Sarah does not. Now, the intensity between them centers on the hire, but this is not the true issue, it is a pseudo-issue. The real issue is that neither Juan nor Sarah has faced the conflict between them. While directly dealing with their disagreements would initially feel more challenging and uncomfortable, over time, it is the more emotionally mature and responsible thing to do.

In fact, one of the hallmarks of increased differentiation is our ability to tolerate and manage short-term spikes in anxiety in order to decrease long-term chronic anxiety. Allowing the parties to experience and manage their immediate pain is necessary in order to reduce enduring tensions. But, instead of addressing their concerns directly, the issues between Sarah and Juan are now transferred to the hire and the original problems between them are deflected. In this way, disagreements around the hire are really a side show and not the main event. Enrico is now a part of an emotional triangle between the partners. He detours and absorbs the emotional conflict between the partners and, in this way, becomes the anxiety binder between them.

The greater the attachment to an anxiety binder, the more *emotional fusion* exists between the triangulated parties. Emotional fusion is the degree to which two or more people give up self to be in a relationship. Emotional fusion signifies a loss of separateness, a loss of relationship boundaries. Self is undercut and merges with other. With this lack of separateness, parties become intensely involved with the anxiety binder. This, in turn, makes facing the conflict and the intensity around it more challenging.

To review: As an automatic reaction to instability in a two-person relationship system, emotional triangulating is a self-generating process whereby chronic and acute anxiety shifts through the relationship system. Triangling is natural and universal—we all triangulate to greater and lesser degrees. This is what makes emotional triangles a central concept in Bowen theory. Emotional triangles highlight all of the previous concepts and theoretical notions: The emotional system acts through triangulation. Reactivity is an ordinary, typical way in which our bound emotional energy of chronic anxiety gets expressed. The more chronic anxiety we carry, the more fuel there is to ignite emotional reactivity. The more chronic anxiety we hold, the less differentiation there is to inoculate our self from the dangers of reactivity. The more chronic anxiety we absorb, the greater the chance for emotional triangling since chronic anxiety is also the energy source that drives emotional triangling. Any initial relief resulting from triangulation is temporary and fragile. Eventually, emotional reactivity increases as these efforts to lessen short-term anxiety often result in amplified long-term reactivity and less stability in the two-person relationship system over time.

The "cure" for triangulation is de-triangulation. De-triangulation occurs when we face our conflicts directly, rather than by detouring them through another person, place, or thing. De-triangulation diminishes intensity when we approach the conflict honestly and frankly with the other person through clear, calm, straightforward, and direct conversation. This is best achieved with a receptive mind, a willingness to listen to and really hear what the other has to say. This approach to the relationship is kind and compassionate. It requires us to accept personal responsibility for our part in the conflict. Lerner suggests that de-triangulation necessitates the use of responsible "I language" instead of the regressive "you language" of blaming.

In this way, de-triangulating *is* differentiating when we attempt a more emotionally mature response and reject escalating reactivity. When de-triangling with another person, it is crucial to ponder what needs to happen. Interacting with the other person in a more emotionally mature manner allows us to find common ground through our common interests.

Learning about de-triangulation, and then moving in a more responsible direction, is critical for increasing basic differentiation. Important components in de-triangling include decreasing our attachment to being "right" and to our egoic sense of entitlement about our position in the disagreement. De-triangling means approaching the other person respectfully, formulating a concerted effort to listen and learn, and using appropriate humor in order to steer clear of "reptilian regressions" into inflexible, steadfast seriousness. In sum, de-triangling means letting go of being correct, of being dependent on a belief, or of being bound up in our positions. De-triangulation is more difficult, but it is a more effective strategy for self and others. It is the path of emotionally maturing.

In summary, the emotional system ties humans to all life on the planet. The emotional system proposes that most of our behaviors are embedded in evolution. The emotional system can be traced, in part, to the oldest parts of our brain, the structures that were present before the development of our thinking/intellectual brain or feeling brain. Think of the emotional system as corresponding to our instinctual, automatic reactions, especially when we are experiencing heightened stress and anxiety.

The individuality life force and the togetherness life force are opposing and balancing life forces through which the emotional system expresses itself. These life forces help establish the extent to which we can live as emotionally detached and separate persons, while at the same time nurturing the important and intimate relationships in our lives.

Differentiation is our ability to manage our thinking, feeling, and acting, along with our capacity to readily describe who we are and what we want in the world. Differentiation includes self-reflection and our skill at self-regulating our emotionality; our capacity to hear others, our ability to speak clearly and calmly; and our willingness to afford others the same opportunity to do so themselves. Differentiation also addresses our aptitude for developing and nurturing important relationships. Differentiated thinking and acting can, in fact, fortify each person in the relationship.

Chronic anxiety is inversely and directly related to differentiation. It determines how we react to perceived threats. When a person's emotional maturity increases, the amount of chronic anxiety absorbed decreases. Inversely, as a person's basic differentiation decreases, the amount of carried chronic anxiety amplifies. Chronic anxiety can be expressed by a person, through a relationship, and even within another person. When chronic anxiety escalates, there is more emotional reactivity, especially under stressful situations, and there is more emotional triangling.

Emotional triangles are automatic, universal ways that chronic anxiety is bound and managed through detouring attention from the source of the threat to another person, object, belief, or thing. Emotional triangles temporarily relieve the anxiety of the moment by binding that anxiety in someone or something else. The greater the emotional triangulation, the more that personal integrity and, therefore, differentiation are compromised. De-triangulation manages the anxiety of the moment by addressing it directly. While this is initially less comfortable, de-triangulation provides people with the opportunity to find long-term solutions to chronic and acute problems by promoting personal responsibility, compassion, and a genuine dialogue regarding conflict and its resolution. In these ways, de-triangling *is* differentiating.

The second part of the theory is more integrative. This theory overview continues in the next chapter as I combine the essential components of Bowen theory to discuss the nuclear family, the multigenerational family, and the larger family of humans.

CHAPTER THREE

BOWEN FAMILY SYSTEMS THEORY: INTEGRATING CONCEPTS

This chapter will review the concepts that tie together the core individual ones, detailing how they all fit together in one comprehensive theory. It will include overviews of nuclear family emotional process, multigenerational emotional process, and societal emotional process.

I will reveal how all of the theoretical concepts function within a family. Then I'll discuss how Bowen theory operates in non-family settings at a societal level such as with businesses, schools, and other emotional systems.

Nuclear Family Emotional Process

Analyzing oneself and one's own family of origin using Bowen theory as a framework is tricky. As an example, most Bowen theorists have learned that it is nearly impossible to accurately describe one's own level of basic differentiation or that of a family member. Nonetheless, we usually try to do so.

While I present the following examples with this caveat in mind, I also want the reader to know that I have extensively examined my family system as a part of my personal therapy, my academic studies, and my work as a Bowen theory practitioner. In fact, this kind of self-reflection is essential in trying to raise one's basic differentiation and lower one's chronic anxiety.

My parents worked blue collar jobs for decades. My mother, a second-generation Italian immigrant, labored in garment factories;

my father, a third-generation Italian immigrant, was employed as a mail carrier and factory worker. They wanted to provide a middle-class lifestyle for their four children, and they pushed education and the promise of professional employment as a way of advancing ourselves in careers that did not require manual labor.

There are three central emotional triangles in my family of origin. (I use the present tense even though my parents are both deceased since, as Kerr and Bowen remind us, at varying levels of activity, triangles are forever, especially in families.) The first emotional triangle is between my older brother Gary and my parents. By all accounts, my father, Gene, was a free spirit as an adolescent and young man. He enlisted in World War II at age seventeen and only served for seventeen months before the war ended. Gene was eighteen when he was honorably discharged from the Navy. This meant that he didn't have to serve in the Korean War as did many of his friends. Some of his friends stayed in the service or joined the reserves after World War II. Others were drafted. Some were killed in the Korean conflict. My father, having served his country, declined the invitation to stay in the Navy or join the reserves.

By his own account, Gene enjoyed early adulthood. At twenty-six he married my mother and settled down with a real job to support his wife and future family. He always felt a loss of freedom with these responsibilities. While he faithfully fulfilled expectations, I believe that my brother Gary was "selected" by my parents as the one who would carry on Gene's extended adolescence and early adulthood. As a deeply talented musician, Gary lived a carefree life for decades, at one point boasting that he never even had a checkbook until he was forty.

I believe that at some level Gary was an offering by my parents to a life that Gene probably wanted to continue living at some level. It was their way of managing this chronic anxiety. It wasn't until Gene retired that he reclaimed the joy of having his own time to do what he wanted to do. I think that Gary was on the inside position of that emotional triangle with Gene, and Antoinette occupied the outside position.

The second emotional triangle in the family is between my younger brother Ronald and my parents, with Antoinette and Ronald on the inside position and Gene on the outside position. Ronald is gay. Growing up, his sexual orientation was not discussed in the family. This was the 1960s and early 1970s. Nonetheless, like all family secrets, it wasn't a real secret. I believe that at some level we all knew Ronald was gay. I regretfully admit to calling Ronald some cruel names when I was young. I knew these names were hurtful; children can be cruel. Ronald is remarkably creative, with an eye for detail and a strong aesthetic, which he shared with Antoinette. As a mother, Antoinette was also very protective of him. Ronald was on the inside position of the triangle with Antoinette; Gene occupied the outside position. As the third son, I wonder if my parents were disappointed that Ronald was not a girl. All of these issues play into the emotional triangle between Ronald and my parents. There was a good deal of chronic anxiety between my parents and Ronald absorbed his share.

The third emotional triangle in my family of origin is between Anne, the youngest and only female, and my parents. Anne occupied the inside position of this emotional triangle with Gene, and Antoinette held the outside position. While both parents were thrilled to have a daughter, my father and Anne were always close. My sister and mother had much conflict when Anne was young and throughout much of their lives. My parents' marriage had its challenges when we were young, and I believe that Anne absorbed some of that chronic anxiety through her closeness to my father and her brushes with delinquency and the law. In many ways, my parents felt done with raising children by the time Anne was a pre-teen and teen. They had already raised three sons, but Anne's "acting out" provided them with a necessary forum to re-engage with parenting.

As Antoinette aged and became ill, the emotional triangle diminished between Anne and my parents along with the conflict between my sister and Antoinette. I do believe, though, that Anne was my father's favorite, as Ronald was my mother's favorite. They were also part of the shifting chronic anxiety swirling around my original family.

I escaped much of the emotional triangling, though, like all children, we all absorbed our fair share of chronic anxiety in the original family.

As a middle child, I observed everything that was going on around me and found ways to escape—into responsibilities of work, into nature, and into an early, intimate relationship. Escaping was my way of dealing with the family's chronic anxiety.

First, I had a paper route at age nine. It was under Gary's name, as I wasn't old enough to have a route. We divided responsibilities, paper deliveries, and payment collections. After a year, Gary had enough of the paper route, and I took it over. I loved the financial independence that the paper route gave me, especially since my parents were always struggling financially, and I didn't want to add to their difficulties. As a youngster, I loved being outdoors and would spend much of my time away from home—with my paper route, riding bicycles with friends, playing sports, exploring. I moved farther away from my family emotionally at age seventeen when I started dating Janet. We spent most of our free time together. I think that my being out of the home so much also protected me from much of the family dynamics. Additionally, my sibling position (birth order) helped.

On Antoinette's side, the second child is a favored position, one that has the greatest freedom and separation from the original family. Second children are explorers and risk takers. My mother's father, Michael, a second child, left Italy for the United States of America as a young man. He immigrated to the United States leaving his wife Genevese, his young son Michael, and his extended family in Italy. His wife and son followed him years later, though he never saw his extended family in Italy again.

Antoinette, the second child, left the Bronx and her family and friends to seek out a new middle-class life on Long Island. Though only an hour or two from the Bronx where they were all born, Genevese was very upset about their leaving, complaining that Gene was taking her daughter so far away from the family.

A second child, I was first to move far away from Long Island and the East Coast to California. My original family all migrated to California over the years. As I said, sibling position offered some protection from the emotional triangles in my original family. The chronic anxiety present in the system affected us all, perhaps me less than others. My family offers an example of how the Bowen concepts are integrated in the nuclear family and through the *nuclear family emotional process*.

Much is currently being made about the changes in the family. Many point to the breakdown of the nuclear family and the rise of single parent families, blended families, divorced families, gay/lesbian/transgender families, and other non-traditional family configurations. Nonetheless, while statistics on non-traditional families vary, even in most non-traditional families there are usually two parents, whether or not the parents are together. As such, Kerr's concept of the nuclear family emotional process is still relevant and endures. Central to Kerr's argument is that the spouses/intimate partners are the foundation of a family and, as such, they imprint the family's emotional process first as partners and then as parents. The degree to which these parents have achieved emotional separation from their parents affects the degree to which their children will emotionally separate from them, as parents. This is relevant whether or not the parents remain together, divorce, separate, were never married, or re-marry.

The nuclear family configures and frames the differentiation and chronic anxiety levels of the children such that the children will attain about the same level of chronic anxiety and differentiation as the parents. Their children may—according to their sibling position, multigenerational emotional field, and current circumstances—achieve a bit more or a bit less emotional separation from their parents than their parents attained from their own parents. All told, though, excluding some unexpected, discontinuous event in the family, levels of differentiation within a nuclear family and with the family of origin will not fluctuate wildly either within the family of origin or within the extended family. Discontinuous family life-cycle events such as an untimely death, a catastrophic incident from war, or a natural calamity may affect this outcome. I address these exceptions more fully in chapter four.

There are, though, progressive and regressive branches in every extended family, so that over the generations, differentiation levels of families and individual members will look significantly diverse among extended family members or even within the family of origin. These fluctuations in basic differentiation are made even more complicated by the range in functional differentiation between people.

To review: Bowen's scale of differentiation highlights emotional maturity from minimal to maximal. Its value is more for explanatory purposes than for clinical research. The upper quadrant of 75–100 reflects those who have achieved a high level of emotional separation from their families of origin, as well as those having a well-developed capacity to function with relative independence in the world. Relationships are based on mutual caring and not emotional need. As the scale decreases, so too does that person's degree of emotional maturity and relationship interdependency. Those in the range of 50–75 on this scale have a fairly well-developed sense of personhood and an ability to function in the world with a moderately high level of adaptability, resiliency, independence, and relationship capacity. Kerr believes that most people function towards the lower end of this quadrant, reflecting a reasonable level of self and a moderate capacity for relationship success.

Those in the 25–50 range on the differentiation scale are more highly dependent on significant others. This is especially true for those lower on the scale. Relationship dependence increases as scale score declines. Often, these relationships create resentments and generate anxiety. Will conflicts are common as people focus more on getting others to change and less on self-reflection and self-responsibility. These individuals operate well in structured, stable environments. They find adapting to unexpected changes difficult. Those in the lowest quadrant 0–25 are those who struggle most in their lives. Due to their reactive behaviors, they find themselves in the legal and social service systems. One distressing event, such as a job loss, can spiral through their families and put them into a tail spin. They have minimal resources to adapt to life's travails.

For purposes of clarification in the following example, I assign numerical values to family members' differentiation levels. To demonstrate how this process operates, I'll use a couple, Francine and Byron. Francine and Byron marry. Bowen theory suggests that we marry at about the same level of basic differentiation. (This occurs because emotional fields "attract.") Francine and Byron have a basic differentiation level of about forty. This is moderately low. They both have stable jobs in a relatively safe community. They appear to be functioning at a higher level of basic differentiation because their life circumstances are positive and secure. While functional levels of differentiation are not scaled like basic levels, for the purposes of this section only, I'll use the same scaling system in order to demonstrate how differentiation works. With their relationship stable, along with their jobs and living situation, Francine and Byron operate in the forty-five range in terms of functional differentiation. They are pretty fortunate, as their basic differentiation levels are lower than their functional differentiation levels.

Francine and Byron have a child, Darren. Darren is a colicky child. Perhaps he is picking up on the added stress in the family since Francine is home and not working, and the bills are piling up. Nonetheless, rather than examining the changing support system between Francine and Byron since Darren's birth, the parents double down on their jobs. Byron is bringing home more and more work in order to court favor with his supervisor. Francine is busy learning how to nurse, feed, clean, and interact with the baby. Neither is as effective as before in supporting the other. Both are overwhelmed, as are most first-time parents. This situational disequilibrium is common in new parental relationships, and it is often distressing.

In Francine and Byron's case, though, neither came from a stable family, and the anxiety that they carry from their own parents' divorces weighs on them. On some level, they decide that talking about all this will make things worse, so they bottle it up inside them. The increased fear, anxiety, and frustration "spill out" onto Darren, who absorbs the excess anxiety and expresses it in colicky crying.

According to Bowen theory, this is part of the *family projection process*, the mechanism by which families "pass on" their chronic anxiety and lack of differentiation to their children. Like emotional triangling, this process is automatic and unthinking. Surely, most parents don't think: "I'll pass on my anxiety about life to my child." It happens over time and with much more subtlety than that.

Chronic anxiety and lack of differentiation can be passed along through specific patterns that exist in the family of origin or extended family, such as alcoholism, an eating disorder, incest, or failure to launch the youngest child. Passing along chronic anxiety and lower levels of differentiation can also be more generalized and not so symptom specific. The family projection process might, for example, be more of a general dread and anxiety about how life is scary and how you cannot trust others.

It seems that we cannot protect our children from absorbing our chronic anxiety. As parents, the only protection we can offer is our commitment to increase our own emotional maturity so that there is less chronic anxiety to pass on to the next generation. In this way, our commitment to differentiating is the best gift we can give to our children. And, as parents, it is important not to berate ourselves for our faults. It appears that all humans have them!

Let's get back to Francine, Byron, and Darren. While their basic differentiation level is forty, their functional differentiation has dropped to thirty-five. Their heightened anxiety "spills out" onto Darren, who, through the family projection process, absorbs the excess anxiety and expresses it in colicky crying. Suddenly, Darren seems like *he* is the problem. In some ways, this supports the couple in not talking to each other, and the child now becomes the focal point of the family's concerns, while the real issue is the marital relationship. Darren's basic differentiation, over time, becomes thirty-five, since he is firmly triangled into the parents' relationship. At thirty-five, Francine and Byron's functional differentiation remains lower than their basic differentiation as well.

Four years later, hoping for a child who is not such a problem, Francine and Byron conceive and give birth to a second child, Nell. Nell is a comparatively easier child. This is due, in part, to much of the couple's anxiety being bound and detoured to Darren, who has developed a speech disorder and is now receiving home services through the local school district. As Nell grows up, her parents see her as a gifted child, and they trust in the school system to provide for her. While they love Nell as much as they love Darren, the parents see Nell as less needy. This allows them to focus more of their energy on the problem child, Darren. Over time, this lack of intense focus by Francine and Byron results in Nell growing up with more emotional separation than her brother or even her parents. Her basic differentiation level in early adulthood is forty-five, slightly higher than her parents' basic level at forty and quite higher than Darren's basic scale of thirty-five.

At one point in their sexual lives, Francine and Byron "slip" and forget to use birth control. Nine months later, and eighteen months after Nell was born, their unplanned child Amber is born. Amber is an average child, requiring neither too much nor too little attention. In fact, while Amber can be a bit immature at times and her parents tend to baby her, she grows up with about the same degree of emotional separation as her parents and, like them, is forty on the scale.

The three siblings are now young adults. At twenty-seven years, Darren has never left home. In fact, his disabilities have grown over the years, and he leads a marginal life, dependent on his parents for much of his emotional and financial support. While his basic differentiation is thirty-five, the stresses from his disabilities and the hyper-focus by the parents have pushed his functional differentiation lower than his basic differentiation. Darren now stands at a thirty on the functional differentiation scale.

The gifted child Nell, in contrast, has been quite successful in school and in her life. She graduated with a degree in microbiology and went on to receive her Ph.D. in Pharmacology. Working as a pharmacist, Nell lives two hours away from her parents, maintains regular contact, helps when she can, and leads an independent life. Nell has achieved greater emotional separation from her parents than either of her parents or siblings, and her life has the structure and challenge needed to make her work exciting and meaningful. Further, she has a strong friendship network and dates when time and circumstances allow. While Nell's basic differentiation is forty-five, she functions at a higher level, given her life circumstances. Her functional differentiation level is fifty.

Lastly, late-comer Amber falls somewhere in the middle between her siblings. While she displays no outward signs of disability or severe challenge, Amber remains fairly dependent on her parents. She stays in her hometown, attends community college, and helps care for her disabled brother. Amber secures a middle-management position at the local Golden Corral restaurant. Her life is fairly intertwined with her parents and older brother. She has achieved about the same degree of emotional separation from her parents that her parents achieved from theirs. Her life is in a routine and in flow. Amber does well as long as there aren't any unexpected surprises or demands on her. Her basic differentiation level, at forty, is about the same as her functional differentiation. It is about the same as her parents' basic differentiation as well.

As you can see, the siblings, while not more than five points apart from their parents' basic differentiation, are quite different in functioning: Darren functions at thirty, Amber at forty, and Nell at fifty. Nell and Darren, while similar to their parents' basic differentiation level, look and function quite differently in the world.

While this example demonstrates how differentiation levels function in a family and how symptoms can develop in a child through the nuclear family, problems or symptoms can also appear in two additional locations. The first is in spouses/intimate partners or parents. This can take many forms, including physical, emotional (psychiatric/psychological), and/or social symptoms. In this scenario, the adult partner disproportionately absorbs the chronic anxiety from the extended as well as nuclear family. By becoming symptomatic and, as a result, the problem, the partner or parent provides some protection against the spread of chronic anxiety throughout the family system. This protection can be overridden when there is more chronic anxiety to absorb than the spouse or parent can tolerate through symptom development. Then, other areas of the nuclear family can also become symptomatic, including symptoms in the other partner, as well as a child or children, which I have already discussed. Symptoms can also appear in the marital/committed/parental relationship itself.

When the relationship itself is symptomatic, there is usually great conflict and intensity within it. This intensity can be expressed through upheaval, blaming, fighting, affairs, and other relationship crises. At more extreme levels of chronic and acute anxiety, this intensity can be expressed through threats of divorce and even threats of violence. At the most extreme levels of chronic and acute anxiety, this lack of differentiation can be conveyed in excessive forms of fusion, emotional abuse, and domestic violence.

Similarly, as with symptoms in a spouse/intimate partner, sometimes relationship dysfunction can offer some protection from symptom development in a child or in the partners/parents. And, again, as chronic and acute anxiety increases, it is common to see symptoms in more than one area. In these circumstances, it is not unusual for family symptoms to manifest in a child or the children, the partner relationship, and even one or both parents. Once again, we see that higher levels of differentiation provide safeguards for individuals and relationships. Higher differentiation offers some immunization against symptom development, especially since it results in much lower levels of chronic anxiety.

Multigenerational Emotional Process

For over a decade in the 1980s, my co-therapist and I worked with incest families. While I document that work more extensively in chapter nine, one family's story stands out as a classic example of multigenerational emotional process (MGEP).

The family was referred to us through social services. The maternal grandfather, Wallace, had molested the granddaughter, Violet, when she was twelve. Violet's mother Molly allowed Violet to spend the weekend with the grandparents, despite the fact that Wallace had sexually abused Molly when she was twelve! It was a striking example of multigenerational repetition of symptoms in a family. Molly had never disclosed her abuse until our family sessions. Molly remembered the abuse, and she was still scarred by her incestuous experiences with her father, which occurred for years. This incest eventually included sexual intercourse. Even though Molly knew that her father was sexually abusive, she still allowed Violet to stay at her grandparents' home overnight. Molly's mother Ester never protected her from Wallace when she was young. Neither Ester nor Molly protected Violet from Wallace. The multigenerational patterns of lack of maternal protection as well as family incest repeated over the generations. The poor differentiation and the extensive chronic anxiety in the extended family were passed down through the generations in the form of incest.

Both positive and negative patterns have a tendency to duplicate in extended families. We see these patterns clearly when we create a multigenerational genogram–a detailed and extensive diagram of the multigenerational family commonly used by Bowen therapists. It includes information on births, deaths, marriages, and divorces. It includes names and essential data on parents and their families of origin, as well as children in the extended family system. The genogram includes the emotional quality of family relationships as well, documenting strengths, symptoms, positive and negative legacies, and patterns of closeness, cooperation, fusion, and conflict.

Creating a genogram is a time consuming and powerful process. It often means interviewing surviving members of the extended family, uncovering important family stories, and trying to decipher the quality of relationships. It requires tenacity, persistence, compassion, and, above all, courage. A genogram can help uncover family secrets, patterns of strength and symptoms generations deep, and stories that highlight myths about the family. Narratives bring to light resiliency and falsehoods; stories expose defeats and adaptability. Genograms help us deepen relationships with others, and they humble us in honoring and recognizing those who came before us.

Genograms reveal. We sensitively gather information and stories from as many sources as possible. We take that data, and we interpret relationships and patterns. These revelations illuminate in their own right. They can also function as guideposts in framing our lives and our choices.

Because of my work teaching Bowen family systems theory courses for graduates and undergraduates for the past thirty-five years, I have worked on my genogram a long time. I still hear new stories and information about my extended family. When I do, I update my genogram. I have presented my genogram to students many times over the years.

A few thoughts come to mind about genograms and presentations: I always experienced anxiety before presenting it. Genograms are highly exposing. I always took care to protect the privacy of my family members as much as possible, while still being honest about my life and my experiences. Most people who write memoirs struggle with this balance between truth and full disclosure—with people, events, dates, and places—and respect for those who never asked for inclusion. My solution to this dilemma was always a function of what I was learning about the family, the dynamics of a particular class, and the teachable moments that occurred throughout the teaching day.

I have uncovered many multigenerational patterns over the years. As I age, I find the genogram helpful in different ways, illuminating generations' deep patterns. One such pattern that is particularly relevant for me now is that in both Janet's extended family and mine, adult children provide direct care for aging parents who were ill or who needed to transition away from independent living and into the home of an adult child.

In 1972, my father's mother, Anne, developed breast cancer. Widowed for twelve years, she lived alone. After surgery, it was apparent that she couldn't live alone during her radiation treatments. Her daughter lived in Florida, and her oldest son wasn't willing or able to help. My father and mother offered our home to my grandmother. She stayed with us during her six months of radiation treatment and recovery. Anne was not an easy woman to like. She always resented her status in life, having come from Italian royalty in her extended family. Queen Regina indeed. There was a perpetual emotional triangle between Gene-Antoinette-Anne.

My father felt pulled between his love for and duty to his mother on one side and his obligations and love as a husband and father on the other side. My parents didn't handle this well. Clear communication was not their forte. My brother and I were exiled to the living room couches as my parents moved into our bedroom. We managed. Young people are resilient. Anne took my parents' bedroom. The symbolism and the reality were there.

What I noticed was the intensity in the house as my mother got into a "will contest" with my father, and my grandmother tried to manipulate Gene to get what she wanted. This emotional triangle had been more and less active for twenty years. Anne never once thanked Antoinette for allowing her to stay and recover in her home. One day, with my parents at work, Anne was up and gone, without telling anyone that she was leaving. Antoinette was enraged by Anne's selfishness and lack of gratitude.

Janet's mother, Helen, was an only child. Her mother, Evelyn, became a widow in 1962 and moved into the Bicknese household the same year, living there until her death in 1972. Janet remembers Evelyn as being an active member of the household for years, until her health began failing. Janet assisted her mother in caring for Evelyn. I think that Janet developed her patience and compassion, at least in part, because of her grandmother. It seemed that Janet's father and mother were both understanding and supportive of having Evelyn live with them over the years. I don't really know the specifics of that emotional process. This was made easier by Lou's twelve-hour workday, which included a daily, four-hour round-trip commute.

While these are the two most relevant examples of multigenerational caring of elders in the extended families, there are others. Janet's paternal uncle helped care for his mother-in-law and father-in-law. Antoinette's younger sister, Josephine, cared for their father, Michael, after their mother, Genevese passed.

Reviewing those six months with my grandmother living with the family, Janet's history with her grandmother, and the other patterns of similar behavior in our extended families taught me many things. The most important lesson was that the marriage or committed relationship must remain *the* priority in a family. Generosity, good will, and family loyalty are not the foundation of a family system. The marriage or partnership is. I'm not saying that a single-parent family cannot be effective and loving. I'm simply saying that when a new person enters a family, especially when that person is an aging parent, it is important to nurture and tend to the primary relationship.

In February of 2012, Janet's father, Louis, had a stroke. At 89, he was living alone, and Janet and I realized that he needed more assistance. We offered Lou the option of moving in with us, which he accepted. This was a multigenerational pattern, and it was the right thing to do. The stroke necessitated him living with us. Knowing family systems theory through my genogram helped me with caretaking my father-in-law, which my wife and I did for seven years. We were all challenged with Lou's declining physical abilities and cognitive capacities. Janet left work, in large part, because he needed more care and oversight. Eventually, we both retired from our employment, though we were not "empty nesters" until Louis died in December of 2019. (Then, Covid-19 hit a few months later.) Despite the real challenges, knowing the pattern of family loyalty, love, and obligation gave us satisfaction that we were replicating something firmly and positively embedded in our families.

Reviewing my genogram helped illuminate the patterns and legacies from our multigenerational histories: that we were a part of a generations-deep pattern of love and loyalty. We were also conscious of the pitfalls to avoid in our sixties and constantly tried to balance the needs of each person, the needs of the marriage relationship, and our caretaking responsibilities. We have had some difficult moments, though, on the whole, we provided for Lou and our marriage during those seven years.

As exemplified above, what happens in one generation is often a playing out of what has occurred in multiple generations. The same nuclear family emotional processes that are active in one generation operate over many generations. In this way, emotional systems are iterative, meaning they repeat over and over again. Why? Because the same emotional processes that operate now, in humans, have operated in humans over hundreds of generations. They are the same emotional processes that have operated throughout evolutionary history, with only slight modifications in humans based on cultural history and evolutionary brain development.

Friedman offers us a model for understanding this pervasive effect of time. He likens time to a collapsing telescope, with the past being pressed up against the present. In this way, the past is ever present in the present, so that even concepts like the past and present are artificial, social constructions. This metaphor can be extended into the future: If the past is ever present in the present, then it seems plausible to think of the future as being pressed up against both the past and the present. Certainly, Einstein's theory of time and space supports this, and physicists (and yogis) generally accept non-linear conceptions of time.

What is useful in this construction is that our willingness to lead a more mindful, intentional, and therefore more emotionally mature life has the potential to change not only our present and our future, but the future of our generational families. The opposite is, of course, also the case. We can "contaminate" these future families through unthinking, reactive behaviors that undermine our differentiation and the differentiation of significant others in our emotional world.

Regardless if it is progressive or regressive, this influence happens through emotional fields and not linear, cause-and-effect interactions. Fields are non-material regions of influence. The influence of fields can occur over vast distances in both time and space. Gravity is one such example of a field. We know gravity is dependent on mass and distance, but we don't really know why gravity exists. It is a non-material field. Gravitational forces are at work throughout time and across the known universe. Its effects span distances from across the galaxy to a stone on a rocky moon.

An example of an emotional field: the traumatic loss of wife Annabelle in childbirth in 1900 results in complicated grieving, secrets, and a severe depression in the remaining children and in Wes, the father. This significant event is a nexus or nodal point in the family's history. That is, everything revolves around and results from this original loss and the way it was mismanaged by Wes.

Wes does not know how to cope with this loss. Annabelle was the primary caretaking parent for the two children, Erica and Marilyn, and he never feels comfortable being alone with them. As a result, Wes gives up the children to Annie's sister, Sophia, to parent. In the language of Bowen theory, Wes creates distance in the form of an *emotional cutoff* between his children and him. This emotional cutoff by the father is just as significant to the grieving children as the painful loss of their mother in childbirth. In this way, chronic and acute anxiety coagulated around these losses. Erica and Marilyn, having lost their mother in a traumatic incident, have now lost their father as well.

The children's lives were significantly impacted by this trauma. While the sisters remained close throughout their lives—they tightly bonded together after they lost their parents—their personal and interpersonal lives were not successful. Erica married an alcoholic and had three children with him. He was always an unreliable husband and father. Marilyn never married. Men scared her, and she always kept her distance. She had a low-paying job cleaning houses and never felt that she amounted to much.

The consequences of these losses reverberated through time. Wes and Annie's loss still has consequences generations later with Terri, their great-grandchild. In 2017, Terri, at twenty-six, enters psychotherapy because she struggles with relationships. She fears abandonment and rejection. Terri is not aware of why this is so, but she has a vague sense of impending doom if she accepts Sid's offer to live together. At some "deep" level she fears that he will leave, and she will be left with any children they have, as was the case with her parents when they divorced and her father disappeared. The "core" of the loss, though, goes back over a hundred years to the death of Annabelle and to Wes having cut off his children emotionally and physically. These traumatic events still reverberate through time and space, influencing what Terri thinks and feels as well as how she acts in the moment.

While Terri is unaware of this nodal point of accumulated anxiety, she experiences a formless sense that something is off. It is not until she is well into creating her genogram as a part of her therapy that she uncovers her great-grandmother's death, her great-grandfather cutting off and abandoning his two children following that death, and the reverberating effects of these losses throughout the generations. Developing a genogram gives Terri a more objective sense of her connectedness across time and especially with her great-grandmother. Knowing the "source" of her chronic anxiety, she begins the long, scary, and exciting period of de-triangling and thereby differentiating from the grief that has overwhelmed the multigenerational family for over a hundred years. This is a courageous undertaking and speaks to Terri assuming a leadership position in her family.

Sometimes, multigenerational emotional processes seem magical or even illogical. How is it possible to be affected by an event years ago? This is where the image of time as a collapsing telescope with the past pressed up against the future is helpful. For, if the past is ever-present in the present, then it still exists today. The grief surrounding Annabelle's death and Wes's abandonment is not some distant event in the past. It survives now, and it continues to exert its power in the present with Terri. In this way, the emotional field is alive and active, influencing relationships across the generations. As Terri emotionally separates from these losses through awareness in the genogram—but even more importantly by getting clear about what she wants for herself in her relationship and in her life—she is able to unambiguously communicate to Sid her hopes and dreams. Over time and with proper coaching, Terri embraces the process of emotionally maturing. As difficult as it is, she begins to view differentiating as a gift—to herself, to her partner, and to her future children and grandchildren. She is altering the emotional field of the generations and begins freeing herself from the oppressive weight of the past. Terri is re-formatting the emotional imprint on herself and her future family so that she and they can be freer in assuming personal responsibility for their own emotional beings and destinies.

There are other ways of emotionally separating from the family than through the kind of detailed genogram study undertaken by Terri. Bowen family systems theory, however, offers a structured way of facilitating greater non-attachment through the theory and therapy.

Multigenerational emotional process is one of the wide-angle lenses of Bowen family systems theory. It is where all of the Bowen theory concepts come together and are expressed across the generations. Emotional process from the nuclear family to the multigenerational family is iterative. That is, multigenerational patterns tend to repeat, as emotional triangles in one generation are often echoes of emotional triangles from previous generations. Differentiation levels often remain fairly constant as well, and chronic anxiety is always transmitted from generation to generation.

Through all of these seemingly deterministic scenarios, though, a concerted, conscious effort over years and decades can begin to alter the form and pattern existing and perpetuating throughout the generations. As we calm down and see more clearly, things begin to change. Like a huge ship on the open ocean, change in direction takes time. Neither an ocean liner nor a person can turn on a dime. Differentiating is a life-long process; it is not a goal attained after fifteen coaching sessions over four months.

Societal Emotional Process

Societies are similar to families in the ways that they manage the forces of togetherness and individuality, emotional reactivity and chronic anxiety, differentiation, and emotional triangles. This is not surprising, as the social systems of civilizations are not really different from the social systems in families. What's different is a matter of scale, not kind. Different eras select different anxiety binders to coalesce the chronic anxiety present in societies. In this way, we see various aspects of Bowen theory played out at a larger, societal level. In today's world, terrorism, fear of immigrants, and Islamophobia are examples of emotional triangulation in the United States and across much of the Western world.

Despite evidence that a person is much more likely to be killed in a car accident, a lightning strike, or even by domestic terrorism by White Supremacists than by Muslim extremism, many people have developed an outsized, irrational fear of Islam in general and terrorism by Muslims specifically. None other than psychologist William James understood the power of emotionality when he proclaimed that "reason is but a fleck on the sea of emotion." Once perceptions are formed, and especially if people believe that they are facing an existential threat, it is difficult to change them. Facts no longer matter.

Add to this the political reality that fear often drives voting as well as public policy. It is understandable that we live in a world of "fake news" and "alternate facts" designed to stimulate emotional reactivity, separate people into categories of us and them, and then use these evolutionary hangovers to demonize groups and their supporters into rigid, emotional triangles.

Again, emotional systems are recursive. They function similarly for families, flocks, and nations. These insights led Murray Bowen to originally propose the concept of *societal regression*, which was later altered and expanded by Michael Kerr to the concept of *societal emotional process*.

Late in his career, Bowen introduced the concept of societal regression to show how the same emotional processes that unfold in humans and human families exist at the larger, societal level. Think of this as "nested systems," or systems within systems. In this way, the same emotional processes that exist in the individual exist in the family. And, the same emotional processes that exist in the family exist in "the family of families" or the human family.

In the 1980s and before his death in 1990, Bowen believed that American civilization had been in an emotional regression for decades. And, as with a symptomatic family, this regression had resulted in and continues to perpetuate emotional triangulation of oppressed groups and individuals, a "scapegoating" of the most vulnerable and exploited members of society. At any given time in any culture, there will be points of contention and eruptions of emotional reactivity. These points of conflict are not random. Rather, they are emotional triangles for the culture, and they often change over time and over circumstances.

Currently, in addition to Muslims, Islamophobia, and terrorism, this list includes the LGBTQ community, people of color, and the social underclass in general. Emotional triangulation also occurs with important policy questions and scientific issues. This triangulation manifests itself around topics that generate fear and anxiety and, therefore, easily arouse passions and emotional reactivity. In 2020, these include Obamacare, global climate crisis, a changing world order or disorder, an ineffective Congress, a remarkably immature president, and the destructive power of concentrated wealth, to name a few of the current but ever-shifting cultural anxiety binders.

Kerr expands the notion of societal regression to societal emotional process. He re-conceptualizes the societal concept to offer a more nuanced, expansive, and intricate approach to understanding emotional process in society through a Bowen theory lens. Through Kerr's expanded concept, there are simultaneously progressive and regressive aspects or "branches" in the culture, as there are similarly progressive and regressive branches in all multigenerational families. We are not simple a society in regression.

For example, gay/lesbian rights seem in the ascension. Marriage equality is now the law of the land. This is socially progressive, as it extends rights to underrepresented and oppressed groups. In addition, we have made progress with civil rights, even though we have a long way to go. And we seem more concerned with and aware of issues of sustainability and the problems of concentrated wealth.

On the negative side, the global climate crisis is an existential threat, and, as journalist, professor, author, and science writer Elizabeth Kolbert and others soberly remind us, we are in the middle of the sixth mass extinction. Clearly, we are not addressing this catastrophe with the urgency it deserves. This is unmistakably regressive. Also, gridlock in government and the rise of nationalism, fundamentalism, and extremism around the globe indicate that large parts of American society, as well as the global culture, are indeed losing headway.

The important point, here, is that societal emotional process is another wide-angle application of Bowen's family systems theory. In this book, many of my chapters are overlaid with the effects of societal emotional process. For example, marriage and family therapists and supervisors often highlight categories of identity, issues of oppression, and social justice in the therapy and supervision sessions. These issues are hot topics in the culture as well.

The American Association for Marriage and Family Therapy supports this approach through their approved supervisor designation training and evaluation process. In chapter eight, I argue that this determination of what is important in supervision reflects the cultural conditioning of society—the societal emotional process of the culture—regarding what is important instead of highlighting the theoretically important concepts in Bowen theory, such as differentiation, emotional triangulation, chronic anxiety, and the emotional processes in the current, nuclear, and extended family.

A case for American civilization in societal regression can still be made today, especially when we examine the fractured, divided nature of the electorate and citizenry. Large pockets of the United States, of all persuasions, seem unwilling or unable to step outside the emotional field of the times. Conflict and polarization seem ubiquitous. This does not bode well for us as a people.

In other chapters, I will describe how the entire social overlay of Bowen theory makes it just as valuable a tool outside of family psychotherapy as it is within the field. My work as a college and university professor, educational leader, mediator, conciliator, supervisor, and trainer were all affected by how I applied Bowen theory in these various career incarnations.

To summarize: Emotional processes play themselves out in all significant relationships. In fact, Bowen theorists suggest that you can work to increase differentiation in a work relationship, love/committed relationship, or in the family of origin and that maturing in one relationship will have a spread of effect to other relationships. This is an important component of this book, since I discuss the various ways I have implemented Bowen family systems theory across disciplines and, therefore, relationship systems.

Nuclear family emotional process describes how the emotional system expresses itself in families. The expression of the individuality and togetherness life forces in action defines differentiating. Chronic anxiety is the "inherited" residue from not differentiating. This anxiety is played out in emotional triangles through anxiety binding. If there is enough chronic anxiety and/or acute anxiety in the relationship, then emotional, social, and/or physical symptoms can develop. These symptoms can appear at three points in a family—in a child or children; in adult parents, spouses, or partners; and/or in the adult relationship itself. The more chronic anxiety that is present, the more it needs binding through inside and outside positions on emotional triangles and through symptom development. The sequence of transmitting symptoms is through the family projection process. This clarifies how families replicate specific or generalized patterns of anxiety from parents to children.

Multigenerational emotional process is a way of viewing the family over the generations "from the balcony," that is, from a more objective perspective. MGEP gives us the ability to see a richer, more complex playing out of family patterns and the influences of both differentiation and chronic anxiety throughout several generations, and it binds together the generations over time and space. Time, in this framework, always exists in the now, and the present can be a source of change for both the present and the future.

A common but destructive way of managing intensity in families is through emotional cutoff. In emotional cutoff, a parent or child (or both) uses extreme emotional distance to deal with relationship intensity. The problems with cutoff are significant. Kerr says that cutoff "reflects a problem, solves a problem, and creates a problem." The problem reflected and expressed is emotional intensity. It is "solved" by creating a lasting distance to avoid that intensity. This solution creates a problem since cutoff in one generation often leads to increased intensity and emotional fusion in another generation or in another significant emotional relationship. For example, a man cut off from his mother will likely have an overly intense and fused relationship with a spouse or child.

Societal emotional process completes this rather quick journey through Bowen's theory. Societal emotional process is an expanded version of Bowen's original concept of societal regression. Through societal emotional process, we see all of the central Bowen family systems theory concepts repeated and expanded at a larger, societal scale. This concept, in particular, allows us to apply Bowen theory to organizations, congregations, mediation, health care, and larger social environments and situations. In essence, the same emotional processes operating in individuals and in nuclear and multigenerational families are also active at a societal level.

As examples, in 2020 we see emotional triangulation with Muslims and Islamophobia, terrorism, Obamacare, and the oppression of women, minorities, and the poor through blaming, scapegoating, and violence. I address many of these social points of contention when I discuss educational leadership, teaching, peacemaking, and supervision.

Selected Support

While Bowen family systems theory has been growing in its implications and applications over time, with a theory that is over sixty years old, what is the evidence of its validity? While this question would also take an entire book to answer, I want to focus on a few areas of neuroscience to present some initial evidence for the theory.

Advances in brain imaging and neurological research in the past generation have largely confirmed or supported many of the theoretical concepts originally put forth by Murray Bowen. For example, Daniel Goleman and Malcolm Gladwell present research on brain imaging that suggests how emotional fields can operate. Limbic systems seem to "link up" so that a strong, calm, i.e., more differentiated presence can have a powerful effect on another person. It seems like the power of presence is real: calm begets calm and laughter begets laughter, as much as anger can beget anger.

Neuroscientists suggest that the mechanism for such "limbic resonance" may have their roots in mirror neurons, and in 2010, scientists from UCLA made a direct recording of mirror neurons in the human brain. Mirror neurons also provide a biological and neurological basis for empathy, compassion, and emotional connection to others, strongly endorsing the presence of the togetherness life force, a concept essential to understanding and applying Bowen's theory.

Other important neurological research suggests that we can increase our success at managing hyper-aroused states–e.g., limbic hyper-arousal into a fight/flight/freeze state–through using our pre-frontal cortex, specifically the left pre-frontal cortex, to calm ourselves and minimize our biologically-wired capacity for reacting automatically to danger. The danger could be life threatening or simply a reaction to an unpleasant situation such as a fight with a spouse or stage fright before a public performance. Unfortunately, our limbic reactions can be similar. But fortunately, there are strong neurological connections between the left prefrontal cortex and the limbic system's amygdalae.

Among its many functions, the amygdalae are the site of our fight/flight/freeze reactions, while the prefrontal cortex, as the brain's executive center, allows us to develop greater conscious control of our thoughts and feelings. This capacity for increasing self-management is itself a product of evolutionary development and is an essential component of Bowen theory's individual life force and differentiation. In many ways, our prefrontal cortex is our personal managerial governing system, and it plays an essential role in our individuality. In fact, our pre-frontal cortex remains the apex of human evolution, developing and refining our capacity to think ahead to the consequences of our actions, planning for the future, meta-cognating to understand how it is that we think and behave, delaying immediate gratification for more long-term satisfaction and accomplishments, not automatically and reactively engaging in emotionally intense environments, and finding more appropriate ways to manage conflict, disagreement, and perceived or actual threat.

We face a number of evolutionary mismatches or what Stanford biologist Paul Ehrlich terms "evolutionary hangovers." These are reflexively-driven and, at times, non-adaptive behaviors that are hardwired from billions of years of evolutionary development and natural selection. The example of hyper-arousal for non-life-threatening situations such as public performance is one such evolutionary hangover. Nonetheless, it seems that humans are also quite capable of moving in different, i.e., more emotionally mature ways in managing our lives and our relationships with the human and non-human natural worlds. Through practice and training, we can coach the pre-frontal cortex to decrease the automatically reactive amygdalae and better manage anxiety and increase differentiation.

Further, recent advances in biology and genetics support Bowen theory. This includes research in understanding epigenetics, an important new area of research that looks at how powerful emotional experiences can affect the turning on and turning off of genes in a single generation and the effect this may have on future generations. This developing area of science is remarkable, as it offers explanations into how genes within the gene pool themselves can be switched on and off based on powerful emotional circumstances, including extreme environmental conditions and intense personal and interpersonal situations. The field of epigenetics offers the biological possibility that the intense emotional effect resulting from efforts at increasing emotional maturity may have significant ramifications not only for the self and the current generation but for future generations as well. Or reciprocally, epigenetics suggest that powerful negative circumstances can decrease adaptability and increase regressive behaviors in the current generation as well as future generations. More and more, it appears that genetics itself is not destiny.

Further, the latest findings on the brain appear to indicate that while certain brain functions seem to be located in specific regions of the brain, the brain has a remarkable capacity for resiliency and healing. Neuroplasticity in brain functioning indicates that, with time and effort, even a brain scarred by injury, disease, or trauma can often re-wire itself to replace damaged areas and functions. This act of developing new neurons and new neural circuits replaces the older notion that the brain is a set organ without the ability to adapt when injured. Brain resilience and adaptability can be correlated with emotional maturity itself. According to current research, the brain is capable of renewal and greater "differentiation." And, like the emotional concept of differentiation, this process requires time to unfold.

These recent advances in biology, genetics, and neurological imaging provide some support for concepts proposed by Bowen's theory. Given the rapidity of scientific breakthroughs, it is deeply satisfying to uncover how salient, relevant, and accurate Bowen's family systems theory remains decades after Murray Bowen first proposed it.

CHAPTER FOUR

THE EVOLVING NATURE OF BOWEN FAMILY SYSTEMS THEORY

Friedman once commented that his relationship with Bowen theory was different than Kerr's relationship with the theory or even Bowen's relationship with his theory. That instantly resonated with me as I realized that my understanding of Bowen theory is also closely connected to my relationship with the theory. This got me thinking about the association between how one "hears" Bowen theory and the nature of change itself.

As an example, Kerr differentiated the emotional and feeling systems. Bowen did not make such a distinction, believing that there was no discernible difference between them. This is one illustration of how Bowen theory does not stand on its own; rather, it is interpreted and implemented based on how one makes sense of the theory, through one's *relationship* with it. With such an understanding in mind, I will share some of my key experiences learning Bowen theory, my thoughts about its evolution, and my suggestions regarding theory expansion and clarification.

Whenever a pioneer like Murray Bowen dies, there are always questions about legacy. This is particularly relevant for Bowen, who left an elegant theory as a part of his life's work. In 1988, Bowen generously proclaimed, "I give my theory to the world." Since his death in 1990, proponents of Bowen family systems theory have sought to understand and appreciate the depth and complexity of his theory and its effects on the personal and professional lives of its advocates.

For those of us committed to understanding and applying Bowen theory, we recognize that an emotional field shift is necessary in order to really *get* the theory. For most theory adherents, this means training that incorporates personal and professional work with a Bowen theory coach in a therapeutic or supervisory capacity. For some, this comprehension and application comes through a peer group support network. For all Bowen family systems theory advocates, keeping the theory alive and central in our lives requires a long-term commitment.

Over the years, I have become more competent and more confident in my understanding and application of Bowen theory to a wide-range of personal and professional endeavors. I first began using Bowen theory as an anchoring theory in my clinical work. Then, I implemented the theory in disciplines other than those addressed in Bowen's original work. These experiences led me to ponder the process of theory revision and extension, considering questions such as these:

• If Bowen family systems theory is to remain relevant in the 21st century, how does the theory evolve when its chief theoretician has passed away?

• If new research shows aspects of the theory incorrect, who makes the decision to officially modify and adjust the theory?

• If a new concept or principle is proposed to the theory, who makes the determination as to whether it becomes a part of Bowen's family systems theory?

• Is there a way to "officially" sanction these new components of the theory or, if not, does Bowen theory go the way of Freudian theory, with "neo-Bowenians" taking the place of "neo-Freudians" and splitting the theory and theoreticians/practitioners into "camps," rather than unifying and expanding the theory?

• Finally, does the theory have to be officially modified and adjusted at all since Bowen gave his theory to the world? That is, need there be gatekeepers?

Paraphrasing the words of one of my blunter students, how do we make Bowen theory meaningful in a changing world, so that it's not simply "another theory by a dead white guy"? As a theoretician and practitioner of Bowen theory for decades, I've thought a lot about these questions. I don't presume to know everything about Bowen's theory or how, exactly, to evolve it. I do believe, however, that Bowen theory needs to evolve. (Bowen, himself, was working on a ninth concept, *spirituality*, before he died.)

In the spirit of adventure, boldness, and radicalism embodied by Bowen and Friedman, I propose an extension to the theory, the differentiating emotional triangle. This extrapolation is based on a non-clinical understanding of emotional triangles and triangulation. It has its roots in Bowen, Kerr, and Friedman. I propose that not all emotional triangles are fueled by regressive chronic anxiety. Some emotional triangles can actually promote differentiation. I will explore the idea of the differentiating triangle.

Also, I will examine the pace of change in advancing differentiation. This is not so much a theory expansion but a modification or clarification to the existing notion of the glacial pace of differentiation accepted by most Bowen theory-based practitioners. Most Bowen theorists focus on continuity in basic differentiation and how achieving even modest increases takes many months if not years of concentrated and determined effort and focus. While I believe that this approach is essentially true, I offer a supplemental understanding of change, which is based in the natural sciences. It is the possibility of achieving more rapid shifts in differentiation due to discontinuous events in the individual and family life cycle. That is, Bowen theory may accommodate notions of swifter changes in differentiation that exists in parallel with findings of how significant shifts occur in the non-human, natural world. If we can better understand the nature of change, we may be able to structure certain environments to take advantage of more rapid opportunities to differentiate.

The Differentiating Emotional Triangle

The differentiating triangle re-conceptualizes the notion of the emotional triangle to include not simply ways of binding and managing anxiety, but also ways of promoting emotional maturity. Bowen's concept of the emotional triangle rests on the observation that a two-person system becomes inherently unstable over time, and, as such, will automatically bring in a third person or third "other" (substance, food, belief, etc.) to create some temporary stability. This triangulation is especially likely during heightened periods of stress and anxiety. The third person, place, or thing helps bind the anxiety for the unstable twosome. In this way, the third point helps achieve some impermanent stability between the other two people, usually through occupying the inside position with one member of the emotional triangle, with the second member occupying the outside position.

Alternately, this triangulation process attains transitory strength through the third other occupying the outside position on the triangle, allowing the inside two to come together, at least momentarily, against the outside third. This second scenario is what occurred in my two case histories as dean and charter school director that I discuss in chapters six and seven.

The emotional triangle is a perfect example of the sophistication and complexity of Bowen theory. Once we understand the concept, we can observe emotional triangles, as well as interlocking triangles and triangulation, all around us. Emotional triangles reveal themselves in personal relationships, families, professional associations, novels, movies, cable programs, politics, work environments, international relations, and a host of other human systems. They are widespread, pervasive, and ubiquitous. Emotional triangling is a natural systems phenomenon and, as such, triangling is automatic and universal. That is, everyone triangulates, and so it exists in every family, culture, and society. We even find examples of emotional triangles in non-human animal systems, especially with primates and other mammals.

While it may be self-evident that regressive emotional triangling is omnipresent and widespread, is the reverse not also true? Rather than simply being a regressive process whereby anxiety is shifted through the emotional triangle, essentially undercutting the twosome's opportunity to directly and maturely manage their anxiety and conflict, is it not also possible that a twosome may create a more differentiating triangle between the two of them and a third person or other?

We must think less like clinicians observing the "dysevolutionary" and regressive effects of emotional triangling and more like observers of *all* evolutionary processes, both progressive and regressive. In this way, we can discover instances of triangles that promote the differentiation of the system or create a product or outcome in service of progression, as well as personal and systemic evolution.

In fact, I believe that this is exactly what Kerr accomplishes in re-conceptualizing Bowen's original concept of societal regression. Societal regression describes one aspect of evolution, one that is degenerative. Societal regression identifies how problematic societal processes undercut evolution. While accurate, it only reflects half of the story. Kerr understands this when he expands societal regression to emphasize societal emotional process. He recognizes that progression and regression both exist in systems, large and small. Kerr expands the concept to include both progressive and regressive emotional features in social systems. In this way, Kerr's societal emotional process does for societal regression what the differentiating triangle does for emotional triangles: expanding the concept to also include its progressive function.

Indeed, if the only function of emotional triangles is regressive and since the process is automatic, universal, and pervasive, it is likely that, as a species, humans would not have evolved. This is clearly not true, as humans have been remarkably adaptive and resilient over time and over vast geological distances and locations and have therefore "progressed" in terms of evolutionary biology. Isn't it likely, then, that something else besides regressive emotional triangling must be occurring? It seems so, and, as such, it appears necessary to posit a counterpoint to the maladaptive and all-encompassing phenomenon of emotional triangulation in order to account for the evolutionary success of humans as a species.

In searching for answers to these questions, I reviewed the literature on Bowen family systems theory and found evidence for this assumption. First and foremost, multiple Bowen theorists, including Kerr and Friedman themselves, suggest that when working with a couple, the therapist must create a "therapeutic triangle." But what exactly is a therapeutic triangle? It is an emotional triangle where the therapist takes personal responsibility for self, develops a positive rapport with each member of the couple, and keeps the anxiety within the couple rather than absorbing it, becoming emotionally triangled by that anxiety, or having the couple emotionally triangulate another.

This strategy and process essentially leverages therapeutic rapport to help the couple learn self-soothing, assume personal responsibility, become more emotionally consistent as individuals, and manage anxiety. (Of course, the more differentiated therapist accomplishes this emotional dynamic through the power of presence with any client system, whether that system is an individual client, a couple, or a family. With an individual, for example, the third point on the emotional triangle is someone or something outside of the therapeutic encounter. With a more differentiated therapist conducting the individual session, the positive results are the same.)

The key to forming a therapeutic triangle is to connect with each party equally and impartially. Doing so replicates Euclid's axiom about triangles, an insight over two thousand years old. He states that "things which equal to the same thing also equal one other."

Extrapolating to emotional triangles, I believe that if a therapist can hold an equilateral and equidistant emotional position relative to the couple, the couple will not only experience the therapist as authentic, compassionate, and equal, but also experience the *self* as emotionally equal to the *partner* as well.

This process does not occur through logical, deductive reasoning. Rather, it takes place through the power of presence in which the leader of the encounter, i.e., the more differentiated therapist, helps to create an emotional field shift such that the resonance of the encounter elevates the couple in ways that promulgate emotionally mature interactions *between the twosome*. Essentially, the therapist's differentiated stance and perspective help increase the functional differentiation of the couple. The Bowen therapist acts like the rising tide that lifts all boats.

This may not happen during every therapeutic encounter, especially as emotional maturity levels decrease in more poorly differentiated pairs. Nonetheless, the possibility of developing and perpetuating a therapeutic triangle amplifies as the emotional maturity level of the therapist (and the couple) increases. The therapist's ability to craft more differentiated and equal relationships between self and the couple is consequently augmented. Through this emotional field shift, the relationship between the couple becomes clearer and calmer, and, consequently, of greater equality.

Rigid over-functioning/under-functioning reciprocal relationship patterns decrease and they begin to function more evenly and effectively. The capacity of each partner to manage personal anxiety more responsibly, i.e., not triangling it out to another, amplifies as well. In sum, a more differentiated therapist (or mediator or leader) assists each individual to not only see and experience the therapist as an equal partner in the therapeutic process, but also allows the person to begin experiencing the other partner similarly, as emotional equals. In this way, Euclid's axiom supports this concept of the differentiating triangle, as "things which equal to the same thing also equal one other."

Kerr and Bowen support the differentiating triangle in their book *Family Evaluation*. Kerr states:

> A basic tenet of systems theory is that the tension in a two-person relationship will resolve *automatically* when contained within a three-person system... It only requires that the third person be in adequate emotional contact with the other two and able to emotionally separate from them. The process of being in contact and emotionally separate is referred to as 'de-triangling' (p. 145).

I believe that this description of de-triangling is consistent with the notion of the differentiating triangle. Staying in emotional contact with each person, being emotionally separate from them, and preventing the couple from re-triangling their anxiety out to an alternate anxiety binder are all hallmarks of higher differentiation. In fact, if emotional triangling is a regressive, pervasive phenomenon that binds anxiety in the triangulated third, then the act of de-triangling is not simply and inherently differentiating. The act of de-triangling itself becomes a differentiating triangle, whereby the emotional maturity or *differentiation of all members* of the triangle is promoted.

In the footnote on the same page, Kerr suggests this notion of a differentiating triangle when he writes, "The ability to be in emotional contact with others yet still autonomous in one's emotional functioning is the essence of the concept of differentiation" (p. 145). Kerr continues: "a twosome regains *emotional equilibrium* (italics added) in the presence of a detached third person" (p. 146) and, finally,

"A third person who can maintain his differentiation in face of emotionally charged communication from others does not permit the problem to be triangled out of the relationship. The effect of having an involved but 'untriangled' third person is to 'nudge' each marital partner toward accepting increased responsibility for the problem and attaching more importance to working it out *between* them" (p. 148).

These descriptions are entirely consistent with the concept of the differentiating triangle. The therapist or third other person, with a higher level of emotional maturity and in a leadership position within the system, affects the entire system by calming anxiety through mere presence. The differentiated emotional resonance of the therapist provides the opportunity for the couple to achieve greater "emotional equilibrium" between them.

In essence, having created an equilateral and equidistant triangle based on rapport, compassion, detachment, and connection—I like to call it passionate nonattachment—the therapist's emotional field influences the couple to self-soothe, self-regulate, and act with greater responsibility and connectivity. This results in each treating the other as equals and not undercutting one another other through reactive behavior and blame displacement.

It is a similar process when coaching a client to de-triangulate in one or more of his central relationships. Promoting greater emotional maturity in managing significant relationships can encourage de-triangulation and support increased differentiation in that person and the entire system. This is the essence of the differentiating triangle.

In my book, *Applying Family Systems Theory in Mediation: A Practitioner's Guide* (2011), I address the notion of the differentiating triangle. In discussing how, in mediation, the conflict itself is the anxiety binder for the disputants, I describe both the structure and the function of the emotional triangle, as well as the role of the mediator in forming what I call a mediation triangle, which is the mediation equivalent of the therapeutic triangle. Both the mediation triangle and the therapeutic triangle are clear examples of how differentiating triangles operate.

In sum, a triangle can be "fueled" by differentiation as well as by anxiety. Emotional triangling powered by anxiety is regressive, activating the chronic anxiety in the system. Triangles powered by differentiation are progressive as they promote the emotional maturity of all members of the system.

As an example, Janet and I have sought to develop our parenting skills in such a way as to promote the emotional maturity of all members of the family. This necessitated our having regular conversations around parental and child expectations, as well as allowing the family members to develop and mature in their own way, at their own rate, and in their own time. We promoted the positive emotional, physical, spiritual, and social development of our family through helping family members to accept personal responsibility, stay in close relationship with each other, and practice self-regulation when anxiety inevitably increases over the course of the family life cycle. We have had our share of family crises, regressive triangulation, and symptoms over the years. What family hasn't? Fortunately, though, we both understand the theory and have used it to successfully promote differentiated triangulation.

In non-family examples, two musicians can work cooperatively and maturely together to write an exquisite piece of music that neither could write alone; two scientists can work synchronistically and creatively to unlock a mystery of the natural world; three friends can develop a remarkable depth of friendship with each other through promoting the mature functioning of each other in their relationships; and a leader in a system can encourage the emotional maturity of all members of the system through differentiated leadership between the leader, the followers, and the goal or vision for the organization. Through all of these examples, anxiety doesn't drive the structure and function of the triangle. Differentiation does.

It may be that the development of family systems theory within a clinical framework has limited our ability to conceptualize the differentiating triangle. As clinicians, it is often easier to monitor regressive processes than progressive ones, since we observe so many regressive emotional triangles in our work. And, as clinicians, we may even be framing our discussions surrounding progressive processes from observations of regressive ones. While Kerr suggests that de-triangling may be the term that describes a progressive emotional process, de-triangling may not be the most appropriate term. De-triangling relates to a *process* of getting unstuck from an emotional triangle; but, it is still rooted in the regression effects of the emotional triangle itself. While de-triangling may, in fact, promote greater emotional maturity in the system, something more positive and evolution-focused, such as the differentiating triangle, gets at the notion of emotional maturation as a natural, growth-promoting process.

Nonetheless, what seems clear is that while the vast majority of people automatically triangulate (hence reducing adaptability, resilience, and functionality between people), evolutionary psychology, observations, and common sense dictate that a counter force is likely present in understanding the human condition as well.

The natural world offers some supportive homologies (parallel evolutionary pathways) here. In quantum physics, all particles have a corresponding opposite. There are particles and anti-particles, including matter and anti-matter; magnetic positive and negative charges; protons and anti-protons; and electrons and anti-electrons (positrons).

I am suggesting that the natural process of opposites that exist in the natural world may be similar to the "anti-regressive" force of emotional triangling. That is, the differentiating triangle seems to offer one such opposite solution since all of human behavior is decidedly not regressive. In fact, differentiation itself already has a natural and opposite "force" and concept in chronic anxiety. Differentiating triangles seem consistent with all of this.

One final example: In the film *Shakespeare in Love*, the fictional William Shakespeare has a passionate and secret affair with Viola de Lesseps, who has been promised to another man by her father. Though both understand that their romance will soon end, they act on their passion for each other physically through their sexual and emotional involvement; but perhaps just as importantly, Shakespeare uses their emotional intensity to create a stirring play, *Romeo and Juliet*. William and Viola's relationship not only helps to break William's writer's block but to co-create a work of lasting beauty that neither of them could have created alone. Though fictional, this film provides a clear and compelling example of what is possible through a differentiating triangle.

Differentiation and Discontinuous Change

Both continuous and discontinuous change occurs throughout nature. We see this, for example, in evolutionary biology and geology. In my second proposition for clarifying Bowen theory, I investigate the probability that more rapid shifts in differentiation are possible.

Discontinuous events can provide a unique catalyst for promoting differentiation, even in those who come from regressive, intractable families not receiving the support they need to mature emotionally. For example, why is it that certain people, trapped in harshly regressive and calcified family systems, nonetheless find ways to differentiate more fully despite their multigenerational emotional process and family history? Again, in *Family Evaluation*, Kerr hints at this possibility: "Basic level is fairly well established by the time a child reaches adolescence and usually remains fixed for life, although *unusual life experiences* (italics added) or a structured effort to increase basic level at a point later in life can lead to some change in it" (p. 98). Here, Kerr suggests that differentiation levels are fairly set by adulthood unless there is a determined effort over time or a person experiences an extraordinary life event.

In nature and across the natural sciences, including evolutionary theory, we find that change often occurs in two ways, through continuous and discontinuous processes. Continuous change is often slow and incremental. It is sometimes referred to as gradualism. This seems to be what Kerr signifies when he says that a "structured effort to increase basic level" can lead to some increase in basic differentiation over time. It is what Lerner refers to as the glacial speed of change.

Much biological evolution falls into this category of gradualism. For example, over time, genetic mutations occur. Those that are regressive for a species are weeded out; those that promote resiliency and adaptability are naturally selected, retained, and strengthened. This process is usually quite slow. That is, evolving as a species takes time.

In geography, there is relative consistency in the Earth's features and formations, from the development and erosion of mountain ranges to the structure and shape of the continental masses. In human development, most emotional, physical, spiritual, and social growth also occurs slowly, predictably, and gradually. As Friedman often reminded us, the process of maturing takes time.

Nonetheless, there are other, countervailing forces at work individually and systemically besides measured, continuous change. In fact, forces of discontinuous change occur naturally as well and are often much more significant over the long run. In biology, for example, discontinuous change is sometimes referred to as "punctuated equilibrium." According to biology-online.org, this process of evolutionary development is a "theory that describes evolutionary change happening rapidly and in brief geological events in between the long periods of stasis (or equilibrium)." It is "evolutionary development... marked by isolated episodes of rapid speciation between long periods of little or no change."

In geography, the term "discontinuity" gets at the same notion of rapid shifts that are articulated in biology through punctuated equilibrium. A seemingly random incident–such as a meteor collision or a tipping point on pressures in tectonic plates–releases forces responsible for radical, severe change. This occurrence results in changes such as elevating mountains, massive volcanic eruptions, and blanketing the Earth in smoke and noxious gases that can lead to extinction events and new geological and biological realities. In effect, something significant and irreversible occurs, changing the face of evolution on the planet and for all species.

There have been at least five previous extinction events in the history of life on Earth, which have led to the decimation of most species and the eventual evolution of entirely new species. Unfortunately, we are currently in the middle of the sixth extinction event, one brought about by the climate crisis and global warming and the first one human-made and human-perpetuated. As is evident throughout history, discontinuous change is built into nature and evolution, providing opportunities for some species to thrive and resulting in a biological dead end for many others.

Finally, advances in epigenetics suggest that genetics and DNA are not necessarily destiny when applied to humans and human systems. Epigenetics is the study of how environmental conditions and genetics interact to influence an individual's behavior and health. Epigenetic research suggests that profound and significant events, including prenatal environments, smoking, parental affection, diet, exposure to toxins, and even experiences with other critical environmental conditions, may switch on or off genes in the gene pool not only in an individual but in the offspring of that person as well. In effect, epigenetic research suggests that momentous events can affect the expression of genes for the individual and one's progeny. The implication for humans in increasing (or decreasing) differentiation is profound. For, if noteworthy and powerful environmental events and conditions can alter the expression of genes and therefore human behavior, the seeming randomness of some people devolving or evolving significantly from the differentiation level of their parents begins to make more systemic sense. For example, how and why is it that some children demonstrate more flexibility, resilience, and adaptability than others, given the same conditions and similar levels of differentiation between parents? Why do therapeutic boarding schools, Outward Bound-type wilderness experiences, and therapeutic communities *sometimes* succeed, even when parents are not involved? Why is it that Tammy Duckworth, an Iraq-war veteran helicopter pilot who lost three limbs in a combat-inflicted helicopter crash went on to a successful career first in the executive branch of government and then in Congress, when other veterans with similar or much less severe injuries develop alcoholism or drug addiction, become homeless, and/or suffer chronic Post Traumatic Stress Disorder (PTSD)?

The unanticipated and unplanned effects of discontinuous change, whether it is through epigenetics or some similar process, may provide an answer. I believe that these events fall into the category of "unusual life experiences" to which Kerr refers. In effect, systems are complex and we cannot always draw a clean, straight line between multigenerational and nuclear family emotional processes and family outcomes in each and every situation. We may not be able to always predict the outcomes of these discontinuous events that can promote higher levels of differentiation. These events are often painful and are usually unexpected. Friedman suggests, however, that more differentiated leaders often seek out adventure and the unknown, since it is through adventure and experiencing new and unexpected environments that we can encounter the very serendipity sometimes necessary for growth and change.

In this way, it may be that certain structured and planned experiences, such as those encountered through a wilderness therapy program or a therapeutic boarding school, may provide for the kind of serendipity some need to overcome the intransigence of their emotionally-regressed families. A 2017 study by Roberts, et al focusing on Outdoor Behavioral Health Care demonstrates symptom reduction through an eighteen-month follow-up with young adults separated from their parents and participating in wilderness therapy programs. Structured planning of unusual life experiences may provide a catalyst for differentiating. Experiencing something new through adventure and exploration can also offer numerous opportunities to adapt, display resilience, and emotionally grow.

The best wilderness treatment environments mimic healthy families, with leaders providing clear, predictable structure; a caring, supportive environment; and consistent guidelines applied fairly to all. Treatment systems designed to take people out of their normal environments and out of their comfort zones may provide unexpected opportunities to emotionally mature, especially if these programs focus on promoting self-regulation, self-identity, and the capacity for relationship building.

Another example: Several years ago, my two adult daughters, my wife, and I journeyed to Italy for an unexpected three-week vacation. While some of the trip was, by necessity, planned, other portions were not. The entire trip required a high degree of adaptability by all of us, as we negotiated traveling through a society with a different language and a different culture. Sometimes, the experience was frustrating, and often it was exhilarating. For all of us, though, that collective experience strengthened us as a family and as individuals, as we worked our way through Italy's cities and towns, traveling by trains, buses, and on foot through unfamiliar landscapes and new environments. This kind of adventure brought serendipitous opportunities to personally and collectively strengthen and stretch our resiliency muscles and return home with greater confidence, competence, and commitment to each other.

While this is a simple, non-traumatic, and positive example, it indicates that nothing is ventured and nothing is gained by "playing it safe." In effect, when we are called to adapt to new environments and new situations, we are forced to grow more quickly than if we play it safe in our comfortable worlds and our contented lives. From this perspective, then, the quest for safety and comfort, at least in the extreme, may, in fact, be ultimately regressive for self and society.

Of course, my personal example is small-scaled, at least relative to those in more severe environments. These extreme environments include but are not limited to: life in a war zone or combat region, coping with environmental disasters, managing life in highly oppressive environments, and other harsh and troubling situations. Through these crucibles, people are fiercely and brutally tested. Some are transformed, and some are irrevocably damaged. Some thrive; many don't survive.

In understanding adaptation, Friedman suggests a two-factor graph that includes both the condition and the response. The condition is the degree of environmental strain and is marked on the x-axis; the response is the level of differentiation or resilience and is placed on the y-axis. The x–y point on this theoretical graph documents a person's functional level of differentiation. What is lacking in Friedman's elegant graphic representation, however, is *why*, after similar trauma and crises, some people increase their functional and even basic differentiation—for example, becoming public servants after losing limbs in a war—and some collapse or regress, becoming less capable or even permanently impaired.

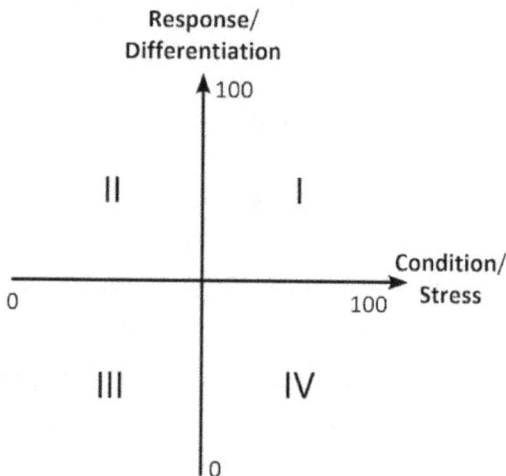

Response/
Differentiation

```
                    ↑ 100

        II           |           I



 ──────────────────────────────────────→  Condition/
 0                   |        100   Stress



        III          |          IV


                     | 0
```

Why is it that after a tornado or hurricane some people shatter like glass and some are tempered like steel? While it may well be that one's basic level of differentiation prior to the event is the most significant variable in parsing out those who adapt and mature and those who eventually collapse, regress, or even die, I wonder what other factors are involved. Ultimately, the answer to the question why some mature and some collapse may be unknowable.

What *is* observable, however, is that extreme environments and traumatic situations affect many people negatively–temporarily or permanently disabling them through the overwhelming acute anxiety of the moment. Others, though, respond to these challenges by helping others, taking a leadership position, and even thriving in bringing a semblance of order to the chaos. Communities strengthen in times of crisis when individuals demonstrate compassion and adaptability.

In effect, while higher levels of basic differentiation provide some inoculation against the most severe forms of emotional regression, it seems as if there are other forces at play. In his 1987 essay, "How to Succeed in Therapy without Really Trying," Friedman said that after decades of observing multigenerational families, he was unable to predict which individuals and families would succeed and which would fail years later. We observe resiliency in unlikely places.

In fact, many people will admit that their most emotionally challenging experiences were also those in which they grew the most. This is the nature of resiliency. The Chinese characters for the word "crisis" combine two elements: "danger" and "critical point." This notion of danger at a critical point underlies how resilience can be strengthened when confronted with peril at an emotionally difficult period in time. For example, my clinical and personal observations over the years and decades are that some marriages thrive after a crisis generated by an affair and others collapse; some people who experience a life-threatening illness reform their lives and their lifestyles so as to alter the fabric of their lives and work, while others don't learn or evolve from the same or a similar experience; some people lose a job and use it as an opportunity to start that business that they always wanted to start, while others surrender to despair and never recover.

No one plans to be thrown into dangerous or severe environments. Many who experience these situations and their consequences do not survive but struggle in marginal existences with the traumatic event permanently scarring their lives. Others, however, emerge from their brutal environments and traumatic events capable of great things, willing and able to help others, and dedicated to making the world a better place. For some, these events provide the crucible for learning, growing, and emotionally maturing. In effect, the crisis reveals the character and even strengthens it. Stepping into the unknown has risks, but it also has rewards.

One of the beauties of Bowen's theory is that it can stimulate us to ponder possibilities previously unconsidered, inspiring questions about the theory itself, the limits of its calculus, and the revelation of new possibilities. The challenge is how to grow and evolve the theory. Earlier, I used Freud and the neo-Freudians to illustrate the difficulties in evolving Bowen family systems theory after Bowen's death. A second example, perhaps as relevant, concerns Darwin's theory of evolution. Over the past one hundred and fifty years, Darwin's theory has been subjected to scientific scrutiny and has continued to evolve. While researchers and theoreticians have modified aspects of evolutionary theory over the decades, in its basic form, Darwin's theory of evolution has stood the test of time and scientific inquiry, and it has become stronger, more relevant, and more valid in the process. The "neo-Darwinians" combine Darwinian evolution with Mendelian genetics in a "modern synthesis." Through this "evolution of evolutionary theory," the scientific community grappled with integrating findings from scientific experiments, technological advancements, and naturalistic observations in order to propose modifications and extensions of the theory without rejecting Darwin's basic theory in the process. When people speak of Darwin's theory of evolution, most people understand what this means. Perhaps, we can evolve Bowen theory in the same manner, though significant challenges remain.

Confirming or refuting a social science theory is more problematic. Humans and human systems are vastly more complex and immensely more challenging to manipulate in traditional scientific experiments. There are also limits to the scientific method, which works through methodological reductionism, an attempt to reduce explanations to the smallest units of measurement. Systems, being complex, do not lend themselves to this kind of scientific inquiry. As such "testing" Bowen theory presents unique challenges, as this theory is not reducible to hypothesis testing through traditional scientific methods. And, the more predictive a theory of humans, the less "freedom" people have, since their behavior would be predicted by the theory. Nonetheless, we continue to make observations, interpret them, develop hypotheses, construct theories, and hopefully, modify those theories over time based on evidence. In doing so, we must be open to new possibilities as Bowen family systems theory, like all scientific theories, needs to evolve.

Finally, each person interprets Bowen theory through her or his own personal experiences, academic study, and training. The knowledge and skills required to learn and apply such a comprehensive theoretical system are significant. Each of us filters our understanding of Bowen theory through these life events and trainings. What results is not an unalterable, rigid set of beliefs and behaviors, but rather, a structured set of theoretical principles and concepts from which we make sense of the theory and its application to our personal and professional lives. My personal relationship with Bowen family systems theory has progressed to the point that I have my own ideas about theory expansion or clarification. In effect, my experiences with the theory result in my assertion of the importance of evolving the theory and what some of that evolution might include.

SECTION TWO

_____

TEACHING BOWEN FAMILY SYSTEMS THEORY TO UNDERGRADUATES

CHAPTER FIVE

TEACHING BOWEN'S FAMILY SYSTEMS THEORY TO UNDERGRADUATES

"If you want to learn something, teach it."–Max Lerner

In 1992, my family and I moved to Prescott, Arizona, where I had been offered a full-time faculty position at Prescott College. Prescott College is a small, progressive, four-year, liberal arts college in the central highlands of Prescott, Arizona. I was hired in the Human Development-Psychology Program specifically to develop courses in family systems theory. For years, Prescott College had been recognized for its work as an environmentally-oriented college, with its experiential approach to teaching across programs. As such, the college was uniquely situated to understand the value of applying family systems theory to humans, as well as the systemic way that people organize and operate.

Ecologists, of course, view the natural world through systemic, evolutionary processes. Prescott College was interested in expanding this understanding to human systems as well. Also, Prescott College was on the forefront of interdisciplinary education. They recognized and appreciated the value of not isolating the faculty or courses into "silos" of knowledge. Instead, Prescott College encouraged faculty to develop courses that stretched and overlapped disciplinary boundaries and to work with faculty in other programs in offering a unique interdisciplinary education.

When I arrived at Prescott College, I joined a faculty and college receptive to experimentation, interdisciplinary investigations, active pedagogy, cross-departmental collaborations, and the application of ecological, evolutionary principles to people and their relationships. Given my excitement about the possibilities of developing Bowen theory beyond the psychotherapeutic realm, I began creating undergraduate courses in applying the theory across a variety of disciplines and environments.

The other relevant variable in my academic odyssey was the students. Students at Prescott College were often different from those at larger, more traditional colleges and universities. Historically, they were a bit older, as many of them transferred from other institutions. Prescott College was often their second, third, fourth, or even fifth college attended. Many were disillusioned by the impersonal structures of traditional colleges and universities, and many had failed to thrive in previous settings. As such, when they arrived, they were clear about what they wanted in an education, and they were highly motivated to earn their degrees.

The age of our students decreased over the years when the college decided to target first-year students. Other student characteristics have remained remarkably constant. Perhaps most importantly, Prescott College students can be differentiated from more traditional college students by their motivation, self-direction, and deep commitment to being forces for positive change in the world. They tend to be risk-takers, hard workers, and profoundly committed to social justice and environmental awareness and activism.

Classes at Prescott College are small, often no larger than twelve to fourteen students. As a result, the students' education is more personalized, and their relationships with their professors are similarly individualized. Students attend Prescott College because they want an education based on an active pedagogy. The college calls this approach experiential education, and it is contrasted with the traditional model of the lecture-based classroom, in which students are passive recipients of information. Besides the fact that research on learning continues to demonstrate that a "sage on the stage" model is among the least effective ways to teach and learn–and our students have always rejected this approach–educators and educational institutions are highly resistant to change, even when the benefits of that change are clearly demonstrated through research and practice.

In contrast, Prescott College embraces project-based and thematic-based learning or learning by doing. With small classes, there is no place for students to hide, so they know that if they attend Prescott College, they will be dynamic participants in their own educational journeys.

For me, this was a "perfect storm" of opportunity that I had been searching for. In 1991, I took a leave of absence from United States International University (U.S.I.U.) where I was an associate professor and program director. The university had moved in a more conservative direction, seeking out additional accreditations (which tend to restrict innovation), increasing class sizes, and moving away from some of the creative, participatory approaches to learning that I believed in.

Besides, I had lived in San Diego for twelve years and wanted something different. Professionally, I was looking for new challenges. Personally, my wife and I had two young children, and we wanted to raise them in a smaller community and not in the large city that San Diego had become. It was time for a change.

All the pieces were in place for me to begin a decades-long experiment in teaching Bowen family systems theory to under-graduates. Given the highly personalized nature of understanding and applying Bowen theory, I hoped that students would be up to the task of learning a complex theory that I had taught only to graduate students, as well as applying this theory to themselves, their families, their communities, and their work in the world. And, for me, it was an opportunity to expand my academic and professional interests.

During my twenty-three years at Prescott College, I can say that this experiment was an unqualified success. Students not only enjoyed their studies in Bowen theory, but a sizable percentage said, in college and after graduation, that learning and applying Bowen's theory profoundly changed them, their families, and their activism. In fact, many students have gone on to attend graduate programs that included Bowen theory and family therapy in their curriculum. These students routinely tell me that they are better prepared for and more knowledgeable about systems theories in general and Bowen theory in particular than most of their graduate school peers. What better testimonials can a professor hope for in making a difference in the lives of students?

First, I will review the courses that I developed and taught using Bowen theory as the central focus and theoretical foundation. Then, I will discuss courses that I infused with Bowen theory to make them more comprehensive. Finally, I will present a detailed examination of one course, Psychohistory of the American Presidency, demonstrating Bowen theory's applicability to assessing presidential leadership.

Family Systems Theory

When I arrived at Prescott College, there were no Human Development-Psychology courses in family systems. To be sure, the Human Development-Psychology curriculum included many interesting and innovative courses, including classes in depth psychology, eco-feminism, holistic health and wellness, and even transpersonal psychology. While as a regionally-accredited college we still taught the basics in psychology, including courses needed as pre-requisites for graduate school, even those courses were taught imaginatively. In this spirit of innovation and encouragement, I immediately created a course that I had taught in graduate school called Family Systems Theory.

As a central text I used Michael Kerr and Murray Bowen's *Family Evaluation*, often fondly referred by those in the field as "the Bowen Bible." I supplemented the academically dense text with Augustus Napier and Carl Whitaker's book, *The Family Crucible*, which details a family's case history over the course of several years of treatment. While Napier and Whitaker's approach to treating the family is based on Carl Whitaker's theoretical model called Symbolical-Experiential Family Therapy, the basic approach to understanding and treating families as complex interactional units with multigenerational histories supports Bowen's theory. (Whitaker and Bowen, like most of the family therapy founders, were friends and colleagues who shared ideas and borrowed freely from one another's work, so this replication of core systemic ideas is understandable.) In effect, I used a theory book supplemented with a book applying family theory to therapy. I also included readings from other family therapy masters, including Salvador Minuchin and Structural Family Therapy; Peggy Papp's Brief Family Therapy, which is a form of Strategic Family Therapy; and Ed Friedman's particular take on Bowen theory.

Even though these were the same texts that I had used with graduate students at U.S.I.U., the students seldom flinched. They loved the theory-therapy combination, as they got to read and understand how to think in systemic ways and then how to apply the theory clinically.

Also, Bowen theory cannot be learned simply by reading about it. It must be personalized and internalized. You have to learn the concepts behind the theory and spend time, often years, working with a mentor or coach to really understand the theory and regularly apply it to one's work and one's life. I used this basic understanding in designing all of my systems-based courses. This theory-practice combination was especially important for Prescott College students, who wanted practical and functional applications to complex theories. Borrowing a phrase from social psychologist pioneer Kurt Lewin, Edwin Friedman was fond of saying, "there is nothing so practical as a good theory." I informed students that they will experience an "aha" moment when the depth, expansiveness, and profundity of Bowen's theory hits them. Then, they will not only understand the Bowen theory concepts but, perhaps more importantly, come to appreciate what Bowen theorist, therapist, and feminist Harriet Learner has written about: the limits of applying the theory are only restricted by one's motivation and persistence.

To better personalize the theory, I used a variety of pedagogical activities to comprehend the concepts and understand how this theory applies to all life and not just human families. So, for example, we reviewed universal aspects of the togetherness life force and the individuality life force in trees and plants; chronic anxiety as manifested in the larger culture and the world through newspaper articles and stories; and emotional triangles in film and television programs.

We examined differentiation through the life-cycle. We explored examples of individuals who were traumatized and then who went on to make important contributions, in part, because of their trauma, such as Senator Max Cleland.

Step by step, they built a working knowledge of the central Bowen family systems theory concepts, tracking the first nine weeks in parallel with the first eight chapters in *Family Evaluation*. If you are familiar with this important text, you know that it is written for graduate students and mental health professionals. While *Family Evaluation* can prove challenging since it is so all-inclusive, students rarely resisted reading it or embracing the concepts.

Students also began applying theory to their lives. The culmination of the class, in week nine of the eleven-week semester, was genogram presentations. Genograms are diagrams depicting the multigenerational family. They detail important relationships, dates of important events, and progressive and regressive branches in the extended family tree.

Students worked for two months collecting and organizing information from their nuclear and multigenerational families. This was a deeply emotional process, of course, as students managed the challenge of contacting distant or extended family members. They began to understand their nuclear and extended families through the lens of family systems theory. They were confronted with powerful family themes and myths about scapegoats and symptom bearers. The theory further challenged them to look at their own symptoms and family relationships through a Bowen theory lens, which rejects blame and promotes personal responsibility throughout the family and the family life cycle. Students from physically and sexually abusive families and those who experienced untimely loss often struggled most with this assignment.

As young adults, students were in the middle of dealing with their emotional legacies, including some who experienced traumas. The idea of facing their family histories and confronting their abuse and loss required a great deal of courage. I provided additional coaching during office hours, and students always had the option of presenting their genograms to me privately if they felt safer doing so. (Interesting, it was rare for students to select this option. Generally, no more than one or two students per class decided to present privately. More often than not, all students in a particular class selected the public presentation option.) Essentially, all the work students put into their genograms created pride in their products. And, many times, their increased objectivity led to decreased self-consciousness about themselves and their families.

Guiding students through creating their three-generational genograms, I coached them to balance multigenerational family strengths with multigenerational family challenges and symptoms. And, if the task proved too difficult, I recommended that they do their best with the information they had and not push family members or themselves too hard. I reminded them that timing is everything, and if the time was not right for such an emotionally intensive project, then they should complete it at the level that felt safe and doable for them. I also offered guidelines for listening, responding, and asking questions of others' genogram presentations.

To better model the process, I presented my genogram a week before the students presented theirs. I have been working on my genogram for over twenty-five years, so I reminded students that I didn't expect theirs to be as complete and intricate as mine. Nonetheless, I believed that the value of their genogram presentations and the power of their learning depended on my capability and willingness to be vulnerable and share my extended family genogram, warts and all.

I was always moved by the courage of the students in undertaking this exercise, the compassion for their fellow students during and after their public talk, and the inherently transformative power of this critical assignment. To better help them prepare, these presentations occurred after students had read Kerr's chapter on multigenerational emotional process.

They were given fifteen minutes to present and five minutes to field questions. I used this tight timeframe in order to ensure that everyone had the opportunity to present and to help students properly format their presentation. I was captivated not only by students' bravery in this process (many felt like it was a kind of "coming out" about their histories and their families, since it was such a deeply revealing project), but by their creativity and willingness to embrace this kind of personalized learning. Often, students created their own unique symbols about health, pets, culture, and other important aspects of their genograms. Many of these symbols and understandings went beyond the basics of genogram construction that I taught, inspiring me with their eagerness to enlarge the theory.

At the end of each semester, we de-briefed the class. The genogram process and the three days of presentations were invariably viewed as the most powerful and important part of the course. Students remarked that genograms personalized the theory and made it come alive. Sharing the stories of their lives and that of their extended families provided a common emotional experience that deepened and transformed the dynamics and cohesion of the class. Students were not only willing and able to step up and do this revelatory work, but they embraced it and sought it out. This remained constant for over twenty-three years and throughout the various incarnations of the class.

Family Systems in Film and Literature

When I was hired at Prescott College, I arrived with a number of other new faculty members. One professor was Kenny Cook. Kenny's professional, publication name is K.L. Cook. Kenny is a fiction writer, literature professor, and all around remarkably intelligent person and beloved teacher. Kenny and I quickly became best friends, as we shared not only professional interests but, personally, we were at the same family life-cycle stage of raising young children. As a writer, Kenny became fascinated with Bowen's family systems theory. I gave him key articles to read, and he wanted to teach a class with me integrating Bowen theory with film and literature. I was very interested in this proposal, since I had been thinking of adding a Family Systems in Film course. I was inspired by Jim Framo—a family therapy founder, friend, and distinguished professor of psychology and family therapy at U.S.I.U.—who had offered a similar class in applying family systems to film for graduate students. This course would be different, though, since we would include a central literature component as well, which was Kenny's expertise.

We proposed a course titled Family Systems in Film and Literature. We offered this as an upper division class through the Arts and Letters Program, cross-listed in Human Development-Psychology. We taught it in a compressed block format of four days a week, four hours per day, for four weeks.

In 2006, Kenny and I published a full description of this work in the edited volume *Teachable Moments: Essays on Experiential Education* (see chapter twelve). Suffice it to say that this course was similarly structured to my Family Systems Theory class to learn the central components of Bowen theory. We did this by replacing clinical case studies with short stories, novellas, plays, short films, and feature-length films. We read the short stories "Sonny's Blues" by James Baldwin and "Goodbye My Brother" by John Cheever, Jane Smiley's novellas *Ordinary Love* and *Good Will*, and the play *The Glass Menagerie* by Tennessee Williams. In addition, we used a variety of other short stories including those by Mona Simpson, Andre Dubus, Louise Erdrich, Melanie Bishop, and others.

Kenny was so influenced by family systems theory that he began to consciously incorporate elements of the theory into his fiction writing. In 2004, Kenny published the short story cycle, *Last Call*. Many of these stories were directly influenced by Bowen's theory. *Last Call* was awarded the prestigious Prairie Schooner Book Prize for Fiction. Prior to its publication, in earlier incarnations of the class we incorporated several of these short stories. After the publication of *Last Call*, we read the entire book as a case study, since so many Bowen theory concepts, including multigenerational emotional process, differentiation, chronic anxiety, nuclear family emotional process, emotional triangles, and symptom development were demonstrated in the linked story cycle.

For films, we selected scenes from Lawrence Kasden's *Grand Canyon* and Alan Parker's *Shoot the Moon*. We watched short films from Rodrigo Garcia's *Nine Lives,* Martin Scorsese's short film *Life Lessons,* and feature films including Woody Allen's *Hannah and Her Sisters* and

Lasse Hallstrom's *What's Eating Gilbert Grape?*, among others. We used all of these films as entry points to highlight how the best artists, screenwriters, and filmmakers seem to have an intuitive understanding of family systems theory processes. We demonstrated how such concepts as functional and basic differentiation, acute and chronic anxiety, emotional triangles and triangulation, and nuclear family emotional process are illuminated in the work.

We ended our film adventure with a full day of viewing Frances Ford Coppola's first two *Godfather* films at my house. And, we made a full Italian lunch with pasta, salad, and dessert to enhance the experience. Using *The Godfather* and *The Godfather II*, we not only tracked the central family systems concepts but we explored the power of multigenerational emotional process in formatting emotional legacies, as well as symptom development from a family systems perspective.

For example, in the first *Godfather* film, as much as Michael Corleone wants to escape "the family business," multigenerational emotional processes overwhelm his free will. Even though he seems the most differentiated of Vito's sons and a decorated World War II veteran, the family's emotional field still pulls him in. When Michael says to his wounded father, the current Godfather Vito Corleone, in the hospital room after an assassination attempt, "I'm with you now, Pop," he commits to the family business and is never able to escape his fate as the next Godfather. In fact, eventually Michael's brutality goes even further than that of his father, ultimately regressing and then destroying himself, the family, and the family business in the process.

Through these literary and film entry points, Bowen theory became clearer and more emotionally relevant for the students. Essentially, students were getting to practice family systems theory on fictional families. Analyzing fictional families is often less intimidating then assessing their own or clinical families.

Multiple writing assignments helped students deepen their understanding, analysis, and application of the theory through film and literature. And students in Family Systems in Film and Literature not only learned about genograms as a way of comprehending and evaluating the film and literature families but they also developed and then presented their personal genograms to the class using the same format described earlier–instructors' presentations of their genograms and fifteen-minute student presentations with five minutes of Q&A, using a minimum of three generations in their formats and exhibitions.

Similar to the Family Systems Theory course, students in Family Systems in Film and Literature consistently reported how profoundly this class in general and the genogram assignment in particular had influenced their understanding of the world, how they were now seeing systems, and how they were beginning to act differently based on what they had learned. Many students from these classes wanted additional opportunities to learn and apply systems theory. I was just getting started!

Community Mediation and Principled Negotiation

By the 1990s, I wanted to expand my work outside of psychotherapy and family therapy. And I wanted to align my teaching with my emerging professional interests. To this end, I attended a number of mediation training courses in California, Arizona, and Colorado. I thoroughly enjoyed the trainings and believed that I had a knack for mediating conflicts. So, I set out to expand my professional competence to include mediation. Perhaps as important, I saw the potential of using Bowen theory as a theoretical framework for conducting mediations, and I wanted to try my hand at it.

After obtaining the necessary trainings and local certification, in 1992, I began working first at the Prescott Justice Court and then at the Superior Court of Arizona in Yavapai County practicing as a mediator and initiating an approach based on Bowen theory. I researched if anyone had ever applied Bowen theory to mediation, and I didn't find any articles, books, or chapters on the topic. (In fact, at the time, the field of mediation itself was largely a techniques, skills, and stage-driven process, lacking any comprehensive theory at all.) So, after developing competence and an evolving expertise with this process, I wrote a journal article applying Bowen theory to mediation, which was published in the Winter 2000 issue of *Conflict Resolution Quarterly*. (See chapter eleven for a reprint of the article.) Favorable feedback from the article led me to begin writing a comprehensive manuscript detailing a Bowen theory approach to mediation.

I developed the course Community Mediation and Principled Negotiation and used Bowen theory as the theoretical underpinning. In 2008, Prescott College professor Steve Pace—my co-instructor with this class—and I published a chapter in the book *Theory and Practice of Experiential Education,* called "The Personal Intelligences in Experiential Education: A Theory in Practice." (I have re-worked this paper, and it appears in chapter thirteen.)

In the class Community Mediation and Principled Negotiation, students learned that mediation is more than simply applying a set of skills and techniques to conflict resolution. They discovered "the power of presence" of the mediator in determining success, and the meaning of success in mediation. Mediation success is difficult to operationalize. Those who subscribe to an outcome model of mediation define success as an agreement between the parties. For me, my fellow mediators, and the program at the Superior Court, though, success was not simply about reaching agreements, though agreements were important. Rather, success included promoting a more positive view of conflict, decreasing intensity between the disputants, and even returning to court better prepared to present their cases and accept the judge's decision if an agreement was not reached in mediation. Defining success this way is more difficult to measure.

In training students to become mediators, I focused on micro-skill development and theory integration. Learning by doing, students discovered the importance of acquiring specific skills, understanding the stages of mediation, moving from positions to interests, and developing competence in brainstorming and shaping proposals. They learned that effective mediation is also includes the ability to reframe conflict and create workable agreements. But this was not enough. So, students began applying Bowen theory to their work as mediators.

For example, students created mediation triangles in order to gain rapport and strengthen the relationship between each disputant and mediator. Students practiced mediator self-regulation and self-soothing in difficult, high-conflict situations. And students experienced the mediator's critical role as leader in the mediation system. By including the mediator's differentiated power of presence in the equation, students were involved in an ongoing process of self-assessment of their performance, in addition to learning each stage and each skill. They recognized that their individuality, and as such their differentiation, had the power to decrease emotional reactivity in the disputants, to shift disputants from rigid positions to more flexible interests, and ultimately, to affect positive change in mediation.

When I first started teaching this class, I relied on my 2000 article in *Conflict Resolution Quarterly* to supply the cornerstone of Bowen theory's application to mediation. Students enjoyed reading the journal article, though, of course, it didn't provide a complete picture of what I was trying to accomplish. Back then, I supplemented this article with a variety of readings in Bowen theory and tried to tie everything together. After I started writing my book applying Bowen theory to mediation, I distributed copies to students and used it in the classes and in my training system. Students provided a tremendous amount of useful feedback that helped me to shape the final version of the manuscript, and I remain grateful for their input.

After publishing my book, *Applying Family Systems Theory to Mediation: A Practitioner's Guide*, I assigned it as one of the two principal texts for the class. (I used the classic *Getting to Yes* as the second text. This book provided the basis for the principled negotiation portion of the course.) With a completed book in hand, the course became a wonderful addition to the Bowen theory courses that I was developing at the college. And, it was the first (and, in 2020, still the only) book applying Bowen theory to mediation. Here was yet another opportunity to learn and employ Bowen family systems theory, and here was yet another course for students to gain greater mastery in Bowen's theory.

Models of Leadership: Leadership through Differentiation

Almost from its origins, many people saw the potential for Bowen family systems theory as a comprehensive "theory about everything." Many practitioners began applying the theory to a host of different disciplines—health care, education, business, and others. One such application that has been extensively developed over the decades is Bowen theory's relevance to leadership, business, and organizations.

In fact, there have been several gatherings of Bowen theorists and practitioners exploring these intersections. Two such conferences, hosted by The Bowen Center for the Study of the Family/The Georgetown Family Center, resulted in compilations. The first, *Understanding Organizations: Applications of Bowen Family Systems Theory,* was published in 1982; the second, *The Emotional Side of Organizations: Applications of Bowen Theory,* was published in 1996.

Also, Friedman was actively involved in writing, lecturing, and consulting on his approach, based on Bowen theory, to "treating" leadership and organizations. His first book, *Generation to Generation: Family Process in Church and Synagogue,* was an instant classic. Many still considered it the seminal work for pastors, priests, rabbis, and other religious leaders in understanding systemic processes in congregations.

As I describe in my chapters on educational leadership, I became fascinated with Bowen theory's relevance to my work as a dean and charter school director. I began my work in this area when I assumed executive leadership responsibilities. I realized that I wanted to learn this approach and teach what I was learning at the same time. In this way, the course Models of Leadership: Leadership through Differentiation was born.

For readings, I initially used many chapters from the two published compilations from the Bowen Center for the Study of the Family. These included articles by illustrious Bowen theorists and practitioners Michael Kerr, Daniel Papero, and Roberta Gilbert. I also included a chapter from Friedman's *Generation to Generation.*

In 2007, eleven years after Friedman's passing, his estate published his work-in-progress, *A Failure of Nerve: Leadership in the Age of the Quick Fix.* Simply put, I was blown away by the book. Here was Friedman's tour de force, a dazzling culmination of his life work. While incomplete, in my mind, this book, alongside Kerr and Bowen's

Family Evaluation, remains the most important and expansive book about Bowen theory's relevance. Friedman brilliantly demonstrates how Bowen theory is germane over time and across disciplines as diverse as immunology, history, physics, and evolutionary biology. I was hooked and began using this book as the cornerstone for the class. The second text that I settled on was organizational consultant Jeffrey Miller's *Anxious Organization.* It is a delightfully insightful and humorous case history that applies Bowen theory to Miller's consulting work with an advertising agency. It is as quick of a read as Friedman's book is a dense read. In this way, the readings replicated the reading in Family Systems Theory—one theory-heavy book and one easier, more entertaining but still important application's book. This combination gave students the benefit of a solid theoretical underpinning with concrete examples of how to implement the theory in practice. Generally, students loved the two texts and the supplemental articles and chapters that we used.

I taught this class in a block format, which, as stated earlier, is four days a week, four hours a day, for four weeks. The beauty of this format at Prescott College is that it allows faculty and students to intensively concentrate on only one course. In typical Prescott College fashion, I wanted this class to be about both theory and practice. So, students completed the Emotional and Social Competence Inventory, University Edition, which is based on Goleman's work on emotional intelligence. It is a self-administered and self-scored test measuring sixteen sub-variables. Students then used their results to begin detailing their strengths and weaknesses in areas of differentiation/emotional intelligence.

A wide variety of initiative activities engaged the students, and we processed their performances, always using the theory of differentiated leadership as a guide. These activities made the class more exciting and involving. The point of these experiential education or participatory pedagogical exercises was more than simply entertainment. They were designed to help students learn the theory and begin to think systems. The initiative activities also required students to manage second-to-second "problems" as the basis of building effective problem-solving skills on a larger scale.

And, perhaps most importantly, the tasks (and Bowen theory) required each person to focus on her or his own personal functioning in order for the group to succeed.

After completing the initiatives, I used the de-briefing process to highlight Bowen theory concepts. For example, we discussed that each person's attitude and behavior affected the group collectively, and the students' success in completing tasks was affected by the group's decision-making processes and its ability to work together constructively. We discussed how Bowen theory views the group as a collection of individuals and that a high functioning group requires each person to self-focus, self-regulate, and assume responsibility for his or her own behavior and not the behavior of others in the group.

The de-briefs often led to discussions of the individuality and togetherness life forces and how each is enriched when part of a deliberate, respectful, and reciprocal process that protects personal integrity and thereby enhances group functioning. Discussing the life forces naturally transitioned to the concept of differentiation and how strong individuals create strong groups. We also discussed how each person had to manage his or her own "performance anxiety" in order to succeed and how self-management is a significant part of differentiated leadership.

The initiative activities were designed with specific outcomes in mind: Students experienced challenging situations. Some didn't see themselves as very coordinated; others struggled with their self-concepts and capabilities in front of their peers and me. Still others found that these exercises generated a lot of performance anxiety. This learning by doing, a hallmark of education at Prescott College, is wonderfully isomorphic (similar in form) to the Bowenian notion that you cannot learn the theory simply by reading about it. You need a mentor and guide. And perhaps most importantly, you must have multiple experiences that challenge you to think systems and then live that thinking through your behavior. While Bowen theorists know that this process takes years, students began their journeys into the theory through many of these courses.

For the first week of Models of Leadership, the class learned theory and progressed through a number of challenging initiatives and theory-based de-briefs. In week two, I added other types of activities and experiences. For one, we watched the original version of *12 Angry Men*. This remarkable film highlights the power of presence in differentiated leadership. We watched using a start-and-stop approach. Students, with a blossoming, embryonic understanding of Bowen theory, analyzed the film and its protagonist, an architect who demonstrates non-reactive leadership based on relationships and clarity of thinking in an emotional whirlpool.

One important assignment involved interviewing a leader. In week three, students collectively developed leadership questions using Bowen theory and differentiated leadership as their guides. They were tasked with creating a common set of twelve questions. Again, this was not merely an academic exercise but an emotional one requiring more differentiated responses. At this point, students realized that it was their class, and they must step up to do the work. Most often, a leader emerged from the group to lead the discussion, and most classes sought a consensus model in developing their final questions.

In the end, each and every time, the students developed a quality set of Bowen-based questions and used them in interviewing leaders. Typically, these questions included those in the areas of vision, managing recalcitrant and resistant employees, self-management of emotional reactivity, use of humor in connecting with others, self-care for leaders, maintaining persistence and stamina, and other important differentiated leadership variables. Students selected leaders from the community to interview—college deans, directors of local non-profits, etc. Students' leadership interviews, their papers based on these interviews, and their class presentations of their interviews formed a significant component of the class. Students developed an important sense of what it means to be a more effective or less effective leader.

In the final phase of the class, students worked in teams of two or three to develop and implement their own initiative activities. These activities gave students a chance to apply their learning and demonstrate their differentiated leadership skills to the rest of the class, including me. These activities were approximately an hour to an hour and a half in length. Students wrote up their lesson plans and met with me prior to implementation. I reviewed the lesson plans for appropriateness in both academic content and safety. When needed, I provided guidance on pedagogy and content delivery. Mostly, though, having been at Prescott College for a few years, students understood the structure and parameters of experiential learning initiative exercises. Afterwards, as a class we de-briefed their activities, their effectiveness in presenting and facilitating the lesson, and the Bowen theory concepts the exercise was designed to reveal. Also, students completed anonymous feedback forms for the leaders, which provided them with additional information.

There were other important assignments and activities for the students, but this sampling provides a helpful overview of the class. Models of Leadership provided an additional opportunity for students to learn Bowen family systems theory at an undergraduate level. As with the other courses discussed, students not only embraced the theory and its application to differentiated leadership, but many went on to study the theory further in additional classes, independent studies, senior capstone projects, and graduate study.

Social Psychology: The Meaning of Contemporary Events

Through our program's commitment to preparing students for graduate school, we offered many of the same-titled courses as other, more traditional colleges and universities but we delivered them in decidedly different ways. For example, many students need a course in social psychology as a graduate school prerequisite. I taught this course with a different theoretical lens than most. I used Bowen family systems theory as the "umbrella theory" to understand social psychology and significant contemporary events.

We reviewed many of the historical social psychology experiments and investigations, including Milgram's work with obedience to authority; the Kitty Genovese murder and the bystander effect; Zimbardo's prisoner-guard demonstration, and other noteworthy studies. Not only did we discuss the research itself–its value, the ethical issues involved in conducting the work, how many of these investigations could no longer be undertaken, and the results–but students learned the basics of Bowen theory to understand, for example, the characteristics and abilities of those who resist authority, who refused to punish prisoners and degrade them as people, and who stepped up to help a stranger when others stayed away. Using basic differentiation and functional differentiation as guides, we delved into understanding how one loses or retains the self in a group, how emotional intensity can undercut integrity, and how best to "inoculate" the self from reactive events.

And we tied historical research to contemporary events. As other examples:

- Zimbardo's prisoner-guard study at Stanford is juxtaposed to the criminal activity by guards in their torturous treatment of Iraq prisoners in Abu Ghraib. What made most of the guards, by all accounts largely "regular troops," depersonalize both the prisoners and themselves by giving up their humanity and sexually mistreating others? What compelled Joe Darby to release the pictures from the prison in an attempt to stop this abuse?

- What made soldiers in the My Lai Massacre brutally kill women, elders, and children in a mindless rage? What personal and interpersonal qualities made helicopter pilot Hugh Thompson put his own life on the line to prevent the murders of so many of the villagers?

- Why did Joseph Dimow say "no" in the Milgram demonstrations when so many others "shocked" their colleagues well past the supposed danger level?

Using Bowen theory as our guide, we tied the theory to issues of morality, de-personalization in crowds and groups, basic and functional differentiation, and differentiated leadership for self and towards others.

Students appreciated this meta-perspective in tying together many of the research studies and investigations in social psychology. They came to understand how to defy illegitimate authority, to hold a strong "I" within the "we" so as to not become a mindless protester or unwittingly support the agenda of a malevolent group, and to self-soothe and self-regulate emotionality in order to see more clearly and act more ethically and morally.

While the content of the course was similar to other undergraduate social psychology courses, the process of learning and incorporating Bowen theory as an umbrella theory exposed student new to the theory with a useful perspective and provided additional opportunities for students with a background in Bowen theory to apply it to both macro and micro levels.

I supplemented the two social psychology-based texts with theoretical material on Bowen theory, and we referenced the theory throughout. We also followed social movements and "tipping points." One of the fun and exciting aspects of teaching this class was the unpredictability of contemporary events occurring during the eleven weeks of the course. One year, for example, I taught the class during the autumn of the Arab Spring. How did a man in Tunisia who set himself on fire become a tipping point for regional democracy movements in Egypt, Libya, and other Middle Eastern countries? During another year that I was teaching the class, the Occupy Wall Street movement was in full force and then it died. What made that movement fizzle out but not the Tea Party movement? Since Bowen theory is so comprehensive, looking at both large-scale events and personal behaviors, it is well suited to providing the very meta-perspective often lost in more traditional approaches to teaching social psychology.

Counseling Skills

During the 1980s and early 1990s, I taught a counseling skills course at U.S.I.U. A graduate class, we used video-tape training and live supervision to guide students in developing core counseling skills. Prescott College already had a counseling skills course as a part of their curriculum when I arrived. A hands-on course teaching basic counseling skills is uncommon at the undergraduate level. For effective training, a small enrollment is required, making a course like this hard to justify. I was impressed by the college's innovation.

In preparing the teach the course, I wanted to keep the direct skills training; provide additional emotional safeguards as students were discussing real and, at times, painful issues; introduce Bowen family systems theory, and demonstrate how the theory can guide our work as counselors and in understanding clients. I re-configured the class, implementing a similar training system that I successfully offered at U.S.I.U.

I divided students into A, B, C triads, with A providing counseling to B, B providing counseling to C, and C providing counseling to A. The third person in the team observed and offered feedback. Students learned micro-skill development around important foundational skills, such as unconditional positive regard/respect, authenticity/genuineness of the counselor, basic and advanced empathy, reframing, relational immediacy, and confrontation/challenge.

As with mediation training, I taught that effective counseling is more than simply applying a set of skills. The other area of importance is the personhood of the counselor, and this is where Bowen theory was particularly useful as it teaches students about the primary importance of emotional maturity and how one's level of differentiation affects counseling outcomes.

Students taking risks in revealing themselves, learning new skills in a public forum, and being open to scrutiny necessitate a lot of trust, between the students and between students and me. That trust developed over the term as I offered individual feedback to budding counselors, gave extensive comments on students' weekly assessment and reflection papers, and took risks myself in conducting counseling sessions in front of the class and receiving their remarks and observations.

During the training sessions, I rotated through the groups, providing counselors with my observations and suggestions. My supervision model used Bowen theory to help them understand what they were doing well and what needed attention. As this was primarily a skills training class, we never discussed the personal issues of the client. Maintaining boundaries in such a class situation is important for emotional safety. If a student needed something beyond what she was receiving from her peer counselor, I provided appropriate resources locally and through the college counselor.

While I used a more traditional text to help students understand and learn counseling skills, I supplemented this with Harriet Lerner's classic book, *The Dance of Intimacy*. Lerner's books are very accessible, as she discusses the essentials of Bowen family systems theory in simple, layperson terms. She covers most of Bowen's key concepts, and she brings a feminist sensibility to her writing and her clinical work. Lerner demonstrates how she uses the theory to guide her practice, so her books are peppered with lots of clinical examples of theory in action. As it is written for the general public, *The Dance of Intimacy* also provides an overarching perspective for students in terms of Bowen theory's usefulness professionally and personally.

I used an assortment of activities to help students understand their counter-transference (their personal sensitivities) in counseling, how to self-soothe in difficult situations, how to avoid conflicts of will with clients, how to remain playful, and, in general, how the counselor's deep presence is so critical to counseling efficacy. These areas are all excellent entry points into discussing Bowen theory—emotional reactivity, differentiation, chronic anxiety, triangulation, and so on. While increasing students' emotional maturity is a goal beyond the classroom, exposing students to the theory, learning new skills, and understanding the importance of being a relatively non-anxious presence provided an important foundation for those interested in the helping professions.

We watched a few films of therapists in action. Over the years, these have included *Ordinary People, Good Will Hunting,* and sessions from the HBO series *In Treatment*. We critiqued the therapists' interventions according to the skills they were learning, assessed the film clients and their families using Bowen theory, and made predictions of client outcomes. These films were helpful in proving an alternative way of knowing and learning, and they were emotionally easier to manage. It is important to offer a variety of ways to reach students using an assortment of activities and learning styles.

Students with a background in Bowen theory appreciated learning another way to apply the theory. Students new to Bowen theory were often intrigued by it and enrolled in additional courses in order to gain a better understanding.

What made this all work were the students. Prescott College students thrive on a relevant education, whether fieldtrips to the border, environmental education in nature, or developing new skills. With their eagerness to learn, we accomplished our goals for the class.

Theories and Methods of Couple and Family Therapy

The course Theories and Methods of Couple and Family Therapy completes my journey in developing and teaching courses in family systems theory at Prescott College. In the winter of 2013, a Human Development-Psychology colleague at Prescott College required a medical leave for the spring semester. As a small department, her departure left a huge hole in our curriculum. We needed to cancel two of her fully-enrolled classes unless the program could find someone to teach them.

The dean asked me to take over one of her classes but I was reluctant. In the past several years, I had taught a number of overload classes as a way of helping the college. But I was disinclined to do so again, especially since I had a pattern of over-functioning in these kinds of professional situations. Also, a new class preparation would have been a massive undertaking given the short time frame. And, I wasn't particularly interested in teaching her specific courses.

Also, during this time, my youngest daughter Sage was enrolled at Prescott College and was finishing her B.A. in Psychology, with an emphasis in Family Systems Theory. During her time at the college, Sage had demonstrated a keen ability to understand and apply systems theory in general and Bowen theory in particular. She completed a number of my Bowen theory classes, and she was my teaching assistant for Family Systems Theory during the spring of 2012. While Sage enjoyed learning and applying Bowen theory, she correctly assessed that the Human Development-Psychology curriculum lacked an overview class covering all of the family theories and therapies. As such, as a part of her senior project-capstone experience, Sage was working with another faculty member in the program to develop a course incorporating all of the major marriage and family theories, past and present. She was making solid progress on her senior project when my colleague's emergency medical leave occurred.

Sage and I both envisioned the medical leave as an opportunity to develop and teach such an overview course. I proposed to the dean that instead of picking up one of the open courses, I teach, with Sage as a teaching assistant, a class titled Theories and Methods of Couple and Family Therapy. He readily agreed. So, Sage and I created a special topics course proposal. It was quickly approved by the program and program council, and we offered it in the spring of 2013. We contacted students in the open classes, and we recruited advanced students who had succeeded in my previous courses. The class quickly filled, and we even increased enrollment to accommodate the high demand.

Sage and I got to work creating the course. Alas, we only had two weeks to pull everything together. Fortunately, Sage had already completed a good deal of her senior project, so we had access to her significant research on MFT theories and therapists, as well as relevant books, articles, and chapters. We read voraciously, framed out the eleven classes, designated historical and contemporary theories and therapists to cover, compiled a comprehensive reading list that we turned into a class reader, and selected Goldenberg and Goldenberg's classic text, *Family Therapy: An Overview*, and Peggy Papp's edited volume, *Family Therapy: Full Length Case Studies*. We developed an array of participatory pedagogical activities, including small group projects where each group was responsible for researching and presenting a particular theoretical and therapeutic approach.

The small groups were essential to the success of the class. Students researched their theory, investigated the central therapists associated with the theory, presented their work to the class, and wrote papers detailing their research.

We taught the class once a week, for four and a half hours. This workshop format allowed us to intensely focus on one or two theorists and therapists per class. We worked from the past to the present, starting with Nathan Ackerman and moving to Susan Johnson and the post-constructivists. The basic class followed a similar format: a presentation and discussion of readings from a highlighted theory and the therapists most associated with it. We followed this up with a DVD of a therapist working with a family from that theoretical perspective. Lastly, we developed activities to highlight the theory through case study vignettes, demonstrations by me, and other ways to personalize the theory.

We covered a lot of ground. For some of the theories and therapists, students took the lead in their research investigations and presentations. For most, Sage and I constructed the classes, the activities, the readings, and the assessment systems.

This was an exciting time, and the group was exceptional. Most students were graduating seniors, and there were a few juniors. And, since we recruited students and had motivated students throughout, the quality of the class, like that of most of my other classes, was more of a graduate seminar than an undergraduate class. In fact, I place this class among the top three of all classes that I have taught over the decades. Not only did I get to co-teach this class with my daughter, but I was able to bring my experience and expertise to bear in a unique way. This was because I knew many of the original family therapists and second-generational therapists either professionally through my directorship at U.S.I.U. over the years or through trainings I attended with them.

After Sage's graduated in May of 2013, we had a second opportunity to teach the class in the Spring Semester of 2014. In this incarnation of the class, Sage was an adjunct co-instructor. Also, as this was the second time around, we modified and adjusted the curriculum, added a few higher quality DVDs, edited and streamlined the reader, and changed the group presentations so that they occupied a smaller percentage of the class time. It always takes two to three iterations of a course before it feels right. This second offering was a productive, informative, and well-received class. This course, which included Bowen theory, but not exclusively, became a permanent addition to the Human Development-Psychology curriculum.

Psychohistory of the American Presidency: A Case History

When I was a graduate student at U.S.I.U. in San Diego from 1979 through 1982, Max Lerner—a journalist, columnist, and historian—flew in from New York City to teach there every other weekend. Max was a remarkable man who had interviewed every United States President from FDR through Reagan. Max was a self-identified "civilization watcher" and commentator. At the time, he was one of U.S.I.U.'s "superstars," the kind of people that the university president liked to bring to campus to provide new perspectives to and opportunities for graduate students. Not only was Max a wise and thoughtful man, but he was a master teacher as well. I remember being in awe of Max as he worked a lecture hall of over a hundred students, answering questions, presenting material, and most importantly parsing out the best parts in a student's comments when, at times, I would see nothing of value from a particular remark. I learned a great deal about teaching from Max, especially his respect for all students and his willingness to listen. I took all of his classes during my three years of graduate study.

As I progressed from first-year graduate student to associate professor at U.S.I.U., I got to know Max personally and was fortunate enough to work with him professionally. As he was only on campus for a limited time every other weekend, Max always worked with a team of professional assistants to help him with course logistics and to work with students in smaller, seminar-style classes after his main lecture-discussion. Several of us were co-teaching his classes with him, providing those important support services as well as offering supplemental thoughts and perspectives during his lecture-presentation. In this capacity, I taught with Max four times. One such class was entitled Psychohistory of the American Presidency.

As a journalist and reporter, Max had first-hand knowledge of the presidents from FDR through Reagan, His classes were not only highly academic as we sorted and analyzed presidents according to his two-factor theory of presidential leadership, but he peppered his lectures with remarkable anecdotes and stories about these important leaders.

Looking for new ways of thinking about and applying Bowen theory, I had wanted to revive some version of this course for many years. I proposed a new course titled Psychohistory of the American Presidency, and it was approved in 2010. To my delight and advantage, my oldest daughter Carly had recently graduated from Northern Arizona University. With her degree in political science, we discussed the possibility of her co-teaching the class with me. She would bring her substantial knowledge of political theory and American history, and I would bring my knowledge of Bowen theory and political history. We offered this course twice; the first time was in the Spring Semester of 2011.

This was an interdisciplinary course that stretched the boundaries of both the Human Development-Psychology program and the Cultural and Regional Studies program. It fully enrolled. Students with a background in Bowen theory wanted more opportunities to study and apply the theory. Others were simply intrigued by the course.

Our version of Psychohistory of the American Presidency was distinctive from Max's course. For example, ours focused on the emotional imprints of Washington, Adams, and Jefferson, the first three presidents, the history of the presidency and the nation, as well as several other significant presidents in U.S. history, including Jackson, Lincoln, and Obama.

We focused on the first three presidents, the history of the presidency and the nation, as well as several other significant presidents in U.S. history, including Jackson and Lincoln. There is only so much that we could effectively accomplish in eleven weeks, so Carly and I decided on depth with a few presidents rather than breadth in numbers.

The course was formatted around Bowen theory as applied to differentiated leadership and the shaping of the nation. This was a new and exciting experiment for me. One of my hobbies and interests over the years has been politics, especially at the national level. But I also needed Carly's expertise in political theory. She, in turn, took her own "crash course" in Bowen theory and soon developed a solid working knowledge. She and I created this class and most of the pedagogical activities that we used throughout the semester. In developing the course, I was continually reminded of what Max used to say about teaching and learning: "If you want to learn something, teach it." Learn it we did, from the class resources, from each other, from our research, and from the students. It was an extraordinary experience for all.

To prepare, we voraciously read many books on the founders and key presidents, especially biographies on Washington, Jefferson, Adams, Jackson, Lincoln, and Obama. We divided the class into two parts. The first half of the class focused on the three founding presidents, as well as Andrew Jackson. The second half of the class addressed Lincoln, Obama, and selected presidents from Theodore Roosevelt onward chosen for their importance. These included TR, FDR, JFK, Johnson, Nixon, and Reagan. Working in small groups, students selected a modern-day president for their research and presentation projects. Obama was president at the time, and as his presidency was historic, we included him in our curriculum.

Students were divided into teams. Each team selected a 20th century president from the list that we created. Working together, their assignment was to create three-generational genograms of their president and apply Bowen theory and differentiated leadership to that president's life, relationships, accomplishments, and challenges. Students wrote comprehensive papers on their investigations, and presented their findings to the class.

We approached the class from a two-pronged perspective. First, we investigated the role of human enslavement in formatting the nation. You cannot understand the origins of the United States of America and the issues we still face as a nation without understanding the role of enslaving people and the continuing significance of its overwhelming emotional imprint. To this end, we read and discussed a seminal article from professor and historian Edmund S. Morgan called "Slavery and Freedom: The American Paradox." In it, Morgan provides a detailed overview of the development of slavery as a way of substituting for the single, young men who were coming to the colonies from England for work. With guns and without mates, these men became more and more problematic for the local authorities as their economies struggled. For landholders, creating an enslaved workforce "solved" this social problem.

We discussed the historical notion of "presentism," that thorn in the side of people who study history and bring modern-day sensibilities and morality to bear when critiquing the past. For example, we looked at the sheer number of early presidents (ten of the first twelve)—including Washington and Jefferson—who enslaved people, why they did so, how they treated them as property, and what happened to these men, women, and children following their deaths. Students, of course, were appalled when they learned of the sheer number of enslaved people in the colonies, how significant they were to the economies of the time, how many of the Founding Fathers and non-founding presidents "owned" enslaved people, and the decision by those opposed to human enslavement to push the problem ahead for future generations to solve. Those opposing human enslavement were brilliant and pragmatic. However repugnant this was to them, ultimately, they were realistic men who knew that the issue of slavery, if confronted too early and too intensely, would destroy the embryonic nation before it was even birthed. Presentism provided a contextual perspective for students' righteous rage about the entire issue.

We taught students how to create and interpret genograms. They learned about the power of genograms and multigenerational formatting. Students came to better understand their selected presidents and their generational families through these genograms. In addition, we studied the genograms of all of the presidents that we investigated. Their genograms revealed how these men's multigenerational histories expressed themselves in how they governed as presidents and how they formatted the presidency from its infancy.

These genograms were deeply revealing about the men, their wives, their lives, and their past and future multigenerational histories. In fact, some of the genograms, such as JFK's, were downright spooky in terms of multigenerational emotional process and presidential legacies. A history of deaths and injuries through plane crashes in the Kennedy family, for example, occurred through multiple generations.

Using genograms as a guide, we delved into the multigenerational histories of the presidents. Some, like Washington, are sketchy. Facts about Washington's lineage are not always clear. And, since "the Father of our Country" did not have any children, his influence on future family members was limited to his step-children. Adams' genogram, by contrast, may have been the most interesting of the founding generation. The emotional intensity and closeness between Abigail and John are well known, as are her contributions to and influence on his presidency.

We also examined the descendants of presidents. Franklin Roosevelt once said that being a child of a president is a curse. As we studied presidential families, we came to discover that many children of these remarkable men would likely echo his sentiments.

We used a number of books, articles, and chapters in the class. We distributed the theory chapter from my mediation book, *Applying Family Systems Theory to Mediation*. This chapter helped students acquire a working knowledge of the significant concepts in Bowen theory. We also disseminated writings from several biographies by presidential historian Joseph Ellis, including chapters from *His Excellency: George Washington*; *First Family: Abigail and John Adams*; and *American Sphinx: The Character of Thomas Jefferson*. As a class, we read Ellis's Pulitzer Prize-winning book, *Founding Brothers*, and Barack Obama's memoir *Dreams from My Father*. And, in order to provide a historical context to all of the presidents and to learn more about their times and accomplishments, we used a more traditional textbook by Sidney M. Milkis and Michael Nelson, *The American Presidency: Origins and Development*. We also read the first chapter in Friedman's *Failure of Nerve* to focus our discussions of differentiated leadership.

I presented Lincoln's genogram, which I had been actively developing over the years. Lincoln was a significant president that we studied in depth. We discussed Lincoln's history of noteworthy and untimely losses (mother, sister, fiancé, etc.) and his subsequent severe depressions. We contemplated how those unexpected deaths helped prepare Lincoln to face the profound personal losses of three children and wife Mary Todd's deepening psychosis, as well as the traumatic effects of the Civil War on him, Mary Todd, and the nation.

We discussed Bowen theory's concept of emotional fields, the way emotional fields are "alive," and how they are influential across time and space. Ed Friedman likened time to a collapsing telescope with the past pressed up against the present. Borrowing a phrase from evolutionary biologist Rupert Sheldrake's remarkable book on morphic resonance (another field theory, this time in biology and evolution) titled *The Presence of the Past,* Friedman said "the past is always present in the present." In this way, the effects of human enslavement live on not only in the collective psyches of people but through our economic policies, laws, and prejudices.

In fact, the concept of emotional fields–how they develop and their effects–was central to the class and was even included in the course description. This was especially critical in formatting the presidency in the beginning. Washington, Adams, and Jefferson in particular, emotionally shaped the presidency for generations to come.

Emotional fields demonstrate the power of presence across the centuries. Unwrapping and understanding this power was essential to the class and its integration with Bowen theory. Emotional fields are part of multigenerational emotional process. These were reoccurring themes that became cornerstones to the essential questions posed in the class and the theory underlying them, ones that we came back to again and again over the semester.

For example, as the first U.S. President, Washington had no model and no historical context for being president. The entire idea of a strong executive leader was not even universally accepted in his time. For many, the power of the federal government was through the legislature, not the executive branch. Also, the Federalists and the Republicans fought for years over issues of states' rights vs. the power of the central government.

This struggle has always existed and still exists in this country today. It was emotionally formatted through the origins of the country and the power of the presidency. We were of two minds since the beginning of our country, just as it seems like the nation, today, remains of two minds when it comes to executive power and legislative authority and the power of the states vs. the power of the federal government. Our hesitancy around centralized power was emotionally imprinted by the founding generation's contempt for English tyranny and their despotic rule over the colonies.

It wasn't just the debates around centralized vs. states' powers that informed and formatted the country, though. Each of the first three presidents was essential in defining the power and customs of the presidency. Another example: Washington was clearly and unequivocally the pre-eminent power of his time. In fact, most historians doubt that the country would have survived its early challenges and stayed intact if it weren't for Washington's uniqueness as a leader. Of all the founders, only Washington had the authority, recognition, respect, gravitas, and indeed size to effectively rule. He singlehandedly figured out what the presidency meant.

Washington was always the ambivalent leader. He voluntarily and willingly gave up his military authority as Commander of the Continental Army after the Revolutionary War ended. He reluctantly agreed to become president, knowing that he alone was best positioned to begin binding together the new nation. He tried to give up power and didn't want to run for re-election but, again, he reluctantly did so for the sake of the country. Then, he definitively said that he would not run for a third term, setting the stage for perhaps his greatest contribution to emotionally imprinting the new republic: voluntarily stepping aside after eight years and saying that no one should hold power indefinitely.

While this self-imposed limitation was not in the United States Constitution, it held sway for all presidents until Franklin Roosevelt's decision to seek third and fourth terms during World War II. (This emotional imprint became a legal mandate that was enshrined with the passage and ratification of the 22nd Amendment to the U.S. Constitution in 1951, limiting presidential terms to two.) In addition, many of his other emotional imprints live on today as well, including civilian control over the military, president as head ("CEO") of executive branch, presidential ability to fire cabinet members, public education as a way of binding the nation together, westward expansion, adding "so help me God" to the end of the constitutionally-required words in the Oath of Office, and the concept of executive privilege, among others.

As unique as Washington was as a leader and a president, not everything that he did to institutionalize the presidency lasted. For example, Washington only vetoed legislation that he believed was unconstitutional vs. vetoing bills that he did not agree with. He also integrated the army but this integration did not last until Truman permanently integrated the armed services in 1948.

In summary, Washington's influence on the presidency was enormous but not absolute. Remarkably, much of what he defined for the office lives on today.

Next, we investigated Adams and Jefferson in the same way, reviewing both their contributions and emotional legacies to the nation prior to their presidencies and their contributions as presidents. Adams' emotional legacies were significant but most were not a result of his presidency. Rather, these accomplishments included his enduring contributions regarding the structure of the states as quasi-independent entities and his role as Secretary of War in the American Revolution.

Adams was a staunch advocate of the colonial revolution for independence, selecting Washington to head the Continental Army and acting as Secretary of War during the American Revolution. His writings in *Thoughts on Governance* recommended that each state adopt a constitutional blueprint with three branches of government including separation of powers, a bi-cameral legislature, and a fully independent judiciary. This was eventually taken up by all of the states and is considered one of Adams' most noteworthy and enduring legacies.

In 1779, Adams singlehandedly wrote the Massachusetts Constitution, which remains the oldest written constitution still in use in the English-speaking world. Slavery was ruled unconstitutional by Massachusetts Supreme Court based on his state constitution.

Adams, as we know, was less successful as president, though, who, in fact, could have successfully followed Washington? He was the only one-term president until his son, John Quincy Adams's re-election defeat in 1829. (Their elections and failed re-elections are excellent examples of multigenerational emotional process.) Nonetheless, there are a few emotional imprints worth noting from his presidency, including his insight, which still exists today, that nations view their international policies through their sovereign interests, a view shared by Washington.

In 1800, at the end of his presidency, Adams selected John Marshall as the Chief Justice of the United States Supreme Court. Marshall, himself, is regarded by most historians as one of the most important and influential Chief Justices in U.S. history. He almost singlehandedly shaped and formatted the power and influence of the Supreme Court as an equal partner in the U.S. government, alongside the executive and legislative branches. In essence, Marshall helped create a differentiated triangle between the three branches of government. This emotional and legal imprint still exists today.

Next, we looked at Jefferson as a man, writer, visionary, president, and slave owner who, unlike Washington, failed to free most of the people he enslaved after he died. We compiled his contributions both as the third President of the United States, as well as his membership in the Revolutionary Generation. These included his pre-presidential accomplishments such as singlehandedly drafting the Declaration of Independence, perhaps his greatest accomplish-ment prior to his presidency. To this day, the Declaration of Independence is considered the most sacred text in American history, and arguably, one that has the most emotionally defined us as a nation. It is one of Jefferson's enduring legacies and one of three contributions that he asked be placed on his tombstone—along with his authorship of the Virginia Statute on Religious Freedom in 1786 and his founding of the University of Virginia.

In addition, Jefferson served as a one-term governor of Virginia. He eliminated primogeniture (the oldest inherits all land), reformed criminal law to limit the death penalty, extended voting rights to more free men, expanded the public school system, and established complete separation of church and state. Many of these legacies, especially the separation of church and state, were vital to the new nation and would eventually become institutionalized through state and national legislation and the U.S. Constitution.

At a national level, Jefferson tried to address the problem of human enslavement through the Ordinance of 1784, which failed by a single vote. This ordinance would have ended slavery in new states by 1800, and established how the Union would admit new states. While not passing, Jefferson's Ordinance established the basis of limiting slavery's geography to the original enslavement states. This fight to limit and finally eliminate slavery continued for another 80 years.

Regarding his presidential emotional imprints, Jefferson was the first president to head a political party, an emotional imprint that spans the centuries and still exists today. Jefferson was also the first president to be elected without a clear electoral mandate and so was also the first president selected by the House of Representatives. While wrenching for the country, as the Democratic-Republicans threatened revolution if Jefferson was not seated as president, the eventual resolution of the disputed 1800 presidential election formatted the processes and procedures, enshrined in the U.S. Constitution, for selecting a president without the necessary electoral majority. This allowed for peaceful transitions of power in this and future disputed elections.

In 1803, as president, Jefferson, who ironically backed a limited federal government, negotiated the Louisiana Purchase from Napoleon and France. This purchase doubled the size of the continental United States. It opened up American settlement west of the Mississippi and removed all major European powers from North America. The purchase was made for three cents an acre! This acquisition is considered by many as the greatest accomplishment of the Jefferson presidency and was one of the most important executive decisions made in American history. Regarding its relevance to Bowen theory, it "formatted" the notion of westward expansion, which was eventually formalized through the Monroe Doctrine and its logical extension through Manifest Destiny.

As a retired president, Jefferson was active, foreshadowing the dynamic role of ex-presidents, exemplified by 20th and 21st century ex-presidents Jimmy Carter, Bill Clinton, and Barack Obama. His greatest accomplishment post-presidency was founding the University of Virginia, the first secular university in the country. He contributed both educational ideals and most of the significant architecture, which is still considered one of the great architectural accomplishments in the United States.

While not all of these accomplishments by Adams and Jefferson can be considered emotional legacies for the country, many are. Others are significant accomplishments in their own right and were, in fact, formatted into other areas of the developing nation, most notably the U.S. Constitution.

Perhaps most uniquely, our class delved into the multigenerational histories of the presidents. Some, like Washington, are vague. An extensive review of Adams's multigenerational genogram reveals that the children and grandchildren of John Adams and Abigail Adams were not very happy people. And, it seems, there was only one child per generation that went on to "succeed." The price of that success, unfortunately, was often very high personally. For example, while John Quincy Adams became the sixth president, he was a brilliant but decidedly unhappy man. He, too, had children that struggled in their lives, with only one achieving any success of note. And, like his father, he was not a popular president. John Quincy won a difficult, contested election and then overwhelmingly lost his re-election bid to his same bitter rival, Andrew Jackson. This was similar to how John Adams won a difficult election and then overwhelmingly lost his re-election bid to his own bitter rival, Thomas Jefferson. (Adams placed third in the presidential election of 1800.)

One of the best features of Prescott College is its commitment to interdisciplinary learning. Even with Carly's assistance, the two of us never considered ourselves experts on the American Presidency. Yet, through intensive preparation, creative pedagogical exercises, and the good work of students, we all left the course far richer, intellectually and historically, than we entered. Here was a unique way of understanding and applying Bowen family systems theory to presidential leadership, leadership through differentiation, emotional fields, and American history.

There is no doubt that I had a unique opportunity at Prescott College. Not only had the college encouraged my expansion of courses teaching and applying Bowen theory, but I found that the students absolutely loved the theory itself. In general, Prescott College students were more naturally systems-oriented thinkers than graduate students that I had taught elsewhere. Further, they embraced the theory and its application with all of the enthusiasm and passion of young adults in their early 20s. They demonstrated intellectual eagerness, a courageous willingness to share themselves and their vulnerabilities, and a deep-seated commitment to applying what they learned to making the world a better place through their activism.

While not every student's life was changed by studying Bowen family systems theory, a great many were. At the beginning of my systems-oriented classes I would audaciously proclaim, "If I do my job correctly and you do your job correctly, this class will change your life forever." This statement always got their attention. In de-briefing these classes at the end of the term, the majority of students not only remembered my statement from the first day, but they agreed with me that Bowen's family systems theory had changed their lives for the better.

The student demand for education and training in Bowen theory increased over time. By 2012, due to student interest, as well as my having developed the cadre of courses listed above, the Human Development-Psychology program added a new specialization to our undergraduate psychology degree. With four concentration courses, students were able to graduate with a degree in psychology and an emphasis in family systems theory. To my knowledge, we offered the only family systems theory emphasis area at an undergraduate level in the country. I was proud of the college's confidence in offering this specialty area, the students' passion about pursuing it, and my efforts—over more than twenty years—in developing such wide-ranging courses in Bowen family systems theory.

After graduation, many students furthered their education in systems theory through graduate school and in their work in the world. Over the years, I can confidently say that I have helped birth and launch many next-generation Bowen theorists and practitioners.

SECTION THREE

BOWEN FAMILY SYSTEMS THEORY AND DIFFERENTIATED LEADERSHIP

CHAPTER FIVE

MANAGING EMOTIONAL TRIANGULATION IN EDUCATIONAL LEADERSHIP: TWO CASE STUDIES

One of my professional careers over the decades has been that of educational leader. First was my appointment to chair the master's and doctoral programs in marriage and family therapy and psychology at United States International University (U.S.I.U.) from 1986 through 1991. I was also elected to the executive council of the faculty senate as vice president. In these roles, I learned a lot about managing students, collaborating with faculty, working with administrators, developing and executing budgets, and implementing innovative academic programs.

After moving to Prescott College in 1992, I served in my first executive leadership role as dean of the undergraduate Resident Degree Program (RDP) from 1995 until 2000. The college is dedicated to "experiential education," that is, an active pedagogy designed to help students investigate social, environmental, and educational problems, explore aesthetics and the arts, challenge themselves in outdoor wilderness environments, and, do so in classes averaging ten to fourteen students.

In my role as dean of this small program of approximately five hundred students, I served in many capacities, including academic dean, student dean, and faculty dean. In addition, I provided supervision and leadership to many administrative sections of the college, including the library, student services, and admissions. In many ways, given the small size of the college, I acted as provost for more than half of the college.

My second supervisory leadership position in Prescott was two non-consecutive, two-year terms as the executive director of Skyview School, a K-8 charter school based on the theory of multiple intelligences. Similar to Prescott College, Skyview School was likewise dedicated to project- and thematically-based learning within an active and aesthetically-rich pedagogy. As the director of a one-district school, I performed all functions normally associated with that of a superintendent as well as a principal for this organization.

Executive leadership offered multiple opportunities to do what I love to do: apply Bowen family systems theory in new settings. I was first exposed to the theory of differentiated leadership at U.S.I.U. as program director in 1987. We hired Ed Friedman to teach an advanced graduate and post-graduate seminar. Ed Friedman led a two-week long symposium on clinical and non-clinical applications of Bowen theory. While I had studied a bit of Bowen theory in my graduate program, after Friedman's seminars, I began applying Bowen theory to my administrative work. Years later, I was interested in expanding my understanding and application of differentiated leadership beyond middle management and into executive leadership in educational systems.

In this chapter, I will explore emotional triangulating in these leadership positions. I will present case examples in which I found myself caught in an emotional vortex of triangular processes as the anxiety binder in the marriage of two couples, one from Prescott College and one from Skyview School. I will discuss how my reactions contributed to this triangulation and how I attempted to work through these emotional minefields by thinking systems and applying the principles of Bowen theory.

In the chapter seven, I will describe how I used differentiated leadership during my second term at Skyview in order to re-stabilize the school, which had had a series of failed leaders who brought the school to the brink of fiscal and organizational insolvency. I will discuss how Bowen theory re-oriented the school back to its mission-driven course, stabilized the school's finances, and shifted the emotional atmosphere of the school back to its founding vision and principles.

In the summer of 1995 and only weeks before the beginning of the new academic year, the current dean, Peter, stepped down from that position to seek his fortune as a stockbroker and analyst. With some reluctance, I put forth my name to the faculty and sought appointment to this position. I had left U.S.I.U. less than three years earlier, in large part to get away from administrating programs and back to teaching, the central love of my professional life. Unfortunately, with such short notice and few internal candidates qualified for the position, I believed that I was the best candidate for the job.

To complicate matters, Prescott College had a tradition of selecting deans from within the faculty. And while those appointments were conceptualized as rotational, with deans returning to the faculty after completing their terms of service, the historical fact was that dean appointments were always an "up and out" affair. The fact that Peter was leaving the college for greener pastures reinforced this pattern. I hoped to change this emotional imprint and had every intention of returning to teaching after completing my tenure as dean.

I temporarily vacated my position as dean to take my sabbatical for the 1999-2000 academic year. I had already delayed my sabbatical due to my dean responsibilities. The college was in a strong position and so a sabbatical for 1999-2000 seemed appropriate. I was scheduled for a one-year leave, after which time the president and I planned my return to the dean's position. There were many reasons why that did not happen. The president and chief financial officer (CFO) of Prescott College had been feuding throughout my terms as dean, and I was often triangulated into their intense conflicts. In a dramatic turn of events, in the fall of 1999, the board of trustees decided not to re-hire the president, and the CFO also left during this time. With all of the upheaval at the college, the board of trustees selected an acting CEO from their own ranks until a new president could be hired. Unfortunately, this trustee had no executive or administrative experience.

Simultaneously, while my contract retained my dean's appointment at the time, I was in a disempowered position from the sidelines, as I was on sabbatical. Given the changes at the college, I became less than enthusiastic about retuning as dean, though I had a great deal that I still wished to accomplish. To make matters more complicated, it seemed to me that as a remnant of this collapsing administrative system, the acting CEO wanted me out.

Parallel to the goings on at Prescott College, Skyview School was in the middle of its own crisis in leadership. I, along with a small group of educator parents, had been intimately involved in founding and running Skyview since those first planning meetings in 1994. Since receiving our state charter in 1995 and opening the school in 1996, I had worked as educational and board consultant. I had also served on the board of directors for several terms. By the time of my sabbatical in 1999, I was board president.

The current director, Dr. Sally Redland, had served less than two years when she decided to return to Colorado to care for her aging and ailing mother and to fully retire from education and educational leadership. Sally was a competent director. She was, though, more accustomed to the role of principal than superintendent. As such, while providing an array of important functions and services for Skyview, she lacked the vision necessary to take the school to the next level as the leader of a multiple intelligences-based organization. Also, Sally was at the tail end of her successful educational career. Even when we hired her in the summer of 1998, we understood that her term would be short. By most accounts, Sally was a successful caretaking director. By December of 1999, however, Sally was interested in a quick transition away from her directorship.

Having successfully served as a dean, I wanted to try my hand as a CEO and apply differentiated leadership to a system where I had the maximum opportunity to effect change in an organization. The challenge was real, and it was an exciting time for me as well as the school. In the winter of 2000, I resigned my board presidency and applied for the position as director. I was hired and began my directorship in March of 2000.

The transition from Prescott College dean to Skyview School director was a natural, smooth one for me. I always felt that I was moving towards something, rather than leaving something. I served as director for twenty-eight months from 2000-2002.

I returned to Prescott College in July of 2002. To make this transition complete, I also left Skyview to the next generation of leaders and did not serve on the board of directors again until January 2009, well after my second term as director.

My second term as the Skyview School director came in January of 2006, at a more difficult period in its development. Once again, I was on sabbatical from Prescott College. In January of 2006, I was approached by Skyview Board President Julie Stenson about accepting a temporary appointment for the remainder of the school year. The previous three directors between 2003 and January of 2006 had failed to provide the kind of effective leadership that Skyview needed. As a result, the school was in terrible shape, financially, administratively, and emotionally. I agreed to return to help but after several weeks on the job, I realized that I would need time to clean up the mess that the school was in. The original four months that the board allotted me wasn't enough time to turn the school around. The school was slowly sinking, and I needed to immediately and forcefully intervene to stabilize it.

Months before, Julie, who was an original member of the parent group that developed and chartered Skyview School as well as a founding board member, was asked to return to help save the school. Before recruiting me, Julie was busy enlisting new board members that would be up to the challenge. Fortunately, most board members, including those recently recruited by the board president, agreed with my assessment and granted me a two-year appointment to re-stabilize the school and get us back to being an educational leader in the community.

As an educational leader in the 1990s and 2000s, there were two decidedly challenging times for me, one at Prescott College as the dean and the second as Skyview School director. In both instances, there was remarkable consistency regarding how I was emotionally triangulated into failing marriages. I'll discuss how that triangulation provided temporary opportunities for the couples to develop greater relational cohesion, at my expense, describe my initial reactions to being emotionally triangled, and my conscious attempts to de-triangulate myself from these intense environments.

As dean, Peter exerted strong control. Even as he was training for a new career, Peter retained his underlying faculty status, and I wondered about his ability to re-enter as a faculty member, his expectations about how a dean should function, and his willingness, in general, to allow someone else to lead. To complicate matters, I had served in Peter's administration as a trusted ally, friend, and confidante in my role of coordinator of the Human Development-Psychology program. Along with other friends and colleagues, Peter and I worked closely in running the RDP. Peter's wife, Cynthia, who served as program coordinator before me, was also a family friend and colleague.

Peter and Cynthia had a chronically strained marriage. By the time that Peter stepped down as dean, his marriage to Cynthia was, by many accounts, once again on the verge of collapse. All this complicated my transition to dean.

During my first year as dean, I supervised a number of national searches for new faculty. One such search involved hiring an education faculty member. As is the case in many academic institutions, there were internal as well as external candidates for the position. Of the four search committee members, two were friends and associates of a particularly strong internal candidate. The other two committee members had no such allegiance and only seemed interested in selecting the strongest possible candidate. Cynthia served on this committee, as did two other faculty members and a student. As dean, I held an "ex-officio" role on this and all faculty search committees. In this capacity, I was responsible for ensuring that the committee conducted its affairs properly and according to policy. As dean, I also approved or rejected for hire the search committee's recommended candidate.

As the search progressed, it became evident that the two committee members who were friends of the internal candidate, one of whom was Cynthia, would only accept the internal candidate, Jeffrey, as their choice to fill the position. The other two committee members were equally adamant that there was a superior external candidate in Richard and that he should be selected and advanced to me for final approval. At the committee's request, I attended one of their committee meetings to listen to their deliberations and discussions. (Later, the college's faculty search procedures evolved to avoid these kinds of conflicts of interest because of dual relationships and the dilemmas that follow.) I was faced with a conundrum: if I didn't find a way out of this impasse, the search would fail and no one would be hired into this important position. We would lose the opportunity to enlarge the faculty and there was no guarantee that the funding would be there next year for a new search and hire.

After listening to the two camps, I asked all members if they believed that both candidates would be acceptable to them, if they would be willing to, in effect, submit both Jeffrey and Richard as unranked but acceptable candidates for the position. All said yes, but stressed that they could only formally accept their own recommended candidate. After securing this unranked acceptance, I selected Richard as the candidate of choice. While Jeffrey had distinguished himself as an important lecturer and member of the Prescott College community over the years, I believed that Richard brought a fresh perspective that would enhance the education program.

I reported to the faculty that Richard was successful in the search. I failed to present the complexity of the issue and how I had managed the impasse. My thinking, though flawed at the time, had to do with preserving confidentiality of the process. I also did not want to inflame the debate over the value of internal versus external candidates that had been raging for years. However honorable my intentions, my actions contributed to the development of several emotional triangles.

As a member of the "pro-Jeffrey" coalition on the search committee, Cynthia, and later her husband Peter, said that I had manipulated the process and had acted unethically, and perhaps illegally, in selecting Richard as the successful candidate. They each, in turn, threatened to go before the full faculty and expose what they saw as my manipulation. After meeting with Peter and Cynthia separately, I began seeing their alliance as emotionally strategic, as a way of building relational support for each other through their criticism of me. In other words, I began feeling emotionally triangled into their marriage. It felt as if I was being used to temporarily strengthening their marriage, at my expense.

This, of course, is the nature of emotional triangles and triangulation. Peter and Cynthia were in the more "comfortable" inside positions of the emotional triangle, and I was in the less comfortable position of anxiety binder on the outside position of the emotional triangle.

Simultaneously with my systemic assessment, I quickly came to realize the rookie nature of my actions and therefore my mistake. While I had sought to salvage an important search during a critical search season, I had sacrificed transparency for expediency and quickly figured out that I needed to correct this error and come clean with the faculty. I also saw this as my way of de-triangulating or extricating myself from this emotional triangle.

I called an emergency faculty meeting the next day and included a single agenda item: my mishandling of the search. While I had already offered Richard the position, I thought that it was important to provide full disclosure to the faculty. It was time to fess up.

The next day's meeting arrived and both Cynthia and Peter attended. Oddly, Cynthia was a bit late because she had to pick up their oldest daughter, eight-year-old Theresa, from school. Theresa sat between her parents, reinforcing this pattern of emotional triangulation that they were so expert at activating through Peter's misbehaviors and affairs, their children, and now me.

I apologized to the faculty for my lack of transparency. I explained my dilemma. In the end, the faculty was largely forgiving, since I was a novice at these national searches, especially with a strong internal candidate. I had already proven my integrity early in my term when the co-president of the college and her financial consultant believed that a cash flow problem equaled insolvency and attempted to close the college. During this chaotic time, I had quickly stepped into a leadership role at the college, exposing this falsehood and the incompetence behind it. As a result, I had gained a measure of political and social capital, respect, and thanks from the faculty and some of my fellow administrators. So, while the faculty expressed some concerns about the thinking behind my decision, as well as the decision itself, they were, in the main, quite tolerant and understanding. Not Cynthia and Peter. In rapid fire synchronicity, they attacked not only my decision but my integrity.

With their daughter sitting between them, Cynthia and Peter expressed a kind a unity of purpose that had been largely missing from their marriage for years. The obvious nature of their emotional triangling with me was reinforced through a second, interlocking emotional triangle with their daughter and them, and a third interlocking, complicated emotional triangle that they tried to develop with the two of them on one inside position of the triangle, the faculty on the second inside point of the triangle, and me on the outside third position of the triangle.

This all contributed to a uniquely bizarre moment. I did my best to remain calm and allowed them to express their concerns. I stopped them, though, from dominating the meeting. Interestingly, while their marriage had attained a degree of temporary stability by using me as their anxiety binder, the faculty was less forgiving, as they saw Peter and Cynthia's attacks as ways in which neither could let a new person successfully assume the position of dean previously held by Peter. In an unexpected way, their attempts to triangulate me actually strengthened my position as leader of the faculty. In short, the faculty rejected Peter and Cynthia's attempted triangulation.

Despite all of this, however, there were still feelings of remorse and regret in this small faculty community with the impending loss of Jeffrey as a community member. Fast-forward three weeks to the end of the semester and the spring faculty retreat. Prior to beginning the retreat, the new college president, Charles, asked me if he could make an announcement before we got down to business. He seemed eager, though a bit nervous, to do this and I, of course, afforded him this courtesy. He began the spring faculty retreat by reviewing the challenges with the education search and saying that, in recognition of this time of emotional upheaval and needed healing, he was unilaterally appointing Jeffrey as a full faculty member in the Adventure Education Program, a position that he was qualified to fill.

Needless to say, many faculty members saw this as a win-win situation for the college: appointing a new faculty member, which is always coveted, and resolving the issue of Jeffrey, so that he could remain a productive and fully-valued member of the community.

There was only one problem: Charles never informed me of his decision, and so I was completely blindsided by his announcement. In effect, rather than the dean and president working together in the best interests of the college, the president emotionally triangulated me into a complicated triangle. The inside positions were the faculty and Jeffrey together at one inside point and Charles, the president, at the other inside point. As for me, I was left on the third, outside position of the emotional triangle. I felt humiliated, confused, and angry at this turn of events. I used all of my self-management skills to stay calm, at least on the outside, and thought about how best to handle this situation. Internally, my heart was beating rapidly and my hands were sweating. I was deeply worked up. Emotional reactivity indeed.

At the morning break, I requested a private lunch with the president away from the retreat center. At lunch, I offered my resignation, which Charles refused. I explained to him that I saw his decision, no matter how positively intended, as an emotional triangle that resulted in his increased political capital with the faculty, i.e., him assuming an inside position with the faculty. I told him that his decision was implemented at my expense, since I became the anxiety binder in the system. His actions had undercut my authority with the faculty, since I was now on the outside position.

In simple language, Charles gained favor with the faculty at my expense. Given my exclusion, though, I couldn't support him by presenting a united front. The faculty needed a cohesive executive team. What they got, instead, was a power play that cracked the foundations of Charles' administration.

I said that if this happened again, I would resign, despite any protestations or refusals from him. I also told him that I was going to explain to the faculty exactly what happened, from a Bowen family systems theory perspective, and I invited him to be a part of that discussion. Perhaps, we could, together, get beyond this unfortunate turn of events and celebrate his appointment of Jeffrey. In effect, I wanted to de-triangulate myself from this situation and use this as an opportunity to better differentiate the entire system. Charles thanked me for the offer but decided against joining me in my discussion with the faculty after lunch, which was rather unfortunate. This was his second serious miscalculation and one that resulted in a lost opportunity for everyone.

I gathered the faculty and detailed for them the nature of emotional systems. I diagrammed how emotional triangulation works in general and in this situation in particular. I explained the effect of triangulation and anxiety in the leadership system and what I was trying to do, which was to de-triangulate myself. I didn't blame Charles for what he did. After all, emotional triangles are automatic and often "mindless" processes. And, even if his decision *was* calculated, I was aiming to explain the way emotional systems worked rather than to ascribe motivation or blame.

Since becoming dean, I had begun teaching Bowen family systems theory to the faculty. It was my way of helping all of us begin using the same language and theoretical system in our work together with each other and with our students. Nonetheless, the faculty sat in stunned silence following my presentation. They had assumed that the president had discussed Jeffrey's appointment with me and that I had offered my encouragement and blessing. When they found out that I hadn't been consulted and, worse, that I hadn't even known about his decision until they learned about it, they were rightly flummoxed. Nonetheless, I had begun to de-triangulate myself, at least temporarily, from this active and potentially insidious emotional triangle around the search, Jeffrey, the president, and the faculty.

Even as I write this, I recognize that the words don't do justice to my state of mind. In both circumstances, with Peter and Cynthia, and again with Charles, I experienced a great deal of turmoil. As a Bowen theorist, it is common to reiterate the importance of keeping a non-anxious presence in an intense emotional environment, though, in truth, we only have so much control in situations in which anxiety is heavily sprayed on us.

From a theoretical perspective, I suppose that had my level of basic differentiation been higher, I might not have fallen into these emotional traps, or if I did, they wouldn't have felt so toxic. Unfortunately, nothing could be further from the truth. Acute anxiety layered on chronic anxiety can be powerful, overwhelming, even debilitating. The effects of anxiety can feel deeply noxious. During these times, I had difficulty sleeping. I felt taken advantage of, and I wanted to fight back or escape by fleeing the field, the characteristic "fight-flight-freeze" reactions of humans and most animals when threatened. Nonetheless, my training and experience with Bowen theory provided me another avenue, one in which I tried to think through my responses, try as best I could to calm my emotionally hyper-aroused state, and act based on the power of my theoretical and personal convictions.

These examples are instructive, for they suggest that we must learn to apply the same degree of compassion, kindness, forgiveness, and empathy to ourselves as we often provide to others. Rather than judging myself for my high level of reactivity at the time, or blaming myself for my inability to sleep at night during those troubled days, slowly, over years and decades, I am learning to accept myself as someone who is attempting to grow emotionally, who is committed to a path of mindfulness and equanimity, but who is, ultimately, human and so will get reactive from time to time, regardless of my best efforts.

Despite some of these emotional challenges, or even because of them, Bowen family systems theory successfully guided me over hostile terrain. The theory provided a roadmap on which to navigate. In these ways, Bowen theory proved invaluable, especially during those difficult moments.

The second example of getting trapped by emotional triangling occurred during my first term as Skyview School director. There was a Skyview family with two children, Annie who was in second grade and her brother Michael in fourth grade, and their two parents, Bert and Bertha. Bert was a minister at the local progressive church, and Bertha was a stay-at-home mother. Bertha maintained that she suffered from chemical sensitivity. She claimed that she experienced significant physical reactions from chemicals in the local environment. Annie was immature for her age, though she was reasonably well behaved at school. Interestingly, whenever her mother came to school, usually around lunchtime every day, Annie would have a meltdown in front of her. It was a common observation by the teachers and staff that Annie was manipulating her mother through her behavior, and her mother responded by reinforcing Annie's daily tantrums by over-focusing on them.

One day, Bert and Bertha came into my office and informed me that Annie was being chemically poisoned by one of our new modular classrooms, claiming that the classroom was outgassing chemicals. That, they explained confidently, was the reason for Annie's temper tantrums. They wanted Annie classified as chemically sensitive, and they wanted us to develop a 504 plan for her. 504 plans are similar to Individual Educational Plans (IEPs), which are required for students with documented disabilities. 504 plans, though, are developed as a part of the Department of Civil Rights. They are designed to create reasonable accommodations and adaptations for those with conditions that might violate their civil rights, should these provisions not be provided. The parents requested a meeting to legally designate Annie as chemically sensitive.

I had observed the family over the past several months. It seemed to me that the parents had a great deal of interpersonal conflict in their marriage. Bert was a classic over-functioner, holding the family together through his occupations as minister and primary homemaker. Further, Bert was an important and respected leader in the local, progressive community. Bertha, on the other hand, under-functioned in her life and in the family. She claimed to be incapacitated, and so Bert, in addition to his professional duties, assumed most of the responsibility for the functioning of the family.

It seemed to me that Annie was reacting to the chronic and acute anxiety in the family, which was manifested through the parents' rigid, reciprocal relationship of over-functioning and under-functioning. Annie's acting out when her mother arrived at school had the characteristic feel of her being the anxiety binder in a stable but unsatisfactory marital system.

As a result, when the parents decided that Annie's emotional meltdown was a consequence of the chemically outgassing modular buildings and not, as I saw it, a consequence of their emotionally triangling her into their chronically anxious marriage, I rejected their conclusion. Further, as a part of their solution, they demanded that the primary students in the two combined first, second, and third grade classrooms of about fifty students plus teachers and aides, change classrooms with the two intermediate classes of fourth, fifth, and sixth grade students, also numbering about fifty students plus teachers and aides. From their perspective, this "solution" protected their daughter from further, harmful exposure. The fact that they would be disrupting over one hundred students and staff was of little consequence to them.

In addition to my reluctance in accommodating their request to dislocate the majority of the school, I also had ethical reservations about diagnosing their daughter as chemically sensitive without proper evidence. Once diagnosed with a particular disorder, a diagnosis often stays forever. I did not want Annie to carry a diagnosis without evidence, especially given its repercussions in the future. Rather than granting the parents' requests, I asked Bert and Bertha to provide me with a diagnosis of chemical sensitivity from a physician. I said that I was willing to convene a 504 meeting after receiving this confirming medical diagnosis.

The parents also demanded that I test the new modular classrooms, since they were convinced that the modulars were outgassing formaldehyde and other toxins. While I didn't believe this was so, I decided to spend the substantial funds for chemical testing to "clear the air." Also, if indeed the modular units were toxic to some children, the school would find ways to protect them all. But, I refused to move the four classrooms to accommodate what I saw as an emotionally-driven reaction on the part of the parents.

The parents balked at my request for a medical diagnosis prior to our meeting to determine a 504 status. They also displayed anger to my refusal to move four classrooms to accommodate their daughter's perceived needs. 504 regulations allow for *reasonable* accommodations. From my perspective, inconveniencing the majority of students and staff at the school seemed anything but reasonable.

My rejecting Bert and Bertha's "solution" created a chain reaction of events that activated emotional triangulation across the organization. The parents had created an interlocking triangle with me that generated and amplified the anxiety in the original emotional triangle between the parents and the daughter. That emotional triangle had Bert and Bertha on the inside positions and me, as the anxiety binder in their relationship, on the outside position. Once again, I was being used by a couple whose marriage was failing as a transitory way of binding their anxiety and temporarily stabilizing their marriage. Bert and Bertha filed a complaint with the United States Office of Civil Rights, who initiated an extensive investigation.

In his classic book, *Generation to Generation*, Ed Friedman asserted that the most reactive and dependent members of a family or organization often set the agenda. If the leader of the system capitulates to their demands, the system can go into emotional regression. "Peace over progress," as Friedman suggested, is never a helpful strategy if it undermines the integrity of a person, family, or organization.

During the following weeks, several things happened. I held fast to my convictions—no, I wasn't going to move all of the classrooms and disrupt the entire school for Annie's sake. I refused to let these people set the agenda and run the school. I was trying to prevent the school from regressing. Further, the data from the chemical testing came through and, as I suspected, there was absolutely no outgassing in the classrooms. And, as I also suspected, this scientific information did little to calm the emotionally riled-up parents. It is common that objective data is no match for reactive thinking and subjective self-justification and rationalization. In the minds of Bert and Bertha, they had a chemically-sensitive daughter and no facts and no testing results were going to change their minds.

Also, during this time, the parents had been keeping Annie home from school for several weeks. Our attempts to get her to attend school failed. After missing over 10% of the school year, more than fifteen absences, we withdrew her from school, as is allowed and required by state law. This, of course, activated more emotionality on the part of the parents. In response to Annie's withdrawal from school, they filed a grievance against me through the State Department of Education and with the Skyview School Board of Directors.

With the board in particular, they were trying to split the members through triangulating them into the emotional tornado that they created and perpetuated. In order to prevent this from occurring, I met with the board president and vice president to discuss the situation. Over the course of several meetings and several days, we strategized how to proceed. The board vice president, an attorney, helped us prepare for the board meeting and offered important legal assistance. The board president, a local psychotherapist though not a Bowen theorist, initially understood my systemic assessment of the situation. With some guidance about systems, she understood that the couple was emotionally triangulating targeted individuals and groups—first me, then the Department of Civil Rights, then the State Department of Education, and now the board of directors. I explained to them how emotional systems operate and the importance of the board sending consistent communication about acceptable and unacceptable behavior by members of our community. I also highlighted for the board officers the need to establish limits on the invasiveness of parents. I reinforced my belief that labeling a child with a permanent disability in response to parental anxiety and marriage instability was unethical and that, as a psychologist and as a director, I would not do this.

Regrettably, by the time that the board meeting convened, tension was high, and it became a bit of a circus. The board president lost control of the meeting. The parents managed to agitate the most reactive and immature parents in the school to support their cause. They inflamed several other parents, painted me as an uncaring bureaucrat operating outside the scope of the law, and as a rigid administrator who did not understand the suffering of their daughter or their family. Due to legal restrictions about discussing students in a public forum, I was limited in what I could say in response to their accusations. Nonetheless, I patiently described and defended my actions as best I could and the law which supported me in removing any student from school due to excessive absences.

My goal was to establish a clear and consistent position for the school, through myself and the board. I wanted to highlight for the parents and the community the impracticality of the parents' request to move four classrooms of students and staff, and my legal authority to withdraw a student for too many absences.

Unfortunately, rather than a unanimous vote supporting my actions, due to the pressure by Bert and Bertha and the intensity of several parents, two board members, including the board president, lost their nerve and voted to support the parents. This was unfortunate, as it gave a mixed message to the larger community. These board members caught the anxiety of the least mature parents at the school. They got trapped in the "peace over progress" mentality commonly perpetuated by leaders. Unfortunately, in an effort to make people feel better, those board members undercut the integrity of the community by their capitulation. Though the majority of the board continued to support my actions, this split decision made it more difficult to maneuver within this emotional environment.

In particular, the board president encouraged us to sit down and work things out. She couldn't get past her individual training and failed to understand the importance of *not* capitulating to irrational demands. In effect, as Friedman would argue, the board president let her empathy get the better of her when she supported the parents. This is, unfortunately, common in organizations and families who believe that communication itself can solve difficult problems.

From a Bowen theory perspective, staying calm, setting limits on others' invasiveness, and being clear about what is and what is not acceptable behavior is more important. Said differently, personal responsibility is more important than communicating or empathy. (In truth, Bert and Bertha had been communicating clearly for months, though that communication was about the poor quality of their relationship and how they decided to deal with that problem.) At the time, I was surprised and disappointed by these overly empathetic board members. In retrospect, though, this is a clear example of how someone in the mental health field can view empathy as more important than responsibility. It is a critical but common error, from a Bowen perspective, that can erode emotional maturity. And, perhaps more importantly, it corrodes institutional and personal integrity and is, therefore, quite regressive.

In *Failure of Nerve*, Friedman discussed this regressive tendency in psychotherapists, counselors, clergy, and leaders in general. He cautioned that while empathy is an important variable in establishing rapport with others, an overreliance on empathy can undercut the promotion of personal responsibility, a characteristic that he saw as more significant in fostering emotional maturity in individuals and organizations. In fact, Friedman distinguished between empathy, feeling *with* another, and compassion, feeling *for* another. He suggests that compassion allows us to understand and acknowledge the pain and struggle of others, while empathy can result in a loss of self with others, since you are feeling with someone. That is, you are feeling what they are feeling. Excessive empathy can be regressive.

After a lengthy investigation, the Department of Civil Rights determined that I was non-compliant with only one aspect of the law: I was required to have an initial meeting, based on the parents' request, and there ask for more data. Instead, what I asked for was a diagnosis *prior* to meeting with the parents to determine 504 status. While I had routinely convened a number of IEP meetings in my role as school director, I had never conducted a 504 meeting before. My error was procedural, involving the sequencing of events, not in rejecting unreasonable accommodations. Also, the State Department of Education supported my decision to withdraw Annie as legally justified and required, as did the board of directors.

Bert and Bertha enrolled their daughter in a different school, and another family withdrew their children because they believed that the modular classrooms were outgassing chemicals. They, too, feared that *their* children were being poisoned as well, despite evidence to the contrary. Anxiety is contagious, and this family absorbed the anxiety generated and amplified within the system by Bert and Bertha.

Curiously, weeks later I received a call from the school nurse where Annie had transferred. She wanted to know what was up with Bert and Bertha, who she believed were being disruptive at their new school. The parents claimed that Annie was experiencing chemical sensitivity at the new school and wanted extraordinary accommodations and modifications. The school was willing to accommodate the parents, she said, since to fight them would take too much time and money. As a larger, traditional school and district, they opted for "peace over progress," and I'm left wondering what became of Annie and her permanent "diagnosis."

While the price was high for me and the school emotionally, we had successfully resisted Bert and Bertha's attempts to flood the school with more anxiety through emotionally triangling the board and me. I had, with assistance from some board members, largely de-triangulated myself from Bert and Bertha's emotional intensity.

At Skyview School, we hold an annual end-of-the-school-year celebration and graduation. We commemorate the students' accomplishments, graduate the 8th grade class, and transition the other students into their new levels. Bert and Bertha attended this year-end celebration since their older son was still a student at the school. After the celebration, I was assisting with taking apart the P.A. system when an angry Bert came up to me. He began ranting about how I had ruined his daughter's life and created such emotional upheaval in their family. (From a Bowen family systems theory perspective, the opposite was actually true: their emotional triangling had created temporary stability in their marriage.) I told Bert that this wasn't the time to have this discussion. He came right up to my face and said, "Suck my dick." I said, "That's great language from a member of the clergy, Bert." He stormed away.

While the intensity within the emotional triangle had been reduced at Skyview, it was not gone. As often happens in the process of de-triangling from an intense emotional environment, those efforts often activate *more* emotional intensity, at least initially, and Bert's out of control behavior illuminated this portion of the theory as well.

As with Cynthia and Peter's tumultuous situation, Bert and Bertha had successfully gotten under my skin. While I could readily see what was happening systemically, I was still affected by their anxiety. In truth, some of my actions generated more anxiety. I'm not immune to the effects of emotional triangulation. Knowing what was going on did not provide emotional protection for me. And, as with the situation with Cynthia and Peter five years earlier, there were days when I had difficulty sleeping and ridding my mind from their effective invasion into my world and my psyche.

Anxiety is transmittable, pernicious, and contagious. The best that can be said about this kind of overwhelming anxiety is that it provides us with multiple opportunities to differentiate. However, these two scenarios demonstrate how emotional triangulation can contaminate a system and undercut the efforts of leaders in moving an organization ahead. They also demonstrate the effectiveness and importance of de-triangling.

The scenarios with both couples were similar in many ways. Both marriages displayed the hallmarks of emotional triangulation. The couples were responsible for generating the conflict and then amplifying the anxiety. In both instances, I was the anxiety binder, which temporarily stabilized the parents' marriages. Interestingly, within several years of each incident, both couples eventually divorced, which supported my initial assessment of these situations.

Ed Friedman said that successful leadership can activate internal sabotage. If a leader is effectively facilitating movement towards a vision shared by most, others may have a different vision. If a leader is requiring respect and responsibility, others may not share these goals. In these ways, Friedman suggested that sabotage can be a marker of leadership success. I have witnessed this firsthand on these and other occasions.

Bowen theory provides clarity about what is going on around us. Understanding the nature of chronic anxiety, how it is bound through triangulation, and the means to de-triangulate from emotional intensity are important lessons and tools for all leaders. Appreciating that reactivity is automatic and knowing how anxiety binding operates helps us, as leaders, to not take it personally and provides opportunities for us to manage our own emotionality with compassion and acceptance. Humans get reactive; most of us are not fully differentiated. Bowen theory even suggests that our degree of reactivity is less important than knowing what is happening and taking responsibility for how we manage it.

The fact is that emotional triangulation, and its harmful effects, challenges all leaders. Understanding emotional triangles and, especially, the importance of de-triangulating, afford leaders and organizations the opportunity to evolve, despite the difficulties involved in achieving these goals.

In these ways, I suppose I should thank these couples for helping me evolve and differentiate.

CHAPTER SIX

CLEANING OUT THE PIPES:
REORIENTING EMOTIONAL SYSTEMS FOR SUCCESS

Each time that I assumed an executive role, I became more successful, but not without substantial and systematic challenges that forced me to critically examine my own role within the emotional field of the organization. My first executive position was as the dean at Prescott College. I was thirty-nine at the time. With my experiences directing programs at U.S.I.U. and at Prescott College, as well as my tenure as a vice president of the faculty senate at U.S.I.U., I believed that I was prepared for the challenges of becoming the dean. In fact, despite the mishaps and challenges, my stint as dean was quite productive. The years from 1995-2000 are often referred to as "the golden years" by the college faculty.

Enrollments soared to our highest level ever. We bought a new van fleet for our field courses, doubled the size of the faculty, tripled the size of our library, developed a performing arts center, added classrooms, improved labs, increased salaries to more sustainable levels, experimented with curricula such as adding a new student seminar and a new program in peace studies. This was, by all measures, a stable and productive time at Prescott College, especially after Charles Marcum was hired as president.

But it took a while to get there and that time was not without controversy. When the faculty was transitioning in deanship from Peter to me, Prescott College had adopted an experimental co-presidency model, with one co-president, Leslie Bennett, managing the internal affairs of the college, and the other co-president, James Houser, responsible for fundraising and other external relations.

The problem was that Leslie was not competent in finances. Her financial advisor, Brian Matheson, had convinced Leslie that a severe cash-flow problem equaled fiscal insolvency that necessitated closing down the college. By the time of my first meeting in President's Council—the senior management team—Allison Skyler, the newly hired Chief Financial Officer (CFO), and I couldn't believe the incompetence of the leadership team. Leslie and Brian were drawing up plans to close the college, and we rejected their analysis. That afternoon, I gathered the students and faculty to disclose their plans. I then assembled an emergency faculty meeting the following Saturday. The faculty, after serious debate and discussion, took the lead in voting no confidence in Leslie's leadership and Brian's fiscal competence. Soon after, the board of trustees convened and removed Leslie from her co-presidency role. James Houser emerged as the sole college president on an interim basis, while the board searched for a permanent replacement.

In 1997, after a national search, Charles Marcum was hired as president. During Charles's tenure as president and mine as dean, we accomplished the goals that I listed above. It was a time of excitement, innovation, and accomplishment.

I championed the addition of peace studies in the curriculum, so that students could develop majors and minors in this area. In order to expand this new curriculum, I developed several Bowen theory-based courses that I later went on to teach, including Community Mediation and Principled Negotiation as well as Models of Leadership: Leadership through Differentiation. Under my guidance and with my insistence, President's Council committed to the "Zero Discharge" initiative, which today at other colleges and universities is more commonly called the carbon neutral or green campus initiative.

Unfortunately, despite the successes at the college, relations between the president and the CFO were often strained and secretive, and more than once I got caught in their power struggles. An example, I became emotionally triangulated when I contradicted the president and CFO publicly at a board meeting. They presented material that refuted financial data that President's Council had discussed the day before. For some strange reason that I still can't fathom today, Charles and Allison decided to withhold information from me and the external dean and present data to the board that was not vetted by us. I publicly challenged Charles and questioned the information given to the board. After the board meeting, Charles told me that he would fire me on the spot if I contradicted him at a board meeting again.

Fortunately, my training and application of differentiated leadership assisted me in thinking clearly about what I was seeing and helped me maneuver in the politically-laden world of higher administration power politics. Voice quaking, in a hastily gathered meeting between the president, CFO, Sean Wendell (the dean of the external, limited resident programs), the board president, and vice president, I told everyone that I would not support information presented to the board in the future that wasn't properly evaluated by President's Council, regardless of the consequences. I would not be bullied by Charles into capitulating to this bizarre fiscal spectacle.

Even now, years later, I'm not quite sure of the motivation behind Charles and Allison's board strategy. After dealing with the repercussions of a flawed national search for a faculty member, I had learned my lesson about transparency, but, apparently, not everyone felt the same way that I did. For many, information is power and how information is used or shared reflects how power is gathered, consolidated, and exercised.

In another instance, the board offered bonuses to all senior administrators. I felt uncomfortable accepting a "secret" bonus when the faculty was struggling with not having a livable wage. I spoke to Sean, the second college dean, about my misgivings. He advised me to accept the bonus and not make waves. I struggled with balancing the need to be a "team player" with the senior administrators and the board of trustees on the one hand and my ethical concerns about fairness and justice on the other. I didn't want to turn down the bonus, which was a direct thank you from the board for a job well done in expanding student enrollments, increasing student retention, and significantly increasing revenue. If I turned down the money, I was told that I would be insulting the board and the president. In the end, I accepted the bonus but gave a significant portion of it back to the college as a charitable donation. I reluctantly made a choice that sometimes peace may be necessary over progress, as long as it doesn't compromise integrity.

Nonetheless, by the time that I went on sabbatical in the spring of 1999, I had accomplished many of the goals that I set out for myself as dean. With the continuing and escalating battles between the president and the CFO, I grew tired of the politics and began thinking about what it would be like to run the show; that is, what would it be like to be the leader of an entire organization. I was itching for a change, but for now, I had decided to enjoy my year-long sabbatical and write.

During my sabbatical the board scheduled a formal presidential review. After completing this review, Charles's contract was not renewed. Allison, sensing that the end might be near for her as well, secured a new job out of state. When the board replaced Charles with a board member without any executive experience, I considered whether to remain or leave as dean. It was at this time that the directorship at Skyview School opened. After meeting with Stu Roberts, the new CEO of the college (the board withheld the title of president from him), I realized that he didn't want me as dean. He refused to negotiate the terms of my returning contract. As the remaining executive in Charles' administration, I sensed that he wanted new people at all senior-level positions. Not finding a receptive audience in Stu and believing that I needed a new challenge, I turned my sights to the director/CEO position at Skyview School.

I wanted to try my hand at the helm of the charter school, so I resigned my dean position, secured an 18-month leave of absence from the college, applied for the director position at Skyview School, and after a national search, I was offered the contract.

During the next twenty-eight months, I applied differentiated leadership to my role as charter school director. I re-established the importance of the mission in operating the school and educating the students. I developed procedures and policies to professionalize Skyview. I authored a document that became an appendix to the charter school contract with the state of Arizona. This document summarized the core principles of the school and how we were going to use those principles in actualizing our vision with students, parents, staff, and community. This defining document, designated Appendix I, became the core of the school's educational and pedagogical philosophy. In writing Appendix I, I was inspired to articulate the uniqueness of the school through our mission.

In his landmark book *Failure of Nerve*, Ed Friedman proposed that all new leaders give an "I Have a Dream" speech to their constituents in order to define for themselves and others the vision for the institution and how the leader plans to implement that vision with the help of the stakeholders. In retrospect, I consider Appendix I my "I Have a Dream" speech.

I was enjoying my work as a CEO. I began moving the school into new territory through academic recognition and grants; increased student enrollments, community outreach and presentations; and improved staff and faculty morale. My understanding of Bowen family systems theory and its application to differentiated leadership effectively guided me throughout. In the previous chapter, I described the significant challenges at that time with Bert and Bertha's family and their supporters. But even with those difficulties, my time as charter school director was deeply fulfilling. At a personal level, I was walking to school every day with my children who attended the school and my wife who was the integrated arts coordinator and creative movement/dance teacher. At a professional level, I was satisfied with the results of the hard work by the entire community of students, parents, board, staff, and faculty.

Near the end of my term, I was faced with a choice of staying on as director or returning to Prescott College as a professor. I always saw my career more in teaching than administrating. So, after twenty-eight months, I left Skyview School and returned to the college. I departed Skyview with a legacy of established policies and procedures, carefully crafted communication guidelines, a vision for future expansion, greater clarity with core curriculum, state recognition for the quality of the school and its programs, and the largest cash reserves in Skyview School's history.

When I reflected on my first two terms as an educational leader, I was pleased with my ability to manage complex issues, develop and implement clear, workable budgets, support faculty and staff in delivering high-quality curriculum to students, and effectively work with stakeholders in advancing the mission of the two institutions. I also reflected on the challenges that I faced, and I tried to understand my role in perpetuating or exacerbating them. From a Bowen theory perspective, was I needlessly generating anxiety when faced with recalcitrant parents? To what degree was I amplifying anxiety in emotional triangles?

Of course, it is always easier to point the finger elsewhere, as there will always be the Peters and Cynthias or the Berts and Berthas in the world to deal with. Nonetheless, from a Bowen family systems theory perspective, it is neither emotionally nor intellectually honest to continually blame others for one's problems. Bowen theory proposes that most blaming is regressive. So, I began asking to what degree was I a part of the problem and not a part of the solution in these highly-charged emotional situations? To what degree were, as Friedman suggests, "the demons of resistance" activated with effective leadership, and how is it that the least emotionally mature members of the organization continue to sabotage the progress being made? These are questions that I pondered and wrestled with for years.

My fiercest critics called me "rigid" and "holier than thou." I tried to examine this criticism to uncover how I could more effectively operate both professionally and personally, and I used Bowen theory as a guide in this process. It is true that I sometimes hold a firm line on a policy or opinion. Sometimes I struggle to differentiate self-definition from inflexibility. And, I do not "suffer fools lightly." I can be curt and dismissive when being verbally harassed or harangued. I will close someone down verbally if he or she is dominating a meeting or speaking disrespectfully to others. I understand how some may find that arrogant or righteous.

On the other hand, I self-reflect on my thoughts, actions, and motivations. I accept responsibility when I'm wrong, and I'm always willing to listen to a respectfully-offered difference of opinion. My training in psychotherapy and mediation assist me to listen deeply, even when being criticized. I don't, though, do well when treated dismissively or when threatened. Firmness and rigidity are different, and I self-reflect and get feedback from those I trust so as to not disrespect others with any rigidity. Even today, my friends, wife, and colleagues versed in Bowen's approach provide insightful feedback to me, and I continue with my commitment to becoming more differentiated and effective in all of my relationship systems.

My next sabbatical was approved for the 2005-2006 school year. During the first half of my yearlong sabbatical, I immersed myself into writing my book, *Applying Family Systems Theory to Mediation: A Practitioner's Guide.* My wife had also left Skyview School to pursue her teaching credential. (Arizona was becoming inflexible in who could teach in publicly-funded charter schools, and Janet, though her degree was in Arts for Children and she had taught for twenty years, lacked teacher certification.) So, at the time, I wasn't much attuned to the workings at Skyview. In November of 2005, I learned from a friend that Skyview was once again struggling. The school had experienced a series of ineffectual directors and was on the verge of fiscal, emotional, and organizational collapse.

As mentioned previously, Julie Stenson had recently been asked to return to the board, and she became board president in order to try to salvage our local educational treasure. In January of 2006, the Skyview School board offered me the position of interim director until July, with the hope that I could bring some fiscal order and discipline to the school and re-energize the staff, faculty, and parents. I was tempted. Though I had my own sabbatical goal of completing my book, I had recently turned fifty, and I thought that I was ready for another turn as an educational leader.

I had come to recognize that sometimes my responses to "crazy" and reactive people were, in truth, too rigid. In my attempts to not let the most immature members of an organization gain inordinate power through their incessant critiques, I sometimes erred by distancing myself from the problem. When pushed too hard, I quickly disengaged from these conflict-saturated people. My attempts at non-attachment sometimes resulted in the very rigidity that made finding common ground so difficult. And, even if common ground was not possible, couldn't I at least keep compassion and kindness front and center? So, I believed that turning fifty presented a new opportunity to stretch my systemic muscles in leading this organization.

I accepted the interim position. This time, as director, I needed to get the school's budget under control to stop the hemorrhaging of money. Skyview School had gone from a school with healthy cash reserves to a school with a cash flow problem and a significant budget deficit. In fact, deficits were projected out for the next several years. Also, the staff and parent community had split into two factions under the most recent director, James. Many parents, staff, and faculty wanted James gone. He still had a smattering of support, though, since he had contracted with Expeditionary Learning Schools (ELS) to improve the quality of the curriculum and the delivery of educational training services.

The problem was that ELS was not quite properly aligned with our multiple intelligences-based mission. Also, Skyview was still designated by the state of Arizona as an "Excelling" school, a classification that, despite poor leadership at the top, hadn't changed because of the quality teachers. Frankly, ELS didn't seem to know how to help us improve, as most of their work nationally went into improving failing schools and assisting start-up schools. We were already a top-tiered school, so we didn't quite fit their models of reform and innovation. We were already reformed and innovative.

In addition, the size of the school's deficit and the exhaustion of its financial reserves were directly tied to the ELS contract. Without this contract, the budget would be close to balanced. If Skyview School had never contracted with ELS, there would have been abundant financial reserves. So, ironically, the very contract meant to "strengthen" the school was actually killing it. As I began settling into the directorship, I realized that if I simply approached the job as a caretaker, the school wouldn't survive. I needed longer than six months in order to affect a turn around. Once again, the college dean granted me a leave of absence, and I remained at Skyview for two years to help the school secure a more sustainable footing.

Despite the hemorrhaging of finances from the ELS contract, extricating Skyview from the ELS school network proved challenging and took over a year to accomplish. Some parents and staff fought me on this and two board members and several families left because of my focus on reactivating and re-focusing on the mission of Skyview School as a multiple intelligences-based institution and not an ELS school. I found it interesting that even when presented with clear evidence for how the ELS contract was bankrupting the school, certain teachers, parents, board members and, of course, the ELS coordinator and his supervisor refused to acknowledge the connection. The thinking was that if Skyview wanted to remain an ELS school, we would find a way to prioritize the funding.

This is a perfect example of emotional logic. It was almost an example of magical thinking: if I ignored the problem it would go away, or the money would somehow mysteriously appear if we wanted that relationship with ELS strongly enough. For me, the majority of the board, the core teachers, and the majority of the parent community, extracting us from the ELS network made sense: Skyview wasn't an ELS school, and the fit wasn't quite right. While I value and respect the ELS organization, it simply wasn't the best match for Skyview. And, even if we had wanted to stay with ELS, there wasn't the money to do so.

My second term as director was largely successful. After almost two years, using differentiated leadership as a model, we once again clarified the mission and vision of the school through educating parents, students, board, and faculty about who we were and the type of education we provided. I carefully culled the bloated staff ranks, which wasn't fun. Terminating contracts, even for those employees that I believed were non-essential to the school's mission and vision, resulted in layoffs and hence hardships for people. But, for the school to survive I did what was needed, as the largest expense in most organizations is for personnel. Unfortunately, these actions alone weren't enough for long-term sustainability.

We faced a budget crisis at Skyview School. Arizona is consistently ranked at or near the bottom of states in per pupil funding for education. Also, Arizona does not finance the purchase or rental of buildings for charter schools the way that it funds district schools for capital expenses. As a result, rent and mortgage money must be taken from the school's general fund. Finally, charter schools cannot raise bonds to pay for school construction, improvements, technology, or renovations. Only district schools have this advantage.

With funding flat, and with increases held to a maximum of two percent a year, we were quickly pushing against some real limits. Health care, utilities, insurance, salaries, and general inflation were all higher than two percent increases per year. Unless we expanded, and quickly, we would be unsustainable in the long run. The simple fact was that we needed more students in order to generate more state income. (As charter schools are public schools, they are free for students and funded by the state.)

To manage this challenge, we embarked on an expansion project to add a second kindergarten and enlarge the primary and intermediate classrooms. Through these actions we projected enrollment to increase from 125 students to 185 students, which it eventually did. Also, we were interested in providing a more sustainable teaching model for faculty. This meant reconfiguring our three-year, multi-age classrooms. Differentiating curriculum for three levels was becoming untenable for teachers.

We divided our two primary classrooms, grades 1-3, into two primary classrooms with first and second grade children. And we reconfigured our two intermediate classrooms, grades 4-6, into two sets of intermediated classrooms. These new intermediate configurations consisted of two early intermediate classrooms of third and fourth grade students and two late intermediate classrooms of fifth and six grade students. Through decreasing the grade and age spread, teachers reduced the scope and size of developing and implementing such a vastly differentiated curriculum. These alterations made teaching at Skyview School more sustainable and fun for the teaching staff.

With these changes in place, we were ready to meet the future re-energized and re-focused. Overall, the faculty and the parents were accepting and enthusiastic. Morale was high in the community; student enrollments were growing. I felt satisfied that my work had more flow, and there were fewer dramatic conflicts. Skyview School was coming out of its emotional regression and fiscal crisis stronger, healthier, and more focused than it had been in years.

As a part of this restructuring, and due to the new educational mandates imposed by President George W. Bush's *"No Child Left Behind"* legislation, I worked with the faculty and curriculum coordinator to significantly modify the kindergarten program. Prior to 2005, Skyview offered a half-day kindergarten program. As kindergarten was not required in Arizona, and as we wanted to encourage kindergarten children to maintain important time with their parents whenever possible, the original charter contract called for a half-day kindergarten program. Times had changed.

With all of the new federal and state educational and academic mandates, kindergarten was being turned into the new first grade, and academic expectations for kindergarten students were increasing as well. In order to satisfy these new academic mandates, and keep the high level of artistic enrichment so central to success in life and at a multiple intelligences school, the teaching staff and I proposed a voluntary full-day kindergarten program to the board of directors.

This process took several months to complete. During this time, two mothers vehemently objected to this proposal and resisted this recommendation. They were quite vocal at the board meetings, with me in my office, and even through the local newspaper condemning this change, even though they could opt for a half-day contract for their children. Honestly, I never understood what their concerns were, given their options.

Once again, I felt myself reacting to the anxiety of parents. In fact, on several occasions, despite my best attempts to reach out and be more "reasonable" with them, conversations degenerated with one mother in particular yelling at me several times. During a particularly difficult board meeting, this mother was over the top, accusing me of manipulating the system and creating an unsafe environment for her child. Somehow, because we were moving towards a *voluntary* full-day kindergarten, these parents thought that their children would suddenly be unsafe.

Needless to say, I was stunned by this turn of events. Despite my best efforts, I once again felt caught in the emotional swirl of others, and I struggled to make systemic sense of it all as the accusations hurled at me. It was then that I began looking for a deeper, more historical and systemic understanding of these attempts at sabotaging my leadership.

I stepped back and began trying to uncover where this emotional blockage was coming from. What immediately came to mind was a particularly unpleasant situation that I found myself in during my first year at Prescott College, thirteen years earlier. While I was originally hired as a fulltime faculty member, the dean, Peter, recognized my administrative history and skills, and after only three months on the job as a new faculty member, he asked me to take over as coordinator for the Human Development-Psychology program from his wife, Cynthia. I was soon a reluctant member of Peter's leadership team at the college.

In a parallel development and also during this time, Peter and then-president Daniel Norris were caught in a political battle for leadership at the college. Peter was convinced that Daniel and his CFO, Angie Mansfield, were mismanaging the college's resources and that the college was headed for a fiscal crisis.

President Norris asked to meet with me. He wanted me to provide some counseling for him. I felt extremely uncomfortable with his request. I could feel the emotional triangling between Peter, Daniel, and me, and I resisted this "dual relationship" as a faculty member in Peter's administration and as counselor to the president. I told Daniel that I couldn't be his counselor, as I considered this a dual relationship. Daniel asked if I could at least meet with him on a regular basis to discuss his struggles, even if it was not "counseling." What could I say? In retrospect, I should have just said "no." But, the president of the college was asking for help, and I was new to the college. I was in a vulnerable position that I shouldn't have been put in. I reluctantly agreed to meet with him on a regular basis. Big mistake!

Things escalated. Within several months, the faculty and staff had divided into pro-Daniel and anti-Daniel factions. During this time, the board of trustees was largely composed of internal staff and faculty.

As such, it wasn't a particularly professional board. During the next board meeting, staff and faculty were allowed to speak about their support for Daniel or their lack of confidence in his leadership. At Peter's urging, the program faculty had already voted no confidence in Daniel.

Taking my cues from the dean, I gave public testimony against Daniel. I'll never forget the pained look on his face as I was speaking. It was a combination of hurt, betrayal, and dismay. I felt like I was committing patricide. It wasn't my proudest moment. While the college president should not have asked me to provide counseling and put me in such a precarious position with my supervisor, nonetheless, I had been severely caught in the emotional triangle represented through Daniel's and Peter's power struggle. This ugly incident eventually resulted in Daniel being ousted from the presidency of the college.

At the time, I remember thinking that I wouldn't speak at any future board meeting about any concerns that I had concerning the college's leadership. What I didn't know at the time, but came to realize later, was that this event emotionally "clogged the pipes" for me with regard to my own leadership. By sabotaging Daniel's leadership, I set myself up for disruption in my future leadership. Call it karma or emotional fields, the result was the same.

In fact, Bowen theory is all about emotional fields. Fields are non-material regions of influence, such as gravity or electromagnetic radiation. An emotional field imprints certain actions or processes for a person, family, or other human system. As one example, multigenerational emotional process demonstrates the power of emotional fields within a family. While we can't see these fields, we can "feel" them. Who hasn't walked into a room with people and said something to the effect that the tension was so high that you could cut it with a knife?

We create emotional fields in our lives, in relationships, and with all people and systems. These fields can generate conflict, hope, confidence, lightness, anxiety, fear, love, and so on. These fields are a part of our cumulative experiences. Through emotional fields, we often attract people to us that replicate the issues we have not resolved. In other words, people and events can "stick" to us if we are not active in differentiating from these emotional concerns. In this way, we cannot escape our "self" or our emotional fields. We can only work to unclog the pipes so that there is a decrease in built up emotional energy, energy that can increase resistance and decrease efficiency in relationships and in life. We are left to either resolve our major hang-ups or "attract" people that will force us to address these issues. We can't run from our emotional fields!

One way to think about these fields is as a kind of "instant karma." In other words, we get what we put out into the universe, and I had put out an irresponsible use of self during a board meeting that led to the CEO of the organization having to deal with a decidedly hostile audience. Sound familiar? This was exactly what I did to Daniel at Prescott College. When I recognized that dynamic, I realized that these emotional field disturbances around my leadership were, in part, residues of unfinished work with Daniel. After he lost his presidency at Prescott College, Daniel became president of another university, where he remained as a successful leader for years until his retirement.

Peter, on the other hand, led a much less successful and less honorable life. After leaving the dean's position at Prescott College, his life took a tragic turn. He was arrested for the murder of his ex-wife, Cynthia. After years of appeals and a very troubling set of circumstances, including the untimely death of a trial judge and Peter's attempts at swaying the jury through planting false evidence through his underage son, five years later he was convicted of murder and sentenced to life in prison without the possibility of parole. For both Daniel and Peter, the true nature of the man revealed itself over the years.

It had been years since I had any contact with Daniel. And, over the years, I had always felt a lack of resolution, as well as guilt over my actions and my betrayal. It wasn't a stretch for me to understand that this distance with Daniel and my unfinished business with him could more accurately be described through Bowen theory as a cut-off. This cut-off, like all cut-offs, left the relationship unresolved. This, in turn, led to a spillover of my emotional field onto others, who then replicated my unprofessional behavior when dealing with me as a leader.

I realized that I needed to confront my past with Daniel. In doing so, I hoped that I could bridge that cut-off and restore my honor and integrity with him. My hope was also that this shift in the emotional field would be replicated in my dealings with difficult parents in board meetings. Whether it did or not, I realized that bridging this cut-off was the right thing to do. I was further inspired to bridge this cut-off when my friend, a fellow Human Development-Psychology professor, told me that he had apologized to Daniel years ago, as he felt that he, too, had acted unprofessionally at that same board meeting.

So, I looked up Daniel's email address and wrote him. I congratulated him on his successful tenure at his university. I formally apologized for the way that I conducted myself at the board meeting that resulted in his departure. I also apologized for contacting him at such a late date but said that he deserved an apology. I wished him well and let him know that he was missed at Prescott College.

Daniel's response was affable and generous. While I want to preserve Daniel's privacy with his response, he gracefully accepted my apology, and we have had additional emails to communicate both our good wishes to each other and thoughts about the future.

I felt fortunate that Daniel was receptive to my apology. Nonetheless, "cleaning out the pipes" emotionally is less about the person's response to you, since no one knows how another will respond, and more about accepting personal responsibility for thinking, feelings, and acting in ways that are less than kind, compassionate, forgiving, mindful, and intentional. In this instance, I was fortunate that Daniel gave me his blessing when he accepted my apology.

The act of taking personal responsibility and bridging the cut-off helps clear the blockage. Cleaning out the pipes means, in essence, that you flush out the blockages that you created through statements of accountability to another. Apologies are particularly powerful avenues for re-connecting, especially if there is something that you need to apologize for. Apologies reflect your understanding and acceptance of your role in a conflict. They allow you to begin bridging the cut-off by re-connecting to an important relationship. Oftentimes, bridging a cut-off, especially in family relationships, necessitates multiple communications over long periods of time to repair relationship damage. For me, my ability to see what needed to be done and Daniel's graceful acceptance of my apology made the process far easier and more effective than most initial efforts at bridging a cut-off.

The results of my systemic intervention were instant and significant. From that time until my leaving the directorship in December of 2007, I never again had to deal with a severely problematic parent, and board meetings ran smoother without conflict or unnecessary anger.

To me, my reparative actions demonstrate the beauty and non-linearity of systems theory. I shifted my focus from viewing others as the problem to better understanding my position *in* the system and how my past actions were still gumming up the pipes of my leadership. Through my actions, I helped to unblock my obstacles to effectively providing Skyview with the resources it needed to flourish. I succeeded in cleaning out the pipes.

Finding the correct intervention for implementing effective systemic change is not always easy. Thinking systemically and applying differentiated leadership to my work at Skyview School enabled me to transcend the divisions I inherited, leave the school with the largest cash reserves in its history, position the school for sustainability with a re-organizational plan that succeeded beyond our original expectations, and take the school to its next level.

After leaving the directorship in December of 2007, I resumed full-time teaching at Prescott College. I returned to Skyview School as a board member in July 2008 and remained on the board as president and secretary until I retired from the board in June 2013. At the time that I left the school, we were enrolling almost 200 students annually, and we were ranked by the state of Arizona as the top school in Yavapai County. I remain deeply pleased with my results in applying differentiated leadership and Bowen theory to this executive work.

SECTION FOUR

———————————

SUPERVISION AND TRAINING FROM A BOWEN FAMILY SYSTEMS THEORY PERSPECTIVE

CHAPTER EIGHT

THE CHALLENGE WITH SUPERVISION: DUAL RELATIONSHIPS, CATEGORIES OF IDENTITY, AND WHAT'S REALLY IMPORTANT IN SUPERVISION

For the past thirty-five years, I have provided a wide range of supervision and training services to a diverse group of professionals. I have offered supervision and training as a nationally certified advanced family mediation practitioner, licensed marriage and family therapist, and licensed psychologist. And, over the decades as a part of my responsibilities as a university and college professor and dean, as well as my work as director of psychology and MFT graduate programs at United States International University (U.S.I.U.), I worked with hundreds of student interns as psychotherapists in training, providing practicum supervision and graduate training opportunities.

In addition, as co-founder and co-owner of Integrative Psychotherapy Services, my professional partner Sally LeBoy and I provided supervision and consultation services to a number of social service agencies in San Diego County, including many of the Marine and Navy Family Service Centers. We offered training and supervision to the mental health counselors and professionals staffing these centers. Lastly, for years, I trained and supervised interns and therapists-in-training who were applying for their licenses as California Marriage and Family Therapists.

All in all, I have been active in applying Bowen theory to supervision. I approach supervision with an eye to assisting the therapist, professional, or intern to self-reflect and increase emotional maturity. In that way, my goals for supervision are aligned with my goals for psychotherapy, and my approach to supervision overlaps with my approach to therapy.

Traditionally, the roles of therapist and supervisor have been distinct. Personal therapy assists counselors in becoming better people; supervision assists counselors in becoming better therapists. The thinking has been that crossing roles results in dual and multiple relationships, and these kinds of relationships must be avoided whenever possible.

Others have written about Bowen-based and systemically-based approaches to supervision. Most of these authors try to inculcate systemic thinking in assessing and treating couples and families. Few have gone as far as Ed Friedman in their approaches. Friedman highlighted the importance of aligned goals between supervision and therapy, that being increasing differentiation. In 1991, Friedman discussed his approach to supervision when interviewed by the American Association for Marriage and Family Therapy (AAMFT)'s *Supervision Bulletin*. Friedman stated that, from a Bowen theory perspective, the distinction between therapy and supervision is artificial. He said that this division perpetuates non-systemic ways of thinking since the therapist's level of emotional maturity is a critical, if not the most relevant, variable in therapy outcome.

Promoting and encouraging increased basic differentiation will positively affect a person's personal and professional life. It matters little, then, how one gets there. So, for Friedman, distinctions between personal therapy and supervision can block potential avenues for maturing. Many found his perspective unacceptable and even dangerous. (Friedman loved his role as provocateur, and he played it well throughout his professional life.) I believe that Friedman was correct in his understanding of the overlap in goals and even methods between supervision and therapy.

So, what information is important in supervision and therapy? Detailing what is crucial for assessment and diagnosis is affected by one's theoretical perspective, which, in turn, is a product of what is prominent in the culture and in the profession at the time. Today, for example, categories of identity, issues of social justice, and recognition of systemic oppression are all considered critical. Over that last thirty years, these societal factors have grown in importance for therapists and their professional organizations. What role do these factors play in Bowen-based therapy and supervision?

In a second interview with the AAMFT *Supervision Bulletin* in 1994, Friedman critiqued the recently-implemented AAMFT supervision rubric, which required inclusion of categories of identity when supervising others and within the Advanced Supervision designation application process itself. Friedman believed that the profession was focusing on the wrong information. As with his critique of the artificial distinction between therapy and supervision, this critique was similarly rejected by many in the profession, including Monica McGoldrick, the illustrious writer and feminist family therapist. McGoldrick attacked his position as unethical, short-sighted, misinformed, and even dangerous.

In recent times, the marriage and family therapy profession, like most disciplines in the social sciences, has been trying to integrate historical and contemporary issues of social justice and oppression. This inclusion of categories of identity was one such attempt to do so. According to McGoldrick (and others), it is critical for psychotherapists to understand how categories of identity and historical oppression have operated within society. These cultural overlays, she suggests, must move to the center of the figure-ground (proximate-distance) relationship for family therapists, rather than remaining in the ground position, i.e., as a background force. From her perspective, failure to do so promotes and enables power imbalances, historical inaccuracies, and the very systems of oppression that have created and perpetuated some of the most intractable problems in society, including poverty, inequality, injustice, and, in general, white hegemony.

Over the years, I have struggled with these issues of identity and justice, and their relevance to my own role as a family therapist, clinical supervisor, and trainer oriented to a Bowen theory perspective. It is true that portions of our society have been systemically oppressed for decades, if not centuries. Many live in closed-systems of oppression and neglect, largely forgotten by the dominant culture. It seems evident that these individuals, families, and institutions carry a heavy burden of oppression and injustice throughout their lives. The generations-deep chronic anxiety accumulated in these families includes both multigenerational emotional process and societal emotional process.

It also seems obvious that self-differentiating within these suffocating systems is difficult for all and impossible for some. So, it makes systemic sense to understand these larger cultural variables and try to include treatments that extend past one hour a week in a therapist's office. Bowen theory, itself, provides the opportunity to understand the impact of these larger systems through the concept of societal emotional process. Through the decades—as my supervisory and training roles extended beyond the therapeutic world into mediation, conciliation, and teaching—these cultural concerns, and how to address them, have remained relevant and pressing for me. Bowen theory supervision, if conducted properly and according to the theory, challenges some of our basic assumptions about the nature of therapy, supervision, and dual relationships.

Bowen Theory and Supervision

While I focus on the role of the Bowen theorist as supervisor and trainer within the mental health field, the same factors and critiques are also relevant in other supervisory situations that I have been involved with, including my roles as supervisor and trainer in mediations, conciliations, and even teaching. As such, the same points that I outline regarding supervising and training for psychotherapists and family therapists are relevant with supervising and training in other human services disciplines.

The core challenge is always the same: assisting supervisees to conduct more effective therapy. Most supervisory systems use a similar format in case presentations and supervision. I have documented these approaches in a previous publication by the California Association for Marriage and Family Therapists. The counselor, intern, or trainee presents her case. This presentation may be oral, written, or both, and may include audio or visual components. (Today, clinical supervision more commonly involves use of one-way mirrors and/or visual and audio presentations of cases.) The supervisor helps the counselor, intern, or trainee with assessment, diagnosis, prognosis, treatment planning, and treatment procedures. In addition, legal and ethical issues are routinely discussed as necessary and appropriate. The key point, however, is that the supervisor and supervisee alike usually focus on the individual, group members, couple, or family in treatment; how best to manage "resistance"; and the most effective ways to promote client or client system progress. In this way, the nature of the supervision is client (system)-centered and client (system)-focused.

Some supervisory systems and supervisors, especially those with a more psychodynamic orientation, may include a section in the supervision presentation and discussion that addresses "counter-transference," that is, the degree to which a client, couple, or family activates personal issues for the supervisee. This is especially so if those activations are getting in the way of therapy progress. Psychodynamic theorists refer to this as "inhibitory-negative counter-transference." To the extent that this focus on counter-transference occurs, though, most supervisors tread what they see as a fine line. They may be willing to address such important concerns but they are careful not to delve too extensively into the personal lives and interpersonal systems of their supervisees. After all, too much uncovering of personal process runs the risk of mixing therapy with supervision.

This co-mingling of roles is considered unethical as it promotes dual or even multiple relationships between the supervisee and the supervisor. It is more common for the supervisor to recommend personal therapy for the supervisee, if needed, than to fully explore those personal touchstones that create therapeutic blocks. As a result, while some supervisors understand the importance of the self in the therapeutic system, even those that do are reluctant to fully engage with the supervisee in this realm lest they transgress the rather rigid ethical boundary lines between providing supervision and providing therapy.

As Friedman reminds us, a supervisor from a Bowen family systems theory perspective questions the very assumptions of traditional supervision itself. While a Bowen theorist supervisor may provide many of the common structures of more conventional supervision–assessment, (systemic) diagnosis, prognosis, treatment planning, and treatment procedures–the very nature of the client-therapist relationship, as well as the supervisor-supervisee relationship, is seen as part and parcel of treatment effectiveness itself.

For example, when I'm providing supervision services and the supervisee is experiencing challenges or impasses in therapy, one of the first questions that I ask myself and, hence, one of the first areas of focus becomes to what degree is the supervisee contributing to the lack of progress in counseling? In this way, as supervisor, I immediately highlight the central importance of the therapist as a critical component of the client's therapeutic system.

It is helpful to think about the client-counselor relationship as a reciprocal relationship. (This reciprocity is the same whether the client is one person, a group, a couple, or an entire family.) From a Bowen theory perspective, a two-person relationship is naturally reciprocal. As such, both parties are making continuous, automatic adjustments to each other based on developing patterns of mature functioning, over-functioning, and/or under-functioning. In this way, resistance in psychotherapy, and consequently challenges to successful treatment, cannot be examined with a unilateral focus on the client or the client system. *That singular focus on "other" is akin to blaming and externalizing the problem to only one part of the system–the client or client system.* This "other focus" actually replicates the problem that most clients have in managing their lives and the lives of significant others in their world: too much blaming and not enough acceptance of personal responsibility and accountability.

In other words, from a Bowen family systems theory perspective, the client-counselor relationship becomes a centerpiece of supervision and examining this relationship, too, as a reciprocal relationship becomes an essential component of successful supervision. Thinking systemically requires that the client-counselor system not be separated out and reduced to one portion of the system–the resistance of the client. While it may be important to examine such traditional variables such as client motivation, timeliness, resources, and other relevant components of supervision, the very act of separating individual components of the therapeutic system and focusing on only one part is analogous to treating a couple or family by scapegoating one person, such as a child or a spouse, for the problems in the relationship. To paraphrase the words of Harriet Lerner, a well-regarded feminist Bowen therapist, in supervision, as in all important relationships, it takes two to dance.

As a reorientation to the supervision system itself, here are examples of the kinds of questions I might address with my supervisees:

- To what degree are you over-functioning in the relationship? Is your commitment to the therapy greater than that of the client/clients? In other words, are you trying harder than they are, or do you care more about their progress than they do?

- To what degree are you under-functioning in the relationship? Are you bored with or by the client/clients? Do you feel stuck? Are you angry or resentful? To what degree are you frustrated by their lack of progress or lack of motivation? Have you emotionally or professionally "backed away" from your commitment to the encounter and the process? Do you dread seeing the client/clients on the day of the appointment?

- What is coming up for you with this client/clients and situation? To what degree are their issues activating emotional reactivity with you? What are the roots of this emotional reactivity? What do you need to do in order to fully engage, while at the same time remaining as non-attached as possible to the outcome of the therapy? What in your current relationship world or family of origin activates this reactivity with your client/clients?

As may be obvious from the above questions, one of the singular differences between more conventional supervision models and supervision by a Bowen theorist is the Bowenian belief that the influence of the therapist—who is also the supervisee—on therapy outcome is paramount. The therapist's "power of presence" or emotional maturity level has a significant if not overriding effect on the process of therapy, as well as the outcomes themselves.

As a result, Bowen theory-based supervision focuses on assisting the supervisee to reduce emotional reactivity, promote responsible engagement with the client/clients, address tendencies to either over-function or under-function, and trace the nuclear family and/or multigenerational roots of the therapist's emotional blocks and distortions. (Again, all of these issues and questions are the same, regardless if the supervision is, for example, for clinical interns or mediators in training.)

This Bowen-based approach is contrasted with more customary models of supervision, especially in counseling and psychotherapy, since it has the potential, according to these models, to cross over from a supervisory relationship to a therapeutic relationship. Doing so potentially creates and perpetuates dual and multiple relationships. As professional codes of ethics in counseling and psychotherapy state, dual and multiple relationships can be an anathema to best practices and, just as important, a violation of these professional codes. These ethical codes advocate for avoiding dual and multiple relationships whenever possible.

To summarize: The therapist's influence on therapy progress and outcome is paramount. As such, a Bowen theory supervisor may intervene at any level of the supervisor's life in order to help reduce resistance, remove impasses, promote emotional maturity, and assist with therapy progress. In contrast, traditional approaches to supervision focus on the supervisee's client or clients. Conventional interventions come from clearly established goals aimed at eliminating or minimizing symptoms. Treatments, especially those deemed "evidence-based" can be prescriptive. If the therapy is not working, then it's often because the method is not being properly employed. Supervision is designed to help treatment procedures get back on track.

The Bowen-based approach understands that the supervisee is a part of the therapeutic system. As a consequence, a natural focus of supervision on the supervisee highlights the paradigmatic shift that Bowen-based supervision offers, as well as the limitations of the dominant paradigms in psychology and counseling. You cannot separate the therapist and the client or client system. This limits supervisory effectiveness and seems like a "two-dimensional" approach. Most therapeutic, supervisory, and theoretical models in psychology/counseling operate this way. Bowen theory's incorporation of the therapist in the larger client-counselor system is more comprehensive, a "three-dimensional" approach.

A systemic understanding of human relationships–especially the nature of hierarchy and the power of influence in any leadership system, including psychotherapy and family therapy–necessitates an approach to supervision based on personal responsibility and accountability. It requires a conscientious focus on the self of the practitioner within the client-counselor system, rather than what is often an "other-focused" approach more common to conventional supervisory systems.

In fact, an approach to supervision that is exclusively other-focused is akin to regressive systems that seek to assign blame rather than promote responsibility and accountability for everyone in the system. It is, therefore, reasonable to conclude that a restricted focus on the client or client system– resistance, psychopathology, lack of motivation, passive-aggressive tendencies, blaming a spouse or a child for the problems in the system, and other indications of non-compliance with the professional "program"–may not only contribute to the lack of progress in the interactional system but may, rather, aid in further regressing the client or the client system. That is, it can make things worse. Consequently, it seems essential to address the reciprocal relationship of the professional system, including and perhaps even predominantly focusing on what the counselor is doing or not doing to contribute to any impasse or resistance.

At this time, I anticipate that many psychotherapists and supervisors who are reading this are saying to themselves, "Yes, that may sound all well and good, but how do you address the *real ethical problem* of avoiding dual relationships, since the supervisor becomes both supervisor and therapist in your system of supervision?" In fact, the very definition of psychotherapy in a Bowen family systems theory approach mitigates against this dual relationship problem.

I am guided here by Bowen's seminal 1970 presentation and article called "From Couch to Coach." In it, Bowen offers a metaphor about how different his approach is to traditional psychoanalysis. In conventional psychoanalysis, the patient lies down on the couch and free associates to a rather-removed psychoanalyst, who jots down notes and offers an occasional comment or interpretation. Even in more contemporary approaches to psychotherapy, where the couch is replaced by the chair, the central component of effective treatment includes the therapist and client developing a trusting relationship so that the client will eventually feel safe enough to explore crucial issues and challenges. Bowen suggested that, though there is value in this arrangement, the central characteristic of the Bowen theorist is one of *coach* and not therapist. The analogy is apt.

With sports, the coach helps to bring out the best in the players, but the coach does not go on the field or floor during the game and, certainly, the coach does not play in the game itself. (The rare exception is the player-coach.) In a Bowenian approach to counseling and psychotherapy, the Bowen theorist likewise helps to bring out the best in the "players" but is not actively involved in the clients' lives. This means that the coach is not so caught up in the life of the players that she undercuts their successfully playing their own "game" in life.

If the coach metaphor is accurate, and I believe that it is, then, as Friedman has correctly noted, there is no dual relationship at all, since the Bowen coach is working the same, whether the client is a patient or supervisee. A coach is not a therapist. A coach is not a clinical supervisor. A coach is a coach. The difference is more than semantics: it is foundational to all Bowen theory work. It extends not only to the thinking of the therapist, but to the core assumptions of the therapeutic relationship itself and the pragmatic process of therapy.

Further, a Bowen theory approach to therapy or supervision, along with most therapeutic approaches, recognizes that developing basic rapport is essential to creating an effective, collaborative relationship in therapy. Strong rapport is a necessary but not sufficient condition for change. That rapport is commonly developed through empathy. Most approaches and training programs highlight the importance of both basic and advanced empathy in developing rapport and in demonstrating effective technique in psychotherapy. For a Bowen theory-trained coach, developing a therapeutic relationship and building rapport is best accomplished with compassion instead of empathy.

Compassion creates understanding *with* and connection *to* the client. The therapist's compassion is demonstrated by a respectful and full presence with the client as the client explores her suffering. Compassion allows for two (or more) people to understand, witness, and affirm the pain of another. Empathy is more about feeling what the client feels. In this way, empathy, especially at high levels, can weaken individuality. It can seep into the therapist with lasting negative effects for both the therapist and the therapeutic system. Clients may come to overly rely on therapists with limited capacity to separate self from client. Also, the client of an overly empathic therapist may rely on the therapist to do her emoting for her. This is a recipe for therapist burnout.

Indeed, too much empathy may be one of the most problematic aspects of supervisees in their clinical work. Honest supervisees recognize that they are too bound up with their clients and their clients' systems when they are overly involved. Getting caught in the system might result in behavioral and emotional over-functioning or under-functioning. This, in turn, highlights an important area of focus in supervision. Beyond a commitment to rapport building, excess empathy is often a significant obstacle, *imposed by the supervisee,* to systemic change. An over-focus on empathy can promote a lack of willingness to accept personal responsibility or accountability by the client or client system.

Friedman goes so far as to suggest that excess empathy may be psychotherapists' greatest limitation. He makes a compelling case for differentiating compassion from empathy, and this distinction is central in differentiating a more conventional psychotherapist from a Bowen theory coach.

Empathy, Friedman says, is a relatively modern word that doesn't even appear in the 1931 Oxford English Dictionary because it was considered "too rarified, too new, or too technical" for inclusion. The use of empathy didn't become prevalent until after World War II. The word empathy means "to feel in." In this sense, empathy is the ability to feel what the other is feeling, to feel for another. That is, it is the ability to put yourself in another's shoes and walk around in them for a while.

Mirror neurons may even activate empathy in others. Do you remember wincing when someone smashed a thumb in a car door? This is empathy activated by mirror neurons. Empathy, then, is a *shared experience* in which someone's feelings are experienced by another. While there may be some benefit to experiencing the pain of another as if it were your own, from a Bowen theory perspective, empathy, especially at high levels, can undercut the self and, in doing so, destabilize the therapeutic process. Too much empathy can weaken the solid core needed for effective intervention and challenge. It blurs the boundaries between self and other. Therapy burn out is also a common outcome.

In effect, by excessively "feeling for" another, the therapist risks losing objectivity with the client or client system. This loss of objectivity is a kind of fusion. Fusion means loss of self-integrity. Loss of integrity is regressive not only for the therapist but for the therapeutic system as well. Since the quality of the therapist's emotional presence is a critical variable for effective treatment, if the therapist loses herself in the suffering of others, her power of presence and, as a consequence, the treatment itself is compromised.

According to Friedman, the term compassion, by comparison, can be traced back to 1340. Its origin means "to suffer with" or "to feel with" but not "to feel for." This is an important distinction, and one lost on most mental health professionals, teachers, parents, mediators, and others in human services. *Compassion preserves and promotes a durable self and connects the self with other*. Preserving and promoting the self, while also connecting the self with another, are differentiating experiences. In contrast, excess empathy, because of its focus on *feeling for another* can actually promote chronic anxiety and emotional fusion.

To go one step further, I have observed that ineffective therapists, parents, mediators, teachers, and other human services professionals often "suffer" from their excessive "suffering for" another. In other words, a common element in ineffectual interventions by human service professionals may well be this very confusion of empathy with compassion. Over-empathizing can contribute to professional burnout, since the distinction between self and other gets blurred.

The suffering of clients is real, and traumas are brutal. The therapist must connect with that suffering but not absorb the pain. Compassionate caring helps to thread that needle. Excessive empathy undermines effective interventions. If you do not stand *beside* your client/client family, and instead stand *in* your client's/clients' emotional shoes, you will not have that critical distance necessary for effective intervention.

I call this optimal distance "passionate non-attachment." You must be fully involved with your relationships without being attached to the outcome or your own expectations about what the other person should or must do. These "shoulds" and "musts" have all of the hallmarks of a will conflict, which is one of those universal quagmires that all people get stuck in. Will conflicts are universal ways that many people interact, and they are especially common in troubled relationships. Mother tries to force her son to come home by curfew; husband tries to get wife to drink less when company is over. Teacher tries to compel students to complete their homework. People push back. Most people don't respond well when told what to do. These push backs create conflicts of will between people and within relationships. Will conflicts, by definition, undercut both the person "willing" change, since the focus is on other and not the self, and those being "willed" to change, since it engenders intensity or capitulation.

In therapy and supervision, too much empathy promotes excessive will conflicts. There is too much investment in outcomes. This can result in over-functioning behaviors rightly resisted by the other, who, in reciprocal response, will often under-function as a result. The act of being more committed to change than the client/client system forms the backbone of resistance problems reported by supervisees.

Excessive empathy can also result in a shared hopelessness or helplessness between the supervisee and the client or client system. This, in turn, can promote under-functioning, an under-involvement by the supervisee. Both therapeutic over-functioning and under-functioning, then, is often the result of too much investment, i.e., excessive empathy by the supervisee.

If this systemic assessment is accurate, then a supervisor cannot ignore the effect of the supervisee's level of involvement and excessive empathy with the client or client family and its potential roots in the supervisee's nuclear family, multigenerational family, or current relationship systems. It seems to me that to *not* focus supervision interventions on the supervisee is, itself, unethical since the goals of supervision are to promote therapist effectiveness in improving therapeutic outcome. Ignoring the role of the therapist in the system can limit the client in meeting her therapeutic goals.

As a result, Bowen-based supervision may involve work in the supervisee's nuclear family, multigenerational family, and/or current relationships and work environments, the triumvirate of emotional touchstones. Exploring any and all of these three areas become grist for the supervision mill as well. Attempts at differentiating the supervisee can have the effect of reducing excessive empathy and promoting compassion. Compassion and rapport allow the therapist to calmly sit with the client's pain and trauma, without absorbing it or needing to reactively do something about it.

As a supervision coach, then, I am free to explore how a blockage in one part of the therapist's personal system—family of origin, current relationships, and/or work system—can contribute to a block in the therapeutic system itself. The focus of the work is less on the client and the client system, though supervision can focus there when needed. It is also less feeling-based, as it might be in traditional therapy and supervision.

A feelings-based approach explores and uncovers complex sensations existing in a person: anger, confusion, resentment, love, joy, etc. From a Bowen-theory perspective, feelings are surface manifestations of "deeper" emotional states. The work in a Bowen theory and supervision approach, in contrast, is more about emotional exploration and differentiation, meaning investigating the roots of reactivity, managing intensity, and strengthening resiliency and adaptability. This approach is particularly helpful in supervision when the therapeutic relationship activates emotionality in the therapist.

It is this therapist intensity that becomes an important focus in supervision. The supervision helps the therapist develop the cognitive capacity to "go to the balcony," meaning, to get some distance from what's going on and to see one's self and one's position in the system in question. With practice over time, the supervisee, like all of us, can learn to experience less anxiety and therefore move more freely within all of these systems, hence unfreezing the therapy. This kind of exploration in supervision by the supervisee may have therapeutic value, though it is decidedly not therapy. The goal for the supervisee, increasing basic differentiation, will have a positive "spread of effect" on the therapy and the clients.

For example, I worked with a supervisee, Delia, who was struggling with a mother in a family she was treating. The mother was a classic "enabler," meaning that she defended the husband's alcoholism and made excuses for his under-functioning as a husband, father, and co-provider in the family. The oldest daughter, age sixteen, had previously run away from the family. Treatment was currently focused on the dynamics of the family that created the environment in which the daughter fled. The daughter's acting-out developed and existed within the context of a family that was failing in its role of developing the resources needed to promote separation and individuation, i.e., the independent and mature functioning of the family members.

The father's immaturity expressed itself through his alcoholism and resulting under-functioning. The mother's immaturity revealed itself through her over-functioning relative to the father's under-functioning and her hyper-focus on the daughter's rebellion and lack of gratitude as a family member. And the daughter's immaturity manifested itself through her fleeing the family, which she described as "delusional." (In fact, the daughter was the family member most capable of seeing the family clearly, as she observed the distortions and denials in her mother and father's marital relationship and the family itself. This was ironic since, as a sixteen-year-old, she is justifiably immature.)

Delia was stuck in treating the family. Previously, she had been making progress in her systematic assessment of the family: detailing the family's structure, roles, rules, themes, and emotional patterns through the nuclear family; discussing the central emotional triangle that existed between the mother–father–daughter; and delineating important multigenerational legacies regarding alcohol and the role of oldest, responsible daughters on both sides of the family. Delia was even able to reframe the daughter's running away, relative to this "oldest, responsible daughters" mutigenerational legacy, as the daughter's willingness to sacrifice her "self" in order to get the family the treatment that it needed. Regardless, what started out promising had now floundered. The family was stuck in scapegoating the daughter and failing to accept responsibility for its members.

In exploring the nature of that impasse, I had Delia pull out her genogram, which all Bowen therapists have developed for themselves. In exploring her genogram, it became obvious that Delia had over-identified with the daughter. As an oldest daughter from an alcoholic family herself (it was her mother who was alcoholic and her father who was the over-functioning enabler), Delia had emotionally sided with the daughter against the parents. She had gotten triangulated into the family system, and it was this triangling that led to Delia's decreasing effectiveness as their family therapist.

As the daughter's advocate and surrogate, Delia's frustration with the fused and closed nature of the marital relationship reflected her excessive empathy with the daughter. This family had replicated some of the important emotional events in Delia's family of origin, and she reacted by reproducing the reactions of the daughter in the family. In effect, with too much empathy there was too much identification and too much emotional fusion. Delia had lost her objectivity within the system and was now a part of a complicated emotional triangle with the daughter and Delia occupying the same outside position of the triangle and the mother/wife and father/husband occupying the inside positions of the emotional triangle. In her triangulated position, Delia's reactivity amplified the anxiety in the family in response to the parents' anxiety generation.

Father—Mother—Daughter Emotional Triangle

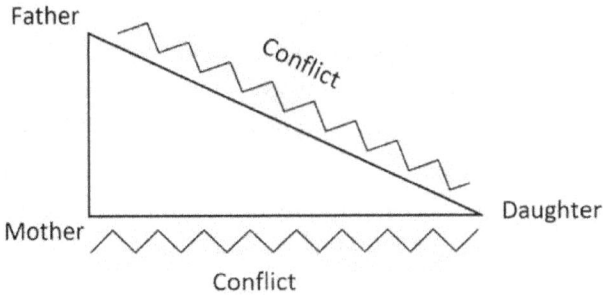

becomes

Father—Mother—Daughter/
Therapist Complicated Emotional Triangle

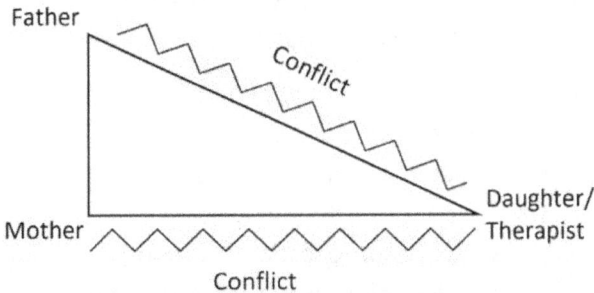

As we explored how the therapy family's patterning imitated the emotional patterning in Delia's original family, Delia became more aware of the automatic and reflexive posturing that she had assumed. Delia realized that she needed to continue and even accelerate her work on separating from *her* original family as a way of de-triangling from her client family. Without going into too much detail, Delia developed a fairly detailed plan for re-engaging with her parents through greater lucidity about her own functioning as an adult within that family system. She further clarified her role in her original family, defining personal expectations for what it meant to be an adult daughter with her parents. Delia also reconnected with her younger sister who had distanced herself from the family in reaction to the parents' emotional immaturity.

Eventually, Delia was better able to dial back her excessive empathy for the daughter and provide greater clarity and compassion for the entire family and their predicament. This, in turn, reduced her blaming her own parents for their alcoholic lifestyle. As Delia worked to strengthen her maturing self, she was better able to work with the treatment family with greater clarity, confidence, and personal responsibility for her role in the therapeutic system. As a result of her de-triangulating efforts, Delia learned to more effectively promote her own differentiation by reducing her empathy and increasing her compassion.

In summary, Delia became more successful in helping her treatment family differentiate their family system as she became more focused on differentiating from her own family of origin. As mentioned previously, while this work with Delia was certainly therapeutic for her, it was not therapy in the classic psychotherapeutic sense of the term. It was, rather, an example of coaching based on a supervision model using Bowen theory as its basis.

Delia's personal work with her family of origin was an on-going process of separating and individuating. What became obvious—to her, to me, and to others in the supervision group—was Delia's interconnectivity between her efforts to more effectively engage as a family therapist and her willingness to assume greater personal responsibility for herself, her family relationships, and her life in general.

From a Bowen theory perspective, then, this kind of supervision is more comprehensive, inclusive, and relevant. That is, it is a multisystem assessment focused more fully on the role and function of the therapist's "self" in multiple, overlapping, and emotionally congruent systems. And, Delia's work on differentiating promotes her in becoming more effective as a therapist and more effective as a person. This, in turn, promotes differentiation in her family of origin and family of procreation. The results of her work were widely systemic.

While I understand and appreciate the importance of ethical codes to promote best practices by minimizing dual and multiple relationships in order to protect the public and the profession, this kind of coaching approach to supervision, based on Bowen theory, is a departure from more traditional models with its focus on the therapist herself as a significant variable in promoting change within a therapeutic system. Through the lens of Bowen theory, the supervisor and therapist each become coaches in a change process. The emotional atmosphere or emotional field of the therapist significantly influences the therapy. Therefore, the therapist's differentiation cannot be separated from the processes and outcomes of the therapeutic environment with the clients.

In fact, a significant change in emotional functioning within any relationship system will have a direct and powerful effect on the emotional functioning of other relationship systems. That is why promoting differentiation in one system will encourage differentiation in other relationship systems, including that of the therapeutic encounter. And conversely, that is why if therapy is at an impasse, it is important for the supervisor to begin a multi-systemic assessment of the supervisee's role in that impasse. A supervisor cannot and should not "turn off" her systems lens when conducting systemic supervision.

To take this thinking one step further, an understanding of systemic processes must occur at the level of the supervisor-supervisee relationship as well. If "stuck," it is the role and function of the supervisor to examine *her* role in the supervisor-supervisee system that may be blocking progress in the relationship and for the supervisee's therapeutic work. The same variables in reciprocal relationships—mature functioning, over-functioning, and under-functioning—exist in the supervisor-supervisee relationship as well.

This final variable in the supervision system, then, is equally important. If the supervisor gets ensnared in the same trap as the supervisee—blaming the supervisee for any impasses in the supervisory system—then the supervisor replicates the problems in the therapy by putting all of the responsibility, and even blame, on the supervisee. This type of "meta-supervision" requires that the supervisor be aware, then, of the three levels in the therapeutic-supervision system: that of the client system itself, the therapist-client system, and the supervisor-supervisee system.

To recap, first, all supervision, including supervision from a Bowen theory coaching framework, is concerned with assisting the client or client system to become more effective in life. This includes symptom reduction or elimination, greater adaptability by its members, and promoting multi-systemic resources to enhance the client system in interacting in the world. Bowen-based supervision adds the primary goal of increasing basic differentiation of the system. A quality supervisor or coach is always looking for pieces of the supervision puzzle in trying to understand the dynamics of the individual, couple, group, or family. True resistance is common. Symptoms can become overwhelming; systems are often calcified into rigid, non-adaptive interactional sequences. Long-standing patterns of poor functioning can be generations deep. Assisting clients in their efforts toward greater emotional maturity takes many forms and requires a determined effort over time.

Second, supervisors recognize that effective counseling requires effective counselors. While theoretical systems can be radically different, most graduate schools and training programs accept their responsibilities for monitoring their students and interns and weeding out those not capable of becoming more emotionally mature, effective therapists. Some supervisors understand and recognize that personal issues can affect professional competence in psychotherapy and systems therapy. Many colleges and university training programs require students to attend their own personal therapy in order to understand what it is like to be a client in counseling and to strengthen the student's self-capacity so that she becomes a more aware, mature, and effective therapist.

Other theoretical models view psychotherapy as a set of skills to master and implement. In fact, many of those promoting "evidence-based treatments" rely on the assumption that treatment techniques and treatment procedures can and should be standardized so that specific treatments are tied to specific diagnoses. In these training systems, the current and multigenerational histories of the therapist are either not relevant or only minimally so. It is here that a Bowen theory coaching model breaks from more conventional models of supervision, arguing that the power of presence of the therapist is infinitely more important than mere techniques and methods.

Third, Bowen theory coaching and supervision also provides a rather unique understanding of the role and function of the supervisor in the supervisor-supervisee system. How many supervisors, in working with an intern or supervisee who is stuck, assess the supervisee's "stuckness" by looking at *their* role, as supervisors, in the supervisor-supervisee system? It is remarkably easier to displace the blame for the supervisee's impasse on the supervisee, or even the supervisee's client or client system, rather than to examine what it is that they, as supervisors, bring to the relationship. As such, supervisors need their own peer supervision and support groups in order to see more clearly and reduce emotional reactivity in their work as supervisors.

I have found that a peer group of Bowen theory supervisors is an excellent way for supervisors to get the supervision that they need and to examine their personal reactions and limitations that may be negatively affecting their supervisees and, consequently, the supervisees' therapy. If we, as supervisors, do not accept *our* personal responsibility for examining our role in any supervision impasse, then we replicate the problems in the client or client system, as well as the supervisee-client/client system, which often results in faulting others or life's circumstances, rather than accepting personal accountability for our role in the relationship.

By thoughtfully reviewing the reciprocal relationship between the self and the supervisee, we can provide more effective supervision. Otherwise, that replicated fault-finding pattern will continue to exist on many levels, with each reinforcing the other and undercutting the differentiation of the systems in question. Blaming can take the form of the client blaming others, the supervisee blaming the resistant client, and even the supervisor blaming the supervisee.

Such automatic reactions undermine thinking that promotes self-management, self-containment, self-responsibility, and appropriate engagement with others. Supervisors are the leaders in these therapeutic systems. The power of *their* presence, including their willingness to "see systems" at all three of these levels, is critical for promoting their effectiveness as supervisors.

Categories of Identity, Social Justice, and Supervision

The second, important variable regarding a Bowen-based approach to supervision is the figure-ground relationship in supervision between categories of identity and social justice, and therefore such issues of identity, oppression, hegemony, victimization, and, ultimately, responsibility. From the conventional systems perspective promoted by AAMFT, these categories of identity and cultural concerns are considered "figure." That is, they are essential to understanding clients and client systems, and are thus central components in assessment and treatment as well. In fact, much of the field has moved in this direction in the last thirty years.

In trying to understand the nature of systems large and small and their impact on one another, I continue to reflect on what information is noteworthy for systemic assessment, diagnosis, and treatment. While it is important to recognize that systems are nested in larger and smaller systems, Bowen theory provides the essential information needed in working with families, while recognizing the importance of larger systems in family therapy and supervision.

Friedman critiqued AAMFT and the field in general for embracing social justice and categories of identity over theoretical perspectives rooted in family systems theory. His central critique, first articulated in 1994, remains provocative and insightful today. Friedman said that requiring a therapist to provide a supervisory analysis that seeks a primary place for categories of identity and social justice, a figure placement as it were, seeks to impose a kind of political or cultural rigidity on the field. This approach may even undermine the free thinking and free exploring required for innovation and experimentation as it makes an a priori assumption about what is important.

Friedman believed that this approach imposed a theoretical inflexibility that runs counter to the entire history of experimentation and radical thinking in the marriage and family therapy profession. For, if the *institutions* of therapy decide what information is correct and necessary for assessment and treatment, it dislodges other competing, alternative narratives about supervision, theory, and practice.

AAMFT is a multi-disciplinary organization consisting of psychologists, counselors, marriage and family therapists, psychiatrists, clergy, and social workers, among others. Professionals working within different psychotherapeutic and systems orientations have their own ideas about what constitutes essential information for assessment, diagnostic and treatment. For example, pastors may consider the spiritual life of the couple as more important than categories of identity and issues of oppression.

This critique has merit. For AAMFT to decide on its own what is indispensable undercuts the value in having such a diverse, multi-disciplinary, and multi-licensed profession. While a basic systems perspective seems essential when working with couples and families (and even individuals), there are many ways, theoretically, for people to conceptualize their client and patient populations. We must approach our responsibilities without rigid assumptions that can undercut our work. The field was birthed by innovative psychiatrists, psychologists, and social workers who rejected the very disciplinary dogma that trapped psychoanalysis and psychodynamic theories. Flexibility, openness, and creativity are the emotional imprints and legacies of our profession, not doctrine, intolerance, and sameness.

This distinction is more than simply a philosophical difference. It is ultimately more insidious and potentially damaging to the profession. It reminds me of the literary and historical concept of "presentism." To review, presentism says that we interpret past events and people through the lens of present morals, values, beliefs, and context. In literature and history, for example, such analysis can result in unfairly dismissing events and people because of their imperfections and flaws, hence failing to recognize important contributions. This happens, for example, when schools ban *Huckleberry Finn* because of the language in the book, language that was common during its time but not acceptable now. It happens, also, when historians and citizens de-value Thomas Jefferson as a thinker, writer, and leader because he enslaved people. As horrendous as enslaving people was and is, it points to how flawed Jefferson was, as are we all. His efforts in birthing the republic may be scarred because of his enslaving people but it doesn't disqualify his writings, ideas, and contributions as critical to the foundations of the country.

Presentism, then, critiques the past and assumes that present attitudes and values are superior. This seems consistent with AAMFT's approach to issues of categories of identity and social justice. The problem occurs not only when we view the past through the lens of the present, but when we don't consider the future. Will future social scientists have the same sensibilities? Might a future AAMFT make an a priori assumption that issues of climate change and carbon footprints are more important than issues of class or ethnicity? It doesn't seem a stretch to assume that future practitioners may look back at the early 21st century and wonder why issues of sustainability weren't primary in any assessment and diagnosis of families, couples, individuals, and other systems. The point is that the multi-disciplinary profession embodied by AAMFT may be better served by allowing for different theoretical perspectives and practitioner postulations.

In sum, lacking the proper distance needed to understand and assess present events places an assumptive theoretical screen over all supervision. Deciding what is important today renders other versions of supervision and theories about systems and society of lesser importance or even irrelevant. I, therefore, understand, accept, and advocate for Friedman's initial critique of the AAMFT Supervision tract, which requires a focus on categories of identity and social justice. Creativity and innovation occur when research meets practice, and when both recognize the limits of what they each have to offer. I don't believe that requiring sameness in assessment and treatment is in the best interests of the profession. Best practices in systems thinking recognize that each clinical situation has unique features, treatment must be personalized and attainable, and resources are limited.

Further, Friedman said that from a Bowen family systems theory perspective, categories of identity and cultural concerns form more of a "ground" perspective. That is, they are ever present, and they are noteworthy, but they are not figure, meaning that they are not central to understanding and treating people and their relationship systems. So, for example, knowing everything about categories of identity and societal variables—including gender, class, race, religion, geography, etc.—will only provide a limited degree of systemic clarity and therapeutic assistance. These categories, though important, are not essential in systemically assessing, diagnosing, and treating individuals, couples, and families. Rather, knowing about the central concepts of Bowen theory and how they present themselves in a family are all vital components in understanding and treating the client and the client system. They include:

1. Expressions of individuality and togetherness through differentiation.

2. Evaluating the effect of chronic and acute anxiety on the system.

3. Identifying emotional triangles and crucial anxiety binders.

4. Assessing reciprocal relationships.

5. Understanding the role and function of nuclear family emotional processes.

6. Highlighting patterning in multigenerational emotional transmission.

7. Recognizing symptom development as a family systems phenomenon.

Understanding and articulating these universal variables tell us more about family and individual functioning and will form the basis for implementing effective treatment options, more so than knowing all about the clients' cultural issues and categories of identity variables.

Each family and each culture provide their own, unique "coloring" on emergent family processes, allowing them to become more visible, unique, and clear. Categories of identity are ways that people identify with a group. They can provide a sense of belonging and meaning for people. They can offer a shared experience that connects individuals with communities. Socially, categories of identity provide context, perspective, and relationships for people. Nonetheless, the emotional processes themselves, as articulated through Bowen's central theoretical concepts, are more germane and, hence, more important to assessment, diagnosis, and treatment.

While Friedman provides a relevant critique concerning these categories of identity relative to the central concepts in Bowen theory, Friedman misses an important opportunity to articulate how Bowen theory can address these social justice categories. Bowen theory itself provides opportunities to understand culture, class, race, and other categories of identity. Rather than simply rejecting categories of identity as a figure component in assessment, diagnosis, and treatment, these categories of identity are themselves embedded within a cultural context through societal emotional process.

Societal emotional process assumes that the same Bowen-based processes are active at the larger systems level of the culture or civilization. The manner in which we emotionally react as a culture, triangulate and therefore exploit marginalized groups, and bind societal anxiety through this emotional triangulation exemplify this. For example, U.S. society, like all societies, finds ways to divide people into "us" and "them." This natural sorting (it appears that we are pre-wired for such in-group/out-group evolutionary categorizations) often leads to displacing blame on the other. Through triangulation, in-grouping and out-grouping propagate racism, LGBTQ discrimination, anti-Semitism, Islamophobia, and other hate-based rationalizations. The in-groups bind societal anxiety onto its most vulnerable members and these groups are pushed to the outside positions in the emotional triangles created by society. The result: systemic oppression and racism centuries deep, generations-entrenched poverty, social policies designed to keep cultures and races separate, and politicians willing to attain and retain power and wealth through fear and intimidation.

Societal emotional process also helps us understand the effects of societal regression: segments of the society forever mired in poverty, illness, family breakdown, and community unraveling. These are the individuals and families most challenged to do something different when the weight of the world is always on their shoulders. So, categories of identity can best be understood through societal emotional process. In this way, Bowen theory can provide the more prescriptive assessment required by AAFMT, while doing so within its own theoretical matrix.

Also, there is a danger is delving too deeply into the social justice worldview as therapists. Overreliance on categories of identity and social justice as a critical feature of assessment and diagnosis can create its own problems. For example, over attachment to these categories of identity and societal oppression, *by the therapist or by the client or client system*, can construct significant blocks to understanding and treating therapeutic systems. People can get trapped within their perception of an identity.

Let's return to the family Delia was working with. A therapist with a strong social justice perspective may view the symptom development of the daughter's running away as a reflection of limited opportunities and choices available to a Latina youth and member of a working-class family, an oppressive society where racism runs rampant, and a culture that disempowers and sexualizes girls. The family has been victimized by the hegemonic, dominant culture and the social system. This kind of assessment has value. Certainly, family systems exist within larger cultural and societal systems, so you cannot isolate larger systems any more than you can ignore the micro-system of the family and isolate treating the runaway daughter from her family system.

Nonetheless, the central therapeutic questions remain: what do you do with all of this information about larger systems, and what data are most important for treatment purposes? In answering these questions, Bowen theory proposes that addressing the family system's primary variables—in this case, the emotional immaturity of family members, the overt and subtle triangulation, the under-functioning of the parents, the daughter's binding of the family's anxiety through her flight, the emotional field of family alcoholism, etc.—will have the most significant, long-lasting impact on the family and its multigenerational legacy. While social and critical theories of identity and systemic, societal exploitation are important to understanding and even effecting change at a macro level, at the level of the individual or family, the family therapist has a different role.

The family systems therapist's role is always to promote and enhance differentiation. This includes encouraging responsibility and accountability for all family members, regardless of their situation. It includes reducing blame through enhanced self-reflection and self-awareness. It includes training to recognize and reduce emotional reactivity. It includes teaching about emotional triangles and de-triangulating symptoms and people. It includes advancing emotional maturity, improving adaptability, and endorsing other family systems solutions to more accurately differentiate the family through second-order, systemic change.

Developing treatment options that take into account cultural concerns and categories of identity may have pragmatic value as a part of an overall treatment process. Unfortunately, those in most need of family services are often those who have the least resources and who are the most desperate and vulnerable. A true systems perspective would incorporate many levels of systems. In fact, many therapies already integrate multi-systemic approaches to solving some of these intractable problems. For example, today it is increasingly common to conduct "mobile therapy," which includes sessions outside of the therapist's office. These include home visits to understand the family environment and to effect changes in the home. Family therapists also visit schools to assist teachers and students in adapting and adjusting to the educational environment. Family therapists also work closely with probation officers, medical personnel, and the courts.

The problem is that families who are unraveling require significant and sustained efforts to help parents and children become more emotionally mature in coping with life's challenges. We are not a society attuned to our most desperate members. Income inequality is larger now than any time in the last hundred years. Rural and inner-city communities face a familiar scourge of symptoms when societies regress: alcoholism, violence, drug addiction, food insecurity, and homelessness.

Further, insurance companies, including Medicare and Medicaid, are more interested in "evidence-based" approaches that reduce symptoms. They are concerned with effecting first-order change. System-level change—second order change—requires lots of time, money, and motivation. It necessitates a deep commitment by society to relieve the long-term suffering of those most in need.

Unfortunately, as a culture it's easier to blame the vulnerable than to show compassion, especially if you, yourself, are only one paycheck away from losing your home. Fear and hatred squash empathy and compassion.

So, given the incomplete resources and the restrictions of medical insurance provisions, more often than not, family therapists are working with limited time, access, and resources. I applaud multi-systemic therapies and efforts to alter cultural inequalities. To the degree possible, systems therapists can and should contribute to furthering these important changes.

At the level of the family, Bowen theory-based therapy provides opportunities for systemic solutions that hold the promise for second-order change within the nuclear family as well as multi-generationally. The family is the entry point of change. And, change at the level of the family system itself is a remarkably difficult task.

It bears repeating that the family systems therapist's role is always to promote and enhance differentiation. The Bowen theory approach to this is universal: encouraging personal responsibility and accountability, reducing blame through enhanced self-reflection and self-acceptance, minimizing reactivity, and teaching about emotional triangles and de-triangulation. As emotional maturity increases, over time people have more successes, and they learn to better manage themselves and their lives.

This level of care and follow-up will require a one-hundred-and-eighty-degree reorientation of society away from rewarding the elite and privileged with more wealth and power. It will require a reorientation towards understanding and providing for the needs of the least fortunate, as well as a willingness to work with these impoverished families and communities to figure out how best to break cycles of spiraling family and societal regression. It costs money and requires time. In the end, this "lifting the bottom" approach provides benefits to all, including a social order that is more stable and more equitable.

There are other dangers with an approach that is too emotionally attached to social justice and societal concerns. Promoting a more macro-assessment understanding of families within larger systems runs the risk of institutionalizing victimization and, therefore, undercutting personal authority and agency in encouraging self-maturity and maturity in relationship systems. It is certainly possible and positive to include sociological issues within a systemic assessment, I simply caution therapists to avoid labeling others or using labels with others, since labels ("victim," "abuser," "white hegemony," "oppression") mean different things to different people. Finally, the family therapist must be careful to not join the system in such a way as to lose hope or be overwhelmed by how the family expresses its fears.

In sum, my problem with the approach to supervision and even treatment by framing what is important a priori is essentially my critique in articulating "the challenge with supervision." I don't reject categories of identity and cultural analysis as having value and relevance in understanding systemic processes. Indeed, as I have stated, Bowen theory allows for such an assessment. My concern is, rather, that these formulations are of *relative* importance but are not *the* central components of effective systemic assessment, diagnosis, and treatment. Insisting that they are correct, those adhering to the centrality of categories of identity and cultural concerns in supervision, including AAMFT's supervisory track, relegate other, alternative explanations to secondary or even tertiary importance. Innovation rarely progresses when innovators are forced to accept orthodoxy, no matter how well intended or politically and culturally correct that orthodoxy seems.

Whether we are discussing the nature of dual or multiple relationships relative to coaching or the figure-ground relationship relative to Bowen's central theoretical concepts and categories of identity, it is clear that Bowen's family systems theory offers some provocative perspectives on what is important, how supervision is provided, and how change occurs. I have found that, while these issues may be controversial, they have contributed to an important dialogue about advancing family systems theory across professions and disciplines.

SECTION FIVE

SELECTED WORKS: INTRODUCTION

This section includes my selected publications. I included these book chapters and journal articles for two reasons. First, I wanted my most significant published work in one place. This makes it easier to access my selected works, rather than tracking them down in different publications. Second, I believe that these publications best represent my thinking at the time in applying Bowen family systems theory to a variety of clinical and non-clinical situations.

I arrange this section chronologically, from oldest to most recent. I explain the context of each chapter and article, and what I wanted to accomplish with these writings. Several of these pieces were originally co-authored. For these co-authored publications, I have worked with each co-author to slightly modify the original work, while preserving their original intent. Also, I did not update these chapters and articles with new research or my new thinking about the topics. I wanted them to stand on their own. Of course, writers are notorious for being self-critical about their work, so I "cleaned up" each chapter to make it more readable. When I have modified a chapter significantly, as with the chapter on teaching undergraduates mediation using Bowen theory, I explain why and how I did so.

Each co-author assisted me with preparing their respective chapter for this publication. And, of course, each has given me permission to include these older chapters in this book. I want to acknowledge and thank Sally LeBoy, Gina Simmons, Steve Pace, and Kenny Cook for their feedback, creativity, suggestions, and insights. They are all remarkably creative and energetic individuals, and I enjoyed working with them again on this project.

CHAPTER NINE

INCEST FAMILIES:
INTEGRATING THEORY AND PRACTICE
-BY WAYNE REGINA AND SALLY LEBOY

Introduction

An earlier version of this chapter was originally published in Family Dynamics of Addiction, Volume 1, Number 3, 1991. I have largely preserved this chapter from the original.

In the early-1980s, Sally LeBoy and I were family therapists working in San Diego with a variety of struggling families. We earned a reputation for effectively treating families with significant child abuse and spousal violence. Many were referred through the military's Family Service Centers. Other families were referred through Child Protective Services (CPS). One day, a CPS social worker called us and asked if we wanted to work with a family who had been reported for father–daughter incest. She believed that they were amenable to family therapy, though she was getting some resistance from CPS about referring directly to family therapy and not waiting until treatment for individual family members was well along.

Sally and I always believed in family therapy, and we were willing to work with difficult families, including those families where parents had characterological diagnoses (borderline personality disorders, narcissistic personality disorders, etc.), where child abuse ran rampant, and where other therapists had given up.

So, it wasn't too much of a stretch for us to accept an incest family. After all, the same family processes operate in all families. While highly symptomatic families are generally less differentiated and often exhibit symptoms in multiple parts of the system–in the children, in the spouses, in the relationships–our overall understanding of any family, as well as the process of therapy, is generally the same, regardless of presenting problem. That is, we are always promoting the differentiation of all family members, through strengthening the selfhood of each person; clarifying, amplifying, and reinforcing parental leadership; and creating and elucidating boundaries. The self–other relationship system is best enhanced with more differentiated individuals. So, from our perspective, incest families are more similar to than different from other families.

We were surprised by the pushback we received from various social systems–the psychotherapy community, the Parents United community, the legal community. We persisted. We researched what other family therapists in the field were doing with incest families. A turning point arrived when we attended a training workshop by Noel Larson and James Maddock, and they presented their work with incest families. We became excited about what they were doing–family therapy–and how they categorized incest families into functional typologies for better screening.

We came away convinced that we were on the right track. Sally and I continued our work with incest families for almost ten years. While we had successes and setbacks, the incest ended for all families. Though not the only goal of therapy, it was an important one. Some families transformed; others muddled along. I suspect that all psychotherapists understand the range of outcomes in therapy.

Sally and I believe that, overall, our approach was successful. As always, we viewed the family through the lens of Bowen family systems theory, and we used "techniques" from the theory, especially de-triangulating, to build and strengthen self-functioning for all members. In addition, we always found Structural family therapy a useful complementary system for assessment, systemic diagnosis, and treatment. For example, more poorly differentiated spouses naturally create a more problematic spousal subsystem. In incest families, these marital subsystem boundaries are rigid, as if there's an emotional and transactional wall between the couple. Also, the generational boundary is missing, with the daughter in the role of spouse. So, creating, strengthening, and reinforcing boundaries are essential to differentiating these families.

This paper presents our efforts with incest families and what we learned over the years.

Chapter Nine

Incest Families:
Integrating Theory and Practice
-By Wayne Regina and Sally LeBoy

This chapter presents a method of conceptualizing and treating incest families integrating Bowen family systems theory and Structural family therapy perspectives. We discuss the inter-generational, structural, and process similarities between incest families and substance-abusing families. We briefly review the etiological theories of incest, and we present a method for treating incest families from the initial disclosure of the incest. We review systematic assessment procedures and address treatment goals, with specific attention being given to establishing or re-establishing a functional generational boundary, increasing differentiation in the family, and breaking the multigenerational cycle of incest.

The systematic study and treatment of incest is in its infancy. Clinicians who have worked with incest survivors, perpetrators, and families in which incest has occurred agree that the ramifications for violating the safety and trust of that generational or familial boundary has lasting effects on all involved. Beyond this, there is little agreement as to the etiology of incest or the most effective treatment for this pathological behavior.

Many clinicians have embraced theoretical perspectives that may limit their ability to seek alternative treatment approaches that could yield positive outcomes and effective healing of the family system. For example, some seek to remove the child from the home and deny the young person any kind of relationship with the perpetrator

(O'Connell, 1986). This reaction may be due, in part, to the exploitative nature of the offense and the instinct to protect children from harm. Who among us has not felt strong feelings when confronted with the abused child? What seems more important, however, is to remain as calm and rational as possible when considering this population. While recognizing the severity of the symptom, as family therapists, we consider incest families as being more similar to than different from other maladaptive families and, therefore, as being amenable to traditional family therapy treatment goals and methods.

Incest families are often multi-symptomatic. For example, others have documented the relationship between incest and alcoholism (Forrest, 1883; Herman & Hirschman, 1981; Liles & Childs, 1986; Martin & Walters, 1983). Barnard (1983) estimates that 80% of incest families have substance abuse addictions as well. In addition, Barnard (1983, 1990) delineates the structural and process similarities between alcoholic families and incest families. He points to the strong homeostatic influences that incest and alcoholism have on the family. These symptoms temporarily decrease anxiety in the system and bring about a kind of impermanent stability.

Symptoms, in general, can have homeostatic effects. They may relieve anxiety in the moment. If the causes or major influences on a symptom are not addressed, however, long-term anxiety will increase, along with symptoms. The net effect of these ineffectual attempts at anxiety management, through severe symptoms like alcoholism and incest, is an increase in chronic and acute anxiety, and a corresponding decrease in differentiation in the family.

Further, Barnard (1983, 1990) discusses that both incest families and alcoholic families lack clear generational boundaries, resulting in children who are parentified and spousified. With both family types there are impaired marital relationships and subsystems where the adults are not adequately meeting each other's emotional, sexual, and physical needs. Instead, there is collusive dependency and emotional distance. Tied to the weak spousal subsystem, both family types reflect an ineffective parental subsystem. As a result, there is no mutual oversight of parenting responsibilities (Barnard, 1983, 1990).

In both incest and addict families, denial and the perpetuation of "family secrets" exist. These distorted emotional dynamics and communication patterns result in muted family affect, "no talk" rules, inappropriate family role assignments, and a further perpetuation of the isolated family system (Barnard, 1983; Black, 1981). Individuality, emotional maturity, and a sense of separate functioning are lost, and, as a consequence, family fusion, emotional reactivity, and symptom formation flourish (Kerr & Bowen, 1988). The symptoms of incest and addiction are part of a triangulation process in both types of family systems, with the symptoms and the family members occupying inside or outside positions in emotional triangles.

Considering the similarities between incest and addict families, and the frequent occurrence of both incest and substance abuse in highly symptomatic families, it seems important to conceptualize and treat incest families with the same "systemic sense" that we treat alcoholic and other symptomatic families. Lawson, G., Peterson, and Lawson, A. (1983) point out that the field of substance abuse is making great progress in recognizing and treating the systemic elements involved in the development, maintenance, and perpetuation of substance abuse and dependency disorders. We approach and treat incest families with a similar systemic understanding.

For various reasons, many professionals resist this approach. One hypothesis is that sexualizing children brings up powerful reactions on the part of society in general and psychotherapists in particular. Those feelings interfere with seeing these families with the same level of "objectivity" or clarity that directs treating other problematic family symptoms. When theory and treatment are subverted by subjective forces such as therapists' feelings, emotions, and reactive thinking, effective treatment strategies that promote healing of the entire family will be difficult to develop and implement (Kerr & Bowen, 1988).

Finally, incest families share an additional characteristic of other highly symptomatic and poorly differentiated families, including substance-abusing families: a powerful multigenerational transmission pattern often manifested in generational repetition of symptoms in one or both parents or their children. Therefore, merely stopping the incest behavior is not enough. Failure to alter the multigenerational emotional process perpetuates the incest legacy in the next generation.

We propose a method of working with incest families that is integrative rather than exclusive. Our theoretical foundation is based on Bowen family systems theory since this theory recognizes the primacy and therefore the interdependency of both the individual and the family.

Our approach is pragmatic and objective by design. We contend that the family remains the central institutional force for affecting individuals and society alike. As such, family therapy offers a unique opportunity for healing highly symptomatic families and, by extension, society. Methodologically, our approach utilizes a number of techniques, including those employed by intergenerational and structural family therapies.

Etiological Models of Incest

There are various ways of conceptualizing incestuous behavior and incest families. Within an analytic framework, incest emanates from characterological defects found in individuals. It espouses a psychopathological model, and treatment focuses on long-term individual and group psychotherapy (Meiselman, 1978; Swanson & Biaggio, 1985).

Feminists argue that a patriarchal culture that condones violence against women and children is to blame, and they view incest as rape (Brickman, 1982; Quina & Carlson, 1979). This approach advocates that incest be regarded primarily in a legal context that dichotomizes participants as either victims or victimizers. As such, the emphasis is on prosecution of the perpetrators and compensation for the victims (Brickman, 1982).

Clinicians advocating an addiction model believe that incest and sexual addiction strongly correlate. They attribute addictive behaviors to the perpetrators and co-addictive or co-dependent behaviors to the spouse (Earle & Crow, 1989). Treatment focuses on participation in ongoing groups designed to assist individuals in breaking the cycle of sexual addiction and co-dependency. As with other addictions, true recovery is never achieved (Carnes, 1989; Earle & Crow, 1989). The sexual addiction model of incest is particularly appealing when there are substance-abusing elements in the family and when the family is engaged in twelve-step recovery programs to treat the chemical addiction.

Family systems therapists consider incest a systemic maladaptation and the result of a breakdown in family structure and family process (Larson & Maddock, 1986; Lutz &Medway, 1984; Reposa & Zuelzer, 1983). For family systems therapists, incest families, like other symptomatic families, have developed emotional and behavioral coping patterns that are chaotic and destructive, resulting in individual and relationship breakdown. With incest and other forms of family violence, however, family therapists often disagree on the most effective treatment modality (Alexander, 1986; Barrett, Sykes, & Byrnes, 1986; Carter, Papp, Silverstein, & Walters, 1986).

All of these perspectives represent potentially valid points of view and, like the Zen story of the blind men describing the elephant from different placements (a tree trunk, a snake, etc.), they likely articulate some aspects of the incest problem. From an inclusive stance, we view the family system within an expanded systemic context that could easily embrace all the aforementioned models. As family therapists, however, we ask a simple and pragmatic question: What are the goals of treatment?

Theoretically and practically, our over-arching goal is to understand and modify or eliminate the family processes that contribute to, maintain, or exacerbate symptoms. Our underlying ethic advocates for systemic health—intrapersonally and interpersonally. Increased family cohesion, adaptability, resiliency, and vitality are essential for achieving this state. Family therapy, as an initial therapeutic modality, can play a central role in achieving these ends.

Early Phase Family Treatment

Our argument for family therapy as an early component of incest treatment may be viewed against the backdrop of California's Family Reunification Program (California Welfare and Institutions Code 300).

This program dictates what happen to a family when a child is removed from the home because of abuse or neglect. It sets out the time frame allotted to reestablish family safety and achieve reunification.

When incest is discovered, either the child is removed from the home and placed in protective custody by Child Protective Services or the abusing parent is removed from the home (California Welfare and Institutions Code 300; California Penal Code 288). On the assumption of father–daughter incest, which is the most prevalent, the father is more likely to be ordered from the home if the mother is determined capable of protecting the daughter. As a result of the distorted family structure, the emotional reactivity of the family, and the denial that often accompanies the incest, however, it is not unusual for the wife to initially support her spouse over her child. If this occurs, the child is usually removed.

Under California's reunification program, the child must be reunited with the family within twelve months, with a possible six-month extension, or the Permanent Placement Program is activated. This begins the process of finding out-of-home adoption, legal guardianship, or long-term foster care for the child (California Welfare and Institutions Code 300). In other words, the family must provide a safe environment for the child within twelve to eighteen months or the child will be permanently placed elsewhere.

California supports the concept of reunification. Whether that stance is pragmatic (since there is a lack of adequate resources for outside placements) or therapeutic, family therapists have a mandate to do everything in their power to ensure that the family dynamics and behaviors that necessitated the child's removal receive immediate therapeutic attention.

When fathers are forced from the home, additional emotional and financial factors enter into the picture. Wives are often emotionally dependent on their husbands and, in our experience, they often decompensate when the husbands are forced to leave. In addition, these families face extreme financial pressures–managing two households, legal fees, therapists' fees, etc.–that add to the family stress. Increased stress is often followed by increased emotional reactivity. Family defenses are activated, which perpetuate denial, minimization, and an already pre-existing propensity to close out non-family members.

With either the father or the child removed from the family, its coping capacity is further strained. Individual and family resources, flexibility, and resiliency are diminished. Early family intervention, when conducted to protect the victims from further trauma, can mobilize family strengths early on. This constitutes an initial step toward constructing a more functional and safer family environment.

The Parents United programs also advocate for the importance of family therapy. Rather than utilizing family therapy as an initial treatment modality, however, they advocate for family therapy much later in the treatment process, after family members have received individual and group treatment, and after therapy has taken place within various subsystems of the family (Giarretto, 1982). Although the Parents United model has revolutionized the treatment of child sexual abuse with its emphasis on a humanistic perspective, its emphasis on later-phase family treatment limits therapeutic interventions that could positively impact state-mandated reunification.

An additional liability of late-phase family therapy concerns the legal system governing incest families. That is, most families remain in the system for a limited time, after which the external forces that mandate families to cooperate with treatment are gone. As a consequence, unless the family has internalized its motivation for change by accepting responsibility, the window of opportunity for systemic change can be lost. Few families are willing to re-engage therapeutically for something as seemingly intangible as breaking the multigenerational cycle of incest or promoting differentiation. Incest families are often a reluctant population that does not stay in therapy beyond the terms mandated by the courts.

As family systems therapists, we believe that strengthening each person's emotional maturity is best achieved through appropriate structural boundaries within the family system. Our goals, therefore, are to break multigenerational cycles of abuse by encouraging differentiation through early family treatment. This affords the best opportunity to accomplish these goals and for prompt reunification.

Using Larson and Maddock's (1986) functional typology, we screen out the more "violent" forms of incest that are not amenable to early family intervention. We have discovered that incest families categorized as "affection-exchange," which represents the largest percentage of the incest population, are particularly good candidates for early family therapy. Within these families, the incest behavior results from misguided attempts by the adult to have his emotional and physical needs met through the child. These families are often different from other types of incest families in that they are often less resistant to family treatment, have more individual and family resources, and are more willing to engage in therapeutic work designed to keep their families intact.

Theoretical Rationale

We implement the same theoretical and treatment criteria with incest families that we apply to other seriously impaired families. That is, we take a neutral and inclusive stance with symptomatic families, choosing to assess each family according to its unique needs. Although we are not exclusive in demanding that all family members attend therapy for every session, we insist that all family members be present initially, as we attempt to comprehend the family and its symptoms.

As Bowen family systems theorists and therapists, we understand and treat incest in the same way that we understand and treat other families, namely through strengthening the self and strengthening the system. Bowen's (1978) concept of basic differentiation is key here. Basic differentiation is the capacity to enhance a sense of self, or self-definition, through self-reflection that leads to an improved capacity for self-regulation and intimacy. As basic differentiation decreases, emotional fusion increases. Emotional fusion is an undue emotional attachment to another, resulting in a loss of self and a blurring of emotional, feeling, and thinking systems within the individual (Kerr & Bowen, 1988).

Emotional fusion can manifest itself through diffuse or rigid boundaries, the absence of a generational boundary, and emotional triangulation.

In a family manifesting high levels of emotional fusion, individuals operate in a climate of fear and anxiety. This emotional reactivity rigidifies into problematic behaviors and challenging patterns of interaction. Symptoms develop, and the system gets stuck because attempted solutions often recreate and re-rigidify the dysfunctional patterns (Friedman, 1985). In contrast, a more differentiated family respects the importance of both separateness and togetherness. They display appropriate flexibility between managing individual needs and managing the needs of the family (Papero, 1990).

Our theoretical and treatment framework centers on Bowen family systems theory. The particular configuration of family members in any given session is less important than our systemic perspective. At all times, we act on the basis of how we are thinking about the family from this theoretical lens. This theoretical understanding *is* the therapy; that is, the theory always guides the treatment.

Assessment and Treatment

Our treatment model for these families derives from our philosophical stance that a resilient, flexible, and functional family is best achieved through modifying and eliminating problematic family transactions in conjunction with an educational and therapeutic process designed to promote differentiation. We begin with an assessment phase to explore individual perceptions of the self and the family, to gather data concerning the current family system and how it functions, and to obtain information about the parents' families of origin. In fact, we devote several sessions to collecting data and observing family transactions. If at all possible, and we insist on this as much as we can, we require that all family members attend these assessment sessions.

We often hear a common concern regarding protecting the child from further trauma and coping with the strong denial in the system. Although it is wise to avoid treating a volatile and dangerous family together, many incest families are not so severely unstable and are quite capable of being interviewed together. In our experience, however, a co-therapy team that remains in charge of the session and directs the flow of information exchange through them, reduces the stress and defensiveness in the family.

In addition, keeping the family focused in this way demonstrates the therapists' interest in the family, making it easier to build a more differentiated rapport (Papero, 1990). Our concern for the family translates into compassion, as the family begins to see us as allies in their attempt to heal the system. One outcome is that all members, especially the victim, experience more safety. With all family members present, we reduce denial and minimization, and the likelihood of re-traumatization.

As a part of taking a detailed family history, we question the family about factual information concerning the family's life-cycle, gather important diagnostic information about the typology of the incest family, and begin to decrease emotionality as we promote more clearheaded thinking within the family. Next, with the family's assistance, we develop multigenerational genograms for each side of the extended family. Genograms provide valuable data, and we use them as both assessment and treatment tools. For assessment purposes, genograms help track multigenerational patterns, themes, symptoms, and other important processes (McGoldrick & Gerson, 1985). In addition, genograms begin the process of expanding the context of the symptom.

Families become curious about their extended family histories. Revelations about repeating patterns, including that of incest within either or both of the parents' families of origin, help with developing understanding and compassion within the family for each other, since it is often the case that the perpetrator and/or the spouse were themselves victims of child abuse, including incest. Through promoting greater understanding of the context within which the incest developed and was maintained, genograms also encourage an increased acceptance of responsibility for personal behavior. Increasing personal responsibility is always an aspect of Bowen family systems theory and therapy.

Information gleaned from these initial family sessions allows us to assess the emotional field of the family and the structural components of the system, especially their boundaries—within the family, between subsystems, and including the outside world. Understanding, with focus on field and structure, aids in developing effective treatment approaches that promote emotional maturity throughout the family and alter structural configurations away from rigid and diffuse boundaries, and toward clearer boundaries. This is especially important in creating or re-creating and strengthening a solid generational boundary, separating adults and children into more appropriate subsystem functioning.

The goals of our therapy are to assist with promoting and maintaining a more functional and adaptive family structure, as well as to balance and support individual functioning and appropriate intimacy. These outcomes, in turn, foster increased responsibility and suitable transactional behaviors between and amongst members.

We find that the Structural family therapy techniques advocated by Minuchin and Fishman (1981) are particularly effective with these families. Most of these techniques are designed to improve and support effective boundaries within the family. In this way, we operate as boundary makers—breaking rigid triads, forming functional subsystems, and building appropriate boundaries all around. Interventions such as reframing, unbalancing, and enactments are particularly helpful. Structural techniques are action oriented and help bring a sense of order and organization to these often-chaotic systems. We use these techniques even as we stay true to our Bowen family systems theory framework. That is, the techniques themselves are used to promote the goals of Bowen theory and therapy. We take care to encourage individuality rather than fostering "stuck-togetherness" solutions in the family. Promoting and enhancing increased differentiation supports a solid family structure and effective emotional functioning.

For example, as a mother begins increasing her emotional contact with her children, she is encouraged to develop a personal definition of good mothering. She then becomes freer to make choices and decisions regarding her relationship with the children guided by more autonomous processes rather than by automatic reactions.

Family of origin work is also an essential component of this model. It is particularly effective if it can help lower and contain the anxiety in the system. With less emotionally mature individuals, the past remains very much alive and is a powerful force that often impedes progress. As a treatment tool, genograms help imbed the symptom of incest within the historical and emotional dynamics of the extended family system. Increased understanding of the forces involved in the formation and expression of the symptom (emotional triangles, the ways in which anxiety is bound, and the like) often lessens the emotional fusion operating within these multi-generational systems. This, in turn, lowers anxiety, promotes individuality, and fosters personal responsibility. When parents are encouraged to begin differentiating from their own families of origin, they unblock previously bound emotional energy. This released emotional energy is more appropriately available to them and their current family (Kerr & Bowen, 1988).

Finally, we manage the potentially troublesome impact of the therapist's own anxiety in dealing with such rigid and poorly functioning systems. With a solid theoretical perspective and blueprint for a clearly articulated treatment strategy, we reduce our own emotional reactivity as clinicians through a co-therapy model.

Co-therapy grants the clinicians greater freedom to join the system with the knowledge that there is a safe haven from which to process inhibitory counter-transference and other forms of anxiety. Furthermore, an effective co-therapy team provides a powerful therapeutic presence that can help prevent any potential re-traumatization of the victim.

Through these treatment processes, we not only hope to affect the present emotional system but to alter the emotional imprint from the past, freeing the family to create something new and better in the future. Our ultimate goal is to break multigenerational patterns of transmission, allowing families to create more differentiated selves and more functional, emotionally safe families.

With Bowen theory to guide us, we begin the family therapy component of treatment almost immediately after the disclosure of the incest. We initially see the entire family for the purposes of assessment. With regards to ongoing treatment, we may alternate therapeutic modalities–individual, adult couple, and family sessions–as needed.

Reconciling Approaches

Our model of conceptualizing and treating incest families isn't radical, nor is it in conflict with other theoretical and clinical perspectives. We have worked with many families over the years in which one or more members were characterologically disturbed. Who amongst us has not worked with paranoid, borderline, or schizophrenic individuals or families? These families often respond well to family therapy precisely because those patterns that influence the development and maintenance of the disorder can be observed and altered. In addition, the fragility of the family, or of a particular individual within the family, can be lessened by activating the resources of the family as a whole and promoting a greater sense of self in that member. Finally, resistance to treatment can be minimized, even in incest families, when problems are addressed within the context of the family therapy setting. We have rarely found it useful or necessary to isolate any family member for individual treatment.

We do, however, support individual and group therapy for all incest family members. This multimodal approach, *when properly coordinated*, can enhance treatment goals. Care must be taken, however, that therapists do not work at cross purposes and undermine the basic goals of decreasing chronic and acute anxiety, promoting differentiation, and creating and reinforcing appropriate boundaries.

With regard to incest as an addictive behavior, this may or may not be so. Certainly, it is a highly predictive behavior within families that have little emotional flexibility. Regardless, family therapy is considered an essential treatment component for addict families. Twelve-step programs and family treatment can work hand-in-hand to ensure the alleviation of addictions and destructive, co-dependent behaviors (Earle & Crow, 1989). And, there are few co-dependent behaviors more destructive than incest. Safety can best be assured for these families by immediately affecting those aspects of the system that allow the co-dependency to flourish. Realigning and strengthening the parental and spousal subsystem, for example, can help de-triangulate the daughter from her role as "wife" to her father and rescuer to her mother.

In addressing the concerns of feminist therapists, we, too, are convinced that the patriarchy practiced and promoted within our society contributes heavily to the formation and maintenance of many social ills, incest certainly among them. Knowing this, however, does little to alleviate the family's problems and the pain associated with incest. All men, women, and children are negatively affected by these destructive social norms. It is precisely at the level of the family unit that we, as therapists, have some power to intervene and bring about improved social standards. For us, a primary focus on social injustice is therapeutically ineffective. From this position, there is a danger of taking an adversarial stance with individual members or the family as a whole. Therapeutic respect can be easily lost, and the therapist risks getting stuck in or fused with the family. The opportunity for second-order change, systemic change, much less third-order transformational change is minimized. What Bateson (1972) called "Learning III" can only come about from a true healing of the entire family. This, in turn, can contribute to emotional evolution at a societal level and the subsequent advancement of improved mores and values.

We have been treating incest families for years with varying degrees of success. We have learned that not all incest families benefit from an initial focus on family therapy but for families in which there is high motivation to stay together, and in which the incest is of an affection-exchange nature coupled with poor boundaries within the family, the prognosis is good. Working with the whole family—including non-molested siblings who are deeply affected by the incest and who are often left out of many traditional treatment models—allows us to access and modify all aspects of family dynamics that contribute to the problematic behaviors.

In addition, we can encourage the family's strengths to reinforce positive family transactions that promote emotional maturity. The danger of recurrence is diminished when the "secret" is exposed to all family members and when the presence of unhealthy alliances, coalitions, and emotional triangles can receive immediate therapeutic intervention. In fact, we have never had a reappearance of incest in any of the families that we have treated. The family members themselves feel less threatened, and, as a result, they are often less defensive when they are allowed to experience themselves as an intact family with the goal of remaining a family, even if the spouses eventually separate and divorce.

In short, the same benefits that apply to working with any problematic family system apply to working with incest families. To treat these families differently may be more of a reaction by therapists to the complex, troublesome nature of incest rather than a therapeutic necessity.

References

Alexander, P.C. (1986). Procrustes was himself tortured: A reply to "the procrustean bed." *Family Process, 25*, 305-308.

Barnard, C.P. (1983). Alcoholism and incest: Improving diagnostic comprehensiveness. *International Journal of Family Therapy, 5*(2), 136-144.

Barnard, C.P. (1990). Alcoholism and sex abuse in the family: Incest and marital rape. *Journal of Chemical Dependency Treatment, 3*(1), 131-144.

Barrett, M.J., Sykes, C., & Byrnes, W. (1986). A systemic model for the treatment of intrafamily child sexual abuse. *Journal of Psychotherapy and the Family, 2*(2), 67-82.

Bateson, G. (1972). *Steps to an ecology of mind*. New York, N.Y.: Ballantine.

Black, C. (1989). *It will never happen to me*. Denver, CO: M.A.C. Publishing.

Bowen, M. (1978). *Family therapy in clinical practice*. New York, N.Y.: Jason Aronson.

Brickman, J. (1982). Examining the myths: A feminist view of incest. *Kinesis, 15*, 8-9.

Brickman, J. (1984). Feminist, non-sexist and traditional models of therapy: Implications for working with incest. *Women & Therapy, 3*(1), 49-67.

California Penal Code 288.

California Welfare and Institutions Code 300.

Carnes, P.J. (1989). Sexually addicted families: Clinical use of the circumplex model. *Journal of Psychotherapy and the Family, 4*(1/2), 113-140.

Carter, E., Papp, P., Silverstein, O., & Walters, M. (1986). The procrustean bed. *Family Process, 25*, 301-304.

Earle, R., & Crow, G. (1989). *Lonely at all times: Recognizing, understanding, and overcoming sexual addiction for addicts and co-dependents*. New York, N.Y.: Pocket Books.

Forrest, G.G. (1883). *Alcoholism and human sexuality*. Springfield, IL: Charles C. Thomas.

Friedman, E. (1985). Generation to generation. New York, N.Y.: Guildford Press.

Giarretto, H. (1982). A comprehensive sexual abuse treatment program. *Child Abuse and Neglect, 6*, 263-278.

Herman, J., & Hirschman, L. (1981). Families at risk for father-daughter incest. *American Journal of Psychiatry, 138*(7), 967-970.

Larson, N.R., & Maddock, J.W. (1986). Structural and functional variables in incest family systems: Implications for assessment and treatment. *Journal of Psychotherapy and the Family, 2*(2), 27-44.

Lawson, G., Peterson, J., & Lawson, A. (1983). *Alcoholism and the family: A guide to treatment and prevention*. Rockville, MD: Aspen.

Liles, R.E., & Childs, D. (1986). Similarities in family dynamics of incest and alcohol abuse: Issues for clinician. *Alcohol Health and Research World, 11*(1), 66-69.

Lutz, S.E., & Medway, J.P. (1984). Contextual family therapy with the victims of incest. *Journal of Adolescence, 7,* 319-327.

Martin, M.J., & Walters, J. (1982). Familial correlates of selected types of child abuse and neglect. *Journal of Marriage and the Family, 45*(2), 267-276.

McGoldrick, M, & Gerson, R. (1985). *Genograms in family assessment.* New York, N.Y.: Norton.

Meiselman, K.C. (1978). *A psychological study of causes and effects with treatment recommendations.* San Francisco, CA: Jossey-Bass.

Minuchin, S., & Fishman, C. (1981). *Family therapy techniques.* Cambridge, MA: Harvard University Press.

O'Connell, M.A. (1986). Reuniting incest offenders with their families. *Journal of Interpersonal Violence, 1*(3), 374-386.

Papero, D.V. (1990). *Bowen family systems theory.* Newton, MA: Allyn & Bacon.

Quina, K., & Carlson, N.L. (1979). *Rape, incest, and sexual harassment.* New York, N.Y.: Praeger.

Reposa, R.E., & Zuelzer, M.B. (1983). Family therapy with incest. *International Journal of Family Therapy, 5*(2). 111-126.

Swanson, L., & Biaggio, M.K. (1985). Therapeutic perspectives on father-daughter incest. *American Journal of Psychiatry, 142*(6), 667-674.

CHAPTER TEN

BEYOND RECOVERY: HEALING ADDICTION THROUGH DIFFERENTIATION
-BY WAYNE REGINA AND GINA SIMMONS

Introduction

This chapter was originally written by Wayne Regina and Gina Simmons for an invited presentation at the 1992 American Association for Marriage and Family Therapy's annual convention in Miami, Florida. Gina and I have edited portions of this chapter, while preserving its original intention and reflecting the paper's original references.

I met Gina when she was a graduate student at United States International University (U.S.I.U.). I was her dissertation chair. Gina's dissertation, titled *Interpersonal trust and perceived locus of control in the adjustment of adult children of alcoholics*, looked for any differences between Adult Child of Alcoholics (ACAs) and non-ACA controls in a non-clinical population. She found no difference in psychological adjustment between the two groups.

As Gina was finishing her dissertation, we struck up a long discussion about the recovery movement, including the 12-steps. During our conversations, we looked at both the strengths and limitations of the movement. What became obvious to us, as Bowen family systems theorists, was that the 12-steps were an important component of recovery, but not the only aspect. From a Bowen theory perspective, it seemed like the shift from using to the 12 steps was a shift in functional differentiation, not basic differentiation.

As useful as the 12-steps are, they may function as an "addiction upgrade"–from substance to 12-steps. That's no minor shift since being so closely connected to the 12-steps program is infinitely better than using and abusing. Nonetheless, it is a shift in functional differentiation only and not necessarily a shift towards greater emotional maturity, i.e., basic differentiation. We thought that promoting basic differentiation was a way of taking recovery to the next step, toward greater emotional resilience, and therefore greater independence and greater interdependence.

We submitted our proposal for differentiation as the "13th step" if you will, to the Association for Marriage and Family Therapy's annual conference in 1992. The paper and proposal were accepted, and we presented our findings and our ideas. Interestingly, while about 100 professionals attended the workshop, a sizeable minority, maybe thirty percent, left during our presentation. Perhaps the concepts were too antithetical for some in the movement. Perhaps, they weren't Bowen theorists and presenting from that perspective on the last day and the last session required too much processing. Perhaps our ideas simply fell flat on that group. Regardless, the majority of the attendees responded quite positively to our presentation. They seemed to understand that something else was needed rather than a permanent wedding of the addict and the 12 steps program.

This chapter presents our thinking about Bowen theory's concept of differentiation and its relationship to the recovery movement.

Chapter Ten

Beyond Recovery: Healing Addiction through Differentiation
-by Wayne Regina and Gina Simmons

The recovery movement has grown dramatically since Alcoholics Anonymous (AA) was formed in the years preceding World War II (Wegscheider-Cruise, 1989). Borrowing from the 12-step model of AA, recovery programs in the form of support groups and clinical treatment have proliferated in many areas, including Adult Children of Alcoholics (ACA), Co-Dependency (Co-Dependents Anonymous), Adult Children of Dysfunctional Families (ACDF), overeaters (OA), substance abuse (Cocaine Anonymous, Narcotics Anonymous), overtly emotional persons (Emotions Anonymous), and even defectors from fundamentalist religions (Fundamentalists Anonymous).

Clearly, the recovery movement has helped many people fight addictions, leave abusive relationships, and break self-destructive denial and minimizing patterns. Nonetheless, questions remain regarding the long-term effectiveness and appropriateness of the AA model and in the splintering and proliferation of the recovery field. Questions include the degree to which these movements seek to increase a person's capacity to manage life and the degree to which any changes, such as cessation of the addictive behavior, are dependent on forces outside of the self, within the groups themselves.

In addition, with such a linear focus on parental and family pathology, and its direct relationship to addictive behaviors in offspring, many in the recovery movement, including clinicians who work with them, define and label individuals solely on the presence or absence of these addictions in the self, the family of origin, or the current family (family of procreation). We will explore the problems incurred through this labeling process.

Rather than only viewing addiction, disease, and recovery through the lens of the 12-step model, we propose addressing addiction through Bowen's family systems theory, a comprehensive theoretical system that suggests that all "dis-ease" processes are significantly influenced by the level of differentiation or emotional maturity in the person and the family. Bowen family systems theory is alternately referred to as Bowen's theory or Bowen theory. First, a few definitions are warranted.

From a Bowen family systems theory perspective, differentiation is the key variable in understanding the continuum from illness to health. A person's core, internal level of resiliency and adaptiveness, as well as her capacity to form authentic relationships with others, is tantamount to one's level of basic differentiation. Basic differentiation is synonymous with emotional maturity. It also refers to a person's capacity to "see clearly"; that is, to separate feelings and emotions when needed, such as when confronted with intense situations. This ability helps prevent emotional reactivity that can undermine relationships, situations, and an effectively functioning self.

Further, a person's capacity for managing life is a consequence of that individual's basic differentiation plus the degree of strain on that person and her environmental and relationship systems. Emotional strains include intensity in current relationships and stressors that might activate genetic predispositions. These twin factors—basic differentiation and current strains—refer to a person's level of functional differentiation.

In this matrix, functional differentiation varies as strain varies, since basic differentiation is much more stable over time. And, the higher a person's basic differentiation, the more "inoculation" she has against the vicissitudes of life since as emotional maturity increases, so too does her ability to manage what life has in store for her. She is less reactive to others and the environment, and she is more focused on her internal compass. Conversely, as emotional maturity diminishes, so too does the ability to tolerate stress. A person becomes more reactive to others and the environment, and she is less attuned to her internal compass.

Functional differentiation is a consequence of a person's reliance on others–the environmental context and relationships–and not self. Functional differentiation, then, is tied to external factors, including relationships and groups. In other words, change is not the result of a strengthening of the internal core, a solid self. Change, if it occurs, is dependent on what others say and do, and the circumstances of an unpredictable world. This kind of change is externally dependent and does not emanate from inside the person. As a result, it is more vulnerable to outside forces.

While much of recovery is focused on changing the self, the 12-step model relies on many external factors outside the person–attendance in and participation with the group, the support of a sponsor, giving up self-empowerment to a spiritual or transpersonal "higher power," etc. As such, we question the degree to which these recovery programs promote basic differentiation rather than functional differentiation. That is, we wonder the extent to which any changes in behavior, feeling, and thinking are dependent on forces within the self or relationships and context outside the self.

In working with and treating addiction based on Bowen theory, addiction is "healed" through increasing basic differentiation. A Bowen family systems theory perspective also provides a common reference point and language in discussing addiction. For example, we use the term *loss of self* or *pseudo self* to understand the effects of addiction on the individual. To frame the recovery process through reclaiming or strengthening the individual, we use the terms *developing and consolidating a solid self*. With such a theoretical orientation, persons are understood through their actions and reactions in their emotional, feeling, intellectual, and relationship systems rather than through an "inheritance" of family pathology, placement in the abuse—abstinence continuum, or the disease process of addiction itself.

Using differentiation as a roadmap, issues of addiction, recovery, and multigenerational emotional processes are viewed more holistically, emphasizing the uniqueness and strengths of each person and her family system. From this perspective, a person's capacity to make better choices and assume greater accountability for her life becomes more important in the healing process than her or her family's past or current "pathology."

The Self-Help Movement

Certainly, peer identification can be a powerful lever for change. If a person attends an AA meeting, for example, he finds needed assistance in facing his alcohol addiction, breaking through denial and minimizing, and obtaining necessary support. However, while clearly useful for many, the danger exists that people get caught in a "cult of dysfunction," defining themselves and their lives primarily through their behaviors and through their participation in and identification with the 12-step group. This type of group self-definition runs the risk of promoting a pseudo-self or false self, one dependent on an identity formed through togetherness pressures rather than from greater individuality (Kerr & Bowen, 1988).

The togetherness life force is a potent energy that propels people towards union with others and can temporarily relieve anxiety through these connections. Unfortunately, the togetherness life force often manifests itself through a kind of "stuck togetherness" such that those who disagree with the group are dismissed, shunned, or rejected in some way. As togetherness pressures increase in any relationship or relationship system, so too does pressure to think, feel, and act the same. Individuality is sacrificed.

The countervailing force, the individuality life force, is a potent energy that propels people toward separateness, uniqueness, and a more "solid self" (Kerr & Bowen, 1988). Bowen theory suggests that the more solid the self, that is, the greater the emotional maturity of a person, the more enhanced the capacity for relationships and intimacy. With greater emotional maturity, the self is not lost in relationships but, rather, is augmented, allowing for further growth and individuation within relationships. In this way, mature individuality supports mature togetherness and mature togetherness strengthens mature individuality.

So, while 12-step programs unquestionably offer the alcoholic or addict the benefit of support from fellow travelers on the road to recovery, the risk remains that assistance may be more about group compliance than enhancing true independent thinking, feeling, and acting. In Bowen theory, this kind of group identification and subsequent loss of self is referred to as *emotional fusion* with others. Unfortunately, self-definition through emotional fusion is precisely what occurs with addictive behavior through fusion with the substance. In this way, the group identification process with AA itself may be analogous to the prior abusive behavior. And, as external change is not a change to the core self, this external reliance can actually be a driving force towards lowering the functional differentiation level of the addict. Lower functional differentiation makes a person more vulnerable to relapse, affairs, and other problematic behaviors.

For example, Lisa was raised in a home with an alcoholic parent, and she is emotionally reactive to the experiences in her upbringing. She attends an Adult Children of Alcoholics 12 step meeting. Issues emerge regarding her family of origin, and Lisa then defines herself as an ACA. She finds herself consistently in relationships with alcoholic men, and while she does not drink alcohol herself, she begins attending AA meetings to overcome her "addiction" to alcoholic men. While attending AA meetings, Lisa begins to refer to herself as "alcoholic" and "ACA." This new self-concept, tied to parental pathology and the pathology of her partners, is reinforced by those in her support groups, psychotherapists, and the larger culture. As a consequence, as a less differentiated person, Lisa remains emotionally reactive to her family of origin and significant others. She remains dependent on her support group, which reinforces her "powerlessness" and hence her negative self-identity. Used in this manner, the AA/ACA 12 step movement becomes an example of undifferentiated, emotionally clouded, reactive thinking not based on the facts or the reality of her situation.

This reactive thinking has led to the notion that having "pathological parents" is now sufficient to place someone in a diagnostic category in need of treatment. Borkman (1987) criticizes this perspective by suggesting that the label "ACA" may, in fact, stigmatize individuals and create psychosocial problems. Burk and Sher's (1990) research supports this. Their study used videotaped interviews of teenagers and found that mental health workers consistently attributed more pathology to teens labeled children of alcoholics (COA) than those labeled as non-COA. Burk and Sher (1990) also found that teens already view COAs as more like mentally ill people than "normals." A potential stigma will likely ensue if resilient, more emotionally mature individuals are assumed to possess negative characteristics merely as a result of the COA label. In fact, Calder and Kostyniuk's (1989) research suggest that the majority of COAs do not possess the negative personality characteristics attributed to them.

ACA and COA Adaptiveness

While many clinicians may argue that ACAs all have problems with adjustment and therefore should get the help that they need through 12 step programs and "inner child" work, the empirical research does not support that conclusion. For example, in a study using a non-clinical population, Simmons (1991) found no difference in psychological adjustment between ACAs and controls. Similarly, Herjanic et al.'s (1977) and Benson and Heller's (1987) research found no relationship between the severity of the father's pathology and disturbance in the offspring. In fact, Barnard and Soentgen (1986)'s research suggests that ACAs from a non-clinical population actually scored higher than non-ACAs in their capacity for intimacy. Herjanic et al. also found higher self-esteem scores for COAs as compared to non-COAs. With an adolescent sample, Dinning and Berk's (1989) work suggested that there was no significant relationship between social maladjustment and severity of parental alcoholism.

All of this research implies that other variables besides parental alcoholism influence the more adaptive and resilient capacities found in many children of alcoholics. Parental recovery and relapse may be two such criteria. For example, Callan and Jackson's research (1986) and Moos and Billings's (1982) research with children of alcoholics suggests that children of relapsed alcoholics had more emotional problems, including anxiety and depression, than did control families and families in recovery.

From a Bowen theory perspective, these differences in decreased emotional reactivity and increased functioning in recovery families may accompany a family's continued commitment to recovery, even if these differences are only due to increases in functional differentiation. In contrast, relapse would almost certainly bring about increases in the family's anxiety, including a re-triangulation of the alcohol by the family system and a subsequent decrease in functional differentiation.

Barnard and Soentgen's (1986) research also demonstrate that ACAs from non-clinical populations have normal adjustment compared to ACAs who seek treatment. These studies and others question the simplistic presumption that difficulties in adult adjustment are always a direct result of alcoholism or addiction in the family (Beidler, 1989; Burk & Sher, 1989; Clair & Genest, 1987; Werner, 1986). Rather, a more thoughtful and nuanced approach will look for common variables in experience as well as the uniqueness in individual adaptation in order to understand the differentiation process in these stressful home environments.

There appears to be a clear bias in the ACA and COA literature that focuses on clinical pathology but neglects those who function adequately and who may have, in fact, learned to thrive in an alcoholic family environment (Burk & Sher, 1989). When the variable of differentiation is introduced, the key diagnostic determinant becomes the degree of emotional separation from the family system, not the mere presence or absence of "dysfunction" in the family system. With this shift in perspective, clinicians and researchers could focus on the common characteristics and experiences of non-clinical, more differentiated ACAs. This strength-based approach may yield positive results in investigating those achieving greater emotional separation from the many symptomatic disturbances within the family, including alcoholism and addiction.

Undifferentiated Application of the AA Model

The recovery movement has splintered into many facets, with each group modeled after the 12 steps of AA. Their underlying assumption is that if it works for the alcoholic it must work for the spouse or partner of the alcoholic, the child of the alcoholic, the compulsive eater, and so on. Many clinicians, aware of the muddy distinctions in the recovery movement, have begun classifying patients as "adult children of dysfunctional parent" (Bradshaw, 1988; Friel & Friel, 1988; Whitfield, 1987). Rather than providing clarity, however, this widened focus potentially pathologizes nearly every human problem.

For example, Wegscheider-Cruse (1989) states that all adult children of alcoholics suffer "from the illness of co-dependency" (p.243). "This 'disease' of co-dependency," she continues, is "similar to the disease of chemical dependency" (p.243). Wegscheider-Cruse (1989) thus broadens the "illness" of co-dependency to anyone who comes from a family "that is preoccupied with a secret, trauma or some other concern" (p.245). These other concerns include "rigid religiosity, workaholism, sexual acting out, mental illness and chronic physical illness" (p.245). From this vantage point, Wegscheider-Cruse typifies many writers in the recovery field who view virtually any hardship in life as contributing to a lifelong disease in need of treatment.

What family, though, has not suffered difficult or traumatic incidents in the course of its life-cycle? Life itself creates these challenges—people are born, they live, they triumph, they suffer, they die. As family members, we all share these common human experiences, as we are exposed to severe losses and challenges over the decades of our lives. Kaminer (1992) believes that to pathologize common challenges in the family life-cycle trivializes the suffering caused by genuine trauma, severe acute and chronic disease, and great suffering. In addition, this mindset diminishes the rich variety of individual and family adaptations to difficult life events.

This type of definition and expansion of co-dependency to most families extrapolates the 12 steps of AA, with its wide-angle focus, to a vast number of people and their experiences. Further, it keeps individuals psychologically fused to their parents, focusing on unmet dependency needs rather than the integration of these hardships into an interdependent self-concept and self-identity.

To be fair, most recovery experts view recovery as a developmental process requiring a psychological fusion to the recovery process as a beginning step. Bowen theory refers to this as *upgrading the addiction*. Clearly, emotional attachment to a support group in order to stop ingesting unhealthy, brain damaging substances produces far fewer side effects than continuing the substance abuse and dependence. One flaw in the 12-step approach, however, is the notion of recovery as a lifelong process and identity, which, if not embraced, leads to further addiction and eventual death (Brown, 1985; Gorski & Miller, 1982; Wegscheider-Cruse, 1989). This acceptance of a lifelong identity as an addict may stunt the separation and individuation necessary for healthy emotional maturation.

A Developmental Model of Recovery

Recovery experts such as Brown (1985) and Gorski and Miller (1982) conceptualize recovery as a developmental process. Gorski and Miller (1982) list developmental stages beginning with stabilization and continuing through early, middle, and late recovery. Brown (1985) borrows from Piaget's model of development and employs the concepts of assimilation, accommodation, equilibrium, and ego flexibility to describe alcoholism recovery. She views the phases of recovery as progressing from the drinking phase to transition, early recovery, and ongoing recovery.

In Gorski and Miller's (1982) recovery model, the individual enters the recovery process after a motivational crisis, which is an event signaling to the alcoholic that something is very wrong. Following the crisis, the individual begins the first stage of recovery called stabilization. During this stage, detoxification and counseling take place to stabilize the alcoholic individual physically and psychologically. In early recovery, the person processes the emotional and cognitive states that led to the crisis and stabilization phase. Middle recovery is characterized by a commitment to long-term treatment. The final stage of middle recovery requires "building a structured, self-regulated sobriety plan" (p.51). The focus is on spiritual values, life, living, and serenity.

Most recovery experts describe recovery as a practice without an end. If a person attends AA or a recovery program for the rest of her life and doesn't use, then that person remains in recovery. This thinking leads to some rather confusing contradictions. For example, Gorski and Miller (1982) write, "the recovery process ends when a person is in remission" (p.48). Then later, "since alcoholism is a chronic and incurable disease, continuous maintenance of a recovery program is necessary even after remission is achieved. This ongoing period marks the final phase, namely the maintenance period" (p.48). The prevalence of this thinking leads many recovering people to fear ever leaving or moving on from the program since they have been told that "working the program" is the only way to remain sober or cope with the disease.

From a Bowen family systems theory perspective, although attachment to the recovery group may initially help through an addiction upgrade, any changes that arise from this attachment and fusion stem from an increase in functional differentiation and not basic differentiation. This means that a person's core level of self or emotional maturity often remains largely unchanged. As a result, attachment to the recovery system itself has risks, of relapse and other relationship and intrapersonal challenges. Clearly, sobriety acquired with the support of a group represents an important and necessary first step on the road to greater differentiation and development of a more functional and resilient self. From our perspective, though, abstinence is only the first step.

Sobriety itself is first-order change or reduction in symptoms. Continued progress in emotionally maturing is not guaranteed. Sobriety can pave the way for the possibility of second-order change, which is an alteration in the structure of the person and the family system through greater emotional maturity, but this requires more than simply attending a support group or working a recovery program.

While this increase in functional differentiation brought on by sobriety may create some initial stability–which in itself is vital–only an increase in basic differentiation can foster a deeper level of healing, one that has the potential to break the multigenerational transmission of substance abuse to succeeding generations. This greater emotional wholeness comes from developing a more solid core, a self that is more trustworthy, honest, and resilient. This is the process of emotionally separating, from the alcohol or other drug, from role assignments from the family of origin, from destructive relationships and patterns, etc. Greater emotional separation promotes an authentic intimacy based on a growing sense of selfhood. Real choices emerge from the process of wanting, not needing.

Bowen Family Systems Theory and Alcoholism

Conceptualizing alcoholism from a Bowen theory perspective is not new. Bowen (1978), himself, described the essential features of alcoholism as a family "disease." For Bowen, several theoretical assumptions were crucial. First, a person's level of basic differentiation provides a more useful prognosticator than "the intensity of the alcoholism" (p.267). As such, symptoms themselves do not inform the therapist about the system as much as the degree of emotional maturity and subsequent adaptability, flexibility, and resiliency of the system.

Second, drinking increases the emotional isolation of the alcoholic. The degree of emotional isolation is correlated with a lack of emotional separation from the family of origin. The alcoholic's fusion with alcohol as a way to emotionally isolate mirrors the fusion or lack of differentiation in the family of origin. This fusion with a substance then influences the development and maintenance of alcoholism and other relationships.

Third, with married alcoholics, the marital relationship is powerfully reciprocal. This reciprocity, in turn, perpetuates a dynamic equilibrium between the couple with alcohol as a central feature of the marital and family system. Alcohol serves as an anxiety binder for the marriage through emotional triangles. Emotional triangles are ways to manage conflict between two people by bringing in a third "other." That third other may be a person, place, or thing such as a substance, belief, work, or any other attachment. Emotional triangles may create some initial temporary stability, but they foster greater long-term instability. The alcohol and the alcoholic occupy the inside position of the emotional triangle; the spouse or significant other, in turn, inhabits the outside position. Cessation of alcohol use begins the process of de-triangulating alcohol from the marriage. Conflicts "detoured" from the marriage through alcohol are now re-focused back to the marriage itself and to the drinking and its associated problems.

As such, terminating drinking can cause the over-functioning spouse, or "enabler," who "borrowed self" from the relationship to feel threatened by the partner's sobriety. The under-functioning alcoholic begins to halt the functional adaptation of "giving up self" in the relationship and to the alcohol. In these ways, the alcoholic, by decreasing emotional isolation through cessation, threatens the stability of the marital system itself. Marital conflict often escalates after the cessation of drinking as the emotional balance in the marriage is altered. This release of additional anxiety from the couple makes relapse more likely in order to restore the former equilibrium to the system. Therapeutic interventions and treatment can help couples manage the additional anxiety, while maintaining sobriety. Proper treatment promotes the stability and continuation of the marriage as the role and function of alcohol is reduced in the emotional triangle that once bound the anxiety in the system.

Lastly, since the emotional isolation created by the drinking masks an emotional fusion or lack of adequate differentiation from the family of origin and other significant relationships, symptom relief itself–the cessation of alcohol use–must be accompanied by attempts to increase self-capacity or a solid self. Self-capacity is increased, in part, through understanding systemic processes. This, in turn, encourages acting based on a more expansive way of thinking.

Failure to understand and treat the alcoholic system through a Bowen family systems approach, or other approaches that have strong systemic perspectives, can increase anxiety, for the alcoholic, the treating mental health worker, and the family members. This intensification of anxiety may result in a re-triangulation with alcohol or a new emotional triangle with another person, place, or thing in an "automatic" effort to restore some dynamic equilibrium. In these situations, affairs, relapse, substitute addictions, and other symptoms can result (Kerr & Bowen, 1988).

Theory in Relation to Technique

A common critique of Bowen family systems theory is the lack of specificity on how to accomplish therapeutic goals. We have heard this pointed criticism from recovery advocates, as the recovery field is itself a methodology rather than a clearly articulated theory. It matters less to advocates of the generic application of the 12-step model whether or not alcoholism and co-dependency share a fundamental biological or emotional similarity. What seems more important is that everyone can find relief in surrender to the 12 steps.

Interestingly, Bowen theory makes some assumptions that parallel this thinking, for it matters not whether a person is alcoholic, bulimic, "work addicted," or "co-dependent." Rather, what is central is the person's level of basic differentiation and the basic differentiation of the marital and family system within which she resides. Similarly, the focus of treatment does not rely on a prescribed set of techniques. Instead, treatment requires shifting one's thinking about the individual and her relationships to a systems perspective and acting based on that thinking.

As the therapist conceptualizes the family systemically, several things may happen. First, everyone in the family is viewed as important and significant, and not just to the addict's using. Increased comprehension often leads to greater clarity and compassion toward all, since every family faces challenges in growing children and helping them mature so that they can function in the world more independently. The therapist, in turn, can maintain the neutrality necessary for effective treatment if she has a good road map to follow (Friedman, 1985). Though the map is not the territory, a good theory, like a good map, can relieve anxiety and make the journey more pleasant and interesting.

Second, understanding Bowen family systems theory frees the therapist to bring forth the creativity necessary for effective treatment. Each person and family is unique, and understanding this uniqueness helps to uncover and utilize strengths in the system. Rather than a set formula of techniques, a Bowen therapist who works in the recovery field has many options available, including using traditional resources such as 12 step programs like AA and NA.

Third, certain ways of thinking lend themselves to certain ways of acting. *Thinking systems* generates a therapeutic environment that allows the use of many techniques. Through a case history, we will demonstrate how Bowen therapists generate creative techniques to help a family in recovery de-triangulate alcohol and develop greater emotional maturity.

De-Triangulation and the Development of a Solid Self

Papero (1991) makes an essential point about stress and conflict in a two-person relationship. When under stress, a twosome will bring in a third to relieve or "bind" anxiety. These third points on the triangle are anxiety binders such as alcohol, drugs, sex, work, food, and religion. They have their own corresponding recovery groups. Clearly, alcohol and drug addiction carries physiological, psychological, and social consequences more immediately dangerous than some other points of emotional triangulation. Even so, discovering the central and interlocking emotional triangles is more important to the therapeutic process than the specific anxiety binder in the triangle.

Triangulation is defined as a binding of anxiety *by the system* and reflects a *pseudo-self* or false self with others. Emotional fusion reflects an underlying level of chronic anxiety and is inversely related to the degree of basic differentiation.

The substance, food, sex, or other anxiety binder can also *generate anxiety* and so a negative spiral develops, driving levels of functional differentiation lower. Friedman (1991) conceptualizes this process as a graph with "condition" (the stress, strain, or intensity of the symptom) on the x-axis and "response" (the degree of basic differentiation) on the y-axis. As therapists, we can more readily impact the conditions on the horizontal, stress axis than we can the responses on the vertical axis, which is heavily influenced by multigenerational emotional processes. So, methods for decreasing strain on the system can be very effective initially. Stabilizing a system in runaway will almost always increase functional differentiation. However, *the underlying dynamic that created the systems vulnerability lies on the response axis, the y-axis.* Without a concerted effort, over time, designed to increase a solid self and greater independent functioning, the system and the individuals comprising it remain vulnerable to symptom development or re-development, including re-triangulation of the substance or other potent anxiety binders.

As an example, Robert and Jean requested therapy due to problems with Mary, their 16-year-old daughter. Mary had been symptomatic for years. The current symptoms included running away and drug experimentation (sex and drugs). Robert, a child of an alcoholic and a self-described "recovering alcoholic" for sixteen years, regularly attended AA meetings. A frequent complaint by Robert was that Jean never attended Alanon. A frequent complaint by Jean was that Robert spent more time with AA, including meetings, being a sponsor, retreats, and conventions, than he did with his own family.

A further history revealed that although Robert had remained sober for 16 years, religiously attended AA, and worked his program, he believed that AA was central to his remaining sober rather than his own self-regulation. The system simply shifted the emotional triangle from emotional fusion with alcohol to emotional fusion with AA. In both instances, Jean remained on the outside position. The daughter, raised in an emotional field where fusion was the norm, was attempting to separate and individuate from the family system through triangulating sex and drugs. While her impulse to emotional separate from her family was a normal part of adolescence, her attempts at differentiating were clearly ineffective as they were based on a *pseudo-self* or a *false self* and not a true, *solid self*. The multigenerational legacy of alcoholism was repeating itself.

Recovery advocates might prescribe 12 step programs for this "alcoholic family" with a "co-dependent" mother and a "COA/addict" daughter as a way of gaining control of the symptoms and the family system. However, equally essential for us were de-triangulation techniques designed to decrease the emotional isolation between the spouses.

The co-therapists placed themselves in a therapeutic triangle with the family in an attempt to free the daughter. In both family and marital sessions, family members were asked to initially speak directly to the therapists and not each other. We promoted self-focus for all family members, and we blocked blaming and other conflicts of will where people try to get others to change. We challenged the family to use "I language," the language of personal responsibility, to help family members develop self-regulation, self-reflection, and self-responsibility (Lerner, 1989). When the focus drifted to another through blaming or anger, we would simply shift the session back to the speaker. We asked what the speaker thought, felt, and wanted, and we explored alternative choices and new behaviors.

Our therapeutic triangle–promoting a focus on the therapists designed to lessen the emotional hold on the daughter–helped to free the daughter from the spousal conflict and manage the subsequent anxiety released by the changes in the family system. Through therapeutic enactments and boundary making, all family members developed greater self-capacity. They gained a bit more clarity and objectivity about their family and their individual functioning. Our efforts at de-triangulating the daughter began the long process of increasing basic differentiation, which had not been previously advocated or affected during the father's sixteen years of recovery.

The therapists did not discourage the father's attendance at AA meetings. In fact, as AA was a part of his belief system of abstinence, we encouraged him to continue with his regular attendance. Further, we suggested that Jean might find Alanon helpful. We did not, however, insist that she attend this or other co-dependency groups. Strikingly, after one year of treatment, Robert admitted that nothing, including all of the family stress, could ever make him drink again. As he became more accepting of his own personal power, Robert decreased but did not eliminate his AA attendance without any prompting by the therapists. Robert had more time for Jean, and Jean had more time for Robert.

We educated the family about Bowen theory principles. They, in turn, began to recognize their own emotional triangles and to minimize their impact. Finally, as each parent developed a greater self, the system's emotional field began shifting, freeing the daughter to discover more appropriate and empowering ways to separate and individuate from her parents. Problems remained, but the two central anxiety binders for the couple–alcohol and the daughter–had been uncovered and minimized. The family was much calmer and more functional as a result of these interventions.

Conclusion

Much criticism surrounds the 12-step recovery field. These critiques have intensified as the movement has splintered into many factions. Clearly, the recovery movement has highlighted many problems in living previously ignored or minimized. Substance abuse and dependency, eating disorders, sexual addiction, work over-involvement, and other challenges negatively impact individuals, families, and society. These behaviors have exacted high personal, interpersonal, and social costs. However, through the 12 steps, the recovery field risks imparting simplistic solutions to complex problems. Bowen family systems theory offers an examination of these challenges from the lens of natural systems, demonstrating universal human struggles as well as how best to treat them, independent of culture, gender, or family structure.

Traditional solutions rely on a prescribed set of techniques such as those offered by the 12-steps. In contrast, Bowen family systems theory presents a way of thinking about these problems through differentiation and the related concepts of chronic anxiety and emotional triangles. This orientation offers a way of "healing" addictions through the process of making a person more whole and complete. We facilitate this "making whole and complete" or healing process through developing greater emotional separation; increasing self-reflection, self-improvement, and self-regulation; promoting self-responsibility; and improving capacity for more authentic and intimate relationships. Encouraging basic differentiation becomes the universal solution to minimizing states of elevated chronic anxiety, which give rise to these addictions and other significant conditions.

A full elaboration of Bowen theory and therapy goes beyond the scope of this chapter. However, the essential characteristics of addictions are not different from other emotional, social, and physical disorders. All involve multigenerational emotional processes of transmission and influence; emotional fusion and the subsequent lack of emotional separation; the binding of chronic and acute anxiety; heightened emotional reactivity; and lowered levels of functional and basic differentiation. Treatment focuses on increasing emotional maturity through de-triangulation, activating and promoting a more solid, resilient self, and increasing objectivity and clarity within the family system through education, responsibility training, and thoughtful action. Techniques themselves become secondary to theory as techniques are derived from the unique features of each personal and interpersonal system encountered.

References

Barnard, C.T. & Soentgen, P.A. (1986). Children of alcoholics: Characteristics and treatment. Alcoholic Treatment Quarterly, 3(4), 47-65.

Beidler, R.J. (1989). Adult children of alcoholics: Is it really a separate field for study? Drugs and Society, 3(3-4), 133-1421.

Benson, C.S. & Heller, K. (1987). Factors in the current adjustment of young adult daughters of alcoholic and problem drinking fathers. Journal of Abnormal Psychology, 96(4), 305-312.

Borkman, T. (1987). Sociologist looks at COAs. California Alcohol Forum, 3, 1-2.

Bowen, M. (1978). Family therapy in clinical practice. New York, N.Y.: Jason Aronson.

Bradshaw, J. (1988). Bradshaw on: The family. Deerfield Beach, FL: Health Communications, Inc.

Brown, S. (1985). Treating the alcoholic: A developmental model of recovery. New York, NY: John Wiley & Sons.

Burk, J.P. & Sher, K.J. (1989). The "forgiven children" revisited: Neglected areas of COA research. Clinical Psychology Review. 9(3), 285-302.

Burk, J.P. & Sher, K.J. (1990). Labeling the child of an alcoholic: Negative stereotyping by mental health professionals and peers. Journal of Studies on Alcohol, 51(2), 156-163.

Calder, P. & Kostyniuk, A. (1989). Personality profiles of children of alcoholics. Professional Psychology Research and Practice, 20(6), 417-4128

Callan, V.J. & Jackson, D. (1986). Children of alcoholic fathers and recovered alcoholic fathers: Personal and family functioning. Journal of Studies on Alcohol, 47(2), 180-182.

Clair, D. & Genest, M. (1987). Variables associated with adjustment of offspring of alcoholic fathers. Journal of Studies on Alcohol, 48(4), 345-355.

Dinning, D.W. & Berk, L.A. (1989). The children of alcoholics screening test: Relationship to sex, family environment, and social adjustment in adolescents. Journal of Clinical Psychology, 45(2), 335-339.

Friedman, E.H. (1985). Generation to generation. New York, N.Y.: Guilford.

Friedman, E.H. (1991). Bowen theory and therapy. In A.S. Gurman & D.P. Knistern (Eds.), Handbook of Family Therapy, Volume 2 (pp. 134-170). New York, N.Y.: Brunner-Mazel.

Friel, J. & Friel, L. (1988). Adult children: The secrets of dysfunctional families. Deerfield Beach, FL: Health Communications, Inc.

Gorski, T.T. & Miller, M. (1982). Counseling for relapse prevention. Independence, MO: Herald House Independent Press.

Herjanic, B.M., Herjanic, M., Penick, E.C., Tomelleri, C.J., & Armbruster, R.B.S. (1977). Children of alcoholics. In Seixas, F. (Ed.) Currents in Alcoholism, Volume II (pp. 445-455). New York, N.Y.: Grune & Stratton.

Herjanic, B.M., Herjanic, M., Wetzel, R. & Tomelleri, C.J. (1978). Substance abuse: Its effect on offspring. Research Communications Psychology and Psychiatric Behavior, 3(1), (65-73).

Kaminer, W. (1992). I'm dysfunctional, you're dysfunctional. Reading, MA: Addison-Wesley Publishing Company, Inc.

Kerr, M.E. & Bowen, M. (1988). Family evaluation. New York, N.Y.: Norton.

Lerner, H, (1989). The dance of intimacy. New York, N.Y.: Harper Row.

Moos, R.H. & Billings, A.G. (1982). Children of alcoholics during the recovery process: Alcoholics and matched controlled families. Addictive Behavior, 7, 155-163.

Moos, R.H. & Moos, B.S. (1981). Family environment scale model. Palo Alto, CA: Consulting Psychologists Press.

Papero, D. V. (1990). Bowen family systems theory. Newton, MA: Allyn & Bacon.

Simmons, G.M. (1991). Interpersonal trust and perceived locus of control in the adjustment of adult children of alcoholics. Unpublished doctoral dissertation. United States International University, San Diego, CA.

Wegscheider-Cruise, S. (1989). Another chance: Hope and health for the alcoholic family. Palo Alto, CA: Science and Behavior Books, Inc.

Werner, E.E. (1986). Resilient offspring of alcoholics: A longitudinal study from birth to age 18. Journal of Studies of Alcohol, 47(1), 34-40.

Whitfield, C.L. (1987). Healing the child within. Deerfield Beach, FL: Health Communications, Inc.

Chapter Eleven

Bowen Family Systems Theory and Mediation

Introduction

An earlier version of this chapter was originally published in Mediation Quarterly, Volume 18, Number 2, Winter 2000. This chapter remains largely unchanged from the original with one exception: I eliminated a detailed explanation of Bowen family systems theory's central concepts from this version, as I have clearly explicated all of these concepts in chapters two and three. In this way, I have simplified and streamlined focusing on the application of Bowen theory to mediation itself.

Before conducting mediations, in the 1990s I underwent extensive training. These trainings provided all of the logistics of doing mediations—introductions, the stages of mediation, the process of mediation, techniques such as brainstorming, caucusing, agreement writing, etc. What I saw lacking was any comprehensive understanding of the nature of conflict or how mediation itself works. That is, from my perspective, the field of mediation in the late 1990s was not centered in any comprehensive theoretical system. Mediation seemed to me ripe for grounding in Bowen family systems theory, the subject of this chapter.

CHAPTER ELEVEN

BOWEN FAMILY SYSTEMS THEORY AND MEDIATION

Much has been written about training effective mediators and the stages of mediation itself (Gray, 1989; Lax and Sebenius, 1986; Moore, 1996). There is also extensive literature about mediation as a successful example of alternative dispute resolution (Avrunch, 1998; Constantino and Merchant, 1996). The research clearly demonstrates that mediation is an effective tool in creative conflict resolution, empowering others to make healthier choices in their lives and promoting the causes of peace, environmental integrity, community cohesion, and social justice (Maser, 1996; Roberts and Lundy, 1995; Suskind, Babbit, and Segal, 1993; Stamato and Jaffe, 1991; Ury, Brett, and Goldberg, 1988). The field of mediation, though, is largely technique and process-driven and lacks comprehensive theoretical perspectives on which legitimate academic disciplines are based.

This chapter is the first part of a larger work that proposes one such theoretical system to understand conflict and conduct mediations. Referred to alternately as Bowen family systems theory and Bowen theory, this theoretical model was developed in the mid to late 20th century by visionary psychiatrist Murray Bowen. His systems theory seeks to understand humans and human relationships through an ecological model based on evolutionary biology.

Here, I examine the interplay of Bowen family systems theory and mediation. I propose that mediation is an example of a human emotional system. Understanding conflict through Bowen family systems theory allows us to intervene in ways that can decrease conflict and promote peace and empowerment. I contend that, like other examples of human systems, effective mediation is a product of the interplay between the mediation process itself and various Bowen theory concepts, including chronic and acute anxiety, differentiation, and emotional triangulation.

In applying Bowen family systems theory to mediation, I include the role and function of basic and functional differentiation in the mediation system. I discuss emotional triangles and triangulation both within the mediation environment and in de-triangulating conflict so that agreements can be reached. I detail the responsibilities of the mediator to understand, monitor, and reduce anxiety in the mediation system, including the mediator's own chronic and situational anxiety. Finally, I incorporate technique as viewed via the theory and as exemplified through the use of caucusing and co-mediation.

Differentiation and Mediation

The basic differentiation levels of the parties in mediation are critically important. Besides the emotional maturity of the mediator, they may be the most essential variable in successful mediation. Parties with moderate to high levels of differentiation are likely to mediate a solution that will endure over time. They realize that mediation is more likely to get them what they want after exploring their Best Alternative to a Negotiated Agreement (BATNA) and their Worst Alternative to a Negotiated Agreement (WATNA). When they understand that mediation can create a win for them, they are not as attached to their positions, and they are more likely to respond to interest-based negotiations. It may well be that the more highly differentiated the individuals, the more they can undertake interest-based negotiations, as they are less reactive, more clearheaded, and can better separate interests from positions.

In contrast, the less differentiated the disputants, the more likely they will experience emotional reactivity in their thinking and feeling, and the more attachments they will demonstrate to positional outcomes as those positions are often a fused extension of the self. As a result, as differentiation levels of the parties decrease, so too does the likelihood of agreements. Any agreements attained will not likely survive the test of time. Other factors, of course, influence the mediation process and outcome as well, especially the level of current stressors on the parties, as I discuss later.

The basic differentiation level of the mediator is also critically important in securing a successful mediation. More highly differentiated mediators are more capable of responding to a variety of situations and conflicts. They are not attached to certain outcomes in the mediation. Rather, they can function admirably in highly charged environments and can tolerate elevated levels of conflict and ambiguity. Although not attached to outcomes, these mediators are very involved in the process, staying connected with all of the parties. They clearly outline the structure of the mediation and the roles of all involved; are self-defined and confident so as to control the mediation process without controlling the disputants or the outcome; and use appropriate humor to de-escalate the seriousness that highly invested people bring to the negotiating table.

More highly differentiated mediators may find themselves more attracted to one of the parties or one of the proposed solutions over another, but they are capable of remaining fairly neutral, reasonably balanced, and more objective. Like effective coaches for a team, they help bring out the best in the "players" without getting on the field and playing themselves. They neither over-function nor under-function out of anxiety. That is, they help create an environment where all of the disputants can fully and appropriately participate in their respective roles.

In contrast, less emotionally mature mediators see themselves as directors and players rather than coaches. They are often attached to outcomes, becoming triangulated in the conflict by siding with one individual or group over the other. They are more emotionally anxious and react from subjective positions that are usually not in the best interests of the mediation process. Less differentiated mediators do not tolerate highly charged situations well. They seek certainty and control, and they are uncomfortable in ambiguous, stressful environments. Rather than having fun with the process, they experience anxiety, anger, frustration, and other feelings that often emotionally drive the mediation. Anxiety makes them either over-function and so they are too active, influencing the parties to under-function and not take full responsibility for the mediation. Or, conversely, their elevated anxiety makes them under-function as mediators, thereby not providing an appropriate alchemical vessel within which the parties can safely and fully explore the issues between them. Agreements may merely be attempts by the parties to end the mediation and therefore may not stand the test of time. More often than not, mediation breaks down as one of the parties becomes aware of the non-neutrality and reactivity of the mediator. In sum, it may be that the differentiation level of the mediator is the single most important and influential variable in conducting successful mediations.

As mentioned in chapter two, it's important to not dichotomize the concept of differentiation when considering any human system, including that of mediation. Differentiation is not an either-or phenomenon (i.e., one is not either differentiated or undifferentiated). Rather, differentiation levels exist on a continuum of functioning. Individuals in every living human (and non-human) system span the range of differentiation levels, be they in multigenerational families, organizations, businesses, educational systems, or governments. In addition, as humans, we are all capable of modifying some of our behaviors and choosing the timing of many of our actions. That is, we are able to adjust our interactions so that they come from a place of greater clarity.

Certain guidelines are helpful in mediating more effectively, as we are all responsible for co-creating an environment that promotes differentiation. As examples, mediators can self-monitor and self-regulate their stress levels. If possible, mediators can schedule mediations at times when they function best. In addition, mediators must be aware of their emotional triggers. All mediators experience more difficulty with certain individuals or situations than others. For example, if mediating parenting time in a child custody case where child abuse has occurred and the mediator has strong negative reactions against perpetrators of abuse, she can refer the case to another mediator or work with a co-mediator who may not have the same sensitivity in this area.

Also, it is important for mediators to monitor the parties in mediation. Mediation is more likely to succeed when the disputants are fairly calm than when they are anxious and agitated. While the disputants are by definition in conflict, the emotional environment the mediator helps create can assist the parties to reduce their anxiety. This lessening can promote an increase in functional differentiation and, as a result, the likelihood of mediation success. I'm defining success here as the parties becoming clear about what they want, which may or may not mean continuing mediation to find a mutually-acceptable solution.

In contrast, the environment the mediator helps to create can increase anxiety, thereby decreasing functional differentiation and diminishing the chances of success. As leader of the mediation system, the mediator's emotional maturity is central to the emotional tone set in the mediation and, as a result, considerably influences the outcome.

In addition, supervisors and trainers must monitor those being trained. Not everyone functions well in highly stressful, decidedly ambiguous environments. Assisting trainees and beginning mediators to learn techniques may have some benefits. But, working to support trainees and beginning mediators to increase their emotional maturity through promoting self-reflection, self-regulation, and interpersonal relating will ultimately result in more mediation success than simply training in techniques and methods.

There are times, however, when trainers and supervisors would do well to recommend a different occupation for less emotionally mature mediators and trainees. Much of the profession remains self-regulated and peer-regulated. As such, it is in the best interests of everyone—trainees, supervisors, the public, and the profession—that we not shy away from helping less differentiated and less capable individuals self-select out of the profession. This is done in every self-regulated and peer-regulated profession. For example, codes of ethics help define acceptable codes of conduct. Mediators should be vigilant about not fostering those without the appropriate emotional maturity to ethically practice in a new and growing occupation or impose themselves on an unsuspecting public.

Demonstrating a long-term commitment to increase one's own differentiation provides the best opportunity to decrease reactivity and boost personal functioning in difficult, anxiety-soaked situations (Friedman, 1991, 1996). This is true for mediators and trainees alike. Individuals throughout history have faced enormous obstacles and overcome them through personal growth, self-reflection, and transformation. Many avenues exist to increase differentiation, including focused meditation, psychotherapy, martial arts, and spiritual practices. Unfortunately, many disciplines promoting personal growth tend to foster dependency, and while they may temporarily increase *functional* differentiation, they do not necessarily promote increases in *basic* differentiation. Promoting emotional maturity assists people in developing long-term practices designed to help them cultivate equanimity, mindfulness, self-capacity, non-attachment, secure relationships, and/or spiritual grounding. In addition, coaches and supervisors trained in Bowen theory can, over time, assist individuals and groups to achieve some increases in basic differentiation.

Ed Friedman's Two-Factor Theory of Functioning Applied to Mediating Parties

Family therapist, organizational consultant, rabbi, and self-described "Bowen disciple" Edwin Friedman (1991) conceptualized functioning by using a two-factor graph with differentiation levels from 0-100 on the y-axis and current strain, that is, life stressors, from 0-100 on the x-axis. This four-quadrant model examines response/reaction and re-adaptation/ resiliency as a function of one's position on the graph. I conceptualize one's x-axis/y-axis coordinate as reflecting a person's functional differentiation at a given moment in time.

Response/
Differentiation

100

II | I

Condition/
Stress

0   100

III | IV

0

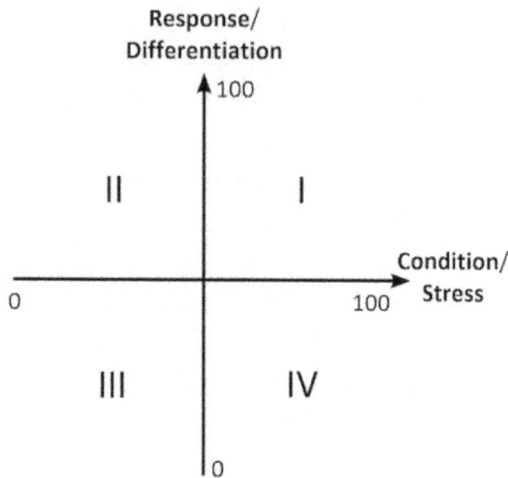

Persons with low to moderate strain (0-50) and moderate to high levels of differentiation (50-100) are located in Quadrant I, the upper left quadrant. Their stress is manageable, and they handle their current life challenges well. Triangulation is minimal. That is, they deal with conflict and stress directly, they have plentiful resources, and they demonstrate heightened levels of adaptation and resiliency. These individuals do the best in mediation as participants and as mediators. They separate positions from interests and remain relatively calm in anxious environments. As a result, these individuals demonstrate more objectivity in their thinking and behavior.

Persons with low to moderate stress (0-50) and low to moderate levels of differentiation (0-50) are positioned in Quadrant II, the lower left quadrant. They find it more formidable meeting their current life challenges. Even though their current stressors are "objectively" not overwhelming and may in fact be about the same as they are for those in Quadrant I, these people do not have the range of resources those in Quadrant I possess.

They carry more chronic anxiety, which makes life adjustments more challenging. As such, their ability to adapt is compromised. They triangulate more; that is, they channel their anxiety through alcohol, drugs, food, blaming others, religion, beliefs, affairs, relationships in general, and so on. They lack resources and often find themselves in the legal and social services systems that force solutions on them. If strain on the x-axis is reduced, these individuals can usually attain a higher level of functional differentiation and often do fine in society and mediation.

I recommend that people in Quadrant II work to decrease their x-axis stressors to the degree possible before undertaking mediation. Of course, this is not always possible, and, in fact, the conflict bringing them into mediation may be exacerbating their maladaptive or reactive functioning. These individuals need more "connection" from the mediator. The mediator must work carefully and consciously to develop and strengthen rapport with these individuals without siding with them, since showing preference can create an emotional triangle with the other party on the outside position.

Individuals with moderate to high stress (50-100) and moderate to high levels of differentiation (50-100) are situated in Quadrant III, the upper right quadrant. For a time, they may appear multi-symptomatic and poorly functioning as many are experiencing moderately high to high stress that is temporarily overwhelming. Others on the highest end of the x-axis have experienced a catastrophic loss or incident and so appear to be less adaptive and capable then they truly are. That is, due to their intense trauma, their degree of functional differentiation is lower than their level of basic differentiation.

High-end x-axis situations include such stressors as the untimely loss of a family member or loved one; being a victim of war, terrorism, or natural disaster; and experiencing a serious illness, trauma, crime, or accident. These individuals respond well with care and treatment and, despite their current life stressors, they have the internal and external resources necessary to assist in their recovery. Prognosis is good. The events themselves may become life lessons, and, often, these people eventually return to their lives scarred but functional. Many are, in fact, transformed by their experiences and dedicate their lives to serving others similarly damaged.

Even though these people are generally high functioning, their current life circumstances mitigate against mediation at this difficult time. If possible, mediators should delay mediating with these individuals until they achieve some semblance of equilibrium and equanimity, after which they are likely to do well in mediation. For example, in victim-offender mediation, a victim in a highly charged emotional state is likely to be re-traumatized in mediation and must re-establish some emotional stability before confronting the offender. With even a modest reduction in stress through providing a safe and secure environment, these people can reactivate and reclaim the internal and external reserves needed to adjust to their new life circumstances.

Individuals with moderate to high strain (50-100) and low to moderate levels of differentiation (0-50) are found in Quadrant IV, the lower right quadrant. These people have experienced difficult or catastrophic life events, and they are the least capable of managing them. They greatly consume society's resources and are ever present in social systems, including the courts, prisons, and/or social services. Their lives are in constant turmoil and crisis, and they are in a downward spiral. Sets of poor decisions, unfortunate events, and/or oppressive environments, sometimes generations deep, create other stressors. These individuals are the poorest candidates for mediation. They tend to see themselves as victims, blaming others for their problems. It is often preferable for them to seek a legal recourse, as this provides the structure that they need, and the solution provided by the courts is at least right or wrong in their eyes. Managing ambiguity and interest-based negotiations is often impossibly difficult for them.

In every quadrant, reductions on the x-axis, that is, reducing acute anxiety stressors, will lead to increased functioning. Less stress makes life easier. Reducing chronic anxiety and increasing basic differentiation are more difficult and take much longer. Even when using a two-factor system for understanding functioning and adaptation, determining a person's basic differentiation level at any moment in time is quite difficult. Basic differentiation can only be evaluated over a period of time and through a variety of situations. Ideally, then, mediators would be wise to observe their clients over time.

Unfortunately, this presents its own challenges, as mediators usually work with people in time-limited circumstances and environments. Nonetheless, individuals who attend mediation with impediments in tracking the process or with high emotional reactivity may be in a temporarily difficult situation but may improve as they begin the process of learning and adapting.

And, attending a mediation can itself feel stressful. People are sometimes court-referred. As such, they may only be present because a judge orders them to attend. Union leaders carry the burden of representing a large number of constituents; business leaders must answer to corporate boards and shareholders. In multi-party mediations, representatives from various stakeholder groups must balance the needs of the stakeholders with the desire to create an agreement that may be the best that they can obtain, given the complexities of the situation and the realities of the courts. Parents in conflict over a dissolving marriage are sometimes predisposed to triangulate the children into their adult conflict, using them as weapons in battles to hurt each other again.

As mediators, we do not work exclusively with the more mature individuals in Quadrant I and Quadrant III, and so we must manage people from across the differentiation spectrum. Bowen family system theory hypothesizes that people marry at about the same level of basic differentiation, even though one spouse may appear more emotionally mature at a given time due to the complex nature of "borrowing and trading of self" that occurs in intimate relationships (Friedman, 1985; Kerr and Bowen, 1988). With divorcing spouses in child custody cases, then, parents are likely to cluster around a similar level of differentiation.

With the exception of mediating these parenting plans for divorcing couples and those leaving long-term relationships, it is more likely that the emotional maturity of the mediating parties will be mixed in the quadrants, making the mediator's task more difficult. The differentiation levels of disputants will significantly influence the mediation and the mediator's ability to facilitate a successful resolution of the conflict.

Understanding the two-factor approach to functioning, however, will help mediators assess functional differentiation both initially and over the course of the mediation, and, therefore, whether or not mediation is or remains a viable option. Recognizing how emotional maturity interacts with current life stress also helps mediators avoid prejudging the outcome of a mediation based on one or two sessions and assists mediators to avoid getting triangulated into the parties' conflict.

Emotional Triangles, Triangulation, and De-Triangulation

As discussed in chapter two, Bowen (1978) said that for humans the basic emotional building block is the triangle. By definition, the two parties in mediation are emotionally triangled by the conflict. The emotional flow of chronic and acute anxiety is bound up in the issue, person, or thing being mediated. The issue, person, or thing, then, becomes the anxiety binder for the parties. Anxiety binders can be people, places, things, ideas, beliefs, religion, finances, children, businesses, and so forth. All anxiety binders help create inside and outside positions on the emotional triangle. All anxiety binders, then, become emotional attachments and are, as such, fused extensions of the undifferentiated self.

In mediation, each party is usually vying for the inside position on the emotional triangle with the anxiety binder. For example, two business partners trying to dissolve their corporation get stuck over the distribution of resources, employees for the new company they each want to form, or even the current company name. All can become anxiety binders whereby emotional attachments create positional stances and detract from interest-based negotiations. The stronger the degree of fusion or attachment with the anxiety binder, the more the person's self is wrapped up and invested with the anxiety binder. This connection makes it more difficult to reach a mediated solution. Positions become hardened, and impasses are likely.

In these situations, which are more or less present in all mediations, the mediator must form what I term a *mediation triangle*. A mediation triangle is an attempt by the mediator to insert herself into the system by connecting equally with each party (similar to the equidistant sides of an equilateral triangle). That connection must be as differentiated as possible. That is, the mediator must have a solid and relatively non-anxious presence, clear boundaries, and a firm capacity for self-definition, self-reflection, and self-regulation. In addition, she must develop a strong rapport with the parties through compassion, understanding, and clarity about each person's role in the conflict and the suffering that the struggle brings them. Through that more differentiated connection, it is possible to lessen the fusion that attaches the parties to the anxiety binder by temporarily increasing the functional differentiation of the mediation system. The mediator initially accomplishes this through shifting the intensity away from the conflict and re-focusing the parties onto their relationship with the mediator.

In a best-case scenario, the mediating triangle transforms into a *differentiating triangle.* I have developed the concept of the differentiating triangle to present a counterbalance to the concept of triangulation. That is, in triangulation, two people in conflict deal with anxiety by bringing in a third "other" to bind it for them. This temporarily creates stability and reduces short-term anxiety. Triangulation, though, simultaneously raises long-term anxiety since the tension between the two is not resolved but rather delayed, and, over time, this triangulated diversion decreases both functional and basic differentiation.

An example of this is a couple that has emotionally triangled alcohol into their relationship. The husband's alcohol dependency may create a temporary decrease in anxiety within the system as his drinking reduces his cravings and diverts the conflict between his wife and him. The alcoholism deflects their problems. The more he drinks, the worse the alcoholism in the system becomes and the more the marriage finds itself on shaky ground. The wife's life, too, is defined by the relationship between her spouse and alcohol. She is on the outside position of the emotional triangle, with her husband and his alcoholism occupying the two inside positions. The tension between the spouses goes unresolved, as alcohol is now regarded as "the problem" instead of it being the temporary binding agent that relieves the anxiety between them in the short term. This emotional triangulation sidetracks them from the serious, enduring problems in their marriage. Long-term prospects for relationship resolution and evolution are decreased, since the focus is now on the alcohol and the problems it has created for them.

In contrast, a differentiating triangle is one in which three people or two people and a third "other" are connecting in such a way that creativity, problem solving, or other higher-order functioning or adaptation is possible. For example, two parents can learn and grow from their child in ways that help each become more emotionally mature, which in turn strengthens the family and promotes differentiation in the child. Two composers can create a differentiating triangle such that together they write an exquisite piece of music.

It is theoretically possible that a mediator can bring such a highly differentiated self to a mediation so as to shift the emotional field to a higher level of differentiation. I believe that the most skilled mediators are capable of such profound emotional field shifts. In these situations, the parties say that the mediator brought out the best in them. The parties may walk away not only with a solid agreement that holds over time but also with a truer understanding of and respect for the other party. In this scenario, mediation itself becomes a transformative experience.

The key to managing emotional triangles and their anxiety is to help people tolerate short-term increases in anxiety for the sake of long-term anxiety reduction (Kerr and Bowen, 1988). That is, by keeping the parties in emotional contact with a mediator who is minimally reactive, moderately to highly differentiated, and calm, the system can explore interest-based alternatives to the current conflict without resorting to habitual, positional patterns of responding. A mediating triangle and a differentiating triangle, in effect, can loosen the chokehold of fusion with the anxiety binder and the positions, freeing individuals to make more autonomous, interest-based choices rather than reactive, positional ones.

This strategy is called *de-triangulation* (Friedman, 1985; Kerr and Bowen, 1988). To effectively de-triangulate, the mediator must recognize that triangulation is occurring. This requires that the mediator label the central and interlocking triangles in the system.

An example: Two business partners, Julia and Roberto, are trying to dissolve their business relationship. The central triangle was between the two partners and their business. Other interlocking triangles interfered with their capacity to manage and, therefore, de-triangulate from this central emotional triangle. Roberto's spouse was over-involved, which complicated the negotiations between the partners. Uncovering the central and interlocking triangles helped me, as mediator, de-triangulate the system by having Julia and Roberto initially focus on me, rather than each other. Through rapport building and deep listening, the parties began freeing themselves from some of the anxiety bound in the central and interlocking triangles.

Second, the mediator must remember that triangulation is automatic and that everyone does it; it is a natural function of all human systems. In mediation, the parties are usually attempting to automatically triangulate the mediator into the system by creating an interlocking or complicated triangle. In attempting to triangulate the mediator, the interlocking triangle becomes Party A and the mediator on the inside position and Party B on the outside position, or vice versa, with Party B on the inside position with the mediator, forcing Party A to the outside position on the emotional triangle. If this occurs, the complicated triangle becomes Party A (or Party B) and the mediator on one point of the emotional triangle with the second inside position occupied by the issue or conflict and with Party B (or Party A) on the outside position of the triangle. (Remember that two or more persons, places, or things can occupy a singular point on an emotional triangle. This makes it a complicated triangle.)

Both possibilities are usually active in mediation, since the triangulating behavior is habitual and, in this way, "mindless." The parties are looking for relief from their suffering; they seek an ally to use as a weapon against each other. Said differently, they want the mediator on their side.

Mediators must be careful not to become part of the triangulated system. Being aware of this automatic process makes it easier to avoid. The triangle is there. Whether or not the mediator is *emotionally triangulated* into the conflict is a function of the mediator's ability to understand the systems dynamics at play and then to remain relatively objective, calm, and unattached in the situation. Developing and strengthening rapport with the parties is essential to remaining de-triangulated. That is, remaining de-triangled is a function of the mediator's ability to remain relatively differentiated in the system and not absorb the anxiety generated and amplified by the disputants. If the mediator is able to accomplish this, he has formed a mediation triangle, which enables him to work within the system without catching its anxiety.

"I Language" as the Language of Differentiating

The language of responsibility is called *"I language."* Sometimes, it is referred to as "I positions" or "I statements." Bowen theorists such as Lerner (1989) prefer the term "I language" as it more accurately reflects a way of thinking that translates into a way of living. The consistent use of "I language" reduces anxiety built up around conflict, and it discourages channeling that anxiety through points in the emotional triangle (Friedman, 1985; Kerr and Bowen, 1988). As a hallmark of de-triangulation, "I language" is effective in any multi-person system that is under strain. "I language" uses definitional statements designed to strengthen the self and stay connected with the mediating parties.

For example, "I am here to understand your situation and to help you resolve your conflict; but I am not here to judge you or take sides." A statement such as this is a standard part of the mediator's introduction. As an example of "I language," its intention is less to communicate the mediator's role to the parties than to define one's role for the self, while staying in contact with others, the twin markers of differentiation. In this example, the mediator is clarifying his role and developing rapport. As a result, he avoids getting caught in the emotional system.

As stated previously, the most important concern for the mediator is to not absorb the anxiety of the mediating parties. If the mediator fails in this, she becomes yet another anxiety binder for the parties. Each of the disputants is likely to automatically vie to bring the mediator into the inside position of the emotional triangle and keep the other party on the outside position. The job of the mediator is to recognize the triangle and to refuse the invitation to participate, that is, to avoid being emotionally triangulated.

Here, too, "I language" is the key to remaining calm and de-triangulated. The mediator must compassionately and clearly state that she understands how upsetting the situation or event is and that her role is not to take sides but to assist the parties in developing mutually agreed on solutions. By remaining compassionate and de-triangled, the mediator can be supportive, encourage (as opposed to direct) a more productive response to the conflict, and avoid absorbing their anxiety. Responses such as these promote role clarity, more effective functioning, and appropriate differentiation in the system. That is, "I language" enhances the system's ability to manage and reduce anxiety on its own and find appropriate solutions.

Training disputants to use "I language" is also important. Usually, the parties come in blaming each other and minimizing their part in the conflict. By having disputants speak for themselves and what they want, the parties practice self-containment, self-reflection, and clarity in interest-based negotiations. For example, saying "I am frustrated by your leaving the business when I needed you most" may be heard differently than, "You abandoned your responsibilities when you left me holding the bag." "I language" increases self-regulation and allows the parties to hear each other more accurately. This, in turn, reduces triangulation and increases functional differentiation.

In summation, in all human systems, including the mediation system, it is essential to recognize that triangulation is a natural reaction to anxiety. Understanding the role and function of emotional triangles is essential for encouraging clarity, decreasing anxiety, and perpetuating calmness. De-triangulating takes constant work and rehearsal, and this effort becomes more effectual the more it is practiced. More differentiated mediators know how to develop and manage a mediation triangle to avoid becoming triangled in the system. The success of any mediation rests on this ability. In this way, the mediator avoids being trapped by the emotionally-charged system.

Technique and Theory

In North American models of mediation, training strongly relies on developing technique (Moore, 1996). Although a technique-based approach to training mediators and conducting mediations is certainly pragmatic, as an academic discipline, the field of mediation will benefit from a stronger and more comprehensive theoretical foundation. Technique devoid of theory will only advance the mediation profession to a certain point. A systemic understanding of the relative roles of the mediator and the mediating parties, as well as the mediation environment itself, will assist the profession to evolve and become even more successful.

Bowen family systems theory applies natural systems to humans. As such, it seems uniquely suited to provide one such comprehensive theoretical model for understanding ourselves as mediators and the mediation process itself. In addition, having an integrative theoretical understanding of systems promotes more success in implementing techniques, for the techniques then become ways of promoting differentiation with the parties, de-triangulation in the mediation system, increased functioning of the mediator, and, ultimately, more durable agreements that succeed over time.

I'll now discuss two examples of using theory to increase the effectiveness of techniques and methods. The first example concerns caucusing and the second example focuses on co-mediation. In both instances, I will demonstrate how viewing the conflict and using techniques and methods from the theoretical lens of Bowen's theory can increase the understanding and effectiveness of the techniques and methods themselves.

Caucusing from a Bowen Family Systems Theory Perspective

Caucusing is a standard tool in the mediator's repertoire (Bethal, 1986; Moore, 1987). Mediators understand the benefits and dangers of using caucusing. Some use it routinely; others refuse to use it at all. When conceptualized through a Bowen theory perspective, caucusing is a technique in which the mediator is extremely vulnerable to triangulation. By definition, meeting in caucus creates inside and outside positions. The emotional anxiety that is part of being on the outside position for one of the parties makes caucusing a high-risk technique.

Nonetheless, caucusing can be a powerful tool for breaking impasses (Moore, 1996). It can uncover important information, conduct reality testing, check for safety concerns, distribute resources, help re-balance the relationship between the parties, and in other ways determine the causes of impasses. On the other hand, caucusing can also create a triangled situation that makes breaking impasses more difficult.

As a technique, mediators are trained to meet with both parties separately during the caucus. At a technical level, mediators know that caucusing can create the illusion of partisanism. The emotional consequences of that partisanism, real or imagined, is emotional triangulation. Understanding triangles, de-triangulation, and the mechanisms by which anxiety is likely to flow in mediation will assist the mediator in using caucusing wisely.

Let's revisit the example of the two business partners terminating their business: During a caucus with Roberto, I found out that he was unwilling to tell his business partner, Julia, about his wife's insistence that any agreement be approved by her. Roberto's wife was angry and fearful over the impending corporate dissolution and was reluctant to agree to any terms that might quicken the end of the business partnership. Roberto asked me not to reveal this information to Julia, and I had stated at the beginning of the mediation that information obtained in caucus would be kept confidential unless the person agreed to its disclosure. I was now in an inside position of the triangle with Roberto (and his wife) regarding this mediation. The degree to which I would be emotionally triangulated into the conflict depended on my response both to Roberto and the mediation when it resumed.

In one scenario, sharing this information in caucus would relieve Roberto's anxiety, while I would absorb it. Roberto would feel better. I would experience more anxiety as I would be emotionally triangulated and could, as a consequence, become more reactive, and the mediation itself would more than likely stall.

In the actual scenario, I refused to become emotionally triangled. This left Roberto to manage his anxiety on his own. While this kind of de-triangulation can take many forms, for me, I determined that the information was essential to the success of the mediation process. I understood the interlocking triangle the wife's involvement created. I said to Roberto, "I respect your wish to keep this information private. However, I do not believe that you will get a mediation agreement acceptable to both Julia and you unless this issue is resolved. How do you suggest that we proceed?" This "I language" kept the anxiety where it belonged—with the parties—and it freed me to respond from a non-attached position, a position of strength rather than of weakness.

As such, rather than deciding when or if to use caucusing as a mediator, using a Bowen theory perspective, the focus becomes *how to use caucusing as a way of promoting differentiation and therefore responsibility in the system.* If that is not possible due to the low differentiation level of one or both of the parties, the highly reactive nature of the conflict, and so forth, the mediator should not use caucusing. Viewed from this perspective, caucusing is not a technique at all but an approach to implement Bowen family systems theory in mediation.

The second example is with co-mediation. Many mediators struggle with whether or not and in what circumstances to use a co-mediator. As a strategy and technique, co-mediation has many advantages and some disadvantages (CDR Associates, 1996; Moore, 1996). Advantages include working with a second mediator to help sort through the complexities of the case, having the opportunity to lead and follow so as to not get too caught up in the parties' conflict, and making the mediation more fun and productive by having a second professional involved. Disadvantages include working with a co-mediator who views the conflict so differently that it is difficult to work together, having a partner who takes over the mediation rather than shares it, allowing the parties to skillfully manipulate one mediator against the other, and the financial constraints of a second mediator's involvement.

As an application of Bowen's theory, the decision to use or not use a co-mediator rests on different assumptions. Perhaps the most important issue in working with a co-mediator is, once again, the emotional maturity of the co-mediator relative to the emotional maturity of the single mediator. The mediator must determine the degree to which the co-mediator has the capacity to remain de-triangulated; has the skill, confidence, and emotional maturity to lead and follow without undue anxiety; and can tolerate the additional ambiguity that working with another mediator brings. In short, from a Bowen theory perspective, the mediator must assess the degree to which the co-mediator is sufficiently differentiated to serve as an asset in mediation and the degree to which the co-mediator's relative lack of differentiation will likely impede the mediation process.

Making this determination is sometimes difficult. For example, at the Superior Court of Arizona in Yavapai County where I worked, mediators were often paired together from an available list. This experience afforded me the opportunity to work with a variety of co-mediators. Through the lens of Bowen's family systems theory, I observed the emotional field that each co-mediator brought to the mediation. As a result, over the years I recognized which co-mediators were more emotionally mature and therefore more effective and which co-mediators were more poorly differentiated and, hence, less effective.

Several years back, I decided I no longer wanted to co-mediate with mediators in this later group. In addition to managing the complexities of the mediation itself, I had to monitor and manage the relationship between the co-mediator and me, as well as the relationship between the parties and the co-mediator. In truth, I found this too time consuming and exhausting.

Co-mediation always presented the opportunity to work on my own differentiation. Over time, however, my willingness to only work with co-mediators that I believed were the most emotionally mature provided a mediation environment that offered a positive experience for all participants. For the past ten years, I was fortunate to co-mediate with my wife, Janet Bicknese, a talented mediator and retired school teacher. Working with a co-mediator whom I trusted, who understood systems dynamics, and who was comfortable both leading and following as needed was refreshingly productive and fun.

Mediation is one form of nonviolent, alternative conflict resolution. It can successfully assist individuals in taking more control of their lives and their conflict, empowering them to make decisions rather than having those decisions foisted on them. Mediation can bring people together in ways that increase respect for differences. It can be a source of positive change through creative conflict resolution in a world that too often relies on an adversarial approach to dealing with problems.

Like all new disciplines in their infancy stage, it is an exciting time that has encouraged creativity, innovation, and experimentation. The field of mediation has been largely driven by techniques and strategies, and it has enjoyed success as well as a growing accept-ance. This chapter grounds mediation in a comprehensive systems theory in order to increase its effectiveness and credibility.

Of course, grounding mediation in Bowen family systems theory or any other comprehensive theory will not ensure mediation success. No theory can accurately predict human behavior and attain unqualified success all of the time. Rather, by viewing mediation through the theoretical lens of Bowen theory, I demonstrated that mediation is a human endeavor governed by the same theoretical concepts and principles as other human enterprises. As a theory of human behavior and functioning, Bowen family systems theory has much to offer the expanding field of mediation. The successful application of Bowen's theory to mediation is a testament to the resiliency and universality of the theory, and it supports my belief that the academic discipline of mediation can greatly benefit from being grounded in a comprehensive theory.

References

Avrunch, K. *Culture and* Conflict Resolution. Washington, D.C.: United States Institute of Peace Press.1998

Bethal, C. "The Use of Separate Sessions in Family Mediation." Mediation Quarterly, 1986, 2 (3): 257-271.

Bowen, M. Family Therapy in Clinical Practice. Northvale, N.J.: Aronson, 1978.

CDR Associates. Mediating Environmental and Public Policy Disputes. Boulder, CO: CDR Associates, 1996.

Constantino, C.A, and Merchant, C.S. Designing Conflict Management Systems. San Francisco, CA: Jossey-Bass, 1996.

Friedman, E.H. Generation to Generation. New York: Guilford Press, 1985.

Friedman, E.H. "Bowen Theory and Therapy." In A.S. Gurman and D.P. Kniskern (eds.), Handbook of Family Therapy, Volume 2. New York: Brunner/Mazel, 1991.

Friedman, E.H. Reinventing Leadership: Change in an Age of Anxiety. New York: Guilford Press, 1996.

Gray, B. Collaborating. San Francisco, CA: Jossey-Bass, 1989.

Kerr M. and Bowen, M. Family Evaluation. New York: Norton, 1988.

Lax, D.A. and Sebenius, J,K. The Manager as Negotiator. New York: Free Press, 1986.

Lerner, H. The Dance of Intimacy. New York: Harper Publishers, Inc. 1989.

Maser, C. Resolving Environmental Conflict. Delray Beach, FL: St. Lucie Press, 1996.

Moore, C. W. "The Caucus: Private Meetings That Promote Settlement." Mediation Quarterly, 1987, 16, 87-101.

Moore, C. W. The Mediation Process (2nd ed.). San Francisco, CA: Jossey-Bass, 1996.

Roberts, K. and Lundy, C. "The ADA and NLRA: Resolving Accommodation Disputes in Unionized Workplaces." Negotiation Journal, 1995, 11 (1), 29-41.

Stamato, L. and Jaffe, S. "Mediation and Public Policy: Variations on a Consensus Theme." Mediation Quarterly, 1991, 9 (2), 165-178.

Suskind, L., Babbit, E., and Segal, P. "When ADR Becomes the Law: A Review of Federal Practice." Negotiation Journal, 1993, 9 (1), 59-75.

Ury, W.L., Brett, J.M., and Goldberg, S.B. Getting Disputes Resolved: Designing Systems to Cut the Cost of Conflicts. San Francisco, CA: Jossey-Bass, 1988.

CHAPTER TWELVE

INTERDISCIPLINARY TEAM TEACHING: FAMILY SYSTEMS THEORY IN FILM & LITERATURE
-BY K.L. COOK AND WAYNE REGINA

Introduction

The original version of this chapter was published in *Teachable Moments: Essays on experiential education*, edited by R. Dean Johnson and published by University Press of America, in 2003. This chapter remains largely unchanged from the original.

Teachable Moments is a series of essays from Prescott College faculty articulating the many ways that we, as professors, create and implement experiential education across the curriculum. These courses ranged from full field courses, to partial field courses, to classroom-based courses. Experiential education, also known as active pedagogy, is the cornerstone of the educational model at Prescott College. Experiential education requires full involvement and participation by both students and faculty. I more clearly and extensively detail the tenets of experiential education in Chapter 15 on teaching mediation to undergraduates, co-written with Steve Pace.

This chapter describes the process by which Kenny Cook and I developed, implemented, modified, and adjusted a curriculum to teach Bowen family Systems Theory to undergraduates using the medium of literature and film.

CHAPTER TWELVE

INTERDISCIPLINARY TEAM TEACHING: FAMILY SYSTEMS IN FILM & LITERATURE
-BY K.L. COOK AND WAYNE REGINA

Interdisciplinary team teaching is not for the faint of heart. It requires stamina, intellectual and interpersonal rigor, and a willingness to step off the firm footing and comfort of one's own discipline and engage with another professional and students in the realm of a less familiar and more unknown discipline. The unique opportunities and challenges in interdisciplinary team teaching, however, offer both students and teachers the possibility of integrating their learning in intellectually and emotionally innovative ways.

This chapter explores the potential and pitfalls of interdisciplinary team teaching through a course, entitled Family Systems in Film and Literature, which we taught a number of times at Prescott College. The first half of the chapter discusses our experience with interdisciplinary team teaching, including how we developed the course, how we created a vocabulary for understanding each other's ways of seeing the world, how the course pushed us to clarify the manner in which film and literature can be used to animate Bowen family systems theory, also known as Bowen theory, and how Bowen family systems theory can illuminate the creative process in film and literature. We also explore our successes and setbacks during the first two times we taught the course and how we modified and adjusted the curriculum to better meet our professional interests and that of our students in future iterations of the class.

The second half of the chapter describes the pragmatics of inter-disciplinary team teaching: institutional support and roadblocks; personal and professional rewards and challenges; and how this kind of course can serve as a model for education that emphasizes inter-disciplinary connections rather than disciplinary specialization. We end by offering suggestions for faculty seeking to emulate this model and for administrators interested in fostering an interdisciplinary curriculum.

While we use our particular class as a case study, our primary intention is to explore the nature of interdisciplinary team teaching. As longtime teachers and administrators at Prescott College, we believe that we bring special insights to this relatively under-explored realm of experiential education.

The Evolution of Family Systems in Film and Literature

Who are we? Kenny is a professional writer and an English professor and has published numerous books, articles, stories, poems, and essays in a wide variety of newspapers, magazines, and scholarly and literary journals. His literary areas of specialty are in modern and post-modern fiction and drama, creative writing, and Shakespeare. Wayne is a family systems psychologist and Peace Studies and Human Development professor, specializing in families, organizations, and mediation. He has published in the areas of education, leadership, mediation, family therapy, and peace studies. Wayne has worked extensively in applying Bowen family systems theory to leadership, education reform, families, and court-based mediation and conciliation.

We both arrived at Prescott College in the summer of 1992. We came here because of our shared passion for interdisciplinary work as well as our attraction to the college's environmental and social justice mission. Entering with the same cohort group of new faculty members, we immediately found a professional and personal kinship, spending many hours discussing our mutual interest in expressions of the human condition through film, literature, and theory.

Over the years, our professional and personal collegiality and friendship blossomed, and we began exploring possible ways to bring our literary, theoretical, and cinematic interests together in an interdisciplinary, team-teaching environment. In essence, Family Systems in Film and Literature evolved from our desire, as friends and colleagues, to see our professional worlds through the eyes of the other. We started with a basic line of inquiry. Why are so many writers and filmmakers natural family systems theorists, intuitively understanding such family systems concepts as triangulation, chronic anxiety, differentiation, and nuclear and multi-generational emotional process? How can family systems theory illuminate the serious study of film and literature? Can film and literature be used as a laboratory for understanding family systems theory, clarifying and articulating complex concepts that are sometimes difficult to observe inside one's original family?

These questions and others ultimately led to more practical, pedagogical questions. Could a psychologist and writer coexist in the same classroom? Would our excitement about and respect for one another and each other's disciplines serve as a model for our student's own interdisciplinary development? How would we go about teaching both disciplines in an intensive, one-month seminar without shortchanging either discipline? And the most important question was this: what special insights lay in the spaces *between* our disciplines rather than in the disciplines themselves, and how would our students help each other and us discover those insights?

These questions were posed against the backdrop of Prescott College itself. In addition to its interdisciplinary focus and environmental and social justice mission, we were attracted to Prescott College because of its commitment to small, student-centered classes (twelve to fourteen students is the maximum class size and most classes have ten students) and its dedication to progressive, experiential education. For example, at Prescott College, students do not have "majors" but rather develop "competences," which include coursework, independent studies, internships, and a capstone senior project that must address five central criteria:

- Literacy in the field of study

- Mastery of methodology
- Application of learning
- Personalization of learning
- Interconnection of learning

Arguably the most important of these criteria for competence, and certainly for an interdisciplinary course, is interconnection of learning. Unlike larger liberal arts institutions, where team teaching and cross-disciplinary learning and teaching raises significant budgetary and curricular turf battles, Prescott College believes that both students and teachers thrive in an educational environment where they are challenged to clarify underlying assumptions about how to understand the world. In effect, students are asked to train their attention on the ways disciplines intersect with and inform each other, rather than simply acquiring disciplinary knowledge and specialization.

Our course developed slowly over a six-year period. Part of this pace was intentional, as we explored different ideas about inter-disciplinary team teaching, and part of this pace was due to circumstance as we both moved into important administrative roles to serve the college that minimized our direct teaching obligations.

Once we submitted the course for curricular approval in the spring of 1997, our preparation and planning began in earnest. Early on, we decided to use a broad-based and flexible model for film and literature, focusing on film clips, short features, full-length features, short stories, plays, and novellas. Due to the condensed nature of a four-week block course, we decided against using full-length novels. Perhaps more importantly, we agreed to target a single theoretical model, that of Bowen family systems theory. Bowen theory had the advantage of being a family systems approach derived from observing natural systems and applying these observations to the family. Among the family systems approaches, Bowen theory was uniquely suited for the minds of our environmental and social justice-based students. In addition, Bowen family systems theory is a comprehensive theoretical system that is intellectually rich, pragmatically sound, and both elegant in its simplicity and complex in its application. It was well suited to handle the variety of cinematic and literary families that we would explore.

Early on, we decided that while we would articulate cinematic and literary elements in films and literature, the central focus of the course would be to help students develop an understanding of family systems theory *through* film and literature. As such, the central goal of the course, as stated in the course syllabus, was "to foster an understanding and application of family systems theory through intellectual and artistic investigation and personal application."

In addition, we decided that the intersection of the two disciplines would serve as the leading edge of the course. Again, from the first goal articulated in the syllabus: "This isn't two courses in one. Instead, we envision this course as a true synthesis to help you discover tools and cross-disciplinary ways of seeing, which you can apply to your explorations of family systems theory, literature, film, the creative process, and your own life." In essence, we wanted to use the theoretical lens of Bowen family systems theory to understand the nature of literary and cinematic expression, while simultaneously illuminating the personal world of the family for both the students and the instructors.

Having defined our theoretical perspective for the course and the nature of our interdisciplinary focus, we began searching for appropriate literary and cinematic material. Part of the challenge was the wealth of excellent films and stories available. We sorted through films, books, plays, and short stories to find fictional families that best illustrated the central concepts of Bowen theory. We initially selected the following films:

- *Life Lessons (New York Stories)*
- *Grand Canyon (excerpts)*
- *What's Eating Gilbert Grape*
- *The Glass Menagerie*
- *Hanna and Her Sisters*
- *Hamlet (excerpts)*

We allowed students to pick several films as well, though their selections reflected cultural influences through the mass media and were less helpful in articulating systemic concepts. In addition, we decided to supplement our classroom time with a local fieldtrip to a movie theatre to view a new release and an outing to a regional theatre to attend a play.

We eventually narrowed our reading list and chose two novellas by Jane Smiley, *Ordinary Love* and *Good Will,* and the Tennessee Williams play, *The Glass Menagerie.* We developed a Family Systems in Film and Literature reader as well. This reader contained extensive articles and chapters on Bowen theory by Edwin Friedman, Michael Kerr, Monica McGoldrick, and Randy Gerson. The reader also collected a number of short stories by a variety of authors, including work by John Cheever, James Baldwin, Mona Simpson, Jessica Treadway, and Alice Walker. Finally, we included a number of short stories by two Prescott College writing and literature faculty, Kenny Cook and Melanie Bishop, and planned on a day in which both authors would talk about the transformation of their own family material into fiction.

In developing the reading list, we were careful to provide balanced gender and cultural perspectives so that we could examine the theory from the works of both men and women, as well as from those of different cultures. As Bowen theory purports universality, we believed it important to explore the theory through a variety of cultural and gender perspectives.

Next, we developed a series of assignments to track student progress, promote interpersonal and intrapersonal development, and encourage creative expression. We designed the class as "writing intensive," a writing-across-the-curriculum designation at Prescott College that imbeds significant writing, revising, and peer review assignments within the content of the course. From the beginning, we chose to try and replicate for our students the kind of fruitful dialogue that we experienced while working with each other to develop and implement the course.

As such, in addition to the formal assignments we asked students to complete, we also expected them to turn in weekly "cover letters"–

lengthy, typed epistles in which they summarized what they'd learned and how they'd been studying, synthesizing, and applying family systems theory to literature, film, and their own lives. The cover letters also created a forum for them to carry on a dialogue with us about how the class was progressing for them–delights, insights, frustrations, questions, and suggestions–and how they were meeting the terms of their individual learning contracts. We would, in turn, respond back with long letters. The letters became, in some ways, our favorite part of the students' weekly portfolios. They offered us greater insight into their lives and learning styles, personalized their education for us, and provided an effective venue for all of us to communicate, make adjustments, and address complicated issues of either the course content or the class dynamics and structure.

Ultimately, these weekly summary and synthesis letters and our lengthy responses allowed us to articulate and record the learning and teaching process. They gave us another way of carrying on a dialogue not only with the students but with each other. This proved especially useful as we returned to the course for its second, third, and subsequent incarnations. We have, in essence, a rich and thorough log of our experiences.

Personalization of learning, another of the five essential criteria for knowledge at Prescott College listed above, became a crucial subtext for teaching the course. We promoted this subtext by having students develop personal genograms, which are factual and emotional family histories that focus on delineating qualitative relationships, themes, patterns, and legacies within a multi-generational context. Through creating these genograms, students would come to appreciate the rich systemic context of their personal lives and begin exploring ways to differentiate or emotionally separate themselves from the automatic and reactive processes inherent in their families. This personalization exercise would culminate with students presenting their genograms to the class.

We realized, of course, that to ask students to bare their family histories and stories to the entire class, we would first have to reveal *our* family histories and stories. It is this kind of emotionally and intellectually challenging work that helps us, as teachers, stay alive and grow, while creating an appropriate climate for our students. That is, to the degree that we, as instructors, would be willing to examine ourselves would be the degree to which students would feel safe investigating and sharing their own stories. In fact, we believed this combination of the theoretical with the personal would accomplish twin goals: students would find intellectual value in analyzing fictional families and personal value in applying these theoretical insights to their own extended families. We hoped this shared experience regarding all of our families would be emotionally moving and also help normalize family processes; students would realize that *all* multi-generational families have histories that include trauma, challenges, and resiliency.

In addition to the portfolio packets, cover letters, and multi-generational genograms, we decided on additional assignments, including an application essay, meant to give students the opportunity to apply specific aspects of family systems theory to one or more of the texts or movies that we would study. This multi-draft essay was designed to deepen students' understanding of the theory through application to the "texts" (both literary and cinematic) that we would be studying. Lastly, we developed a creative application assignment, designed for small groups, to present some aspect of Bowen theory through film and literature that would include an experiential class presentation.

Family Systems in Film and Literature: First Incarnation

We taught the course for the first time in the Winter Block of 1998. We both enjoyed positive teaching reputations and the class fully enrolled. While Wayne's *Family Systems Theory* classes predominantly enrolled human development and psychology students, *Family Systems in Film and Literature* attracted, as we hoped, students from a wider population, including a number of writing and literature students. Drawing students from differing academic perspectives helped us to immediately highlight a cross-disciplinary approach.

While many students initially blanched at the significant reading and writing in this four-week course, most everyone rose to the occasion, completing all of the assignments. In fact, students quickly embraced the theory as they were fascinated by its richness, complexity, and comprehensiveness. All of the assignments were quite valuable, adding to students' learning and our assessment of their progress.

On the very first day of class, we read Raymond Carver's two-page contemporary story, "Popular Mechanics," a tragic five-minute scene, depicting an argument between a couple who are separating. Their tension escalates as they fight over who will retain custody of their child. In a scene eerily reminiscent of Solomon and the two mothers fighting over possession of the baby, at the end of the story the two parents each grab the baby by the arms and literally "rend" the child in two. "In this manner," the omniscient narrator says in the darkly ironic final line, "the issue was decided."

While the class began to decipher what had happened in the story and its symbolic meaning, we quickly focused their attention on the family systems concepts of Bowen theory. Even as the story may resonate as a dark contemporary parable about the tragic ramifications of parental strife, it also brilliantly and efficiently dramatizes the concepts of emotional triangles and triangulation, the nature of automatic emotional reactivity, will conflicts, and anxiety cascades. Our goal in this short exercise was to begin to train the students on how to apply the theory to the text and how to use the text to illustrate and humanize the theory.

On this same day, we watched Martin Scorsese's brilliant short film, *Life Lessons*, about a famous middle-aged painter (played by Nick Nolte) and his young assistant (played by Roseanna Arquette). The film, in Bowen theory terms, depicts the artist's attachment to his art and to the young woman, with whom he is having an affair, and how both sex and art become anxiety binders for him. We see him generating and amplifying his own and his assistant's chronic and acute anxiety and then trying to triangulate (even exorcise) that anxiety through his art. We also witness the stark difference between the artist's *basic* differentiation level (that is, his core emotional maturity) and his *functional* differentiation level (that is, his appearance to the world at a given moment in time), which deteriorates as the film progresses and he becomes consumed by his own violent jealousy.

This kind of exploration and analysis led to a rapid engagement with the artistic and theoretical material and immediately set the intellectual tone for the course. By the end of the first week, students were working in small groups, explicating the theory for the rest of the class, prompted by assigned topics such as these:

- What is the concept of "the emotional triangle"? Using examples from the literature and films we've studied, chart several central and interlocking triangles and compare and contrast the way anxiety moves through the different emotional systems. Specify the anxiety binders.

- "Fusion" and "emotional cut-off" are often two sides of the same coin – contrasting symptoms of more poorly differentiated emotional systems. Define these concepts and clarify them through examples in the texts and films that we've studied.

- Friedman asserts, "Bowen's multi-generational transmission concept is rooted in the notion that all generations are part of a continuous natural process with each generation pressing up against the next, so that the past and the present almost become a false dichotomy." What does he mean by this? Using the literature and the films we've studied, illustrate this concept.

These kinds of group activities allowed students to collaborate, as we had done, and to explicate the theory with specific examples.

By the end of the second week of class, students were asked to write their own application essays, using even more specific topics to force them deeper into the theory. Here is an example of one of the many complicated topics from which they could choose: "Track the level of chronic anxiety in *The Glass Menagerie,* scene by scene, or an in-depth analysis of the chronic anxiety in one of the scenes. Determine the level of differentiation, fusion, and/or will conflict—the source of chronic anxiety and the way the characters cope with that anxiety—through over-functioning/under-functioning, binding of anxiety, or shifting anxiety to a third party."

Viewing films and reading literature provided a relatively safe perspective within which to explore the family system. In many ways, it is easier to explore the artistically created family than one's own family of origin. It is less threatening and more possible to objectively view the unfolding of emotional patterns, thematic legacies, chronic anxiety, and the complex process of differentiation through fiction and cinema. What was (and is) fascinating for us as instructors is that without formal study in family systems theory, exceptional writers and directors display remarkable compassion for and insight into universal family functioning.

In addition, the genograms and family biographies moved the learning from the more objective and abstract to the more subjective and personal. Where students could more easily articulate inside and outside positions in triangles, clearly discuss the role of over-functioning and under-functioning in symptom development, and distinguish between the nature of functional and basic differen-tiation in a fictional family, once students began focusing on their own multi-generational families, objectivity melted away, and their clarity of thinking became blurred with emotional reactivity and chronic anxiety.

Nonetheless, having learned the central theoretical elements in Bowen theory, students were poised to use their own families as laboratories for personal exploration, investigation, and understanding. In particular, the genogram presentations created a depth of compassion, insight, and awareness that was almost unparalleled in both instructors' years of teaching. The presentations became a mechanism to apply what we were learning and a venue to share familial secrets, hopes, and fears from the past and for the future. Truly, the developmental sequence of intellectual understanding through fictional families and personalization of the theory through the genogram and subsequent family biography assignments grounded the students learning in powerful ways.

Modifications and Adjustments: Second Incarnation

Despite its initial success, we realized that there were significant areas in need of modification and adjustment for the second offering. In the first iteration of our class, for example, we allowed the students a lot of flexibility and input into the design of the course. Students not only presented their individual genograms, which took, much to our surprise, an entire week of a four-week class, but we also allowed them to choose films for us to watch as a group and stories for us to read. Uncharacteristically, for the second offering, we modified and adjusted the course by *limiting* student participation in film and literature selection. We normally provide ample opportunities for students to help develop the syllabus and the course. However, the films and stories the students selected the first time either lacked internal systemic consistency or provided only marginal opportunities to integrate theoretical analysis with artistic critique.

In addition, during the first course offering, we had given over the last week of class to collaborative presentations of students' creative application assignments. Group topics included family systems applied to art therapy, improvisational theatre, and even the multigenerational history of elephant families in South Africa. In some ways, this collaboration with other students was effective. Students felt greater ownership of the course, and it did significantly broaden the scope of the course and the application of the theory to other disciplines. We felt, however, that we had given over almost half of the course to the students and that we had sacrificed depth of theoretical understanding as well as practice with application of the theory in both clinical and literary/cinematic contexts.

What we determined was that in an interdisciplinary course, students must struggle to integrate the two disciplines. In order to facilitate their understanding, it was important for us, as instructors, to provide greater structure and create more focused assignments. We were wary this time about relinquishing so much autonomy to the students in designing projects that ranged too far from the already complicated work we were doing. As a result, in the second version of the course, we actually increased the size of our reader, adding more theoretical material on Bowen family systems theory as well as additional literary texts. We modified the film list to better represent the cinematic family and theoretical components of the theory:

- *Life Lessons*
- *American Beauty*
- *What's Eating Gilbert Grape*
- *The Glass Menagerie*
- *Hanna and Her Sisters*
- *Godfather I* and *Godfather II*

We streamlined our assignments, providing more opportunities for students to digest the theory and begin applying it to both film and literature in full-class settings as well as in small groups. As a result, their major application essays demonstrated greater depth and analytical sophistication. We kept the student genogram work and presentations but set tighter limitations on presentation time.

We also maintained the outside fieldtrip components of the class. The first time we taught the course, these fieldtrips were successful in generating a sense of group cohesion, and we wanted to replicate this success. We agreed as a class to see a current movie, *The Royal Tenenbaums*, which had just been released at the theatre, and we saw a regional theatre one-man show, focusing on a Latin-American family. We supplemented the course with an all-day Italian pasta party, where we watched and analyzed the first two films of the *The Godfather* series.

We deleted the collaborative presentation assignment and replaced it with two other assignments that more directly related to the content of the course. The first was a family biography/family systems analysis, where students were able to put their genogram work in narrative form, first describing and then examining a family theme, multi-generational pattern, central emotional triangle, or family secret in their own families. Here is one example, the "family secret" topic:

Family Secret. According to the theory, there are no secrets in a family. The entire system colludes in keeping them. In many of the films and literature we studied, as well as the genogram presentations, you've seen how secrets can be transmitted through generations. Often these secrets are linked powerfully to the family's conception of shame and may be used as a tool for one generation to exert its will (about how to behave properly or ethically) over another generation. For example, in the families we've studied in class, suppression of a Chinese woman's story creates anxiety in her niece, who searches desperately for "ancestral help"; a suicide is covered up to protect the children; a priest and a baroness produce an illegitimate child. Is there a secret in your own family? How has that secret generated chronic anxiety in your family's emotional system? Can you identify the members of the family throughout the generations who bind the anxiety of this suppressed secret? How do they bind it? What is the effect of the secret on the basic and functional differentiation of the members of the family?

This assignment, in effect, allowed students to create a piece of literature—their family story or myth—and then to analyze that story using Bowen family systems theory as a guide.

The final assignment was a take-home exam that allowed students to demonstrate their understanding of the seminal concepts of Bowen theory, using at least three assigned texts or stories that we *hadn't* discussed in class. The second part of the exam allowed students a tremendous amount of leeway. They could write a story, a short memoir, a series of poems, a song, or create a visual collage or series of paintings or photographs, a game for the class, a performance piece, or any other creative means of demonstrating their personalization of the theory.

These final two assignments—the family biography/analysis and the exam—worked especially well. Both assignments allowed students to personalize their learning and to have greater autonomy, characteristics we didn't want to lose from the first class. The assignments, though, were more directly related to the already complicated subject matter of this course and allowed the students opportunities to deepen their analysis and synthesis skills.

When we taught the course for the second time in the winter of 2002, it was over-enrolled with a waiting list. We felt pleased by the "word of mouth" generated by the first class. Most of the students were juniors and seniors this second time around, which helped with the pace of the class, as we were able to proceed quickly through introductory material and gear the class to the high functioning level of the group.

With one class cycle under our belts, we felt more comfortable with the material and with the modifications and adjustments to the structure and content of the course. *The Godfather* marathon was especially effective and engaging. This daylong film festival was intense, as the films, while brilliant, are violent and disturbing and provided a wonderful opportunity for group cohesiveness through cooking, eating, and learning together.

The changes we had made contributed to the increased success of this course. We had streamlined the course and tightened our reading and writing requirements, provided opportunities for fieldtrips and class retreats, and demonstrated flexibility to meet student interest. Also, once again, students embraced the opportunity to construct their family genograms and present them to the class. As instructors, we set reasonable but firm limits for class presentation of genograms. Knowing that they each had twenty minutes to present their genograms and receive feedback, student presentations were much more focused than the first time. Not surprisingly, we found that teaching the class a second time was more effective. Our confidence working as an interdisciplinary team and our comfort with the material and each other's style allowed for greater flow and, perhaps most importantly from a Bowen theory perspective, we felt less anxiety and thus generated less anxiety in the class. In essence, we had more fun and students perceived us as more relaxed and (ironically, given our tightening of the structure) more flexible with assignments. We discovered that by creating more structure for the class, we did a better job of unleashing our students' potential. Their course evaluations and end-of-class debriefs revealed that they seemed happier and better served as well.

While we have continued to make further adjustments for subsequent incarnations of the course, we believe that we have finally found an essentially balanced course design that allows students to become literate in these two fields of study, to demonstrate their growing mastery of methodology, and to apply and personalize their learning.

Interdisciplinary Team Teaching: Reflections and Suggestions

Working with a colleague from another discipline can be an incredibly rewarding experience. For us, the experience enriched both our personal friendship and our professional lives. For example, Kenny's appreciation for and understanding of Bowen theory grew tremendously. He embraced Bowen theory not simply for its application to film and literature but for its usefulness as a theoretical system in his leadership role as the Associate Dean of the Resident Degree Program at Prescott College. He finds the theory applicable and invaluable as he manages the many day-to-day requirements of his job and for long-term planning and development.

Wayne has found that he approaches film and literature with a greater understanding of form and aesthetics, and he has learned not only to see systems in these creative expressions but also to appreciate how writers, directors, and screenwriters approach their craft. This understanding and appreciation have also helped him expand his professional commitment to Bowen theory beyond the family system into artistic expression, leadership, education, and understanding of macro-systems.

Based on our experiences, we offer these four central suggestions for faculty interested in team teaching an interdisciplinary course and administrators interested in fostering an interdisciplinary curriculum.

1. Interdisciplinary Pollination: Choosing Disciplines to Integrate

There are really two issues to clarify here. The first is to distinguish between the team-taught course, in which two instructors in essentially the same discipline collaborate, and interdisciplinary team teaching, in which faculty from different disciplines work together for interdisciplinary pollination.

For example, at Prescott College, we have a heavy field curriculum, so safety issues often require the institution to provide two instructors for a course. One course, Adventure Education is a semester-long, eighteen-credit, eleven-week course in which two faculty members from our Adventure Education program work with ten students in the field on theory, history, practical application, and development of outdoors, technical skills. In-town courses, however, may also benefit from faculty collaboration.

Wayne, for instance, has taught the course Community Mediation and Principled Negotiation with another Human Development-Psychology faculty member, who is also a trained mediator. Because mediation and conflict resolution require significant role-playing to develop basic skills, there is a strong justification for this course being taught by two faculty members, in this case one trained originally as a psychologist and systems theorist and the other educated as a social worker.

Kenny had previously co-taught a course entitled Travel Writing: Journey as Metaphor. While this course took place in the field and consequently required two instructors for safety reasons, it also helped that the other instructor was a literature teacher as well as a poet, which complemented Kenny's training in literature and fiction writing. While both instructors were English teachers and writers, their skills helped broaden the scope of the course and the student opportunities.

A truly interdisciplinary course, however, is one in which the faculty members come from completely different academic disciplines. The course is designed to explore the intellectual and creative space that arises when you integrate the two disciplines. Other examples of this kind of course at Prescott College include Religion and Science, taught by a religion and philosophy teacher and a geologist; and Nature and Psyche, taught by a conservation biologist and a counselor.

In the case of Family Systems in Film and Literature, we were intrigued by the very different ways we examined human behavior, in particular family dynamics. As a systems practitioner and professor, Wayne brought a highly sophisticated theoretical and clinical approach to his understanding of family functioning. As a fiction writer and literature and creative writing professor, Kenny applied a more intuitive method to his examination of family structure and dynamics, informed by a rich literary tradition, ranging from the Greek tragedies and Shakespeare to modern and contemporary storytellers like Tennessee Williams, William Faulkner, Gabriel Garcia Marquez, and Jane Smiley.

We believed that co-teaching that combined our different approaches would be mutually beneficial not only for our own professional growth but for our students as well. For example, one of the challenges of a family systems course is that there is no easy pedagogical way to examine family functioning. The work is clinical in nature but the instructor is forced to rely on case studies, heavy theoretical immersion, and a rigorous analysis of one's own family of origin. While this kind of clinical focus obviously works, literature and film provided a relatively unexplored laboratory for analysis of family functioning, as well as a way of at least informally testing the theory. That is, if the theory does indeed have universal applications as it purports, then the analysis should hold up just as well for a classic text of family functioning, such as *Hamlet*, as it will for a contemporary clinical situation.

Similarly, for literature, writing, and film students, this course would give students a critical apparatus and theoretical vocabulary by which to examine not only the imaginative narratives of classic and contemporary texts but also their own lives. Often a film, literature, or creative writing course is concerned with form and aesthetics. This kind of approach allows literature students an opportunity to step outside their roles as aesthetic or cultural critics and explore in more depth the psychological and systemic issues of a text and the way the characters may clarify and illustrate the complexities of theory. To date, most psychological studies in literature and film have used Freudian or Jungian approaches. A family systems model provides a fresh approach to psycho/systemic-literary studies.

The pitfall of such an interdisciplinary approach is that it can potentially subvert the intentions of both disciplines. Both psychology and literature students may begin to see the characters in a play, novel, or film as clinical patients, in need of diagnoses and counseling, rather than as imaginary figures functioning within a larger ritual of form: tragedy, comedy, romance, naturalism, absurdism, etc. If the artist has done his or her job correctly, then the characters should live, breathe, and provide insight into the complexities, frailties, and foibles of human behavior. The writer or director's goal is not to present a case study. However, we sought to examine this very complexity. Human behavior is never neat. Intelligent and good-intentioned people cannot be easily reduced. Differentiation, chronic anxiety, multi-generational transmission process... these are all qualitative assessments that involve some degree of inference once you apply them to either real or imaginary people. We were convinced that the theory would activate our students' curiosity about the intellectual implications of narratives, while the literature and films would humanize the theory, hence making it accessible.

Our suggestion to prospective interdisciplinary team-teachers? Choose the disciplines to combine carefully. Make sure that the integration stretches you and the students beyond your comfort zones but that the disciplines also effectively illuminate and deepen the understanding of each other.

2. Narrow the Focus

It is important to find a balance between breadth and depth. Remember that the primary goal of an interdisciplinary course is to examine the area *between* the disciplines rather than try to fully articulate both. In our initial plan for the course, this was one of the major obstacles we confronted. Our original course title was *Family Systems in Film*. However, we felt that by limiting our "laboratory" to just film, we would be eliminating great resources. Film, like drama, is primarily an *external* medium. The narrative unfolds almost exclusively through action and dialogue. In fiction, poetry, and narrative nonfiction, the narrative often unfolds *internally*; reflection, lyrical meditation, analysis of character and situation are just as crucial, if not more so, than dialogue and action. We wanted this "double vision." We also wanted to examine a case study of a writer, to show the evolution of a family story in different mediums. This wider focus allowed us, for example, to focus on Tennessee Williams' autobiographical family drama, *The Glass Menagerie*. We were able to read about Williams' own family history, and see how he transformed that history first into a short story, "A Portrait of a Girl in Glass," then into his acclaimed play, and finally to see how that play is realized in a production by a sensitive director and skilled actors, in this case the filmed adaptation directed by Paul Newman.

While this broadening of our focus was initially liberating, early on we still struggled with the problem of having too much material to cover in too short a period of time—a four-week, intensive block session. At first, we felt that we needed to serve our respective constituents: psychology versus writing and literature students. There were complex learning outcomes that were expected in a straightforward family systems course. Those students needed a solid grounding in the clinical applications of family systems theory. Similarly, writing, literature, and film students were expected to hone and deepen their understanding of literary and cinematic theory. Could we accomplish both objectives in this course without subverting our original goal? Something had to give.

We agreed that depth was more important that breadth. We would both have to compromise in order to achieve our larger goal. As described earlier, we determined that the course needed to be primarily a family systems course. The literature and films should be used to explicate and clarify Bowen theory, while also allowing us opportunities to fairly objectively examine the subtle complexities of family functioning. We decided that, first and foremost, we needed to ground students in the theory and to then let them deepen their understanding by applying what they had learned to not only the texts and films we were watching and reading in class, but also to their own lives. Once we agreed on this central objective, we were able to more easily structure the course, breaking it into three overarching teaching imperatives: (1) Introduction to Key Theoretical Issues & Concepts; (2) Application to Literature/Film/Our Lives; and (3) Synthesis and Conclusions.

3. Administrative Considerations: Prerequisites, Curricular Justification, and Workload Issues

In addition to the pedagogical logistics, we were trying to work out with each other, we also had to contend, as all team teachers must, with significant administrative issues. We had to, in other words, sell our course to the administration, to justify it both curricularly and financially.

Prerequisites. One of the minor, though still important, administrative issues that every interdisciplinary course must confront is what level of students to pitch the course to and what prerequisites to require. We designed this course for upper-division students. We wanted to emphasize and help students hone sophisticated analysis and synthesis skills. Yet we also wanted to attract psychology as well as literature and writing students. We knew that the chances were slim that any student would have significant coursework in psychology, literature, creative writing, and film. Here again, we compromised. If this class was to function as a true interdisciplinary think tank, then our students would be very much like us: they would probably have significant academic training in one area or the other but not both. We decided to require all students to have at least first-year composition and *either* significant coursework in psychology/human development *or* literature, creative writing, or film studies. This decision turned out to be fortuitous since we attracted students from across the college, and each brought special expertise to the content area. The course also stretched everyone's intellectual and creative muscles as well; like us, no one had tried to link these two disciplines together in any systematic or rigorous way, nor had they explored the potential benefits of such an integration.

Curricular justification. In addition to creating prerequisites that would effectively attract a wider spectrum of upper-division students, we also needed to make a curricular case for our course. We had to make sure it served both student constituents in their major or minor areas of focus. We believe that any interdisciplinary course must address this larger institutional necessity in order to succeed. Toward this end, Wayne proposed that the Human Development-Psychology advising document allow our course to substitute for the more clinical Family Systems Theory course. Kenny worked with his writing and literature colleagues to adopt a new literature requirement–Cross-Disciplinary Literature, including courses such as American West in Film and Literature, Holy Books, Philosophies of the Interpretive Naturalists, and Women's Literature–which all Writing and Literature students would need to fulfill.

Workload. Perhaps the most demanding administrative hurdle that team teachers must overcome is convincing department chairs and deans that the allocation of resources is worth the cost. At Prescott College, we were serving as the dean and the program chair during the time when we presented our course for approval. Regardless, we are fortunate at Prescott College that all classes have an average college-wide 10:1 student/faculty ratio. Already, this low ratio creates a risky cost-benefit analysis for our administration. When you factor in field courses, which often require double staffing and can drive the ratio down to as low as 4:1, then the prospect of allowing two faculty members to co-teach an in-town, upper-division course can seem highly suspect, if not downright unfeasible, from a budgetary standpoint. It's even more crucial, in these circumstances, to create prerequisites that allow students from across the college to participate and for both instructors to build consensus in their respective curricular areas or programs so that students have an advising incentive to take the course. It also helps if you can acquire outside funding.

For example, the instructors for Prescott College's Religion and Science course applied for and received a sizable grant to help fund their own research and to reward Prescott College financially for supporting such interdisciplinary ventures. While we have not applied for such funding, we have compromised by increasing our course capacity from twelve to sixteen and by offering the course on a rotating basis every two years so that the impact on both our teaching loads is significantly reduced.

While Prescott College generally supports this interdisciplinary team-teaching approach, the institution does impose some general limitations on this work. For one, each instructor can only team-teach once a year. This limit helps ensure balance and curricular continuity. Second, the Resident Degree Program has instituted a Number of Students Served (NSS) system to monitor faculty workload and help ensure equality and balance from all faculty members. Team teaching only credits the faculty with .67 NSS for every student enrolled, rather than the normal 1.0 NSS for each student enrolled in an in-town class. This "reduced credit" also encourages us to over-enroll our class or to balance our other classes or independent study assignments with higher enrollment numbers. In effect, the college still needs to manage its curriculum with limited resources and limited faculty.

4. *Communication: Preparation, Planning, and Student Assignments*

The central myth to dispel when considering team teaching is that it requires less work. After all, with two people teaching the same course, shouldn't the workload be lessened? Unfortunately, the opposite is true. Given the nature of collaboration, the differences in personality and teaching styles, and the complexity of the interdisciplinary material, this kind of team teaching requires more time, more preparation, and more coordination than teaching alone. For Family Systems in Film and Literature, the one exception was with reading, correcting, and critiquing student assignments. The first time that we taught the class, we each read, corrected, and critiqued all of the students' papers. In part, this was due to our unfamiliarity with the other's style and level of detail in the critiques themselves. Being committed "over-functioners" with a penchant for academic rigor, however, we soon realized that much of our reviews and critiques were redundant. As such, the second time that we taught the class, we divided the student assignments, though we made sure to divide the multiple draft assignments so that we both worked with and gave extensive feedback to each student for at least one significant writing assignment.

Even with this splitting of the student written workload, inter-disciplinary team teaching remains a time-intensive commitment. In addition, it functions best when the instructors can check their egos at the door. Fortunately, we have developed enough confidence as teachers to allow each other plenty of leeway in the classroom. For example, at times, Kenny will direct the class, explicating a text or providing the literary or historical context for a film. At other times, Wayne's clarification on a theoretical concept will take center stage. Sometimes, these presentations are planned; other times, they occur spontaneously from "teachable moments." We keep in close contact with each other, with daily discussions before and after class to ensure balance, comfort, and class continuity. In addition, we keep in regular and close contact with the students, ensuring that their needs are being appropriately considered and to monitor and adjust based on their feedback.

Any team-taught course requires a tremendous amount of communication and trust. Rarely, especially in the initial conception and design of the course, does it involve less work. We had been discussing the possibility of teaching Family Systems in Film and Literature for six years before we were able to teach it. Once the course was approved and in the curriculum, our planning was extensive. We both had to master, to some extent, each other's discipline. We had to learn to speak each other's professional language. We had to remember that it was okay to ask dumb questions. Our collaboration humbled us in important ways that we believe benefited our students and our teaching for this and other courses. We were reminded of both the thrill and the struggle of having a "beginner's mind." Also, because we had just struggle to learn the material, once the course began we felt more compassion for our students' struggles to digest the information and their ability to integrate the disciplines effectively. We also felt a great deal of pride in them, since we knew how difficult the task that we set for them was.

The primary piece of advice we offer is to allow more time than you think you need to prepare the course. In fact, double whatever amount of time you think you need. We discovered that it was essential to more fully prepare this course than either of us was accustomed to doing with our own courses. Collaboration depended on good planning, both for the overall design and the day-by-day classes. Paradoxically, we needed to know more so that we could feel comfortable improvising. One of the payoffs for this kind of intense preparation was that we got to learn how the other person taught. Teaching is, ironically, a rather solitary act, especially at the college or university level. There's not much oversight, and faculty are generally given a great deal of autonomy. The downside is that we rarely get an opportunity to discuss and learn, in a detailed way, how our colleagues actually do what they do. In this kind of team-teaching situation, you get that opportunity, and it can't help but enrich your own teaching to see how another person designs a course, prepares for class, improvises from the plan, and responds to the inevitable teaching moments that arise every day. It was truly inspiring for both of us – not just as scholars being allowed to learn a new discipline but also as teachers engaged in an on-going pedagogical colloquium.

Conclusion: Differentiated Teaching

Should differentiated teaching be a goal? We have taught the course additional times. We've both certainly become more adept. We've learned to trust each other with the material. Kenny has no qualms about turning over a literary or film analysis to Wayne, and Wayne regularly lets Kenny explicate the theory. We've both grown immensely. For Kenny, his deepening understanding of Bowen's theory has benefited him not only as a literary and film critic, but also as a writer, administrator, and person. Wayne uses film and literature more fully in his own family systems classes and also teaches a systems approach to differentiated leadership, which draws on our working conversations and our collaborations in the classroom. He's a closer examiner of texts and films, and now has a useful tool for illustrating complex human interactions in a clinical setting.

Could either of us teach the course alone? Perhaps. But we won't do that, nor should it really be the goal for any genuinely interdisciplinary course. In an interdisciplinary team-teaching situation, the source of both intellectual and creative energy is the exploration of the space between disciplines, and it helps to have two people bringing their different professional lenses to bear on the subject matter.

We hope this kind of learning environment serves as a model for our students of the kind of work we'd like them to aspire to at Prescott College: work where intellectual boundaries are permeable rather than rigid, where collaboration is encouraged rather than academically suspect, and where they can apply and personalize theoretical material, moving beyond analysis and evaluation to the truly creative realm of synthesis. Our experiences have taught us that interdisciplinary team teaching can be–if academically nourished, rigorously conceived, and effectively executed–liberal arts education at its best.

CHAPTER THIRTEEN

BOWEN THEORY, MULTIPLE INTELLIGENCES THEORY, EMOTIONAL INTELLIGENCE THEORY, AND EXPERIENTIAL EDUCATION: TEACHING UNDERGRADUATES THROUGH MEDIATION TRAINING
-BY WAYNE REGINA AND STEVE PACE

Introduction

The original version of this chapter, titled "The Personal Intelligences in Experiential Education: A Theory in Practice," appears in the 2008 book *Theory and Practice of Experiential Education*, edited by Karen Warren, Denise Mitten, and TA Loeffler. For this book, we have altered the chapter to more fully represent our work as teachers in the classroom, integrating Bowen family systems theory as a co-principle theory. We also re-wrote the chapter using a first-person perspective.

In the original published chapter, we detailed how we used this course to teach mediation through a systems lens. The theoretical basis of the article combined Howard Gardner's personal intelligences and Goleman's emotional intelligence as a framework. Since many people in the field of experiential education are more familiar with Gardner's work and Goleman's writings than they are with Bowen's theory, we originally decided to write the chapter from the perspective of these more familiar theorists. In truth, though, we actually taught the class using Bowen family systems theory as a co-theoretical foundation.

Those familiar with these approaches to understanding human behavior and human group interactions understand the essential similarities between emotional intelligence, as articulated by Daniel Goleman; the interpersonal and intrapersonal intelligences, collectively called the personal intelligences, proposed by Howard Gardner as a part of his Multiple Intelligences theory; and differentiation, as described in Bowen family systems theory. We re-formatted our chapter for this book, so as to more accurately reflect the actual work of the class.

Chapter Thirteen

Bowen Theory, Multiple Intelligences Theory, Emotional Intelligence Theory, and Experiential Education: Teaching Undergraduates through Mediation Training

-by Wayne Regina and Steve Pace

In this chapter, we explore the Bowen family systems theory (also known as Bowen theory) construct of differentiation and its importance in learning. We investigate the relationship between differentiation and the associated concepts of the personal intelligences and emotional intelligence, and their intersection with experiential education or active pedagogical education. We discuss the essential nature of developing the functional differentiation of learners and educators. Further, we discuss how we applied these theoretical systems through structured, active pedagogy and sequential, experiential education exercises as faculty members in our Prescott College class Community Mediation and Alternative Dispute Resolution. Further, we identify opportunities for field and classroom teachers to increase their emotional maturity in order to improve the quality of the active learning environment. Finally, we consider current challenges to implementing a differentiation-based model in a national environment dominated by high-stakes testing and a content-driven curriculum.

The philosophy and methodology of active pedagogical or experiential education has been applied to a variety of educational settings ranging from ropes courses to academic college courses. Nonetheless, there are certain common threads that distinguish experiential education from other types of educational models and learning experiences.

Joplin (1995) offers a stage-based model defining experiential education. She articulates focus, action, support, feedback, and debrief as important components of experiential education. Her five-stage approach offers a guidepost to structuring an active learning environment for maximal effectiveness: clarity of task; a challenging environment that introduces uncertainty and ambiguity in order to dynamically engage the learner; support for and feedback to the learner to better ensure a positive outcome; and opportunities for a public debriefing so that the learner can reflect on the experience and share what was learned.

Prominent researchers and theoreticians outside of the field of active pedagogical education have articulated and defined educational and learning theories that are remarkably consistent with the theory and practice of experiential education. One such approach is Howard Gardner's Theory of Multiple Intelligences or Multiple Intelligences (MI) theory (Gardner, 1983, 1993). The Theory of Multiple Intelligences is a theoretical system that wielded an important influence on the field of education when Gardner first proposed it. During its time, Multiple Intelligences theory significantly impacted education, providing a robust catalyst for education reform, especially in the 1980s and 1990s (Armstrong, 1994; Campbell, Campbell, & Dickinson, 1993; Gardner, 1993; Lazear, 1993). While that influence has waned, at its heart, MI theory and practice have provided a natural bridge to experiential education theory and practice over the years as it integrated current knowledge of brain-based learning with active and challenging learning environments, a dynamic pedagogy, and opportunities for reflection and review.

Interestingly, Gardner (1983, 1995) did not initially conceptualize the practical applications of MI theory when he first wrote about it in the seminal work *Frames of Mind*. Nor did he envision that MI theory would provide a catalyst for education experimentation and reform. Nevertheless, Gardner's initial writings and follow-up work spurred a generation of educators who were restless to break free from the bonds of tradition and eager to develop and implement curriculum based on multiple ways of knowing and learning.

Gardner's (1983) initial research led him to propose seven intelligences that describe the various ways that individuals learn. They are: logical-mathematical, verbal-linguistic, visual-spatial, bodily-kinesthetic, musical-rhythmic, interpersonal, and intra-personal. A decade later, Gardner added an eighth, the naturalist intelligence (Checkley, 1997). Through proposing a theory of multiple intelligences, Gardner (1995) suggests that *all* of the intelligences are important. He identifies these from studies of brain functioning and defines them based on "biological and psychological potential (p. 2)," emphasizing that they do not simply reflect a learning style.

In an interview with Checkley (1997), Gardner describes intelligence as "the human ability to solve problems or to make something that is valued in one or more cultures… (with) a particular representation in the brain for the ability…(and) an evolutionary history of the intelligence…seen in animals other than human beings…" (p. 8). Gardner (1983) theorizes that these potentials are "capable of being realized to a greater or lesser extent as a consequence of the *experiential,* cultural, and motivational factors that affect a person (p.2, italics added). In effect, by promoting all eight intelligences, Gardner advocates that intelligence is not only based on cognitive processes such as reading, writing, and arithmetic, but, rather, intelligences are also evidenced through nature, the arts—visual art, music, and dance—as well as through knowing oneself and knowing others.

Prior to Gardner's MI theory, the educational system in the United States was focused almost entirely on the verbal-linguistic and logical-mathematical intelligences. These dominant intelligences translated into curriculum models, delivery systems, and assessment structures that were, likewise, similarly limited. Even today, over thirty years after Gardner published *Frames of Mind*, despite pockets of creativity and innovation in some charter schools, public schools, and independent schools, learning and high-stakes testing is still predominantly based on the verbal-linguistic and logical-mathematical intelligences.

While the prevailing educational paradigm still reflects the supremacy of these two intelligences in content, delivery, and assessment, a growing body of research and practice—based on Gardner's theory, those of other educators influenced by Gardner, and the work of similar theorists and reformers—is demonstrating the power of the other intelligences in promoting learning. Gardner says that learners have different strengths and can learn more naturally and efficiently through the strengths of their various intelligences. MI theory and practice suggest that an active and varied pedagogy promotes learning, creative thinking, reflection, retention, and problem solving. These discoveries are not limited to use in education, but are relevant throughout life in the ways that we learn, work, play, and love.

Perhaps most importantly, MI advocates believe that learning does not take place in a vacuum. Learning about self and others through developing the intrapersonal and interpersonal intelligences prepares students to better discover academic content and to make positive contributions to society. As such, the core of the theory lies in the importance of the interpersonal intelligence and intrapersonal intelligence, commonly referred to as the personal intelligences (Gardner, 1983). The personal intelligences are similar in both conceptualization and practice to Bowen family systems theory's central concept of differentiation, extensively detailed in chapter two.

Similarly, Goleman (1995) conceptualizes emotional intelligence as crucial to all other learning. He breaks down emotional intelligence into a variety of subsets—knowing one's emotions, emotional self-management, motivating and working with others, and managing the emotions of others. Each of his core principles is consistent with the characteristics and behaviors found in Bowen's concept of differentiation.

Success in developing and strengthening these core processes, whatever they are called by various theorists and practitioners, significantly influences learning in all content and process areas (Larriveer, 2000; Marzano, 2003). For example, managing oneself effectively in highly ambiguous and anxious situations; the capacity to hear, offer, and integrate support and feedback; and the ability to incorporate public debrief and reflection are all capacities associated not with only experiential education but also with increases in differentiation, the personal intelligences, and emotional intelligence. As the terms are essentially the same, we will use these terms interchangeably in this chapter.

In effect, by strengthening emotional maturity the individual becomes a more capable and ready learner. And, perhaps most significantly, the emotional maturity or basic differentiation of the educator, as leader of the classroom or educational system, is perhaps the most significant variable in influencing the educational environment. Learning environments that encourage development of emotional maturity are best delivered by educators who are dedicated to enhancing their own core or basic differentiation. This is especially true for educators and students involved in experiential or active pedagogical education.

In this chapter, we explore how we use experiential methodology to teach the theoretical concepts and behaviors of differentiation and the related constructs of emotional intelligence and the personal intelligences. We trace the important theoretical and practical implications of focusing on developing emotional maturity as a means of improving content and process learning. To this end, we investigate the intersection of Goleman's work on emotional intelligence, Gardner's personal intelligences, and Bowen theory's concept of differentiation. We present research and theory supporting the use of these concepts as the basis for personal development and content learning as well.

We further demonstrate how promoting functional differentiation is a central component of experiential, active pedagogical education, using examples from our Prescott College course, Community Mediation and Alternative Dispute Resolution, to highlight the theory in practice. In doing so, we discuss how this approach is consistent with the basic tenets of experiential education.

Differentiation, the Personal Intelligences, and Emotional Intelligence

In *Frames of Mind*, Gardner (1983) defines the intrapersonal and interpersonal intelligences. He classifies the intrapersonal intelligence as the:

> Development of the internal aspects of a person. The core capacity at work here is *access to one's own feelings life*–one's range of affects or emotions: the capacity instantly to effect discriminations among these feelings and, eventually, to label them, to enmesh them in symbolic codes, to draw upon them as a means of understanding and guiding one's behavior...At its most advanced level, intrapersonal knowledge allows one to detect and to symbolize complex and highly differentiated sets of feelings. One finds this form of intelligence developed in the novelist (like Proust) who can write introspectively about feelings, in the patient (or the therapist) who comes to attain a deep knowledge of his own feeling life, in the wise elder who draws upon his own wealth of inner experiences in order to advise members of his community. (p. 239)

As defined by Gardner, then, the intrapersonal intelligence allows the individual to know self more fully and to use that knowledge to benefit the self and others. This is precisely what the individuality life force component of differentiation promotes as well. In this way, the intrapersonal intelligence is almost identical to the individuality life force in Bowen family systems theory.

Gardner (1983) goes on to describe the interpersonal intelligence as one where an individual:

> Turns outward, to other individuals. The core capacity here is *the ability to notice and make distinctions among other individuals* and, in particular, among their moods, temperaments, motivations, and intentions...in an advanced form, interpersonal knowledge permits a skilled adult to read the intentions and desires–even when these have been hidden–of many other individuals and, potentially, to act upon this knowledge, for example, by influencing a group of disparate individuals to behave along desired lines. We see highly

developed forms of interpersonal intelligence in political and religious figures (a Mahatma Gandhi or a Lyndon Johnson), in skilled parents and teachers, and in individuals enrolled in the helping professions, be they therapists, counselors, or shamans. (p. 239)

As defined by Gardner, then, the interpersonal intelligence allows the individual to enjoy effective relationships with others, including partners, friends, and colleagues. This dovetails with the togetherness life force of Bowen theory's basic differentiation. Taken together, the personal intelligences are uniquely aligned with Bowen theory. We believe that the two theoretical components of differentiation–the individuality life force and the togetherness life force–are synonymous with the personal intelligences.

Gardner (1983) acknowledges that although all of the intelligences are important, it is the personal intelligences that form the basis for success in both the individual and society. He writes:

> While the decision to employ (or not to employ) one's musical or spatial intelligence is not heavily charged, the pressures to employ one's personal intelligences are acute: it is the unusual individual who does not try to employ his understanding of the personal realm in order to improve his own well-being or his relationship with the community...armed with such a scheme of interpretation, he has the potential to make sense of the full range of experiences which he and others in his community can undergo. (p. 241-242)

In effect, while the other intelligences are important for both personal and social advancement, developing and implementing the personal intelligences are basic and fundamental for success in life and for societal betterment. Again, this is congruent with a person of moderately high or high levels of basic differentiation.

Other theoreticians and researchers echo the centrality of these theoretical constructs. For example, Daniel Goleman and his colleagues have created an industry in promoting emotional intelligence (Boyatzis, 2002; Goleman, 1994, 2006; Goleman, Boyatzis, & McKee, 2002) and more recently social intelligence (Goleman, 2006). Salovey and Mayer (as cited in Goleman, 1994) used Gardner's work in the personal intelligences as a springboard for defining emotional intelligence. Goleman (1994) expounds on their work in defining emotional intelligence to include:

1. *Knowing one's emotions.* Self-awareness–recognizing a feeling *as it happens*–is the keystone of emotional intelligence...the ability to monitor feelings from moment to moment is crucial to psychological insight and self-understanding ...People with greater certainty about their feelings are better pilots of their lives, having a surer sense about how they really feel about personal decisions.

2. Managing emotions. Handling feelings so they are appropriate is an ability that builds on self-awareness...the capacity to soothe oneself, to shake off rampant anxiety, gloom, or irritability...those who excel in it can bounce back far more quickly from life's setbacks and upsets.

3. Motivating oneself. Marshalling emotions in the service of a goal is essential for paying attention, for self-motivation and mastery, and for creativity. Emotional self-control–delaying gratification and stifling impulsiveness–underlies accomplishment of every sort...People who have this skill tend to be more highly productive and effective in whatever they undertake.

4. Recognizing emotions in others. Empathy, another ability that builds on emotional self-awareness, is a fundamental "people skill"...empathy kindles altruism. People who are empathetic are more attuned to the subtle social signals that indicate what others need or want. This makes them better at callings such as the caring professions, teaching, sales, and management.

5. Handling relationships. The art of relationships is, in large part, skill at managing emotions in others...These are the abilities that undergird popularity, leadership, and interpersonal effectiveness. People who excel in these skills do well at anything that relies on interacting smoothly with others. (p. 43-44)

Decades prior to Gardner and Goleman's research and writings on the personal intelligences and emotional intelligence, Murray Bowen (1971) addressed the importance of the personal intelligences as articulated in his family systems theory. It is puzzling that neither Gardner nor Goleman ever cited Bowen in their research, despite the fact that their descriptive language on the personal intelligences and emotional intelligence sounds remarkably similar to basic differentiation.

As stated in chapter two, Bowen articulates two fundamental life forces—individuality and togetherness—and proposes that the interaction of these life forces determines a person's core capacity to manage herself, her life, and her relationships with others and society (Bowen, 2002; Kerr & Bowen, 1988). According to Bowen theory, it is these twin life forces in motion that determine the organism's level of basic differentiation or capacity to function as a distinctly separate organism, while remaining in intimate connection with others and the environment.

Bowen family systems theory conceptualizes differentiation as the ability of the individual to clearly define a self; regulate one's own behaviors, emotions, and feelings; develop personal responsibility; and, simultaneously, relate well to others, work effectively with individuals and groups, develop empathy and compassion, take a stand regardless of the emotional climate or reactivity in others, and follow one's own "north star" in pursuing one's own life goals (Bowen, 2002; Friedman, 1996, 2007; Kerr & Bowen, 1988; Regina, 2000). Synonyms for differentiation include emotional maturity, personal integrity, resiliency, the ability to adapt to life's various situations and challenges, and a willingness to accept personal responsibility and accountability for one's being and emotional destiny (Friedman, 1991, 1996, 2007; Kerr & Bowen, 1988).

Clearly, all of these theoreticians, educators, clinicians, and practitioners have developed a common, converging schema for successful human functioning: one's effectiveness in life, capacity to learn and grow, ability to effectively engage with others, and personal satisfactions are all related to the development of basic differentiation, emotional intelligence, and the personal intelligences. Interestingly, these are many of the same outcomes sought and achieved through experiential or active pedagogical education.

Most educational systems in the United States only glimpse the importance of developing these personal and interpersonal strengths. While many schools and districts now implement character education programs, essentially programs designed to foster and promote emotional intelligence, these programs are usually relegated to secondary or tertiary importance in the average school day or school curriculum. Instead, according to the growing body of research on the importance of the personal intelligences for life and success, they should be essential components in developing effective citizens able and willing to work well with others and having clear goals about self and self-determination.

Those responsible for implementing more innovative educational institutions and programs understand the importance of developing these central capacities and how fostering them not only increases a student's effectiveness in her life and within the life of the classroom but also facilitates learning in the other multiple intelligences. For example, Sylvester (1995) states that "we know emotion is very important to the education process because it drives attention, which drives learning and memory...It's impossible to separate emotion from the other important activities of life (p. 72, 75)."

Caine and Caine (1997) go further, detailing how the brain functions when fatigued or feeling helpless. They offer the term "downshifting" to describe how learning suffers when students do not feel empowered or when they can no longer function adequately due to exhaustion. Their brain-based research model parallels Bowen's family systems theory, which describes how emotional reactivity increases as anxiety increases (Friedman, 2007, 1996; Kerr & Bowen, 1988).

In fact, Bowen theory suggests that as long-term, multigenerational, chronic anxiety increases, levels of core or basic differentiation decrease. This, in turn, lowers resiliency, adaptability, and the capacity to successfully alter one's environment. Bowen theory further proposes that the broadband, emotional "antibiotic" that best protects the self and promotes learning and personal development is increasing one's level of basic differentiation, i.e., strengthening emotional intelligence or the personal intelligences (Friedman, 1987).

Whether guided by MI theory, emotional intelligence theory, Bowen theory, or other similar theoretical and brain-based research systems, some of the most promising work in education reform utilizes an educational strategy that advances the personal intelligences. Effective learning strategies that encourage differentiation are largely based on an active pedagogy that bears all the hallmarks of experiential education as articulated by Joplin (1995). This was the theoretical underpinning for our course, Community Mediation and Alternative Dispute Resolution.

Applying Theory in Practice

Education at Prescott College is experientially based. As such, students learn theory and practice through an active pedagogy designed to involve students directly in their own learning. Classes are small, usually between ten and fourteen students. These small class sizes allow for personalized learning, feedback, and training. The primary goal of the course Community Mediation and Alternative Dispute Resolution is to develop the skills, attitudes, and behaviors necessary to effectively mediate disputes. To accomplish this goal, our eleven-week course helps students increase their emotional intelligence through combining theory and practice.

The focus of the course is on skill development and practical learning activities. Through modeling and guided practice of micro-skill learning and application, students develop proficiency in listening, reflecting, rapport-building, reframing, shifting from positions to interests, and agreement writing, among others. These hands-on, skill observations and development components are supplemented by various readings and discussions around theories of conflict resolution and mediation, including Bowen theory. The reading requirements include Wayne's book *Applying Family Systems Theory to Mediation: A Practitioner's Guide* (Regina, 2011), as well as Fisher and Ury's (1981) classic *Getting to Yes,* which provides practical opportunities for students to apply principled negotiation to their own lives.

Several examples will highlight this approach. Initially, students share why they are interested in the course. This activity is designed to begin the process of developing a sense of personal ownership of the course and for its success. It provides the students with the opportunity to reflect on their personal interests, as well as engage with others to formulate a common vision. This experiential exercise affords us the opportunity to initially assess each of the student's functional level of differentiation.

Within the boundaries of the course description, the students and instructors co-create the learning goals that are addressed during the course. The students are asked to brainstorm specific skills and theories they want to cover in the course. Topics are added and subtracted from the developing list until a consensus is reached. In its final form, the topics usually include an understanding of conflict and conflict resolution, acquiring mediation skills, and improving interpersonal communication.

Through this exercise, students begin the process of developing personal and collective responsibility for the course. They help formulate course topics and goals, and by so doing, they define the course for themselves, manage their own emotional reactivity to the interests of others, and work cooperatively and collectively to include others' perspectives without losing "self" in the process. This initial exercise is specifically designed to help students assess and develop their functional differentiation, and it helps set the stage for what is expected throughout the class. (Functional differentiation is the differentiation of the moment. It is contextually driven. Increasing basic differentiation takes years of practiced effort. Also, basic differentiation is something that can only be approximated and assessed over time and across situations. As such, only functional differentiation, a site and setting level of functioning, can be approximated and impacted in specific situations such as a class environment. While important, functional differentiation should not be confused with basic differentiation.)

Next, we ask students what attitudes and behaviors we can expect from each other in order to successfully achieve our educational goals. We find this "group norming" exercise crucial to the success of the group as a learning community since it promotes clear and shared expectations as well as common agreements for all. Student responses often include: say what you need, help others, have fun, actively participate, respect self and others, maintain confidentiality, take risks, arrive on time, be prepared for class, and so on. The students and instructors then commit to these common agreements, and we all sign a group contract to hold each other accountable.

The symbolic gesture of signing the agreement signifies personal commitment. If a participant breaks one of these common agreements later in the course, the class as a whole can be asked to respond to the transgression using the spirit of the contract as a rubric. This group norming continues the process of creating a sense of group responsibility for the success of the course. In addition, this active exercise asks students to take personal and collective responsibility for their actions throughout the course, further promoting the personal intelligences.

In a second example designed to assess and interpret how students view conflict, students are paired together and given a small cup of M&Ms. They are told the following: "You are going to play a fun game of arm wrestling. The winner of each arm-wrestling contest can eat one M&M. Arm wrestle twice with your partner, using your left arm and then right arm. Then, switch to another player and then another. Please play until all the M&Ms are eaten."

During the activity, much laughter ensues as students began competing. After a brief period of time, many of the pairs discover that if they cooperate they can share the M&Ms by taking turns winning. We then debrief the activity around the concepts of cooperation, competition, and conflict. Students are asked to reflect on how they managed the activity, the level of conflict and cooperation they created, and their degree of anxiety or comfort around competition. Through the de-briefing process, the students discuss what they learned about themselves regarding the central topics. (We do not know the origins of the M&M game, but thank those who created this activity.)

In other activities which occur throughout the term, students learn the specific micro-skills of mediation. While the concepts of differentiation and emotional intelligence provide the theoretical "vehicle" for traveling down the road of skill development and improvement, students have to master a set of specific mediation skills and processes along the way in order to successfully complete the course. These skills are sequentially introduced and include:

- Stage 1 – Introductions: Review, writing, and practicing introductions

- Stage 2 – Getting the Stories/Uninterrupted Time: Review and practice

- Stage 3 – Developing Connections: Review and practice

- Stage 4 – Building Agreements: Review and practice

- Stage 5 – Concluding Comments: Summing up, managing disputants who have not formed a common agreement

Developing specific skills for implementing each stage follow a consistent pattern. First, students read about the stage. Next, we present the micro-skills for each stage through either demonstration or through examples that we discuss and process. Finally, students practice each stage and specific skill through sample vignette mediations. As students develop the skills necessary for each stage, the subsequent stages are layered on, so that students learn the sequence of mediation as well as the skill set required for successfully implementing each skill and each stage. Students rotate through the roles of disputants, co-mediators, and observers so that each person experiences every role in the mediation process.

Throughout the training, we observe each mediation group, provide critique and feedback to the participants, as well as insert ourselves into the mediation process as a co-mediator as necessary to re-direct a mediation that loses its focus, to demonstrate a particular technique or skill, or to prompt the co-mediators into examining issues and interests that they may have missed.

At all times, the integration of experiential exercises throughout the course fosters the development of increased functional differentiation such that a feedback loop occurs through presenting the material, discussing the stages and skills for the lesson, implementing the activity through role plays, receiving individual practice, and de-briefing individually and with the entire class. As students progress through the stages, new vignettes are introduced to keep the mediation role-plays fresh and to give students an opportunity to implement entire practice mediations.

Through this ordered teaching and learning situation, students expose themselves to structured environments with highly ambiguous outcomes. That is, students need the personal strength to develop and implement new skills in a public arena where they are critiqued by other students and by the instructors. The courage that students display throughout the learning process is always inspiring. They come to realize that the best way to acquire skills and expertise is through structured activities that provide opportunities to directly experience and learn the material, risk-take in environments and through activities that naturally raise their anxiety, and de-brief their learning in both private venues, such as portfolio reflections, as well as public arenas, such as small group reflections and large group discussions.

These kinds of challenges require students to learn self-soothing in difficult environments, entertain new ways of defining themselves and their work in the world, work cooperatively with others to foster effective learning, and promote self-integrity as well as the integrity of both the mediation process and the disputants themselves. While it may be possible to begin the process of increasing basic differentiation through this training system, increases in emotional maturity take time, effort, and commitment over years and decades. Rather, it is more likely that students can begin to increase their functional differentiation. By doing so, they come to appreciate the value in this kind of self-reflection, self-definition, self-management of anxiety, and interpersonal relationship work that is necessary for a more committed approach to increasing basic differentiation.

While strengthening students' emotional maturity is an important goal for us in this and in other classes that we teach, we realize that this cannot be achieved in short time frames. Nonetheless, our teaching introduces students to the ingredients necessary for increasing the personal intelligences, and it provides them with the opportunity to begin this important journey. The most motivated and enlightened students understand this approach theoretically as well as personally and emotionally. Many take additional classes with a Bowen family systems theory focus in order to continue learning the theory behind differentiation and the practice of differentiating.

Still, through increasing functional differentiation, students learn about themselves, develop increased capacities to work cooperatively with each other, and, in doing so, acquire academic, theoretical knowledge along with specific skills sets useful for accomplishing the goals of the course and transferable to the world outside of the classroom.

The Personal Intelligences of Educational Leaders

Differentiation enhancement in educational settings must occur holistically throughout the learning community. Students cannot, nor should they be expected to, take risks in isolation. In particular, as an educator and leader of the educational environment, we must be willing to subject ourselves to the same scrutiny and trials that we expect of our students. In his book, *Multiple Intelligences in the Classroom*, Thomas Armstrong (1994) reinforces this point when he writes, "Before applying any model of learning in a classroom environment, we should first apply it to ourselves as educators and adult learners, for unless we have an experiential understanding of the theory and have personalized its content, we are unlikely to be committed to using it with students" (p. 16).

This practice is central for practitioners of experiential education. Teachers and students alike must be active participants in learning. As educational leaders, our willingness to "walk our talk" is not simply a matter of fairness and balance. It is, rather, a function of setting an emotional atmosphere and tone in which learning is prized by all through a challenging environment that introduces uncertainty and ambiguity in order to engage us all as learners. Also, we ask students to support our roles as co-learners through their offering us constructive feedback and providing us opportunities, as instructors, to publicly debrief our own mediation demonstrations so that we, as co-learners, can reflect on our experiences and share what we learn as well.

In fact, both Friedman (2007) and Goleman (2006) suggest that leaders in any human system are the most significant individuals in influencing others and creating the emotional field in which learning and leading occur. Boyatzis, 2002) suggests that if leaders in educational environments are capable of promoting a "positive resonance" or differentiated presence such that they are viewed as equal partners in learning, while maintaining their position of leaders in the system, then classroom and other educational environments can be more readily transformed into learning communities where education is treasured by all.

In other words, leaders with a higher level of differentiation who are committed to developing their emotional maturity are more emotionally congruent leaders. The more emotionally mature the leaders, the greater their capacity to elevate emotional intelligence in the educational environment. For many, the emotional capacity of the educational leader is the most important variable in successful learning and leading (Bowen, 2002; Friedman, 2007; Goleman, Boyatzis, & McKee, 2002; Regina, 2000). Who among us has not experienced this firsthand, where the self-responsible, non-defensive educator with an enhanced ability to engage others creates the necessary and sufficient conditions for learning, while the less emotionally mature leader fails regardless of the sophistication of the lesson plan?

As instructors, we want to set the emotional tone for risk-taking, learning from others, and accepting feedback, since students receive our comments and critiques throughout the course. In part, we do this through role playing two demonstration mediations, which are developed by students. For each mock mediation, we select two student volunteers to create the conflict scenario and role play the parts of disputants. We then demonstrate the stages of mediation through a "stop-and-go" process whereby we de-brief each stage with the entire class before proceeding to the next stage. At the end of each of these role-play mediations, we debrief the entire activity from both personal and theoretical perspectives.

These two role-play mediations are particularly important in developing a class culture promoting increases in functional differentiation. They are examples of our participating in activities where we expose ourselves to the same scrutiny and risk-taking that we expect from students. As instructors, we enter the mock mediations with a substantial degree of uncertainty about the process and outcome. We conduct the mediations and solicit feedback, reflections, support, and critiques from the students in the form of a public debrief. All the while, we are providing a forum for students to learn how to give and receive feedback, and we are working on our own differentiation as we manage our performance anxiety, humble ourselves before of our students, develop rapport with the participants, define and clarify roles and guidelines for the mediation, and provide a template for conducting community mediation.

As instructors, we set the emotional tone of the learning environment through our willingness to be co-learners in the educational process and to accept personal responsibility for managing ourselves as mediators. In these ways, the class activities are specifically designed to help set the best emotional tone for the course.

In sum, we have encountered extraordinary success through integrating the development of functional differentiation and emotional intelligence with academic and skills-based knowledge acquisition. This approach to education demonstrates all of the hallmarks of experiential education, through a theoretical system that promotes the personal intelligences as foundational to ongoing success in learning inside and outside of the classroom. In an interview published in the book *The Project Zero Classroom* (Hetlan and Chalfen, 1999), Gardner reiterates this point when he says, "Personal intelligences are important because life consists significantly in understanding other people and in understanding yourself, and being able to use those understandings productively."

An education that effectively focuses on developing and strengthening emotional intelligence is an education that elevates emotional maturity. More emotionally mature people can, in turn, more efficiently integrate and synthesize knowledge and information to become more involved and productive citizens in the world. Experiential education, because of its emphasis on action and reflection, is a perfect crucible for developing functional differentiation. We believe this is one of the primary reasons experiential education through an active pedagogy can be a life-changing methodology and philosophy.

The success of active pedagogical or experiential education can be witnessed through the proliferation of theory and research articulating its effectiveness as well as its congruence with other theories of education and learning. In particular, this chapter provided a rationale for including Bowen theory, MI theory, and emotional intelligence theory–all essentially congruent theoretical systems–as theories within the broader field of experiential education. We describe the theoretical convergence between experiential education and these theoretical systems as well as their pedagogical consistency. As educators provide multiple ways to instruct a variety of populations, active learning is ultimately effective when learners learn about themselves, others, the world in which they live, as well as specific content that is a part of a given curriculum.

References

Armstrong, T. (1994). *Multiple intelligences in the classroom.* Alexandria, VA: ASCD.

Boyatzis, (2002, April 24). Positive resonance: Educational leadership through emotional intelligence. *Education Week*, 52, 40-41.

Bowen, M. (2002). *Family therapy in clinical practice.* Northvale, NJ: Jason Aronson.

Bowen, M. (1971). Family therapy and family group therapy. In H. Kaplan & B. Sadock (Eds.), *Comprehensive group psychotherapy* (pp. 384-421). Baltimore, MD: Williams & Wilkins.

Caine, R.N. & Caine, G. (1997). *Education on the edge of possibility.* Alexandria, VA: ASCD.

Campbell, L., Campbell, B., & Dickinson, D. (1993). *Teaching and learning through multiple intelligences.* Tucson, AZ: Zephyr Press.

Checkley, K. (1997, September). The first seven...and the eighth: A conversation with Howard Gardner. *Educational Leadership*,

55, 1: 8-13.

Fisher, R. and Ury, W. (1981). *Getting to yes*. New York, NY: Houghton Mifflin Company.

Friedman, E. (2007). *A failure of nerve: Leadership in the age of the quick fix*. New York: Seabury Books.

Friedman, E. (1996). *Reinventing leadership: Change in an age of anxiety*. New York: Guilford Press.

Friedman, E. (1991). Bowen theory and therapy. In A. Gurman & D. Kniskern (Eds.), *Handbook of family therapy, volume 2* (pp. 134-170). New York: Routledge.

Friedman, E. (1987, May-June). How to succeed in therapy without really trying. *Family Therapy Networker*, 27- 34.

Gardner, H. (1983). *Frames of mind*. New York: Basic Books.

Gardner, H. (1993). *Multiple intelligences: The theory in practice*. New York: Basic Books.

Gardner, H. (1995). *Reflections on multiple intelligences*. Phi Delta Kappan, 77, 200-208.

Goleman, D. (2006). *Social intelligence: The new science of human relationships*. New York: Bantam Books.

Goleman, D. (1995). *Emotional intelligence: Why it can matter more than I.Q.* New York: Bantam Books.

Goleman, D., Boyatzis, R., & McKee, A. (2002). *Primal leadership: Realizing the power of emotional intelligence*. Boston, MA: Harvard Business Press.

Hetlan, L. and Chalfen, K. (1999). *The project zero classroom: New approaches to thinking and understanding*. Harvard, MA: Project Zero Harvard University.

Joplin, L. (1995). On defining experiential education. In K. Warren, M. Sakofs, & J.S. Hunt, Jr. (Eds.), *The theory of experiential education* (pp. 15-22). Dubuque, IA: Kendall/Hunt.

Kerr, M.E. and Bowen, M. (1988). *Family evaluation: An approach based on Bowen theory.* New York: Norton.

Larriveer, B. (2005). *Authentic classroom management: Creating a learning community and building reflective practice. Second edition.* Boston, MA: Allyn and Bacon.

Lazear, D. (1993). *Seven Pathways to learning: Teaching students and parents about multiple intelligences.* Tucson, AZ: Zephyr Press.

Marzano, R. (2003). *What works in schools: Translating research into action.* Alexandria, VA: ASCD.

Regina, W. (2000). Bowen systems theory and mediation. *Mediation Quarterly*, 18 (2), 111-128.

Sylvester, R. (1995). *A celebration of neurons: An educator's guide to the human brain.* Alexandrai, VA: ASCD.

CHAPTER FOURTEEN

BOWEN FAMILY SYSTEMS THEORY
AND MARITAL CONCILIATION

Introduction

A version of this chapter, titled "Bowen theory and Marital Conciliation" was originally published in my 2011 book *Applying Family Systems Theory to Mediation: A Practitioner's Guide* by University Press of America. This chapter describes what conciliation is, how I developed a conciliation model using Bowen theory, and the results of my activities conducting conciliations.

I spent over fifteen years creating, implementing, and refining this model. Conciliation counseling is expanding as the courts become more involved with mediation, arbitration, and other alternative dispute resolution processes. What follows is a model for conducting conciliations and evaluating their success.

CHAPTER FOURTEEN

BOWEN FAMILY SYSTEMS THEORY
AND MARITAL CONCILIATION

In Arizona, a marital conciliation meeting is granted when either the petitioner or respondent in a marital dissolution proceeding believes that there is a basis for marital reconciliation. In an effort to support the institution of marriage, Arizona state law grants the married couple a mandatory conciliation session that involves the petitioner, respondent, and court conciliator. The goal of the conciliation meeting is to determine whether or not there is a realistic basis for marital reconciliation.

Although I conducted mediations for years, in 2001 I began conducting marital conciliations with no formal training other than my experience as a mediator, family psychologist, and marriage and family therapist. Arizona state law specifies that conciliation is not marital counseling, so there were no guidelines for how to proceed. During my first conciliations, I stumbled around, trying to find a useful model with which to conduct these interviews and interventions.

As I gained more familiarity with conciliations, however, I realized that although my background as a mediator was useful in organizing the structure of the sessions, it was my experience as a Bowen family systems theory psychologist and marriage and family therapist that was most helpful in guiding my assessment and intervention strategies. As such, I began to conceptualize my role in conciliations as expert consultant, assessing the couple's individual and systemic functioning and providing each person separately and the couple together with my observations regarding their significant strengths and the primary challenges facing them individually and relationally. Over time, I developed a six-stage procedural framework, while relying on my theoretical perspective as a systems practitioner.

Applying Bowen Family Systems Theory to Marital Conciliation

Marital conciliation is a time-limited opportunity to assess a couple's relationship system and help them decide if there is a basis for reconciliation. The role of the marital conciliator is that of systems consultant and not marital therapist.

By the time a couple enters into court-ordered conciliation, the marriage is severely damaged. Hurt and angry feelings abound with accusations of betrayal, disappointment, and blaming as common themes. A host of systems dynamics is also alive and active. Under-functioning/over-functioning patterns are often polarized, calcified, and externalized such that the marital patterns are usually chronically locked. Often one spouse is more symptomatic and the other is more enabling. Drug abuse and alcoholism are common, as are "process addictions" such as gambling and affairs. The build-up of chronic anxiety in the system, the intensity of the couple's emotional reactivity, the severity of symptom development, and the resultant polarization of their positions has resulted in the collapse of the marriage, culminating in one spouse filing for divorce. This is what has typically occurred when a couple is seen in conciliation.

It is common for spouses to over-focus on the other partner in the relationship instead of concentrating on their own expectations, goals, dreams, and self. Other-focused thinking, feelings, and behaviors are the norm and are manifested in blame displacement, anger, fear, and other fight-flight-freeze and defensive reactions. Neither husband nor wife is accepting personal responsibility for the marital conflict. Reactive criticism commonly takes the form of creating distance as a way of managing anxiety or of relentlessly pursuing and blaming the other as a way of getting the spouse to change. Both approaches minimize self-responsibility by emotionally reacting to the other instead of thoughtfully responding to what it is each must do to increase self-soothing, self-management, and personal responsibility.

Other-focused thoughts, feelings, and actions often result in subjective thinking, which is thinking that is driven by anxiety and fear. All too often, subjective thinking has one or both partners believing that if the marriage ends, so will their problems. A common example of subjective thinking is: "If I cannot get my partner to change, I can change partners, or at least get out of the marriage as a way of restoring my life."

Unfortunately, divorce rarely ends the pattern. If there are children from the marriage, divorce often increases the emotional intensity between the couple through triangles created with the children. Without intervention, and especially with more poorly functioning parents, blame displacement, fighting a proxy war through the children (using the children as a weapon against the other), and other forms of emotional entanglement and fusion can last for generations.

In these instances, children are often caught in the middle. They experience escalating anxiety and often develop symptoms. They experience loyalty conflicts between themselves and their parents and/or their parents' new partners, and they may manifest impaired intimate relationships as they get older. Heightened reactivity results in emotional polygamy for the couple, escalating chronic anxiety for the parents and the children, and a psychic battlefield littered with casualties.

Even when a marriage is childless, escape into divorce rarely results in increased emotional maturity, as patterned responses are usually not relationship specific but, rather, stylistic and automatic, reflecting a lower level of basic differentiation. As such, I have two central goals in conducting conciliations.

First, I use the conciliation session to highlight these emotional processes in order to help the couple recognize the relationship patterns that they have created together. I attempt to break or at least minimize the blaming of the other spouse and the acceptance that "it takes two to dance" in marriage.

If I can point out the problematic patterns that they have co-created, we can expand this investigation to uncover positive patterns that were present early in the marriage that may be underused at this point. This is an attempt to highlight each person's responsibility for developing and perpetuating the charged emotional field and ways that they can, individually and together, alter the patterns in their relationship in a more productive, loving direction.

Second, I address each spouse's challenges in decreasing emotional intensity in the self and the relationship and begin moving toward a place of increasing personal accountability. To do so, the conciliator acts to shift the couple from this other-focused perspective—which usually involves conflicts of will to get the other to change—to a self-focused perception. Said differently, I want them to concentrate on changing self rather than changing other.

While the above two goals are paramount, other sub-goals come I to play. For example, I must sort through the couple's central and interlocking triangles. Common central triangles include the couple and affairs; alcohol, drugs, and other substances; physical, social, and psychiatric symptoms; children; and multigenerational legacies of violence and abuse. Familiar interlocking triangles include interested friends and family members all too willing to advise and support one spouse against the other, work, money, pets, the house, and other people, places, or things caught up in the couple's struggles. At the extreme, emotional triangles saturated with chronic anxiety decrease functional differentiation and increase automatic or "mindless" reactivity. The intensity of triangulation processes can lead to the ultimate system breakdown of divorce.

Of course, the same patterns used in the outside world are brought into the conciliation as husband and wife automatically vie for the "inside position" of the emotional triangle with me. To be effective, I must remain de-triangled. In other words, I must not take sides or absorb the anxiety in the couple's relationship. To this end, I establish and maintain a balanced working relationship with each spouse. Similar to the mediation triangle, this "equilateral" position between the spouses assists the couple to view themselves individually and relationally with greater clarity and objectively. In forming this *conciliation triangle*, I help to minimize the complexities created by central and interlocking triangles through focusing on the essential concerns between them.

This is easier said than done and requires me to continually walk the path towards a moderately high level of emotional maturity of my own. I am challenged to remain as non-reactive as possible; to present myself as reasonably calm and objective in intense situations by seeing system's dynamics and not simply individual behaviors; and to view the conciliation as an opportunity for discovery instead of trying to enforce or impose my will on the couple. My systemic assessment is important for both the wife and the husband, and it is crucial to their future individual functioning, regardless of their ultimate decision to reconcile or divorce.

The Six-Stage Marital Conciliation Process Using Bowen Theory

When I began conducting conciliations through the Superior Court of Arizona in Yavapai County, I was allotted two hours for each couple. Over time, however, the court has relaxed the two-hour provision, granting me more latitude to experiment with the length of marital conciliation sessions. I began working with willing couples for up to four hours: approximately two and a half hours to complete a comprehensive initial assessment and consultation, and, if needed, to develop a plan of action for the future, and an additional ninety minutes in a follow-up session to determine their success with the initial action plan, should the couple want to pursue reconciliation.

Greater time and session flexibility significantly increased the efficacy of my conciliations as anxious and agitated couples had more time to compose themselves and concentrate on the matters at hand. The initial single, two-hour framework created a "one size fits all" structure that limited my effectiveness. Most couples enter conciliation in attack and defend mode, replicating the difficult challenges in their relationship. A single, two-hour session did not always provide me with enough time to develop rapport, assess the marriage, calm the system, shift their focus from other to self, and develop a reconciliation strategy. For some couples, even four hours cannot begin to heal the relationship damage self-inflicted over the years. Nonetheless, the expanded format created an opportunity for many couples to push past their entrenched defensive structure and experience a more positive outcome to their marital conflicts.

In evolving my model, I expanded my timeframe, while using the initial structure of a six-stage model that I developed early on. The six stages are organized as follows:

Stage I: Introduction (approximately 10-20 minutes)

During Stage I, I welcome the couple, introduce myself, and have the couple introduce themselves. I discuss the process and stages of conciliation, review confidentiality and ground rules/guidelines, and answer any questions that they may have. I inform the couple that my role is to help them decide whether or not to reconcile and not to impose my beliefs about the appropriateness of their staying married. During this introductory phase, I highlight my role as expert consultant to inform them that my experiences as conciliator, mediator, marital therapist, and family psychologist may offer them a different perspective about themselves and their relationship than the one that they currently have.

I also let them know that engagement in conciliation sessions is strictly voluntary. I tell them that after the introductions are completed and the *Agreement to Participate* is signed, demonstrating to the judge that they have attended the mandatory session, I will ask them if they want to continue or not. If they both agree, we continue to the assessment phase of the meeting. If either partner (or both) does not want to pursue conciliation, I work towards dismissing them, since they can't reconcile a marriage unless both consent to this goal.

This decision-tree process is different from when I began conducting conciliations, where I met with both husband and wife for a full session, regardless of whether both wanted to attend. Over the years, I have come to recognize that if one partner (or both) does not want to reconcile, it does not serve the spouses individually or collectively to pursue a path that will not be successful.

If there is an early decision against reconciliation, I meet with them separately in caucus. In these individual meetings, I check on how well connected each person is in her or his community, including family, church, and friendship support. Also, I offer referrals for counseling, twelve-step groups, and other medical, social, and therapeutic services that they might need. Typically, but not exclusively, it is the women who file for divorce and who do not want to return, especially if there has been significant and repeated domestic abuse and violence in the relationship. Also, typically, women are better at developing and maintaining a broader support system in their communities and are often in counseling already. (Arizona, along with the nation, has recently allowed for same-sex couples to marry. To date, I have not worked with same-sex couples in conciliation.)

The men typically have less community resources, including church, family, and friend involvement. The husbands are often the spouses seeking conciliation, so these individual sessions are important to assess and affirm their disappointments, fears, and betrayals if a conciliation session is rejected by the wife. I work hard to get these men connected— with other family members, the clergy, counseling, and other referrals designed to increase their community participation and decrease their isolation and (often) their drinking and/or drugging.

I estimate that about half of couples decide not to pursue conciliation. After securing their signatures and describing the process of moving out of conciliation court and back to marital dissolution court— including what to expect with their upcoming mediation session if the couple has minor children—I dismiss them after their caucus meetings.

Stage II: Overview (approximately 40-60 minutes)

After securing an agreement by both spouses that they want to at least explore the possibility of reconciliation, during Stage II, I ask each person to explain what has led to the dissolution proceedings and this conciliation meeting. I explain that I need to learn all about them in order to help them. It is usually best to keep this request open so that each person can present the background information and perspective as she or he sees fit. As with mediation, it is important to allow each person uninterrupted time to tell his or her story. I am interested in a historical narrative of the relationship, from initial meeting and courtship through current circumstances. Also, like mediation, I manage their initial reactivity by prompting each through focused questioning and by minimizing interruptions.

My two primary goals at this stage are the initial assessment of each person and the relationship system, as well as developing rapport and a balanced working relationship with both husband and wife. It is important to be constantly aware of the couple's level of emotional reactivity, individually and collectively. Similar to mediation, it is common for each person to try to triangulate me into the inside position of the emotional triangle with the respective spouse on the outside position of the triangle. While this strategy is ultimately self-defeating, it is automatic, and I avoid becoming triangled by balancing rapport building with each spouse without alienating the other partner.

It is also important to remain conscious of amygdala hyper-arousal. Activation of fight-flight-freeze reactions bypasses a person's capacity for thoughtfulness. Evidence of hyper-arousal includes frequent interruptions, angry outbursts, and significant withdrawal reactions. Should I observe any of these indications, I assess if an early caucus is needed to establish or re-establish rapport and to help soothe the husband and/or wife.

A rich history allows me to uncover strengths that have been lost or minimized and significant historical information about each's family of origin—sibling position, parents' relationship, traumas and abuses, as well as resiliencies and adaptabilities. In addition, I'm looking for disturbances in the family life cycle; the roles of alcohol, physical violence, abuse, affairs, drugs, and children in the relationship and with each person; and how things reached the tipping point where divorce was filed.

I ask the couple to speak directly to me one at a time, and I ask the other spouse to listen without interrupting. I carefully choreograph the questions, as well as frame and reframe their answers. In my mind, I want to understand: Who is the pursuer and who is the distancer? What strengths were initially present in the relationship? How are over-functioning and under-functioning managed in the relationship? How have important issues such as sex, finances, children, and emotional needs been communicated? What patterns are repeating from their original families? What are the central and interlocking triangles? And, perhaps most importantly and most challenging, what is their basic and functional level of differentiation?

I actively acknowledge how challenging it is for the other spouse to listen without interrupting, and I encourage the other person to write down what they see differently. I give each spouse about 15-20 minutes to address my questions, to complete some of the couple's important history, and to uncover pertinent family history. I work hard to develop, strengthen, and preserve the conciliation triangle, which is central to this stage in conciliation and, therefore, to conciliation success.

Stage III: Caucus (approximately 20-30 minutes)

Unlike mediation where the caucus is optional for many mediators, in my conciliation model, the caucus is essential. There are two crucial and overlapping goals of the caucus. The first goal is to further strengthen the working relationship with the husband and wife in order to help legitimize my position as expert consultant. Rapport building continues, as does hypothesis-testing to help determine the individual and collective strengths in the system, as well as each person's dominant mode of automatically reacting in the relationship (attack, defend, withdraw, triangulate, etc.).

With a strong conciliation triangle established, I can move to the second and more important goal: promoting differentiation. I highlight the significance of individual responsibility, self-management of emotional intensity, self-reflection to enhance self-improvement, and shifting from other-focus to self-focus.

It is during the caucus that I explore interests, help each person move away from intractable positions, and plant seeds for individual change as I emphasize personal accountability, regardless of whether or not the relationship continues.

I discuss other systems ideas as they are relevant, such as the person least involved in the relationship having the most power. I point out ineffective patterns, often replicated in the conciliation session, which created and perpetuate the current emotional gridlock. We explore over-functioning and under-functioning patterns, as well as patterns of pursuing and distancing. I separately coach husband and wife to respond to the other through clarifying personal goals, stating interests, and defining a "bottom line" as to what is and what is not acceptable in the relationship. This systemic coaching also helps individuals move from critical, other-focused accusations to clearer, self-focused statements of interests and personal responsibility.

While caucus meetings are confidential, I encourage information sharing in the re-convened session if I believe that disclosing specific facts or perceptions are important for progress. Similar to a mediation caucus, I balance the time spent with each spouse to avoid becoming triangulated into the relationship. I make individual referrals, determine issues of safety, and re-balance power.

Stage IV: The Exchange (45-60 minutes)

After the caucus, the couple re-convenes for the exchange. During this part of the conciliation, the husband and wife discuss the possibility of reconciliation. I reinforce initial coaching during the caucus as they discuss the status of their marriage, perhaps with a new perspective and direction. I assist with this discussion and coach them to concentrate on making self-statements accepting personal responsibility and clarifying wants. I help loosen entrenched positions so that the spouses can explore what their interests are individually and for the relationship.

Usually, if the couple can encounter some movement in these discussions, that is, if they can begin to experience a different interactional and emotional pattern *and* if one spouse has not emotionally closed down, with appropriate coaching the couple may begin to uncover some hope where no hope existed before. Sometimes, a softening occurs that allows the spouses to re-experience deep feelings of love and connection.

Stage V: Consultant's Assessment (approximately 20-30 minutes)

During Stage V, I review, refine, and reinforce my assessment of each individual's strengths, dominant interactional style, personal issues, and relationship challenges. I avoid giving an opinion as to whether or not the marriage should continue or dissolve. It is also essential that I not frame the decision simply as a decision to stay or not stay in the marriage but, rather, as a decision to accept personal responsibility for one's own life. In other words, regardless of outcome, my assessment highlights what I have observed and what will lead to more effective personal functioning and relationship functioning. I help the couple consider that fleeing the marriage will not end their personal difficulties. I give a somewhat formal assessment of individual and relationship functioning, highlighting strengths and challenges, recommending appropriate counseling or treatment when necessary, and presenting them with the particulars of their systemic patterning.

Successfully moving a couple from other-focus to self-focus can take months or years depending on the couple's level of basic differentiation, so making this shift in one or two conciliation sessions is not simple. The key variables in facilitating this shift are the differentiation level and, accordingly, the motivation of the couple, as well as the differentiation level and objectivity of the conciliator. I also point out areas that need more self-soothing, self-defining, and self-responsibility. While increasing basic differentiation in one or two conciliation sessions is not really possible, I can often help to increase functional differentiation within the session, which can stimulate hope, motivation, and the possibility of change.

As discussed earlier, one essential feature in maintaining a more differentiated and de-triangled stance as a conciliator is establishing a conciliation triangle. In a conciliation triangle, I enter the marital system without absorbing their anxiety. Instead, like an emotional mirror, I reflect back their anxiety, while remaining authentically connected with them and fully committed to the process.

Conciliations are difficult, and I experience as much failure as success in helping couples make this shift to increase relationship functioning. Through the conciliation triangle, I highlight relationship interests and promote self-focus. I help couples individually and together experience something different from their old, established, and rigidly conflictual patterns. Sometimes the outcome is to continue with the marriage. Even if one or both spouses reject reconciliation, though, strengthening individuals through re-aligning this concentration on personal responsibility can go a long way towards promoting emotional maturity in one or both spouses. In this way, future relationships and future life functioning are healthier. If divorce occurs, our work can set the stage for a functional relationship with the ex-spouse, an especially important outcome if there are children involved.

Stage VI: Decision (approximately 10-20 minutes)

By now, many couples are clear about their interest in reconciling. Some want reconciliation. Other times, one spouse is not sure what to do. Sometimes, the couple is not certain about how to proceed.

For some, the decision is not difficult. They have explored key relationship issues and themes; they have attempted a different interactional style based on accepting more personal responsibility and self-focus; and I have articulated the individual and relationship challenges they must overcome in order for reconciliation to succeed. If the couple decides to reconcile, I offer community referrals for marital therapy. Timely follow-up to the conciliation session helps prevent relapse into non-functional patterns.

I never work privately with the couple after the conciliation. Self-referring to one's own practice is an unethical conflict of interest and may undercut the conciliation process itself. Also, having court-referred conciliation couples available for private referral may negatively affect my objectivity in the consultant's role.

At this point, for many couples, there is a lack of clarity about how to proceed. In these instances, I suggest that we collectively develop an action plan. Actions plans are unique for each couple, based on our collective assessment of what's needed and their willingness to engage with these important behaviors. These action plans typically include some of the following: investigating insurance issues and coverage for marital therapy, agreeing to begin couple's therapy, securing promises to attend 12-step programs, monitoring or minimizing alcohol and drug use, no violence contracts (if needed), and practicing communication strategies carried out in the conciliation session. All of these actions are designed to challenge the couple to re-invest in their marriage in more productive ways. The results of these action plans are usually determinative about the couple's motivation and ability to do the work necessary to begin repairing the marriage.

I write out these agreements in the form of a specific plan, review it with the spouses, and the couple signs the accord. The agreement is then submitted to the referring judge for review and approval, becoming a court order. I schedule a follow-up session between four and eight weeks later. I let them know that we will review progress at this second session, and that they must make a decision about reconciliation at the final meeting.

The follow-up meeting is often shorter than the initial meeting. We review the goals in the action plan, including their successes and challenges with meeting its terms. By now, the couple is usually clear about what direction they want to take with their marriage. Oftentimes, a lack of progress over the previous weeks speaks volumes about the state of the deteriorating relationship. These couples usually select marital dissolution. I file the appropriate paperwork indicating "no reconciliation," and the couple's case is moved back to marital dissolution court. I inform them about the process to come. Sometimes, if the couple has minor children, I coach them on how to proceed with their upcoming mediation to develop a parenting plan.

For those who have uncovered latent strengths and renewed commitment, reconciliation is a real possibility. We review the progress that they have made. I reinforce new patterns of appropriate communication and functioning, and I congratulate the couple for their committed work. I let the petitioning spouse know that she or he must file a motion to dismiss the case. They sign an agreement to reconcile, and I file this with the court.

Three Case Examples

To illustrate the challenges and possibilities of marital conciliations, I will discuss three cases that highlight this model and demonstrate the use of Bowen theory to guide the practice of conciliations.

Anxiety Cascade: Biological Imperatives that Override Conciliation

Early in my work as a conciliator, and before I had established my own model, I was assigned a court-referred couple I'll call Doris and Brian. The spouses had been separated for six months, and Doris requested conciliation. Through her own therapy, Doris said that she had worked on her own issues, and she now wanted to reconcile. When the session began, however, Doris launched into a tirade of complaints about Brian, blaming him for everything that was wrong with the marriage. He reciprocated, blaming Doris for her inability to demonstrate love and affection. Brian was clear that he was attending the session only because of a court order and not because he wanted to reconcile. (This session occurred prior to me developing a system to dismiss non-interested spouses, which I now routinely do.) I tried to gain control of the session by having each person speak individually, preventing the non-speaking spouse from interrupting, asking them to write down any responses, etc. These are all traditional skills similarly employed early in a mediation session. Doris was unable to remain silent, despite my urging. After a few minutes of trying to listen to her husband, she stood up and marched out of the conciliation, saying that she could no longer listen to his lies. Doris was gone.

As I reflected on this conciliation, it became obvious that I had erred in conducting the session. What happened was that Doris began experiencing hyper-arousal. Her amygdala had activated. Once this happened, her cortical thinking processes were overloaded and bypassed, and she was left in a state of fight-flight-freeze hyper-arousal. When I blocked her attempts to fight with Brian, the only survival reaction left to her was to flee, which she did. Doris was experiencing an anxiety cascade, and her body and mind called for an immediate response to alleviate her perceived threat.

I learned a valuable lesson from this meeting. Couples enter conciliation with their emotions charged and their thinking often affected by their strong feelings. This condition can lead to a survival response that is overwhelming, resulting in automatic hyper-arousal in the form of fight-flight-freeze. I learned that it is imperative to track emotional escalation in conciliation sessions. Once activated, the amygdala needs time to calm down and return control to the more rational, cortical thinking centers of the brain. Self-soothing becomes crucial and the conciliator can help by providing a non-threatening, quiet environment.

An early caucus offers the time and place to gather thoughts, soothe passions, re-group, breathe, and calm down. As a conciliator, I support this process. If suitable, finding opportunities to experience laughter can really help as appropriate humor can activate other, less reactive portions of the brain.

More importantly, I learned that as a conciliator, I must be conscious of amygdala activation *before* hyper-arousal sets in. Being observant of the following variables is important: the level of tension in a person; the capacity to listen without interrupting and reacting; the effectiveness of initial attempts to develop and maintain rapport; and one's own "gut" intuition regarding a situation. Should I detect evidence of such emotional escalation by either party, it is crucial to break the three-way meeting and immediately move into early caucus, beginning with the most emotionally reactive party.

In subsequent sessions with other couples, I have effectively managed hyper-arousal using this strategy. Once in caucus, I work to calm the individual, strengthen rapport, and help the husband and wife determine whether or not conciliation is appropriate at this time. Sometimes, mitigating circumstances heighten the person's base level of reactivity, making conciliation counseling more difficult.

In one instance, the wife had recently lost her job and was living with her mother. That relationship was very strained. We re-scheduled the conciliation after she developed stability with her own home and a new job. When her life circumstances settled, conciliation was timelier and, as a result, more effective.

It is also important for me to recognize when conciliation is not appropriate. For example, I worked with a man with a severe bi-polar disorder, and he was actively psychotic in conciliation. In this state, he was unable to function effectively on his own behalf. He declared that if his wife and he were not going to reconcile, he wanted sole legal and physical custody of their son. During caucus, we discussed the present value of conciliation, and I told him that, in my opinion, what he needed was psychiatric treatment and a family law attorney to help advocate for him. I subsequently dismissed the couple, informing the court that, in this instance, conciliation was not appropriate.

Other situations not appropriate for conciliation include couples where severe abuse and physical violence are present in the marriage. Many of these women have gathered the necessary courage to walk away from domestic abuse over significant amounts of time. These spouses do not want to reconcile. In fact, many of these women do not even want to sit in the same room with their abuser. The law requires that the spouses show up, regardless of circumstance.

So, we screen for spousal abuse and, if I deem the couple not appropriate or if the wife is too afraid, she waits in a separate waiting room, isolated from the abuser. Then, I begin the conciliation with a caucus. I meet with the abused spouse first. After assessing for safety, I further investigate the resources and support that the wife has or needs, and I make appropriate referrals. (Typically, it is the wife who is abused and the husband who is the abuser.) I then dismiss the wife through back stairways, so that she doesn't have to see the husband and interact with him.

Finally, I meet with the husband, inform him that the wife chose not to participate in conciliation, manage his disappointment and anger, give him appropriate resources including anger management groups, and coach him to respect his wife's wishes, lest he be arrested for violating an Order of Protection, if one is active, or get in trouble with the law for pursuing her, which could negatively impact parenting time with his children. I usually speak with the husband for 10-20 minutes, which gives the wife enough time to leave unmolested by her husband.

More and more over the past fifteen years, domestic violence and abuse are part of the equation of couples in conciliation. For some, domestic violence is the game changer ensuring no reconciliation. Nonetheless, it is not uncommon for husbands to use the conciliation law as a way of trying to convince the abused wife to come home.

While I protect the wife from this pressure by not meeting with the couple together, being legally required to attend the conciliation meeting creates a great deal of anxiety for the abused wives, as they fear having to face the man they have run away from and have often sought protection from the courts.

For others couples, domestic violence isn't chronic or the couple minimize its effects. These couples need an active intervention strategy–including a no violence contract–to eliminate its occurrence in the family and reinforce the importance of home as a safe place for all. One such couple is highlighted in the third example.

The Cybersex Triangle

This couple was court-referred based on the wife's request for conciliation. They had been married for three years. I'll call them Martha and Jim. Martha was in her early seventies, having been previously divorced for twenty years. Jim was in his mid-sixties and wanted a divorce because he said that their interests had changed and that there was no longer any passion in the marriage. Jim had been married several times in the past, and he established a pattern of leaving first. It was clear from the outset that Jim was only in conciliation because of a court order. (This, too, was an early case prior to my having changed the guidelines for conciliation to include acceptance by both parties to proceed with a full session.) Nonetheless, I conducted the conciliation using the guidelines outlined previously.

Though Martha had been alone and independent for many years, it was clear from the meeting that she was hoping to "grow old" with Jim and spend the rest of her life with him. Jim, on the other hand, stated that they used to hike and fly airplanes together, and that they had led a very active lifestyle. Jim complained that life with Martha was now too dull, and he was not prepared to lead a sedentary life in his later years. During the overview stage, Martha and Jim interrupted each other constantly, and Martha reiterated her litany of complaints against Jim. It was clear that Jim had heard these complaints before. Martha was especially critical of Jim's cybersex life, as he spent countless hours on the Internet, downloading pornography and excluding her from his sex life. I tried to keep them focused on narrating their own stories as best as I could.

At the individual caucus with Jim, it became clear that he had no interest in salvaging the marriage. He was content with his Internet sex life and claimed that masturbating to pornography provided more variety than did sex with his wife. I assessed Jim's interest in pornography as compulsive and tried to have him focus on improving his relationship with himself and on aspects of his life that he could manage without resorting to his cybersex addiction. I was not successful in de-triangling cybersex from the couple's life.

I had more success with Martha during her individual caucus. I asked her if their patterned interaction as a couple was similar to what I observed in conciliation. She acknowledged that it was the same, with Martha pushing Jim to give up cybersex and return to her. She spoke about how, as a woman in her seventies, she could not compete with the physicality of the Internet women and expressed despair, frustration, and anger about even having to try to measure up.

I asked her if she was willing to risk trying something different when we reconvened. She stated that she was, as she had nothing to lose at this point. I coached Martha to self-focus on both what she wanted from the relationship and what she wanted for her own emotional wellbeing rather than focusing on changing Jim. Perhaps out of desperation, Martha embraced my perspective and decided to try something different. I coached her to use "I language," focusing on stating her personal desires and dreams, as well as soothing herself, regardless of Jim's reactions. In effect, I helped Martha to self-regulate, and think and act differently.

When we re-convened, Jim made it clear that he liked his life the way it was, that he wanted a more active lifestyle than Martha afforded him, and that he was perfectly content with his daily and extended cybersex routines. Martha focused on herself, stating what she wanted from the relationship and in her life. She made it clear that she wanted to remain married to Jim. She did a remarkable job of remaining calm and using I language.

In the end, Jim refused her offer to reconcile and left the meeting unchanged. Martha, on the other hand, encountered a profound emotional shift. She told me that she had experienced a strength she had not known in years, and she was committed to re-discovering her own life goals and not being defined by how Jim saw her. She cried over the loss of the marriage and asked me for a reassuring hug, which I willingly provided. I believe that her new determination came from a spark of self-definition and her willingness to begin managing her own life without Jim. I referred her to Harriet Lerner's (1989) outstanding book on marriage and family relationships, *The Dance of Intimacy*, which is an important resource for women that uses Bowen theory as its framework. In this case example, I believe that the conciliation, while not repairing the marriage, provided a foundation and framework for Martha's developing emotional maturity.

I applied what I learned from this conciliation to other cases that I have worked with over the years. Specifically, as stated earlier, I don't keep couples in conciliation unless they both want to attend. As important, though, I use the individual caucuses to reinforce movements toward emotional maturity, sometimes challenging partners on their patterns and even provoking them towards greater self-definition and self-regulation.

With abusive relationships, I am always inspired by the courage of these women to leave. I am similarly moved by some of the husbands who come to recognize the destructiveness of their abusive and controlling behaviors, and strive to change these patterns, even through the loss of their marriages.

Of course, as a conciliator I understand how the abused child becomes the abuser in adulthood, reinforcing and perpetuating often generations-deep patterns. That is, while the abuser may be the perpetrator, once, the abuser was the victim. This understanding helps me find compassion for both parties. I reject judging the abuser for the abuse or the abused for staying in an abusive relationship. Compassion, empathy, and clearheaded systems thinking is needed in these situations, not judgements and criticisms. While rejecting the behavior of abuse, I can still find kindness and caring for all involved, which often translates into stronger rapport and a greater ability to influence parties to do the right thing for themselves and their lives.

Fundamentalism and Emotional Reactivity

This couple was court-referred based on the wife's request for conciliation. I'll call them Susan and Luke. Susan and Luke were members of a fundamentalist church and had a very set, structured view of the husband being the head of the household and the wife being subservient to the husband. Though Susan filed for both marital dissolution and conciliation, Luke willingly participated. The presenting problems were two-fold. First, Susan accused Luke of cheating on her by looking at other women with "lust in his heart." According to her and quoting biblical scripture, looking at other women was tantamount to infidelity and reflected his impure heart and a battle with the devil for his soul.

Luke, for his part, had left the home because of escalating tension, and his increased frustration threatened to erupt into violence. His anger and capacity for violence against his wife frightened him. Separating was his attempt to regulate their closeness and therefore diminish the possibility of becoming violent. According to Susan, if they were not living together, they were breaking their marriage vows.

On the surface, Susan appeared less differentiated. She triangulated biblical scripture to reinforce her positions and used church teachings to strengthen her statements. Susan seemed less mature in her emotional make-up and was limited in her ability to respond through thoughtful discussions and an objective understanding of their situation. Understanding Bowen theory helped me view Luke's relative calm and clarity in creating safety through distancing and Susan's reactive attempts to bring him back to the marriage through pursuing–even at the cost of her possible safety–as two sides of the same "differentiation coin." Luke came from a physically abusive home, and he carried a great deal of anger. He used religion as a way of trying to manage his anger but the conflict with his wife quickly brought that rage to the surface. Luke's distance and his reliance on his own biblical interpretations to justify his actions reflected the same limited emotional development as Susan's pursuing.

In other words, using Bowen theory as a guide, I perceived the couple as sharing a similar level of basic differentiation, even though on the surface the husband appeared more functional and the wife appeared less so. They were engaged in the process of "borrowing and trading of selves" in the marriage. My initial assessment was characteristic of most couples in conciliation: each used "you language" to articulate what the other had done to create and exacerbate the problems in the marriage; each blamed the other for the failing marriage; and each proposed solutions to their difficulties based on how the other needed to change.

Under these emotional conditions, I caucused with them separately. Meeting individually was extraordinarily effective in calming the system. By providing a more differentiated presence—remaining calm and deepening my rapport individually with Luke and Susan—I begin to shift their focus from blaming to assuming greater personal responsibility and self-regulation. I supported each spouse's efforts to clarify what it was that each wanted, including Susan's "bottom line" that she would not wait forever for Luke to return to their marriage and live together, as well as Luke's desire to not re-enter the marriage while the threat of violence was alive for him.

To help de-triangulate the Bible, church elders, and her parents, I asked each of them separately what they wanted, what they were willing to do in response to the other, and what parts of their individual and marital lives were non-negotiable. During this process, I helped Susan and Luke to remain available to each other and not automatically distance or pursue out of anxiety.

Susan became aware that she had no power regarding her husband's separation, and that, in fact, as the person least involved in the marriage Luke had the most power. As such, I coached Susan to define her personal goals and her goals for the marriage. Susan became clear about several concerns and interests. First, she decided that their weekends together (the husband was at this point working out of town and they only had weekends together) would not include sexual intimacy. Susan felt strongly that sexual intimacy should be reserved for marriage, and she defined marriage, in part, as living and working together to make the relationship work.

Susan increased her confidence and clarity as she realized that, while she did not have any power over Luke's need for physical separation, she could control her responses to his weekend sexual advances and not undercut her self-esteem by satisfying them. Susan realized the importance of giving her husband some time to figure out whether or not he was going to return, though she set a "bottom line" timetable of six months, after which she would re-institute divorce proceedings.

Luke also responded well. (Respect for authority is an important component of most fundamentalist churches and, as such, I believe that the couple responded well to my position as an expert who represented the Superior Court and my extensive experience as a family psychologist, marriage and family therapist, mediator, and conciliator.) Luke realized that the most important issue for him was managing his temper and not putting his wife or himself in danger. I made a referral to an anger management group and stressed the point that regardless of Susan's "provocations," he was solely responsible for his behavior and responses. I suggested that until he felt personally empowered and strong enough to ensure that physical abuse was not a possibility, it was essential that he not return home and thereby create a dangerous situation. I coached Luke in understanding that Susan's position regarding his seeming "infidelity," abandonment, and other concerns were all opportunities for him to re-focus on himself and what he needed to do for himself and the marriage. I further coached Luke, as I had coached Susan, that the challenges we identified in caucus were the same challenges that they each faced individually. Whether or not their marriage survived, divorce would not resolve these basic issues of selfhood.

When we reconvened for Stage IV, "the exchange," I highlighted their strengths, including their commitment to the marriage. I coached the couple to communicate using I language and to gain as much clarity as possible as to why their marriage was important to them individually, collectively, and as a matter of faith. I called on them to state what each was willing to do to repair their marriage and helped them clarify to each other what their respective "bottom lines" were. The caucus meetings had helped quiet the system and allowed for progress in these areas.

In Stage V, "consultant's assessment," I applauded Susan and Luke's efforts to communicate differently and to accept more personal responsibility. I carefully reiterated the individual and relationship strengths and challenges. And, I reinforced that whether or not they decided to reconcile, the issues we were discussing still pertained to their functioning as individuals.

During Stage VI, "decision," Susan and Luke decided that, based on their religious conviction and their love for each other, they owed it to themselves and each other to attempt marital reconciliation. Susan agreed to file a motion to dismiss the marital dissolution action that she had initiated. I also referred them to a church elder with whom they each felt comfortable, as well as to two secular marital therapists in the community.

In the end, my attempt to calm the system by providing a more differentiated presence helped shift the emotional atmosphere for the couple, enabling them to gain a measure of clarity about themselves as individuals and their relationship. I reduced the intensity of the active triangles enough for them to communicate in a different way. They were able to present themselves directly to one another without the complications brought on by escalating anxiety in the central and interlocking triangles.

Marital conciliations are always challenging. It is a court-ordered, last attempt to salvage a battered and bruised marriage. Often, one person is only attending because of a court order. Sometimes, spousal abuse is present and safety issues override the importance of this court-mandated session. While demanding and sometimes frustrating, I find conciliations a fascinating and rewarding opportunity to help couples find productive paths in their lives, individually and, sometimes, collectively. Working with this six-stage model, and having a theoretical framework based on Bowen family systems theory to guide me, I am discovering opportunities for success that were not available to me previously.

Over the years I have modified my approach to conciliations. In addition to providing increased flexibility relating to time, I only conduct conciliations when the husband and wife are both willing participants. While a judge can order couples to attend conciliation, once in attendance, I find that voluntary participation follows an important ethical guideline present in mediation, that of self-determination. Also, the court has improved its capacity to screen cases for domestic violence, and, if present, we are careful to provide husbands and wives separate waiting areas. While I have worked with a number of couples where a history of domestic violence exists, voluntary participation is essential, and these cases are carefully managed to ensure safety.

To date, my conciliation "success rate" is approximately 30-40% for those who choose voluntary participation, with success defined here as the couple agreeing to marital reconciliation and withdrawing their dissolution petition. As a family psychologist and conciliator, however, I do not determine success from these criteria alone. (Of course, a couple deciding to divorce more respectfully and with less conflict is itself a form of success.) First, while "successful" conciliations help unclog the overburdened courts, they do not necessarily result in successful marriages. Marital success can only be judged over time, through committed work and sustained efforts. Currently, there is no mechanism to track these marriages in the court system.

Second, living in a relatively small town, there are limited opportunities to make referrals to marriage specialists, especially those subscribing to a systems perspective. As such, I sometimes question whether the work that I accomplish in creating clarity and hope is sustained or whether it all falls apart weeks or months later through ineffective marriage therapy or a lack of follow-through on the couple's part.

Yet, more hopefully, I see myself as a gardener, tilling the soil, planting seeds for change, and giving people a different perspective on how they can grow as individuals and in intimate relationships. I often provide books and articles to encourage spouses to continue their emotional development, and I emphasize that the work done within marriage can often accelerate the emotional maturation process more quickly than does the dissolution of the marriage. While I am not there to witness which seeds germinate and flourish and which do not, I believe that the conciliation opportunity provided by the state of Arizona can spur individuals to take more responsibility for their lives and towards their children, and that a Bowen family systems theory approach helps me become a more effective gardener.

I use marital conciliations to encourage couples, individually and together, to seek out solutions to their complex problems through thoughtful dialogue, commitment, and perseverance, seeing divorce as an option never to be taken lightly and only as a last resort. Guided by Bowen theory with a six-stage model, marital conciliations offer the last, best hope for couples seeking a final opportunity to heal the wounds in their marriage through increasing their emotional maturity.

CHAPTER FIFTEEN

BOWEN FAMILY SYSTEMS THEORY AND PEACEMAKING:
HUMAN EVOLUTION AND CONFLICT RESOLUTION

Introduction

A version of this chapter, titled "Bowen theory and peacemaking: Human evolution through nonviolent conflict resolution," was originally published in the 2013 book *Exploring the Power of Nonviolence: Peace, Politics, and Practice*, edited by Randall Amster and Elavie Ndura, published by Syracuse University Press. My original submission was much longer than the published version, understandably edited for consistency with other chapters in the book. For this publication, I'm including the original draft, as it's a more thorough representation of Bowen theory as it relates to human evolution, conflict resolution, and peacemaking. I've retained some introductory material on Bowen theory, while eliminating many redundant definitions of core concepts, since these are accessible in chapters two and three.

CHAPTER FIFTEEN

BOWEN FAMILY SYSTEMS THEORY AND PEACEMAKING: HUMAN EVOLUTION AND CONFLICT RESOLUTION

During the Vietnam War, one iconic photograph of a divided America was that of anti-war protesters and armed National Guard soldiers facing each other. A young man can be seen placing a flower in the rifle barrel of a guardsman. A closer look reveals that another soldier has two flowers protruding from his gun barrel as well. The year was 1967, and this photograph was viewed worldwide, indicative of a nation torn between war and peace. The competing narratives of the image reached deeply into the nation. For some, it represented a potent statement of non-violent resistance against an overpowering military force. For others, it demonstrated the government's need to act decisively against a youthful population willing to sacrifice the good of the country for their own idealistic and self-serving ends.

Flash forward to 1989 and a second iconic photograph of resistance. In China, democracy supporters congregated in Tiananmen Square, protesting for change from the repressive, communist régime. Bolstered by their "Lady Liberty" statue and propelled by the success of similar peaceful revolutions across Eastern Europe, brave men and women assembled together, risking everything for freedom and democracy. The Chinese authorities, however, decided to move decisively and violently to crush the peaceful protest. Unofficial casualty estimates of the Tiananmen Square massacre ranged as high as 2,500 people killed and well over 10,000 people injured and imprisoned.

The emblematic image from that brutal repression is that of the lone man standing in front of four Chinese tanks, refusing to move, refusing to let them pass. A video of this image is equally striking: the young man moves side to side to block the tank's progress, refusing to give ground. This vision of courage is deeply imbedded in the world's consciousness regarding that tragic day.

In viewing these two images side-by-side, most people in human rights, social justice, and peace movements would agree that both pictures tell a similar story: one of brave protesters willing to risk their lives for their principles, using non-violent responses against overwhelming odds. The Tiananmen Square photograph captures this definition of nonviolent protest. Here, a lone man blocks the tanks from moving forward to crush the democracy movement. This symbolic photograph speaks volumes about an individual's bravery and clarity of purpose to non-violently achieve a positive outcome.

In contrast, however, an alternate understanding of the photograph from the Vietnam War protest suggests something more nuanced and perhaps just as important. On one level, the protesters placing flowers in guns can also be interpreted from a similar perspective of bravery against overpowering and oppressive forces. In fact, from an anti-war or pro-peace perspective, it is easy to invoke a narrative about heroes and villains from this photograph: the anonymous military police threatening the protesters and blocking their right to Constitutionally-protected free speech and assembly, and the ironic gesture of placing flowers, symbolizing peace, in gun barrels, symbolizing violence.

Conversely, those who supported the National Guard embraced a "law and order" storyline, one in which the stability and security of the state was best assured through a strong, disciplinary presence. There is, however, a third narrative. This account suggests that our thinking and our acting either promote nonviolence, through encouraging our own emotional maturity and hence the emotional maturity of others, or undercut peace through thinking and acting in ways that undermine our emotional maturity and the emotional maturity of others.

In this alternative storyline, then, placing a flower in a gun barrel can be interpreted as escalating a potentially explosive situation. The act, ironic or otherwise, increased the intensity of this situation, likely amplified the anxiety of the soldiers who were following their orders, and increased the potential for a more violent outcome.

In this chapter, I articulate the nature and power of nonviolence and peacemaking in ways that are personally and socially responsible. I look at the nature of attachment and conflict, our ability and willingness to assume increased levels of self-responsibility and accountability for our acting and thinking, and a recognition that all of our actions and behaviors either promote peacemaking or undercut it.

I will use Bowen family systems theory, also known as Bowen theory, to provide a framework of what peacemaking means and how our "core" level of basic differentiation, or emotional maturity, is bound to our capacity to promote peace within the self and interpersonally with others. I will discuss the contributions of evolutionary biology in understanding human behavior, how the limbic brain is wired for detecting and reacting to threats, and how cortical management of hyper-arousal can set the stage for nonviolent conflict resolution and peacemaking strategies. I suggest that higher levels of emotional maturity create opportunities for differentiated leadership, promoting personal and interpersonal fields of influence that advance peacemaking. Reciprocally, as emotional maturity levels decline, so too does our capacity for personal peace and, consequently, our ability to positively influence others toward effective, nonviolence conflict resolution.

An Alternative Perspective on Peacemaking

There are many models for discussing, promoting, and investigating peacemaking. Peacemaking is sometimes investigated from the perspective of techniques, methods, outcomes, and other points-of-view that examine end results as determinants of success or failure. For example, during a peaceful demonstration, participants might focus on their degree of media coverage, the effectiveness of their message in reaching a target audience, and whether or not the results of their actions met their hopes and expectations. Others groups may focus more on interpersonal process, such as creating consensus, as a means of advancing their agendas. From this perspective, process *is* outcome as working for and achieving consensus is in itself a form of peacemaking. While other perspectives certainly exist (such as a hybrid of consensus with more clearly established external goals, supermajority voting, etc.), many use results or process as the standard for determining success.

A Bowen family systems theory perspective offers a different framework for understanding the nature of peace and peacemaking, suggesting that we must learn from what nature has to teach us and that the power of personal presence is what creates opportunities for peace (Friedman, 1985; Kerr and Bowen, 1988). From a Bowen theory viewpoint, peacemaking is about seeing systems, i.e., viewing the entire picture clearly, understanding the nature of personal power through acceptance of personal responsibility, and promoting "right action" in others as an outgrowth of self-management, especially in intense emotional environments. What Goleman (2006) refers to as "empathic resonance" or fields of influence is best achieved when we take charge of our own lives, avoid conflicts of will with others, minimize blame, develop self-understanding, and remain flexibly and reasonably engaged in our interpersonal world (Friedman,1987; Kerr and Bowen, 1988).

Bowen theory is a natural outgrowth of evolutionary biology (Kerr & Bowen, 1988), which teaches us, among other things, about the power of in-groups and out-groups. Humans and other mammals naturally sort into in-groups and out-groups. For humans, this process begins early in childhood (Bigler, Brown, and Markell, 2001; Tajfeland Billic, 1974). In order to make sense of our world, humans naturally categorize. From an evolutionary perspective, kinship systems are one such in-group, and these are often the most powerful and important relationships for humans. Kinship connection, including the concept of inclusive fitness, suggests that humans and non-humans take greater care of and offer protection to close relatives who are, of course, those who also share the most genes (Kerr and Bowen, 1988). Clearly, designating in-groups are functional from an evolutionary perspective.

Humans distinguish between in-group and out-group membership for other reasons as well, including for such important evolutionary outcomes as social cohesion. With social cohesiveness, humans form in-groups to more efficiently gather and utilize resources, as well as for protection, social engagement, and mate selection (Medoza, 1984). Activists demonstrate social cohesion in order to find common purpose in determining policy and promoting social action. Meetings are also great places to discover like-minded people.

Unfortunately, as emotional intensity increases, in-group and out-group processes can accentuate togetherness pressures, resulting in both greater "herding" tendencies in thinking and behaving as well as, conversely, a loss of a core self or "solid self" (Friedman,1997). These automatic reactions are more "mindless" and can actually prevent individuals and groups from clearly and objectively assessing the progress of their cause or the effectiveness of a particular campaign (Miller, 2002). In more extreme cases of herding or "stuck-togetherness," attachments to outcomes are high, and the group mindset encourages in-group members to think and act similarly (Kerr & Bowen, 1988). Out-group members are often relegated and denigrated to a fused, de-personalized "other," a sameness characterized by references to a faceless "Corporate America," the "Prison-Industrial Complex," or even "politics and politicians as usual." Certainly, there is comfort and security in "us vs. them" designations, though sweeping generalizations resulting in this kind of reductive polarization actually generate a more conflictual, less mature, and, ultimately, less effectual model of peacemaking.

Bowen family systems theory offers a different way forward. Bowen theory eschews polarizations that create false dichotomies. Creating these artificial distinctions are ultimately less effective attempts at defining a self and being a part of a group since these identities are formed and maintained at the expense of others (Friedman, 1996).

Murray Bowen was an innovative psychiatrist. His investigations with individuals and families helped him formulate his theory. Bowen was an astute observer of human and non-human nature. He noticed that the same basic processes existed in both the non-human and the human world, as well as within the wide spectrum of human functioning. In fact, Bowen and his followers postulated that the fundamental forces that shaped the formation of the cosmos and life on planet Earth are the same fundamental forces that continue to shape humans and their relationships today (Friedman, 1991; Kerr, 1981; Kerr and Bowen, 1988). Bowen family systems theory is an ecological theory tied to nature. It is a universal theory, akin to Darwin's theory of evolution. Bowen theory applies across species, as well as within humans, irrespective of gender, race, socio-economic status, religion, tribe, ethnicity, family structure, or other categories of identity (Friedman, 1991).

From a Bowen theory perspective, all species share a kind of chronic anxiety that is essentially an automatic reactivity to threat. All species mature and differentiate into distinct organisms. All species are "formatted" multi-generationally through genetics, epigenetics, and experience. Consequently, all species are shaped by historical genetic and environmental forces beyond their present circumstances.

Herding behaviors that cluster humans into in-groups and out-groups are automatic and based on evolutionary biology. Togetherness in humans, as well as other animals, is often associated with lower levels of stress; increased group cohesion, and improved collective functioning through an established hierarchy. The outcome is greater calm as members within a group feel connected to each other and emotionally understand their place in the overall system (Ferrera, 1996; Miller, 2002).

As togetherness pressures increase to the point of stuck-togetherness, self-integrity declines, and effective self-functioning through self-reflection, self-improvement, and self-management become more impaired. Out-group members are more likely perceived as enemies or at least threats to the in-group (Miller, 2002). In-group functioning becomes dependent on the out-group's vilification, stripping out-group members of their individualities and even their important contributions to the functioning of larger social, national, or international systems.

We humans pay a significant price for that kind of fused togetherness: *more* conflict, *less* resilience, and a *greater* willingness to seek out heroes and villains in a split narrative based on a right/wrong, us/them exclusivity. Temporary benefits derived from intense herding quickly evaporate as self-cohesion is sacrificed for stuck-togetherness. The outcomes are greater conflict, tension, and emotional reactivity, and the loss of peace and peacemaking opportunities (Friedman, 1996).

While emphasizing our connectedness to all life and natural evolutionary processes, Bowen did not discount what makes humans unique. In fact, as a pinnacle of vertebrate evolution, Bowen understood that humans have unique, or somewhat unique, abilities to go beyond our predetermined and hence automatic behavioral patterns and respond more thoughtfully and independently (Kerr and Bowen, 1988). Bowen discussed our uniqueness as a species through the evolution of a highly developed feeling system (as contrasted with the "deeper" emotional system), as well as a decidedly advanced thinking or intellectual system.

In fact, Bowen said that it was the intellectual system, and its most evolutionarily advanced features in the prefrontal lobe where higher order thinking takes place (planning, foresight, self-reflection, insight, and so forth). This capacity allows us to respond differently from our animal cousins (Kerr and Bowen, 1988). Bowen recognized that the human brain has developed a remarkable capacity for self-reflection, clear thinking, and comprehension of consequences based on actions. This ability assists us in developing and strengthening our authentic or true self. Consequently, we are self-contained within our individuality. The result is that we are capable of greater intentional and mindful responses. Bowen theory demonstrates how, with a concerted effort over time, humans are capable of modifying some of our reactive impulses and responding with greater consciousness and thoughtfulness (Friedman, 1991).

One of the hallmarks of Bowen theory, then, is the notion that humans are social animals who have developed the capacity to move beyond our systems "programming" and respond more intentionally rather than simply reacting instinctively. While most humans have this capacity for independent response, during stressful and emotional times we must cultivate deliberate thinking in order to override reflexive impulses. This defined capacity for greater self-determination is called differentiation. In peacemaking, our basic differentiation level—the capacity to think clearly, act thoughtfully, self-soothe, stay connected to important others in our environment, and self-regulate emotional intensity—is the most significant variable in resolving conflict non-violently. This is especially true since the only person we have power, control, and authority over is our personal self. Promoting basic differentiation or emotional maturity results in a self that is more integrated, more self-contained. We are developed and nurtured through these same processes of self-reflection, self-definition, and self-soothing.

Conversely, when we allow others to define who we are and, consequently, how we should act, think, and feel in the world, the result is herding and a loss of an integrated self. Initially, we may feel greater connectedness, since the in-group and the self are essentially co-joined or fused, but we sacrifice our individuality or authentic self in the process. The wellbeing of the self is now bound up in our definition of belonging to the in-group.

Lastly, a higher level of emotional maturity inoculates the self from some of the negative effects of stress. With feet planted firmly on the ground, it takes more for the winds of change to blow us over. Inversely, as basic differentiation decreases, there is the more variability in functional differentiation over time and across situations. In this way, reflected self—in which the self is delineated through others and not defined by one's internal compass—promotes regression for self, others in the in-group, and those in the out-group.

As peacemakers, we often find ourselves in emotionally intense situations in which our anxiety may be aroused, exposing our pre-disposed ways of managing emotional intensity. In addition to the importance of basic differentiation levels, chronic anxiety levels become crucial variables in peacemaking success and failure. As basic differentiation decreases, chronic anxiety increases inversely. The anxiety of the moment—acute anxiety—is generated and amplified as well. As chronic anxiety and acute anxiety increase, so, too, does the formation and activation of emotional triangles.

Emotional triangles form inside and outside positions. Out-group members are typically relegated to the outside position of the triangle, while in-group members and the self reside on the inside positions of the emotional triangle. Triangling creates temporary stability through shifting alliances but does nothing to peaceably improve relationships between people. In fact, relationships often deteriorate through calcifying inside and outside positions. More conflict results.

The out-group binds the anxiety for the in-group members. That is, the out-group becomes the anxiety binder for the in-group. They are often viewed as the "enemy"–the Tea Party, the Liberal Media, etc. This process perpetuates conflict through extreme generalities and stereotypes, mindless categories, and faceless adversaries. Especially as emotional pressure increases, this triangulation between in-group members—self—out-group members often results in a narrowing of thinking, feeling, and behaving as it is easier to develop and maintain connection with the in-group through vilifying the out-group.

In order to break this "cycle of violence," as peacemakers we must practice differentiated leadership (see chapters six and seven for extensive discussions on differentiated leadership). We must focus on de-triangulating disputants from their attachment to the conflict. This means approaching out-group partners with respect and compassion, making a concerted effort to connect equally with all participants, and maintaining an attitude of good humor to avoid a "reptilian regression" into rigid, unyielding seriousness and attachment to positions.

In all human interactions, the key to managing emotional triangles and decreasing both chronic and acute anxiety is to tolerate short-term anxiety increases for the sake of long-term anxiety reduction and relief (Kerr and Bowen, 1988; Regina, 2000, 2011; Regina and Pace, 2008). In peacemaking and through differentiated leadership, this means keeping the parties in contact with a peacemaker who is minimally reactive to the emotional intensity of the disputants, who is moderately to highly differentiated and, as a result, can maintain some calm in an emotional storm.

Initially, this contact is likely to increase short-term anxiety, as the parties are brought together and differences are aired. But, the power of presence of a moderately to highly mature leader can provide the kind of calm, soothing environment where people can begin to truly hear what out-group members have to say. This kind of differentiated leadership promotes a listening environment for all. If this occurs, the system can seek interest-based alternatives to the current conflict without resorting to habitual, positional patterns of reacting and blaming.

Applying Bowen Family Systems Theory to Peacemaking

Bowen theory provides us with a way of thinking that translates into a way of acting. This focused thinking is not always needed, of course. When we are living in the moment, for example, occupied with our work and our play, involved with friendships, family, acquaintances, and intimate relationships, more differentiated people simply exist—they do what they do when they need to do it. As emotional intensity increases in personal, interpersonal, and social environments, however, we are tested to live with greater integrity and dignity, rather than reacting instinctually. Our capacity to manage ourselves is more challenged, as is our ability to think more clearly and act in ways that are consistent with our values, beliefs, and lifestyles.

If our work takes us to places of conflict, if we are called to action to right injustice, or if we simply get into an argument with a stranger in a grocery store, evolutionary biology can work against us. When threatened, we automatically react accordingly, and we can quickly escalate into a flight-fight-flee stance. Our limbic system's amygdala—the brain's fight-flight-freeze center—is prone to activation even in non-life-threatening but nonetheless difficult situations. While this is the kind of "evolutionary mismatch" discussed in evolutionary biology, we are nonetheless left to manage our reactions or else we are simply at the mercy of our evolutionary history. If we are working with a political organization or non-governmental institution, or if we have simply come together to address a common cause, we are pulled to working with those who see things as we do. As emotional pressures increase, we often shift from our calm selves to our anxious selves. We risk engaging more reactively. This may initially *feel* right but can ultimately be counterproductive to our long-term goals as peacemakers. In these instances, how do we maintain our integrity in the face of these counter-differentiation pressures?

The goal for peacemakers using a differentiated leadership model is a long-term commitment, over years and decades, toward increasing our personal level of emotional maturity. We must manage the emotional forces of the moment, self-soothe our hyper-aroused and reactive impulses, practice self-containment, and avoid triangling as a way of temporarily feeling better. This is not a quick fix, and it requires an ability to see systems as well as a type of persistence and motivation that often runs counter to our quick-fix cultural and biological conditioning. Nevertheless, increasing our basic differentiation acts as a kind of immunization against capricious and emotionally reactive thinking and acting.

Knowing our personal signs and triggers of emotional reactivity and subjective thinking can also provide guideposts when we stumble. Experiencing emotional reactivity, we can choose to self-soothe our agitated beings and calm our racing hearts. We can "hit the pause button" and override our initial impulses and seek more deliberate responses. Committing to developing our emotional maturity strengthens our core self, and the stronger our self the more durable and effective all of our relationships. Being more calm, non-attached, present, and engaged allow us to create resonant fields of influence that can positively affect others. Just as reactivity breeds more reactivity, calm breeds more calm. Encouraging a more differentiated togetherness influences others to self-reflect, responsibly engage, and work toward common interests with in-group and out-group members alike.

This is the nature of differentiated leadership and peacemaking. The goal is not to satisfy everyone all of the time. That is more akin to undifferentiated leadership. More differentiated leaders establish their own vision for an organization, group, tribe, or even family (Friedman, 2007). They accept input; modify and adjust their goals and activities accordingly; and invite others along to implement the group's vision. This approach is based neither on the charisma of the leader nor on a consensus model of decision making. It is based, rather, on clarity of vision; acceptance of personal responsibility to minimize reactivity and blame; ability to self-soothe in emotionally intense environments; and a willingness, if needed, to go it alone in the interests of the group or organization's mission.

In more differentiated leadership environments, less emotionally mature members will initially reject, sabotage, seduce, and in other ways react emotionally to undercut the leader's vision and stance (Friedman, 2007). In fact, effective peacemaking efforts can initially generate greater conflict in those who resist effective change. Over time and with a resolute effort to stay connected with recalcitrant others, greater peace often prevails. This peace comes not from conflicts of will with those opposed to the leader but, rather, from creating an emotional environment that encourages and promotes others in the system to take greater responsibility for themselves, as well as providing support for their efforts. A more emotionally mature leader will promote the differentiation of followers and, over time, generate greater opportunities for longer-lasting peace.

This, too, is consistent with what we know from evolutionary biology. Hierarchy and leadership itself are inherent in nature (Gilbert, 1996). We see hierarchy in multiple species, from mammals to insects. Animals that are a part of tribes, schools, flocks, and families experience less stress within clearly delineated, hierarchical leadership systems. Lacking leaders, social animals struggle and will seek to re-establish a leadership structure.

Denying this part of our animal heritage may make certain human groups feel like they are evolving away from antiquated and outmoded leadership systems, but alternatives such as consensus give power to the most extreme, least emotionally mature members of a system (Friedman, 1985). This is counter-evolutionary. While high functioning and emotionally mature groups can often function effectively with a consensus model, most groups are not composed of all high functioning people. Rather, there is a range of differentiation levels within most assemblages. In these groups, consensus often fails and the groups never reach their potential because of this "weakest link" limitation.

And, while groups led by charismatic leaders seem more closely aligned by purpose and design, there is actually a loss of self in such groups, as self is given over to the leader. As a result, while these groups may be effective in the short term, many if not most rarely survive after the leader dies or leaves, since the social cohesion of the group is dependent on one person rather than the high emotional functioning of all group members. Differentiated leadership, by contrast, provides social cohesiveness through promoting the emotional maturity of all members. It doesn't require the "super-glue" of charisma or the control of the cult to keep the group productive and intact, since the group is made up of differentiating individuals.

The clarity of more differentiated leadership is its refusal to sacrifice progress for short-lived peace. While differentiated leadership's "hell-bent" determination and persistence may be viewed as insensitive to those needing external validation or constant support, more differentiated leaders encourage and support the brightest and most capable–those willing to buck the trend of fused togetherness and to move forward in the best interests of the group, guided by the mission and vision of the organization, family, or tribe.

More differentiated leaders, in other words, facilitate more differentiated followership and, over time, increased levels of differentiation create and stimulate the power of presence in not only the leader but in the followers, who are leaders in their own right. Paradoxically, hierarchy is flattened in this model, leadership becomes more shared, leaders are less likely to burn out, and long-term peace and effective functioning are likely to prevail (Bowen, 2002).

Peacemaking occurs at many systemic levels, from the macro to the micro. The concepts of peacemaking and differentiated leadership that I discuss here are relevant across levels of systems, as systems are "nested" within larger and smaller systems. These nested systems all operate similarly, using the same universal concepts articulated in Bowen's theory. What follows is an example of peacemaking through Bowen theory from my work as a mediator at the Yavapai County Superior Court in Arizona, illustrating the concepts of emotional reactivity and differentiation through triangulation and de-triangulation.

The conflict was between a homebuilder, Ansell, and a homeowner, Jim. The case came to mediation because of several disputes around the quality of the construction, specifically cracks in the concrete driveway and a leak in the bathroom that was dripping through to the basement. These relatively minor concerns had escalated into a major lawsuit. In mediation, it was clear that there had been a number of vicious verbal altercations between Ansell and Jim during the construction of the home, with allegations of incompetence, contract violations over physical materials used in the project, and intentional delays in completing the job. As the two men were unable to civilly and calmly discuss, negotiate, and resolve these concerns, a reservoir of bad feelings had escalated. When these relatively minor problems surfaced, the anxiety between the two became crystallized or "bound" in the concrete flaws and the leak.

Each party became reactive to the other, attached to being wronged by the other, and rigidly locked into his position. The dispute itself became the triangular anxiety binder for Ansell and Jim, and neither was initially capable of moving from his positional attachment to their common interest—successful completion of the home according to common standards. Jim and Ansell were each supported by members of their family and friends, calcifying triangulation between each disputant, their allies, and the other resulting in firmly established in-groups and out-groups.

This is a common thread in high conflict disputes of all kinds: disputants become so attached to their positions that the issues comprising the dispute, as well as the dispute itself, become the anxiety binders that lock the parties into the rightness of their actions and beliefs. This perpetuates and escalates the conflict. By definition, then, the people are triangulated by the conflict and their positions. The issue, person, or thing becomes the anxiety binder for the parties. Each disputant and the conflict become the central emotional triangle, with the parties trying to keep the inside position with the issue and push the other to the outside position of the emotional triangle. Others involved in the conflict, such as friends and family, become part of interlocking emotional triangles, rigidifying positions, attitudes, beliefs, and feelings.

Working with a co-mediator, we attempted to calm the parties, used humor as a way to connect with them and loosen the chokehold of attachment to their "rightness" and the other's "wrongness," and set out to carefully foster an environment that promoted a rational solution that met both of their common interests for fairness, justice, and satisfactory completion of the project. Using a differentiated leadership model, we consciously developed an equally strong rapport with both men. Within the highly structured mediation environment, each person began to feel less threatened and, over several hours, the conflict was somewhat de-triangulated so that they were more capable of listening to one another.

Not having members of each person's in-group present also helped the parties see the other as an individual and not as a part of a cohort group set against them. As the men developed more trust for the co-mediators and the process, they were eventually able to find interest-based solutions to their disagreements, and they left with a mediation agreement that met both of their needs. Self-determination and personal empowerment prevailed, as they peacefully resolved their differences and came to see the other as more reasonable.

This mediation example articulates how applying Bowen theory can increase peacemaking through differentiated leadership. More differentiated peacemakers provide clarity, consistency, and connection in social encounters. They demonstrate more capability in family and work relationships. They can clarify an "I" in intense emotional environments that instinctually pull towards an undifferentiated "we." More differentiated peacemakers, in effect, create a resonant power of presence that positively influences others.

Neurological research supports this alignment of brain patterns in perpetuating such emotional resonance (Goleman, 2006). Mirror neurons mimic brain states and the experiences of others, reinforcing the notion that we influence others for good or for ill. In fact, limbic systems between people can align with resonance. Laughter and humor are powerful tools for cultivating such positive resonance in reaching others and promoting peace. Laughter and humor are also powerful antidotes for regressions into attachment and seriousness.

In essence, a calmer, looser, more humorous, clearer, better defined, flexible, and socially-connected person displays an emotional maturity that makes a significant difference not only for self but for others in the world. More differentiated peacemakers are more naturally differentiated leaders. They avoid polarizing that leads to vilifying out-groups. A sense of group unity is achieved through common cause, not common enemy.

In truth, these notions are quite radical. It is easier to become reactors in the evolutionary game of us vs. them. It is easier to resist change than to assist in shaping it. It is simpler to say "no" than to find ways to say "yes." It is less complicated to put a flower in a gun barrel than to speak to, differentiate, and hence humanize the soldier holding the gun.

Making a long-term commitment to increasing our emotional maturity requires a greater degree of self-honesty, patience, persistence, non-attachment, engagement, and a willingness to live by the power of one's convictions. It means apologizing for mistakes, developing compassion and kindness not only for your friends but for your adversaries, which can be painful and difficult. What might have been different if the Vietnam War protester reached out to the National Guard soldier instead of dishonoring him by putting a flower in his gun barrel? Perhaps, a different kind of peace may have prevailed. An approach to peacemaking through Bowen theory affords people the opportunity to develop long-term solutions to seemingly intransigent problems.

In the final analysis, peacemaking through Bowen family systems theory is about contributing to the evolution of the species (Friedman, 1986). It offers us immediate opportunities to make conscious choices everyday about who we are and what we do. It is about leading a life with dignity, integrity, honesty, intentionality, and mindfulness under all kinds of situations and circumstances. While none of us can expect to get fully there in our lifetimes, we can make the commitment to peacefully resolving conflict through increasing our emotional maturity and enjoying the journey.

Bibliography

Bigler, Rebecca, Christia Spears Brown, and Marc Markell. 2001. When groups are not created equal: Effects if group status on the formation of intergroup attitudes in children. *Child Development* 72 (4): 1151-1162.

Bowen, Murray. 2002. *Family therapy in clinical practice.* Northvale, New Jersey: Jason Aronson.

Ferrera, Stephanie J. 1996. Lessons from nature on leadership. In *The emotional side of organizations: Applications of Bowen theory*, ed. Patricia A. Comella, Joyce Bader, Judith S. Ball, Kathleen K. Wiseman & Ruth Riley Sagar, 200-210. Georgetown, MD: Georgetown Family Center.

Friedman, Edwin. 1985. *Generation to generation: Family process in church and synagogue.* New York: The Guildford Press.

___1987. How to succeed in therapy without really trying. *Family Therapy Networker*, May-June: 27- 34.

___1991. Bowen theory and therapy. In *Handbook of family therapy*, ed. Alan S.

Gurman and David P. Kniskern, 134-170. New York: Brunner/Mazel, Inc.

___1996. *Reinventing leadership.* New York: The Guilford Press.

Gilbert, Roberta M. 1996. A natural systems view of hierarchy. In *The emotional side of organizations: Applications of Bowen theory*, ed. Patricia A. Comella, Joyce Bader, Judith S. Ball, Kathleen K. Wiseman & Ruth Riley Sagar, 130-137. Georgetown, MD: Georgetown Family Center.

Kaati, Gunnar, Lars Olov Bygren, and Soren Edvinsson. 2002. Cardiovascular and diabetes mortality determined by nutrition during parents' and grandparents' slow growth period. *European Journal of Human Genetics.*10: 682–688.

Kerr, Michael. 1981. Family systems theory and therapy. In *Handbook of family therapy*, ed. Alan S. Gurman and David P. Kniskern, 226-264. New York: Brunner/Mazel, Inc.

Kerr, Michael E. and Murray Bowen. 1988. *Family evaluation: An approach based on Bowen theory*. New York: Norton.

Goleman, Daniel. 2006. *Social Intelligence: The new science of human relationships*. New York: Bantam Books.

Mendoza, Sally P. 1984. The psychobiology of social relationships. In *Social cohesion: Essays towards a sociophysiological perspective,* ed. Patricia R. Barchas, and Sally P. Medoza, 3-30. Westport CT: Greenwood Press.

Regina, Wayne. 2000. Bowen systems theory and mediation. *Mediation Quarterly*, 18 (2): 111-128.

Regina, Wayne. 2011. *Applying family systems theory to mediation: A practitioner's guide*. New York: University Press of America.

Regina, Wayne and Steve Pace. 2008. The personal intelligences in experiential education: A theory in practice. In *Theory & practice of experiential education*, ed. Karen Warren, Denise Mitten, and TA Loeffler, 494-506. Boulder, CO: Association for Experiential Education.

Tajfel, Henry and Michael Billic. 1974. Familiarity and categorization in intergroup behavior. *Journal of Experimental Social Psychology* (10) 2: 159-170.

EPILOGUE

PERSONAL REFLECTIONS ON MY RELATIONSHIP WITH BOWEN FAMILY SYSTEMS THEORY

There are challenges in living a life with Bowen's family systems theory as a central focus. There are even greater challenges on reporting about those efforts. Bowen theory says that subjectivity increases as proximity to self decreases. The corollary is that objectivity increases as proximity to the self increases. That being the case, then, writing about my experiences becomes tricky. Discussing my successes may come off as arrogant. Analyzing my failures and challenges may come off as sentimental. Nonetheless, I was determined to personalize this book differently than with my previous writings and to do so with as much clarity as possible.

I wrote chapters designed to highlight theory as it applies to practice in a host of disciplines that I have been involved with over the decades. In doing so, I included personal reflections and examples. My intent and interest were to demonstrate a consistency of application across careers, and how Bowen theory has served me in my work life.

But, Bowen's theory is not simply a theory about engaging in the professional world. According to the theory, dichotomizing the personal and professional is a false distinction. For me and others, Bowen family systems theory is also a theory about how to live a more intentional and attentive personal life. That means developing, nurturing, and sustaining more effective and loving relationships in all of my roles and identities, including that of husband, father, son, brother, brother-in-law, uncle, son-in-law, cousin, colleague, and friend. While a full articulation of this decades-long process is beyond the scope of this book, I want to finish with reflecting on particular moments in time and in my family life cycle and how "thinking systems" has helped.

Over the years in researching, preparing, and presenting my genogram, I became acutely aware of patterns of multi-generational emotional processes in my family. I uncovered strengths like entrepreneurship, nurturing and caretaking elder parents at the end of their lives, and strong family of origin ties with siblings and parents. I also discovered challenges, such as my generation of siblings who are pursuers in relationships and partners who distance. Uncovering patterns is an essential part of discovery through the genogram.

One such pattern that I became conscious of is that of multiple nodal events occurring within relatively close proximity, sometimes within days and at other times within a few months of each other. As discussed, nodal events are significant events in the individual and family life cycle that appreciably impact individuals and systems.

Nodal events also provide opportunities for systemic change. Bowen theorists and practitioners are aware of the potential impact of a structured attempt to increase differentiation during these emotionally fluid times. Theorists and practitioners of Bowen family systems theory—including Bowen himself his 1967 article "On the Differentiation of Self" that he authored with the pseudonym "Anonymous"—describe intentional efforts to extricate themselves from emotional triangles in their families of origin and their attempts to alter the family emotional system during these impressionable times. As Ed Friedman reminds us in his 1971 Family Process article entitled "The Birthday Party," systems are particularly open and malleable to influence during these times, as the emotional field of the family is in flux.

Peter Titelman and his contributors, in the classic 1995 edited volume *The Therapist's Own Family,* say that as Bowen theorists, we can consciously harness nodal events as opportunities for individual and systemic change. All contributors discuss the value and power of differentiating efforts during these transitional times. Even with the most mindful of efforts, successfully negotiating nodal events like marriages, births, and deaths usually takes several years.

I became aware of the emotional pattern of intersecting nodal events through my genogram years ago. An early example of this was in 1985 when my parents moved from their home of fifteen years on Long Island to be closer to my father's sister's family in Florida. Originally, my parents considered moving to San Diego where my wife and I lived and worked. We were, though, in the midst of a marital crisis, so my parents decided to move to Florida instead. Right after their decision, Janet and I separated, a parting that lasted for six months. This occurred after six years of marriage. These were two significant events—my parents retirement move and our separation—closely related in time.

In another example, our oldest daughter, Carly, graduated high school in 2007 and my mother passed unexpectedly less than ten days later on my brother's son's birthday. A third example occurred in 2009, when my youngest daughter, Sage, graduated from high school. The very next day, my father, who was visiting us for the occasion, had a massive seizure due to a brain tumor. This also occurred on my younger brother's birthday. Further, my father passed away in mid-May, 2010 and my mother's brother died two days later.

A final example (though there are many others) centers on my retirement from Prescott College at the end of June 2015, and our youngest daughter leaving to attend graduate school in Philadelphia in July 2015. (Sage had been living on her own and working at a treatment center in Prescott for two years following college graduation. Though she was independent, Sage was situated in an independent apartment in our walk-out basement and helped us care for Janet's father, who had moved in with us in February of 2013.) Also, I turned sixty in September 2015, and received emeritus status at Prescott College in October 2015. While these events were a normal part of the family life-cycle, cumulatively, they are significant as they represent many big changes, departures, endings, and honors. Also, with Sage leaving, more care for my father-in-law fell on Janet and me. There was more upheaval and adjustment for all.

I'll discuss how Bowen theory has helped me navigate my personal emotional landscape, especially during these significant events. As reported previously, genogram development and presentations were a central part of two courses that I taught. Kenny Cook and I co-taught Family Systems in Film and Literature. When we were teaching our course in September of 2011, I noticed increasing irritation and impatience on my part and I wondered why.

In preparing to present my genogram to our class, I became acutely aware of a number of nodal event intersections. I titled my presentation "Rocks in the Pond." I highlighted these events and made an analogy of how the ripples from each nodal event acted like intersecting waves in a pond with many rocks thrown into it.

Like that pond, I felt the chaos of how those forces rocked me. I believe that numerous nodal events, in close sequence, have an exponential quality of emotional imprinting on the family system. The waves become larger, more dramatic, and more de-stabilizing.

By September of 2011, both my parents had passed away. With both my mother and father gone, I came to realize how much they had fully supported me in my life and always believed that I could accomplish whatever it was that I set my mind to doing. Truly, their love was unconditional. I became aware that I "split" this optimism/confidence in me so that my parents "owned" the optimism and belief in my abilities and I, in turn, "owned' my more self-critical nature. With my parents gone, all that was left was my self-criticism. Hence my increased irritation and impatience, especially with myself.

I realized that I needed to internalize their belief in me and their confidence in my abilities. In other words, it was time for me to resurrect the qualities "owned" by my parents within myself.

What this meant, practically, was that I needed to develop the same compassion for my "self" that I had carefully cultivated through compassion for others. This simple truth led to increased awareness on my part that this emotional integration and transition would take time. This deep knowing was quite different from the intellectual knowledge that my parents were gone and that this life-cycle transition would take time. I gave myself permission to be irritated and impatient at times, and I used this insight to decrease my reactivity and judgments around these concerns.

Presenting my genogram to the class was powerful and poignant. Students appreciated the personal depth of my revelations. And, they got to see, first hand, the power of the genogram at different stages in the individual and family life cycle. As we had been teaching them, the genogram became a powerful tool for obtaining greater clarity and objectivity about one's family.

Another significant series of nodal events occurred in a six-month period. In December of 2012, Janet had hip reconstruction surgery to remove benign tumors in her hip area and to replace her damaged hip. Janet had suffered from decades of limited mobility due to a college injury in a dance class. After forty-five years of adapting and suffering, she was ready to have her hip repaired and replaced. The surgery was successfully, and the recuperation was extensive.

A month later, in January 2013, after eighteen years of involvement and service, I resigned my board membership and ended my active involvement with Skyview School. With our children long gone from Skyview, it was time to leave the school to the next generation of leaders.

The next month, in mid-February of 2013, my father-in-law, Lou, had a moderately severe stroke. Janet and our youngest daughter Sage had to fly to Maryland to care for him and to transport him to Arizona for rehabilitation and relocation. After long family discussions, we made the decision that Lou would live with us permanently. At the end of February, he moved into our home to recover. This decision went against the wishes of his lady-friend of eight years, Marianne, who wanted him to move in with her, against medical advice. The entire issue with Marianne was emotionally difficult and challenging. In the end, though, the family decision was accepted, Lou moved in, and we began closing down his life in Maryland after 25 years.

As mentioned in chapter five, also at the beginning of February, a colleague had to take an emergency medical leave of absence from Prescott College, stranding dozens of students without the courses that they needed. I previously discussed how Sage and I created our own course in response to this personnel challenge. Teaching Theories and Methods of Couple and Family Therapy became a highlight of my teaching career and deepened my professional and personal relationship with Sage.

At the beginning of March, Janet declined her contract offer at Skyview School, where she had returned after securing her teaching certification. Janet had spent the previous six years teaching kindergarten students. After eighteen years of service at Skyview School in various positions from integrated arts coordinator, dance teacher, director, and kindergarten teacher, it was time for her, too, to transition away from the school.

Also, in 2013, Prescott College was in the midst of its worse financial crisis since 1995. Poor leadership, ineffectual management, and a down-turned economy had met in a perfect storm that pushed the college to the edge of fiscal insolvency. From February through July, the faculty struggled to respond to these systemic failures in leadership and their reverberations across the college.

As a part of this crisis, a number of faculty members had left. This included my closest friend, co-teacher, and co-writing colleague, Kenny Cook, as well as his wife, Charissa Menefee, a dear friend as well and a Prescott College faculty member in theatre. Less than a year prior, my other close friend and Prescott College faculty member, Tim Crews, had left the college to head up the research program at The Land Institute in Salina Kansas, an agroecology research center focused on developing perennial grains. His wife, Sarah, was also a good friend. So, in less than a year, the backbone of my personal and professional support system was gone.

In early May of 2013, Sage, graduated from college. We began remodeling the basement of the house into an independent apartment to accommodate her returning home prior to her attending graduate school, and our oldest daughter, Carly, came home for the summer from graduate school. This remodeling was a massive construction and renovation project being completed in the midst of these changes.

Janet finished her work at Skyview School toward the end of May. She cleaned out her classroom, and left for good.

At the beginning of June 2013, Janet, Lou, and I went to Maryland to clean out Lou's office, ship his car to Arizona, take his necessary papers, and prepare his house for sale. This was an emotionally difficult trip for Lou. After decades in his house and living independently after the death of his wife, this part of his life, along with his eight-year relationship with his lady friend, was coming to an end. I was formally retired from the Board of Directors in early June.

On top of it all, the family dynamics of Janet's family, active for almost 60 years, became acutely problematic, as her sister was demanding control over her father's health care and finances. She had hired an attorney to assume this control, and Lou hired an attorney to block her attempts to do so.

The clustering of these emotional events was profound. Prior to Sage's graduation and Janet leaving Skyview School, and before Lou became disabled, we had envisioned our summer as a second honeymoon and had begun to excitedly re-imagine our lives as "empty nesters." But, given the difficulties that my father-in-law was experiencing, things changed quickly.

As our family histories on both sides demonstrated patterns of caretaking elderly parents, there was never a question about having Lou live with us, especially as Janet's sister was not emotionally capable of taking him in. Nonetheless, seeing all of these nodal events together, we recognized the importance of patience and mindfulness, as all family members had been affected by all of these changes.

Overall, I believe that we weathered these nodal events well. There were occasional "subterranean eruptions" as the emotional consequences of these situations would boil over into experiences of disappointment, testiness, and frustration. Nonetheless, knowing about these events and talking about them as a family provided some guidance and relief for all of us. These experiences called on me to be more accepting, understanding, and mindful, and less reactive when setbacks occurred. Normalizing all of our struggles at transitioning helped to take away some pressure for all of us, as we recognized that change takes time and multiple nodal events occurring in close proximity can complicate those changes and the timeframe of transition.

While we intellectually understood the crucial nature of these events and the time frame necessary to manage transitions, we also *experienced* this process emotionally. A clear understanding of Bowen's theory, which Janet, Sage, Carly, and I all studied, helped us to track and manage our reactions individually and as family members. We were called to demonstrate a higher level of kindness and compassion for each other. Sometimes we succeeded; sometimes we came up short. We discussed and reviewed the power of these multiple nodal events and how anxiety can act with exponential power and force. This awareness often translated into right action along our life journeys together and separately. When we stumbled, the love and commitment in our family as the emotional center of our lives helped us to grow and strengthen the bonds of our family.

It has been eleven years since the nodal events in 2011 and more than nine years since those transitions in 2013. There have been additional nodal events "layered" on these, including my brother and his family moving away from Prescott and back to California, Sage moving away to graduate school and now working as a family therapist in Philadelphia, and my father-in-law passing away in December of 2019. And, Janet and I retired as mediators with the Superior Court in May of 2017.

While my life, like all others, continues to evolve and change, an understanding of the power of these nodal events and the possibilities provided by Bowen theory afford a window into the power of family systems, the role and function of significant life events, and the ability to approach changes with conscious intention, equanimity when possible, and grace when practiced.

Bowen's family systems theory is a theory of human systems as well as a theory of life. I use the theory as a guidepost through challenging times, to enhance my work in various jobs, and to train others to do so as well. Professionally and personally, Bowen theory has been good to me for over three decades. I believe that I have a unique perspective in that I have held a variety of posts and careers over the years. I have exposed many students and colleagues to Bowen family systems theory. Most have found the theory valuable. Some continue to use it professionally and personally. Others are finding ways to expand its horizons in the 21st century in the age of racial and cultural diversity and inclusion, gender fluidity, and LGTBQ rights. Bowen theory continues to demonstrate its power, relevance, and usefulness. Scientific advancements reinforce many of the concepts of the theory, and it has not diminished in the professional sphere, as have many of the marriage and family therapies and theories of the founders. Thankfully, it appears that Bowen family systems theory is here to stay.

www.ingramcontent.com/pod-product-compliance
Lightning Source LLC
Chambersburg PA
CBHW031457270326
41930CB00006B/132